NAFSA

EDUCATION ABROAD
FOR ADVISERS AND ADMINISTRATORS

EDITED BY

MAGNOLIA HERNANDEZ, MARGARET WIEDENHOEFT, AND DAVID WICK

NAFSA
Association of International Educators

FOURTH EDITION

About NAFSA

NAFSA is the largest association of professionals committed exclusively to advancing international higher education. The association provides leadership to its diverse constituencies through establishing principles of good practice and providing professional development opportunities. NAFSA encourages networking among professionals, convenes conferences and collaborative dialogues, and promotes research and knowledge creation to strengthen and serve the field. We lead the way in advocating for a better world through international education.

CONTENTS

About the Authors. iii

About the Editors xi

Introduction xiii

PART I. EDUCATION ABROAD ADVISING

CHAPTER 1   Marketing for Education Abroad Advisers 3

CHAPTER 2   Education Abroad Advising. 21

CHAPTER 3   Education Abroad Applications:
             Balancing Data Collection and Student Preparation 41

CHAPTER 4   Preparation and Orientation 53

CHAPTER 5   While Abroad. 75

CHAPTER 6   Post Study Abroad 91

PART II. EDUCATION ABROAD RESEARCH

CHAPTER 7   Getting Acquainted with Comprehensive Internationalization:
             U.S. and Abroad 115

CHAPTER 8   Education Abroad Research. 125

PART III. HEALTH, SAFETY, AND RISK MANAGEMENT

CHAPTER 9   Physical and Mental Health of Students. 151

CHAPTER 10   Risk Management Planning for Education Abroad:
             Issues, Challenges, and Resources 159

CHAPTER 11   Insurance for Education Abroad 175

CHAPTER 12   Crisis Management 191

APPENDIX A   Questions for Responding to Emergencies 207

PART IV. DEVELOPING AND
MANAGING EDUCATION ABROAD PROGRAMS

CHAPTER 13   Strategic Planning for Education Abroad Programs. 213

CHAPTER 14   Education Abroad Models. 227

CONTENTS (CONTINUED)

CHAPTER 15 Work, Internships, and Volunteering Abroad 243

CHAPTER 16 Program Administration 265

CHAPTER 17 The Experience of Students On Site 283

PART V. MANAGING AN EDUCATION ABROAD OFFICE

CHAPTER 18 Portfolio Management 301

CHAPTER 19 Human Resources in Education Abroad 315

CHAPTER 20 Effective Utilization of Institutional Data for Strategic
Education Abroad Planning and Campus Advocacy 331

CHAPTER 21 Managing an Education Abroad Budget 357

CHAPTER 22 Partnerships and Advocacy 377

CHAPTER 23 Policies and Procedures 393

CHAPTER 24 The Theory and Practice of Outcomes Assessment
in Education Abroad 407

INDEX 423

ABOUT THE AUTHORS

Kati Bell is the executive director of global education at Dominican University of California. She has been an international educator for more than 15 years and has worked for five universities in three countries, including Ukraine and Australia. In her previous positions, Bell has developed international exchange programs, cocreated diversity improvement plans, served on campus internationalization committees, and managed the establishment of an administrative infrastructure for a university research institute. She holds a BA in German from Sacramento State University, an MA in German literature from San Francisco State University and an EdD in educational leadership from San Francisco State University.

Joseph L. Brockington is associate provost for international programs and professor of German language and literature at Kalamazoo College. He holds a BA, MA, and PhD from Michigan State University. A former SECUSSA chair, Brockington has served as a member of the founding board of the Forum on Education Abroad, the executive committee of the Association of International Education Administrators (AIEA), and the national team of NAFSA's International Education Leadership Knowledge Community. He currently serves as chair of the Ethics Working Group of the Forum on Education Abroad. He has published and presented numerous papers at conferences on topics such as international program administration, campus internationalization, legal and risk management issues in education abroad, and modern German literature. From 2005–09, he organized and led the NAFSA annual conference workshop on best practices in legal and risk management issues in education abroad. He is a coeditor of the third edition of *NAFSA's Guide to Education Abroad for Advisers and Administrators.*

Heidi Buffington works with undergraduate and graduate students from the United States, Europe, Africa, and Asia as an international admissions counselor for Saint Louis University's (SLU) campus in Madrid, Spain. In her 10 years at SLU, Buffington has worked with more than 4,000 students. She is persistent in promoting study abroad to students with nontraditional study abroad majors, such as engineering and nursing. She also enjoys writing and researching and has presented her work at many international conferences. Buffington's first experience with international education was as a student in

Córdoba, Spain, an experience that opened her eyes to a new language and culture. She completed her undergraduate degree in biology and Spanish at The College of Wooster. In 2003, she was invited by the Spanish Ministry of Foreign Affairs and Cooperation to complete an MA in international studies at the Diplomatic School of Madrid.

Eric A. Canny has more than 17 years of experience in educational policy and programming, curriculum development and accreditation, admissions, crisis management, student and staff development, public relations, grant writing and nonprofit event management. He is currently the director of WORLD: International Learning at Stetson University, coordinating the strategic goal to "make intercultural learning vital to the Stetson experience." At New York University, Canny was director of global student services, coordinating operations for the world's largest study abroad program, serving more than 4,000 students annually. He served as team leader for opening of foreign operations of U.S. higher educational institutions in Argentina, China, Costa Rica, France, Ghana, and the United Kingdom, as well as expansion of existing programs in Chile, Czech Republic, France, Germany, Mexico, Spain, and Thailand. He presents globally on a range of topics. He received his BA and MA from New York University.

Holly Carter is the director of the Office of International Education at St. Edward's University in Austin, Texas. She holds a PhD in sociology and health services research from the University of North Texas, as well an MPH, MPhil, MSSW, PGCE, BSW, and a BA in French. Carter teaches in sociology, public health, and in many areas of health care funding and policy. Carter is also a Global Village team leader for Habitat for Humanity, and leads teams to build houses in different international locations each year. She has been a part of 12 international builds and continues to work with the organization on an annual basis.

Eduardo Contreras is a doctoral student at the Harvard Graduate School of Education (HGSE). His research focuses on the history of American undergraduate student study abroad programs and international education at American colleges and universities. Before returning to graduate school, he worked for seven years at the University of Texas-Austin (UT). At UT, his experience with internationalization included web development, community outreach, grant writing, student advising and faculty-led study abroad program development. In 2005, he cofounded UT's first study abroad student mentor program, aimed at increasing study abroad enrollment of students from underrepresented groups. In the spring of 2014 he taught a course at Harvard called "Internationalizing Higher Education: Possibilities, Perils, and Promises." He received his EdM in higher education in 2009 from HGSE, has an MA in Asian languages and cultures, and a BA in history from the University of Texas-Austin.

Steven T. Duke worked as a study abroad adviser and assistant director at the University of Wisconsin-Madison for three years, directed the education abroad office at Virginia Tech for three years, and served as director of international studies at Wake Forest University for five years. He currently serves as executive director for Global Student/Faculty Development, Research, and Risk Management at Wake Forest University, where he directs a cross-cultural engagement program for students, the annual Workshop on International Skills Enhancement (WISE) conference for faculty who teach abroad, and other globalization efforts for faculty and students. His book *Preparing to Study Abroad: Learning to Cross Cultures* was published by Stylus in 2014. He holds a PhD in Russian history from Indiana University, and has taught Russian, Baltic, European, and world history courses at Brigham Young University, the University of Wisconsin-Madison, and Wake Forest University.

Gail Gilbert is assistant director in the Office of International Education at Marquette University. In her role at Marquette, Gilbert manages daily study abroad operations, oversees predeparture and reentry courses, and is responsible for crisis management for international programs. She has worked in education abroad for more than 10 years, and has contributed to the field through various presentations on topics such as managing student workers, responding to overseas emergencies, working with parents, and understanding the Clery Act. Gilbert also serves as the content coordinator for health and safety on NAFSA's Education Abroad Knowledge Community.

Emily Gorlewski is an assistant director in the Center for International Studies at Western Illinois University, responsible for education abroad and institutional partnerships. She is also chair of NAFSA Region V, serves on the editorial team of the *Review of Global Studies Literature,* and is part of the subcommittee on research and scholarship in the TLS Knowledge Community. She holds a MSEd in counseling, adult, and higher education, with an emphasis on higher education administration, from Northern Illinois University, and is working on an EdD for international educators in organizational leadership, policy, and development at the University of Minnesota.

Nick Gozik is director of the Office of International Programs and the McGillycuddy-Logue Center for Undergraduate Global Studies at Boston College. Gozik has held positions in education abroad at Duke University, New York University, and the University of Richmond. He has taught courses at Boston College and New York University in research methodology, international education, and communication studies. Additionally, he has been an active member in a number of professional organizations, including NAFSA and the Forum on Education Abroad. In the latter, he serves on the Forum Council, the outcomes assessment and research committee, and works with undergraduate research awards. Gozik holds an MA in French language and civilization and PhD in international education from New York University.

Corrine Henke is the director of International Learning Opportunities at Boise State University. She has an MA in international and intercultural management from the School for International Training in Vermont. She has worked at Boise State since December 2000. Prior to Boise State, she was the Study Abroad Advising Center coordinator at the University of Massachusetts-Amherst. She has facilitated a number of cross-cultural trainings for professional organizations on the Boise State campus and in the community. In 2009, she received the provost's "Excellence in Advising" award, as well as a $100,000 grant for education abroad scholarships. She led a team of trainers to create NAFSA's e-learning course, "Mapping Short-Term Programs Abroad." She is the Fulbright scholar adviser at Boise State and is a recipient of a Fulbright International Education Administrators award to Germany.

Chelsea Kindred is central regional director of university relations at Academic Programs International (API), a study abroad program provider based in Austin, Texas. As central regional director, Kindred builds and maintains partnerships with institutions of all types in the central United States. Kindred also manages API's alumni development programs, where her responsibilities include drafting curriculum, facilitating training, managing activities, and providing relevant professional feedback for alumni participants. Kindred holds volunteer leadership roles with Lessons from Abroad and NAFSA. She has presented on many topics in education abroad, including alumni development, short-term education abroad programming, social media/technology, and orientation strategies. Kindred earned a BA in English and French from the University of Texas-Austin and is currently working to complete an MFA in creative writing from Chatham University.

Joshua McKeown is director of International Education and Programs at the State University of New York-Oswego. The large international office was recently ranked eighth in the nation in the Institute of International Education's *Open Doors* ranking of students abroad on semester/quarter programs, and recently more than tripled its international student enrollment. McKeown is responsible for leading strategies, directing personnel, and managing priorities for a department of 12 employees responsible for education abroad, international student and scholar services, international recruiting, and campus internationalization. He directs more than 80 study abroad and exchange programs in more than 30 countries, enrolling 400–500 students annually. In addition to his professional presentations and journal articles, McKeown is the author of the book *The First Time Effect* (SUNY Press, 2009), showing that first time study-abroad students achieve significant increases in their intellectual development.

Mary Meadows is currently the assistant director for university and alumni relations at Academic Studies Abroad, where she travels across the United States inspiring students to go abroad in addition to sharing ideas between institutions to maximize their marketing plans for various student groups. She has worked in the United States and internationally in the field of international education since 2005. Meadows specialized in business marketing and international education for her MS in higher education administration and student affairs at Florida State University, where she was dubbed "The Globalization Fairy" by her cohort. Among the range of marketing projects and collaborations Meadows has developed are workshops on networking, social media, and selling an abroad experience during a job search. A NAFSA volunteer leader through Trainer Corps and the education abroad dinner meetups, Meadows consistently encourages new ideas to come to the table for discussion and application in our field.

Catherine S. Meschievitz coordinates study abroad and exchange programs for students and faculty at Florida Atlantic University in Boca Raton, Florida. She also negotiates and manages international institutional agreements for FAU and its overseas partners, and supports the faculty and colleges in the advancement of their strategic priorities for international education. Meschievitz chairs the FAU Council on International Education, and represents the university as the liaison to state, regional, national, and international organizations on international education matters. She previously was associate dean of international studies at the University of Wisconsin-Madison. Meschievitz has a PhD in modern South Asian history from the University of Wisconsin-Madison and a JD from the University of Wisconsin Law School.

Meschievitz is a member of the Florida Consortium on International Education, the Florida Humanities Council, the Association of Asian Studies, the Association of International Education Administrators, and the Wisconsin State Bar.

William Nolting has more than two decades of experience at the University of Michigan International Center, where he leads initiatives for global work, internships, volunteering, and careers. As a longtime member of NAFSA, he served as national chair of education abroad, founded the WIVA Subcommittee, and contributes to conferences and publications.

Anthony C. Ogden is executive director of Education Abroad and Exchanges and an adjunct assistant professor in educational policy and evaluation studies at the University of Kentucky. Ogden earned his bachelor's degree from Berea College and his master's degree in international and intercultural management at the SIT Graduate Institute. He completed his PhD at The Pennsylvania State University in educational theory and policy with a dual title in comparative and international education.

Gary Rhodes is director of the Center for Global Education and the Safety Abroad First–Educational Travel Information (SAFETI) Clearinghouse at the Graduate School of Education and Information Studies at the University of California-Los Angeles (UCLA). He received his PhD and MSEd in education and MA in international relations from the University of Southern California (USC), and BA from the University of California-Santa Barbara. He has published articles, been cited, and presents widely on issues of university internationalization, international learning, safety, risk, crisis management, legal issues, and study abroad across the United States and around the world. He has taught courses at the graduate level at USC and UCLA on administration of international programs in higher education, and has received Fulbright grants to India and South Africa.

Jason Sanderson, PhD, is the senior overseas studies adviser in Georgetown University's Office of International Programs, where he has advised students interested in a variety of programs in Europe and Africa since 2004. He also works closely with faculty on issues related to language learning abroad. Sanderson's current research focuses on language attitudes and identity. His master's thesis focused on perceptions of sexual identity and study abroad. Sanderson is a member of the Center for University Programs Abroad (CUPA) academic advisory board, and serves as the chair of the No Barriers to Study working group as well as the France country coordinator on NAFSA's Consular Affairs Liaison Subcommittee.

Joseph (Joe) Sevigny is associate vice president of enrollment management for IES Abroad headquarters in Chicago. Sevigny, who has been with IES Abroad since 2002, manages the admission, financial aid, and student visa processes for approximately 5,000 students annually. Prior to IES Abroad, Sevigny worked as associate registrar at both Northwestern University and New York University, director of graduate enrollment services at New York University, and assistant director of graduate admissions at Long Island University. Sevigny is a current member and former chair of the NAFSA Visa Education Subcommittee and has presented several times at the national and regional levels on student visa issues and concerns. Sevigny has been a contributing author for *The AACRAO International Guide: A Resource for International Education Professionals,* NAFSA's *Student Visas: What You Need to Know Before You Go!,* the Kaplan/Newsweek *Graduate School Admissions Adviser* and NAFSA's *A Guide to Educational Systems Around the World.*

Angela Shaeffer began her career in international education in the study abroad office at the University of Maryland, where she obtained an MA in international education policy. Her research focused on underrepresented populations in education abroad. After serving in the international studies office at Goucher College—during a time when the institution implemented its unique study abroad requirement—Shaeffer began working at Cultural Vistas. Currently the director of program development at Cultural Vistas in New York, Shaeffer creates international exchange programs focused on professional and career development. A longtime NAFSA member and co-chair of the Underrepresentation in Education Abroad Subcommittee, Shaeffer is also active in a number of other professional organizations for international educators. A Baltimore native, she has studied abroad in Germany, Denmark, South Africa, and Mexico, and enjoys trying foods she can't pronounce.

Thomas Teague serves as an education abroad adviser at the University of Kentucky (UK). In addition to advising students in the College of Arts and Sciences and working with a variety of campus and external constituents, he develops and coordinates the ongoing orientation programming for outgoing students. Teague has presented at conferences both regionally and nationally, on ongoing orientation programming, underrepresented students, and the transition from college into the education abroad workplace. Teague graduated with a BA in French language and literature from North Carolina State

University, and moved to the University of Tennessee to pursue an MS in college student personnel. While at Tennessee, he worked as an intern in both the Programs Abroad Office on campus and at the University of Worcester's International Centre.

Stacey Woody Thebodo is the assistant director of international programs at Middlebury College, where she manages all aspects of Middlebury student participation in externally sponsored study abroad programs and domestic off-campus study programs. Her responsibilities include advising, program evaluation, application review, predeparture and reentry programming, credit assessment and transfer, policy development and implementation, and many other aspects of study abroad administration. Stacey has been assistant director of international programs at Middlebury College since 1997. She is the author of several publications and articles and has presented at many conferences on various study abroad topics, such as predeparture orientation and cross-cultural reentry, sustainability and study abroad, using technology in study abroad advising, blogging as a tool for reflective writing, and strategic student survey assessment. She earned her BA in psychology from Central College in Iowa and an MIA with a focus in international education from the School for International Training (SIT).

Jennifer White is associate director of the Office of International Studies at Goucher College, the nation's first liberal arts college to require study abroad for all undergraduates. White holds a BA in English and East Asian studies from Harvard University and an MA in comparative culture from International Christian University in Tokyo, Japan, where she conducted research on cross-cultural influences between American and Japanese women during the Allied occupation of Japan. During her 14 years in the field of international education, she has held positions at Harvard University, Kalamazoo College, Washington University in St. Louis, and Webster University, and has served as a member of NAFSA's Trainer Corps and as NAFSA's Missouri state representative. She has extensive experience in risk management, health and safety protocols, and student advising, and has recently become an Intercultural Development Inventory (IDI) qualified administrator in order to conduct research on study abroad learning outcomes.

ABOUT THE EDITORS

Magnolia Hernandez has nearly 10 years of experience in international education, dedicating many of those years to matters of access and study abroad funding for students of diverse backgrounds at Hispanic-Serving Institutions (HSIs). Hernandez is the former director of the Office of Study Abroad at Florida International University (FIU). She has recently shifted her career focus to graduate education and academic support services at the FIU University Graduate School.

David Wick, EdD, is director of study abroad at Santa Clara University. He has worked in international education since 1988, with a decade-long break in advertising and design. His professional and research interests center around equity, diversity, and inclusion, and on strengthening study abroad curriculum and pedagogy from outreach through reentry to enhance student learning.

Margaret Wiedenhoeft is the associate director in the Center for International Programs at Kalamazoo College. Her interests include promotion and advising to encourage diversity in study abroad, international service-learning projects, and conducting research about the impact and experience of study abroad on U.S. college students.

INTRODUCTION

As with many areas in the realm of higher education, the context of international education (IE) has changed since the 2005 edition of NAFSA's *Guide to Education Abroad for Advisers and Administrators*. Student demographics, study abroad programming, financial realities, political tensions, natural disasters, and the increasing professionalization of the field have all impacted the structure and content of education abroad. Comprehensive internationalization initiatives in higher education and curriculum integration efforts have also increased the visibility of education abroad and spurred significant growth in the field. We have intentionally designed this volume of the guide to address these current topics. Additionally, we have asked our contributors to frame these topics in a way that is relevant to international educators at all stages of their careers, including those who hold various functional roles.

When the guide's last edition was published, the Institute of International Education's *Open Doors* (2006) had reported a 150 percent increase in study abroad participation over the previous decade.[1] More than half of study abroad participants studied in Europe, with Latin America the second largest destination at 14 percent. The field was focused on encouraging students to explore beyond Europe. Crisis management, risk management, and health and safety emerged as areas of focus for institutions. In addition to these developments, international educators became focused on developing learning outcomes and assessment, curriculum integration, and campus internationalization, all while learning new communication skills for social media.

In the recent past, the field has also focused more on inclusivity of study abroad, STEM student participation, diversification of student demographics and study abroad destinations, and international internships, volunteer opportunities, and research projects, in addition to a "traditional academic" study abroad experience. Study abroad has also expanded to include, in a more comprehensive manner, first-year students, graduate students, and students in the allied health professions. While promoting the growth of international education, it is also important to recognize the developing regulatory federal environment that includes the Clery Act, Title IX, and the Americans with Disabilities Act (ADA), as well as the international environment for student exchange and transit.

---

[1] Institute of International Education. 2006. *Open Doors 2005 Report on International Education Exchange*. New York: Institute of International Education.

The current *Guide to Education Abroad* seeks to be relevant to education abroad professionals both in the United States and abroad, and to serve as a foundation for international educators who work with study abroad in all professional functional roles: direct service, operational management, and senior strategic leadership. We recruited authors with various lengths of experience and positions and charged them to present model practices grounded in research and theory. The format of this guide will allow for interactivity, and is intended to be a tool for both newcomers to the field and those who are looking to learn more about a particular topic. We see this guide as a basis for the knowledge of a particular topic, with references and links to other resources for further reading. Because of the nature of the material, we hope to be able to update the guide at regular intervals, reflecting the continued learning and growth of the field.

Section I: Education Abroad Advising

This section is organized by study abroad stage and includes six major chapters, covering outreach, advising, application, preparation, time abroad, and students' return. Each chapter in this section includes background and infrastructure, content and learning outcomes, and student characteristics and data management. Many of these topics are addressed from a different perspective in other major sections of the guide. Each chapter in this section is aimed at supporting effective advising with systems and structures that can be tailored based on institutional or organizational context, and which can be scaled to differently sized programs. This section is intended for advisers, or the person who provides direct service to students.

Section II: Education Abroad Research

This section provides foundation information on comprehensive internationalization and education abroad research. Of all the sections in the guide, its audience is the broadest. It is written for all education abroad professionals, including those who work at higher education institutions, in organizations that create and manage programs, and with foundations or government agencies that support or fund education abroad initiatives. Furthermore, this section is meant to provide support for professionals who provide direct service to students, manage education abroad offices or programs, and those who lead vision and strategy related to education abroad.

Section III: Health, Safety, and Risk Management

This section includes a comprehensive approach to the health and safety of students abroad, a topic that has gained prominence since the last edition of the *Guide to Education Abroad.* It features a separate chapter on insurance, and its important role in crisis and risk management. Though the context for this section is based on U.S. higher education, it is also meant to serve as a foundation for our colleagues from host institutions abroad, so that they might better understand the U.S. context.

Section IV: Developing and Managing Education Abroad Programs

This section focuses on education abroad programming, particularly the various models for programs and strategic considerations in developing a comprehensive set of international education experiences for students. This section also includes a chapter focusing on the experience of the student on site, bringing in the perspective of an on-site host, to help education abroad professionals better understand a student's environment while abroad.

Section V: Managing an Education Abroad Office

This section of the guide focuses on the everyday management of a study abroad office. With a total of seven chapters, the section includes information on everything from developing, creating, and maintaining budgets, to building or growing the infrastructure of a study abroad office, incorporating assessment and data collection into the office's portfolio, and building partnerships on and off campus. Providing a number of valuable best practices and institutional models for study abroad offices and institutions of all sizes, this section bridges the theory-to-praxis gap that is often faced by study abroad professionals at all levels.

Acknowledgments

We would like to thank the authors and other contributors for their work on this project. As a profession, we are fortunate that so many are generous with their knowledge and eager to share model practices Thank you to NAFSA staff, especially Emily Buckler and Chris Murphy. Finally, we want to thank the previous editors of the *Guide to Education Abroad,* for their excellent work in defining what the guide means to the profession of international education.

PART I
EDUCATION ABROAD ADVISING

CHAPTER 1

MARKETING FOR EDUCATION ABROAD ADVISERS

By Mary Meadows

Overview

In this chapter we will look at marketing education abroad programs and building a network of supporters to help you with your outreach plan. We will review tools to create and develop a marketing plan, from in-person marketing to social media strategies. We will also consider how marketing has an effect on the decision to study abroad, the timing of study abroad, and on program choice. We will introduce you to a decisionmaking theory from the field of career counseling to help better understand some of the effects of marketing, and how to help students become smart consumers in their search for the best program for themselves.

Throughout this chapter we refer to an "organization" as any office or team at an institution of higher education, a nonprofit or for-profit education abroad program provider, or any other governmental or nongovernmental organization marketing education abroad locations or programs to students.

Background and Infrastructure

The structure of your outreach team can vary greatly depending on the size of your organization, the office structure or processes management approach, office goals, and institutional mission, vision, and values.

Many organizations are seeing an increase in the number of students who are provided education abroad services. The benefit to this is that we are seeing new positions being developed that devote a large percentage of time to aid in the education abroad outreach process. As we have moved into using more technology to promote programs, we are seeing new positions for people with the technological skills to manage social networking, online databases, and website maintenance.

Good examples of office structure can be found online through various organizations' websites. If you aren't sure which institution may be similar to yours, admissions office staff and organizational leaders may be able to provide a list of the comparison institutions they use for benchmarking. You can look at staff listings for a particular office to help you understand how that office is structured and the number of people they have for different roles.

As organizations grow, responsibilities are often split between regions of the world, program types, or academic departments on a campus. Advisers may be traveling to certain parts of the world to market programs. They may also be in the office, advising students from a particular college on campus, or advising those who are interested in traveling to certain countries. It's important to consider how your advising responsibilities are divided and the effect that this has on marketing various programs to a limited or broader audience.

Whether or not you have a team of people in your organization to help you to get the word out about the options abroad for your students, there are many initiatives that you can take to increase awareness about programs. We will take a look at some of these options in the "Strategies" section of this chapter.

Principles

Through our marketing and other policies—which students are obliged to examine in order to identify the ideal program type and destination—we can help students develop skills to be smart consumers. Consider how you can improve student outcomes by adjusting marketing practices and creating a meaningful process related to academic and professional goals rather than, for example, slotting each student into a single program based solely on a topic of study.

You can think of marketing education abroad programs—in general, or a particular feature of a program—as promoting something that students already want or need (e.g., academic credits, a unique experience, studying or living in a popular location, etc.). You can also think of marketing as a means for promoting a feature of a program or the entire program in such a way that students develop the mindset that the particular aspect of the program is something that appeals to them and that they believe they need (e.g., specific skills, taught by home institution faculty members, or a unique experience). You might use this second approach if you have a new program that you want students to join or an exchange program that has an imbalance. If you create a list of the things that education abroad programs provide students, you may find that some items can fall under both categories based on a student's previous knowledge and perceptions about the program options.

Examples of different marketing pieces for education abroad are offered in the NAFSA publication, *By Example: Resources for Education Abroad Offices and Advisers.*

We can also use tools from the field of career counseling to aid students in their decisionmaking process, and to help them become smarter consumers who select programs that meet their individual goals. There are several tools that career counselors provide to help students assess their values, interests, and skills. If you do not have access to a career services office on campus, there may be one in your community, which you can turn to in order to understand such processes or receive tools for students. You can also use online resources to help you understand theories from the field of career counseling, such as the CASVE Cycle. The CASVE Cycle is a process theory that helps students consider their values, interests, and skills in decisionmaking. Its acronym comes from inclusion of the following stages: communication, analysis, synthesis, valuing, and execution.[1]

FIGURE 1. Five Stages of the CASVE Cycle, Model 1: Description of Information Processing Skills Used in Career Decisionmaking

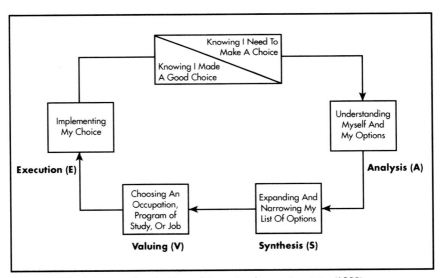

Source: Used with permission from the National Career Development Association (1992).

Figure 1 should help you understand the CASVE Cycle stages in general. Figure 2 breaks down the stages of the CASVE Cycle with examples related to education abroad.

---

[1] Learn more about the CASVE Cycle process theory and tool online at **http://www.career.fsu.edu/** techcenter/designing_career_services/basic_concepts/.

FIGURE 2. Five Stages of the CASVE Cycle, Model 2: Information Processing Skills Descriptions for Use in Decisionmaking for Making Education Abroad Plans

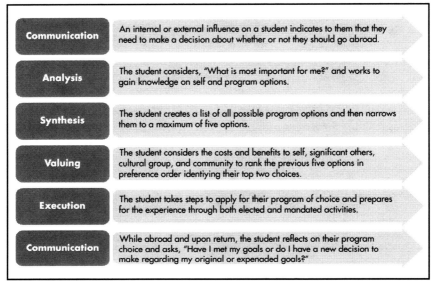

Communication	An internal or external influence on a student indicates to them that they need to make a decision about whether or not they should go abroad.
Analysis	The student considers, "What is most important for me?" and works to gain knowledge on self and program options.
Synthesis	The student creates a list of all possible program options and then narrows them to a maximum of five options.
Valuing	The student considers the costs and benefits to self, significant others, cultural group, and community to rank the previous five options in preference order identiying their top two choices.
Execution	The student takes steps to apply for their program of choice and prepares for the experience through both elected and mandated activities.
Communication	While abroad and upon return, the student reflects on their program choice and asks, "Have I met my goals or do I have a new decision to make regarding my original or expenaded goals?"

Source: Mary Meadows

For a concrete example of putting theory to practice for a student considering a study abroad program, see figure 3 on page 7. (Please note: The top center box and final box left of top center in figure 3 both represent the "communication" stage: The former represents the beginning of the cycle, and the latter represents a reflection, which may in turn trigger additional cycles through the stages.)

In order to better understand how to market a program, you need to understand what communication students have received indicating to them the option of going abroad (e.g., reminder of an academic requirement, poster in hallway, peer pressure, etc.). It is also important to understand why and how your target group of students is making the decision to go abroad or select particular programs. This communication may or may not have been a part of a previous marketing plan put in place by your organization or an unknown source or person with whom you can develop a relationship to benefit your goals more strategically. You can read more about defining and developing your own marketing plan in the "Strategies" section of this chapter. The "Partnerships" section will look closer at how relationships can help you market programs. The "Data Collection" section in this chapter will also provide some tips on how you can understand your students and obtain data to make informed decisions for your marketing.

FIGURE 3. Sample of Student Decisionmaking Cycle When Selecting a Program Abroad

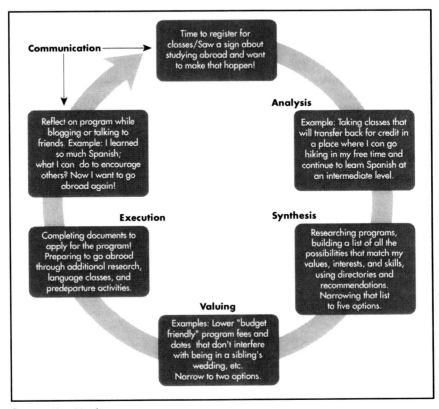

Source: Mary Meadows

By using the decisionmaking CASVE Cycle or other predetermined process to help students make the decision about going abroad, you can look specifically at their decisions to help guide your marketing plan. For example, you can create an advising form that asks students about their values, interests, and skills, in relation to their academic, personal, and professional goals. You can then market the programs that reflect the values, interests, skills, and goals to the groups of students who are seeking that type of program.

Strategies

Your marketing strategies, including items from the different sections of this chapter on partnerships, programming and events, technology, and social networking, will come together to form a marketing plan. In order to get a marketing plan, you need to do some market research, as well as understand the "marketing mix."

One of the most well-known explanations of this marketing mix is the use of the "4Ps" to decide whether or not to market absolutely anything, from socks, to gadgets, to education abroad programs. These "4Ps" are: product (or service), place, price, and promotion (McCarthy 1960). In order to develop a marketing plan, you have to do some research. MindTools and Marketing Teacher both provide information about the "4Ps" and address questions you and your team may have when evaluating your marketing plan and your program options for students.

Partnerships

You can tell, when you visit higher education institutions, where there is a culture of education abroad and where there is not. When there is a culture of education abroad at an institution, you will find that people are talking about it in some way, and that there are multiple lines of communication crossing through the work spaces of faculty, staff, and administrators. This feeds into campus programming and student development opportunities, including those offered by student organizations and off-campus organizations.

How can you create a campus culture where going abroad on a particular program or just going abroad in general is an expected activity for the majority of students? You must look at your formal and informal relationships, and help encourage people to talk about your programs.

Even if you are an O'Po (one-person office), you can develop formal and informal relationships that in effect get others to work with you to enhance your marketing. You may want to get a campus map, world map, or other map of the area you cover to market to students. This map may be printed, or be an online—and if possible, editable—map, such as those you can create with Google Maps.

To develop advocates, think about each building on campus, at your particular workplace, and in your community. Find out what happens in these buildings on a daily basis or for special events. Who works there, and what are their daily tasks? Schedule some informal meetings with people in those buildings to have conversations about what your goals are and see if there are already some direct or indirect matches regarding shared interests. Ask questions to see which of these people could be advocates for promoting your programs. Strategic meetings may be your next step if you have already identified advocates and want to develop a committee of advocates from a particular area or for a particular marketing project.

For example, some institutions have advisers from each of the colleges who are the main points of contact for study abroad. Some program providers have a board of directors from various institutions. Other study abroad offices have connected with student groups interested in travel or alumni of study abroad. More information on peer programs and how they can help increase your outreach can be found in chapter 6.

As relationships evolve, you should put forward efforts to maintain conversations in order for you to understand how your efforts with groups of advocates and their interests may change over time. Rather than trying to talk a person into doing something for you, you should consider how you can build excitement around your goals. There are several books out about "building your tribe," which essentially means finding advocates, bringing them together, and keeping them passionate about your programs so they in turn will talk about them through word-of-mouth marketing or will promote them in other ways. Good references for word-of-mouth marketing, and the inspiration for several ideas in this chapter, are resources by Brains on Fire, including the most recently published *The Passion Conversation: Understanding, Sparking, and Sustaining Word of Mouth Marketing* (Phillips et al. 2013). This book provides groundwork to improve your mission and help develop your marketing plan.

Programming and Events

Word-of-mouth marketing that happens with your advocates can be encouraged by providing outlets for interactions to take place between your advocates, already interested students, and other people you would like to be advocates. These events can also be a great way to help any stakeholders understand what you do and why it is exciting, important, and helpful in maintaining or building a positive culture. These events can also help your community understand how the things you do are connected to a specific part of your organization or institution's mission statement or goals. Consider how you will make these events productive for everyone in attendance and how you can help encourage people to easily interact.

If you are based on a campus working with organizations that are on and off campus, be sure to make your rules and guidelines clear. Many institutions place information on their website where it can easily be referenced. If you are an organization being allowed to promote programs on a campus, be certain to follow the guidelines that have been provided for you and to ask questions about anything that might be unclear.

Education Abroad Fairs

Institutions often hold education abroad fairs, which include opportunities for students to study, intern, research, work, or volunteer abroad. There are many factors to consider before hosting or attending a fair in order to make sure that it will be beneficial for you. Take a good look at your marketing plan, results from previous events, and budget. Guidelines for holding a fair and being an exhibitor at a fair can be found through NAFSA.

Work with other institutions and organizations hosting fairs or other events around the same time as yours. Exhibitors appreciate coordination among institutions as it allows them to maximize their time on the road in a particular area. Consider planning across the state at state conferences or with a recruitment tour organization so that traveling from one place to the next is as easy as possible—and better for the environment. Use GoAbroad's fair calendar (see below) to post the dates of your fair to help exhibitors with their planning.

Fair Calendar

http://www.nafsa.org/Find_Resources/Supporting_Study_Abroad/
Network_Resources/Education_Abroad/Study_Abroad_Fairs_
in_the_United_States/

Guidelines for Campus Visits

http://www.nafsa.org/Find_Resources/Supporting_Study_Abroad/
Network_Resources/Education_Abroad/Marketing__on_Campus__
A_Guide_for_Program_Providers/

Classroom Presentations

Have a method in place for faculty to request presentations and training to maximize the short amount of time that is often allotted for such presentations. Work with your main contact on a campus in order to get approval for class presentations, and always respect the time allotted.

Working with Student Organizations

Informational e-mails about education abroad and ideas for collaboration with the specific student organization are a great way to get started in discussing shared interests and ideas. Some campuses have their own fairs for student clubs and organizations, which is a great way for on-campus education abroad staff to speak in person with student leaders. Campuses may even have their own clubs that are made up of education abroad alumni.

Working with Student Campus Entertainment

Depending on how student campus entertainment is scheduled, you can plan to link your marketing to an event by sponsoring or simply hosting an information table in the proximity of the event. You could also suggest particular entertainment groups.

Working with Other Departments Within Your Organization

If you have used the 4Ps system mentioned in the "Strategies" section above and found that you have advocates in various departments within your organization, be sure to keep the information flow consistent so that you can plan events that connect to the goals of all stakeholders.

Working with Other Groups Outside Your Organization

Whenever you are contacting someone new, be sure to check with your main point of contact within the organization, if you have one, to see if it is appropriate for you to contact them directly. Make sure that the groups outside of your organization have policies in place that match the ethical guidelines of your organization. You can use NAFSA's Statement of Ethical Principles as a reference point.

Fundraisers On and Off Campus

You or your students may want to consider fundraising events with local organizations and businesses. You should double check with the foundation for your institution to make sure you won't be stepping on any toes by trying to work with someone they might already be requesting donations from. However, your institution's foundation can be helpful in developing scholarships, and should be approached about working together to attain such goals. Fundraising events can be powerful marketing events where you can (a) show off all that has been accomplished, (b) acknowledge outstanding students, and (c) acknowledge other contributors to your mission.

Technology and Social Media

Just as you may have looked at every building on a campus to see where your advocates might be, you can also look at various social media outlets. Consider the ways that technology and social media fit into your goals and role. Are these things you should be handling or could they be better handled by someone who is already managing this type of marketing for a larger part of your organization?

There has been an increase in the number of education abroad directories and databases such as GoAbroad, TDS for Study Abroad (formerly Studio Abroad), and Abroad Office. Consider your marketing strategies across the board and determine how to list your programs by working with both the management and clients of those directories. Some of these software providers offer training sessions.

You should also consider how your programs are being listed and perceived on review sites such as Abroad Reviews and Abroad 101.

If you are responsible for social media for your office or organization, be sure to check and see if there are already social media guidelines and policies in place. You can also consider various applications that allow you to set up auto-posting of web content on social media outlets to help manage your time. Different countries will have their own popular social media websites, so be sure to consider who your target market is for social media marketing and survey them to determine which outlets to use and how best to utilize your resources.

You may also find valuable the use of virtual fairs, where you can connect with students on the Internet on a set day and time to talk about your program options.

Outreach Content

Academic Preparation

When you are creating your marketing plan, you should look at when would be the earliest points of contact you can have with incoming freshman to talk about education abroad. This can help increase the number of students on your programs by helping to make sure they are planning ahead appropriately to keep an opportunity abroad available to them and to make sure that they are prepared to maximize their time abroad.

Work together with academic advisers on study abroad options and policies, so that they can also help students prepare for a term abroad and map their course plan. You may want to include a page on your website that advisers can reference. See chapter 2 for additional information and resources related to academic alignment and advising.

You can also market your education abroad programs to students who are required to take a second language as a graduation requirement, or for those students who might be interested in studying in a country where their first language is not the primary language. Encourage language learning prior to departure for such a program, or offer programs that have intensive language learning at the beginning of a term on site.

Students may avoid going abroad because they aren't sure how to make it a reality. To help take away some of the guesswork and anxiety, you can require students to attend a brief orientation about preparing themselves to go abroad and how the processes work for your organization. In addition to encouraging more students to go abroad, this approach can also reduce the workload in your office. You may have prerequisite classes, offer predeparture courses, or combine classwork and travel programs that help to increase the number of students going abroad.

Moreover, consider if it would be of value for you to stretch your brand by being a part of freshman orientation sessions, offer freshman year abroad programs, "gap year" programs, or programs at the secondary level.

Professional Alignment

Study abroad can be a great way for students to enhance their degree and make it unique to their interests. Often, elective classes that are limited, not offered, or closed to non-majors on the home campus may be offered on the program abroad. Take for instance a mass communications student who decides she wants to improve her photography skills, and who goes abroad and takes a fashion or sports photography course. That course and the projects completed through it can be the thing that gets her an interview for a job on a path to their dream career.

Moreover, focusing on unique program attributes in your marketing communications can be beneficial for students valuing opportunities for internships, company visits, research, project-based learning, or community service. Consider ways in which you can market the various programs that provide opportunities for students to gain specific professional knowledge, skills, and awareness in their career field of interest.

Getting students excited about going abroad means that we often need to work with them individually to identify their values, interests, and skills to find a program match. If you already organized your interest and application forms to reflect these questions, you can be more efficient in your advising. There is more information on this in this chapter's "Strategies" section. Additional information on the development of intake forms is available in chapter 2 and chapter 3.

Some of the ways you market the benefits of a program will be in the way it is talked about by returnees. Let's say that you describe a program as an academic program abroad that also provides experiential education opportunities and community outreach—you will start to hear many of those words repeated by students. However, helping them truly communicate the transferable skills they gained from their experience abroad and providing specific examples will help them stand out in future interviews. Work with your career center to develop such a workshop for returnee students, or consider including a session while students are still on your program abroad.

Further reading on returnees can be found in chapters 5 and 6.

Personal Considerations

Have a look at how honest you are with every marketing piece. You are setting expectations for what the experience will be like for your students on each program; the goal is for students to be satisfied with their experience. In print and online marketing pieces, you will want to make sure the photographs and descriptions convey the same seasons, settings, and similar experiences that students are most likely to encounter. Check to make sure that the buildings and monuments in images will be what they will see in their host city or on excursions. Do images and descriptions convey an accurate presentation of interactions that students are most likely to experience with other people on the program and in their host community?

More programs are now offering multiple options for students to not just study abroad, but also to volunteer, intern, and work. A program may have a focus on any one of these types of experiences, and offer any combinations of types of programs. Refer back to your application or advising sheet with the student to determine which program components meet their values, interests, and skills.

As you communicate with a student about a program you are offering and the possibilities to add on other components, include a discussion about students' time management and commitments while they are abroad. Students often have grand expectations about all the places they will travel. With the marketing of the program, be open about how much time will be available for students to plan trips of their own and what will be realistic for the free time they have at the location where they are studying. Also, it is important to remind students of the need to balance their travel plans with academic expectations such as projects and exams, and to wait to book travel until they are aware of such dates and deadlines.

Be open about the amount of language acquisition students should expect to have by the end of the program and steps they can take to improve the chances of improving their language skills while they are abroad. For a more in-depth discussion of program types and relative benefits, please see chapter 2.

Remember to follow the ethical guidelines of your institution and those from the profession, including those available through the Forum on Education Abroad and from NAFSA.

Financial Planning

While a lower-priced program may be the best option for some students, price may not be important to others. However, if the program is very similar to another option at the same location, you may not have as much success recruiting students for a more expensive option. Within the 4Ps mentioned in the "Strategies" section of this chapter, you should certainly review the "price" aspect of marketing your programs. Be aware of whether or not a program that is being introduced as an option for students is more or less expensive than similar options. Compare what is included in a program fee for students and ask for budget estimates, if not already provided, of things that are not included in the program fees. NAFSA offers a budget worksheet to help with advising students on the total cost of going abroad.

Offering scholarships for a particular program is a great way to also help market a specific program or location. You can check to see if local chapters of various clubs and organizations on campus and in your community offer scholarships to go abroad to particular countries. Some examples of organizations that provide scholarships are the National Italian American Foundation and the Rotary Club.

Advising students on how to market their study abroad for fundraising opportunities is another way to promote education abroad as being more accessible for students. Bringing students together to discuss their plans for fundraising and providing success stories can encourage more students to see going abroad as an option. Online crowdsourcing sites are now available for students who want to participate in education abroad programs, and some provide their own advisers to assist students with their efforts. Project Travel is one such resource site.

Student Groups

Data Collection and Use

Where can you gain knowledge about what your future students will want in an education abroad program? If you work at an educational institution, there is likely an office for institutional research that can help you develop and approve a relevant survey. Someone may already be asking the same questions you seek information about, or the data you want to collect may have additional benefits to your office and the institution.

Asking early for assistance will help you with capacity building and finding the right programs through partnerships or when developing your own programs. You can provide a questionnaire at freshman orientations that includes such questions as: Where do you want to go? When? For how long? In relation to which major?

Once you have a student who is interested in going abroad, you can survey them on how they heard about the program and why they chose it. Some people may decide to survey students at several points along the process, including when the student is searching for a program, while they are abroad, and upon return, while others may decide that one survey at the end of the program is sufficient. You should definitely survey students at the end of program at least, and ask about what they see as its value. All of the information you gather from these surveys can help you build a more successful and efficient marketing plan.

You can also work with your organization's alumni or your foundation office to share your data or help survey students as they are graduating—and on into the future—to increase the potential for donated funds to be used for scholarships or other needs of your office.

If you are using a software program to manage your applications, quite often you can add a survey to the processes for each student. You can also pull information from software programs such as Terra Dotta's software for study abroad to find out more information and track patterns with your students.

Consider also using student identification data collection, such as student ID card readers, at fairs or other events where you are promoting. You can also use this type of data collection in areas where you are considering a promotion to better understand what students are in the area, so that you are more likely to market programs that match their needs. For guidelines on surveys, you can read more in chapter 24 on assessment and in chapter 20 on data collection.

Underrepresented Student Groups

It may be beneficial to provide extra time in your marketing and advising processes for underrepresented student groups. You can start building promotional resources and a network of advocates who underrepresented students can relate to, who are ready and willing to encourage students to go abroad. (This is a good example of why you may not always be the best and only person to promote your programs.) Even if you are a one-person office, you should have a community of advocates working with you in order to maximize your promotional opportunities.

Remember that a powerful influence on students is peer influence. Connect with student or community organizations that represent various disciplines or categories of students you are trying to target. Find returnees to share their stories with the appropriate groups about how they made their program abroad a reality, and seek out or create opportunities to bring your advocates and prospects together. Use your network to build these connections, too. For more information, refer to this chapter's "Partnerships" section above.

In addition, try not to filter all your students from a particular underrepresented group into a single program. This can happen with Science, Technology, Engineering, and Mathematics (STEM) students, where a department has developed a single program with core curriculum for a certain major. Not every student is going to want to have the same experience, and opening up or digging in to find options for these students to mix with those from other disciplines should be encouraged.

Consider campus policies and state regulations on targeting specific groups for marketing to make sure you don't violate any policies or laws. You can find tips to market to various groups from allabroad.us or diversityabroad.com.

Conclusion

Outreach efforts and marketing plans will vary greatly depending on the goals of the organization during different times of the year. These plans are often reviewed annually or when strategic changes are taking place at any level of your organization. Marketing is a specific task within an organization that encompasses the opportunity to educate students on their opportunities and become better consumers. From research on your marketing efforts, organizations can also learn about the needs of future participants and how students make decisions. Understanding your organization's leadership, the mission and goals of your organization, and those of your possible advocates, will help you to continue communication with them and increase the awareness about your programs to your target audience.

Additional Web Resources

Abroad 101
www.studyabroad101.com

Abroad Office
www.abroadoffice.com

Abroad Reviews
www.abroadreviews.com

All Abroad
www.allabroad.us

Brains on Fire
www.brainsonfire.com

Diversity Abroad
www.diversityabroad.com

GoAbroad
www.goabroad.com

National Italian American Foundation
www.niaf.org

Project Travel
projecttravel.com

Rotary Club
www.rotary.org

TDS for Study Abroad (formerly StudioAbroad)
www.terradotta.com

References

Breakell, Tina and Bradley Titus. 2013. *By Example: Resources for Education Abroad Offices and Advisers.* Washington, D.C.: NAFSA: Association of International Educators. http://www.nafsa.org/Find_Resources/ Supporting_Study_Abroad/Network_Resources/Education_Abroad/ By_Example__Resources_for_Education_Abroad_Offices_and_Advisers/.

Friesner, Tim. 2014. "Marketing Mix." West Sussex, United Kingdom: Marketing Teacher Ltd. Retrieved May 9, 2014 from http://marketingteacher.com/ lesson-store/lesson-marketing-mix.html.

Manktelow, James. N.d. "The Marketing Mix and 4 Ps: Understanding How to Position Your Market Offering." Wiltshire, United Kingdom: Mind Tools Ltd. Retrieved May 9, 2014 from http://www.mindtools.com/pages/article/ newSTR_94.htm.

McCarthy, Edmund Jerome. 1960. *Basic Marketing: A Managerial Approach.* Homewood, Ill.: R.D. Irwin.

NAFSA. 2007. "Study Abroad Fairs in United States." NAFSA: Association of International Educators. Retrieved May 9, 2014 from http://www.nafsa. org/Find_Resources/_Sidebars/Study_Abroad_Fairs_in_United_States/.

NAFSA. 2009a. *Marketing on Campus: A Guide for Program Providers.* Washington, D.C.: NAFSA: Association of International Educators. https://www.nafsa.org/Find_Resources/ Supporting_Study_Abroad/Network_Resources/Education_Abroad/ Marketing__on_Campus__A_Guide_for_Program_Providers/.

NAFSA. 2009b. *NAFSA's Statement of Ethical Principles.* Washington, D.C.: NAFSA: Association of International Educators. http://www.nafsa.org/findresources/Default.aspx?id = 2475.

NAFSA. 2009c. "Study Abroad Fairs in the United States." NAFSA: Association of International Educators. Retrieved May 9, 2014 from http://www. nafsa.org/Find_Resources/Supporting_Study_Abroad/Network_Resources/ Education_Abroad/Study_Abroad_Fairs_in_the_United_States/.

NAFSA. 2013. *Budget Estimate Creation and Dissemination for Study Abroad Programs.* Washington, D.C.: NAFSA: Association of International Educators. http://www.nafsa.org/Find_Resources/Supporting_Study_Abroad/Budget_Estimate_Creation_and_Dissemination_for_Study_Abroad_Programs/.

Peterson, Gary, James Sampson, Robert Reardon, and Janet Lenz. 2003. "Basic Concepts and Principles of the CIP Approach: An Overview of the Pyramid of Information Processing Domains and the CASVE Cycle." *Basic Concepts and Principles of the CIP Approach.* Retrieved May 9, 2014, from http://www.career.fsu.edu/techcenter/designing_career_services/basic_concepts/index.html.

Phillips, Robbin, Greg Cordell, Geno Church, and John Moore. 2013. *The Passion Conversation: Understanding, Sparking, and Sustaining Word Of Mouth Marketing.* Hoboken, N.J.: Wiley.

Sampson, James, Gary Peterson, Janet Lenz, and Robert Reardon. 1992. "A Cognitive Approach to Career Services: Translating Concepts into Practice." *Career Development Quarterly,* 41, 67–74. Broken Arrow, Okla.: National Career Development Association.

CHAPTER 2

EDUCATION ABROAD ADVISING

By Stacey Woody Thebodo

"Good advising may be the single most underestimated characteristic of a successful college experience," wrote Richard J. Light in *Making the Most of College: Students Speak their Minds.* Light (2001, 81) made this statement after many years of researching the most effective ways for faculty members and college administrators to advise and teach on U.S. campuses. High-quality advising is especially crucial for education abroad. Education abroad advisers play a central role in the entire study abroad process, from the moment students first interact with the education abroad office, until after they return from overseas. Advisers help establish the foundation from which students' education abroad experiences are launched, where study abroad learning begins.

Education abroad advising, like all advising in higher education, is an art, not a science, and it is a complex process. Education abroad advisers must be knowledgeable about the vast assortment of options available to students, including in-depth knowledge of program structures, academic offerings, and requirements. Advisers must be well-versed in the policies and regulations of their institutions, as well as federal, state, and local laws about student privacy, financial aid, and more. In addition to the nuts and bolts of guiding students to make informed education abroad decisions, advisers must understand student development, advising techniques and strategies, and resources to use in advising. Furthermore, education abroad advisers must be familiar with international higher education and should be knowledgeable about different countries, regions, and cultures. An effective adviser must also be able to collaborate and develop partnerships with faculty, administrators, staff from program providers and universities abroad, and parents.

This chapter will address the goals of education abroad advising and the role of the education abroad adviser, as well as student development theories, programming, and advising models and techniques. In addition, this chapter will include practical aspects of education abroad advising, such as student goals, institutional policies, academic planning, program selection, and financial matters.

Advising Principles and Goals

The Forum on Education Abroad's Standards of Good Practices for Education Abroad (2011c) identifies advising as an essential part of the standards of good practices for student learning, development, and preparedness for the learning environment abroad. NAFSA included advising skills as one of the key competencies of education abroad professionals in its *Statement of Professional Competencies for International Educators* (2009).

Education abroad advising should be consistent with the institutional mission and must address students' needs and objectives. The goal of education abroad advising is to guide students throughout the entire education abroad process, helping them to make informed decisions from predeparture through reentry (Forum 2011a). For most education abroad advisers, however, the greatest part of advising takes place prior to departure, which is the primary focus of this chapter.

Student Development Theory

One of the ultimate goals of advising—and of higher education in general—is to guide student development and learning. As such, it is essential for education abroad advisers to be familiar with student development theory. The concept of student development has existed for many years and is defined in various ways. In short, student development is seen as a positive process of growth and progression, resulting in the individual becoming increasingly able to accomplish complex developmental tasks, achieve self-direction, and become interdependent (Evans et al. 2010). Evans et al. asserts that "our student populations and the developmental issues they confront are more diverse and complex than ever in the history of higher education" (xvii). Student development is multifaceted and is more complex than any one theory can explain; it must encompass psychosocial, cognitive, integrative, and social identity theories.

The most well-known foundational theories of student development include the psychosocial developmental theories of Erik Erikson, James Marcia, Ruthellen Josselson, and Arthur Chickering. Erikson was the first clinical psychologist to examine identity development beyond childhood and into adolescence then adulthood, resulting in a theory describing eight stages of development: (1) basic trust vs. mistrust, (2) autonomy vs. shame and doubt, (3) initiative vs. guilt, (4) industry vs. inferiority, (5) identity vs. identity diffusion/confusion, (6) intimacy vs. isolation, (7) generativity vs. stagnation, and (8) integrity vs. despair. Marcia built on Erikson's theory, focusing on individual identity formation and the process through which an individual progresses in questioning then making choices regarding his or her values and goals. Josselson took these theories a step further and explored the differences in identity development in women (Evans et al. 2010).

Many education abroad advisers are familiar with Arthur Chickering's seven vectors of development, the first major theory focusing specifically on the development of college students (Evans et al. 2010). Chickering's vectors of development include progression that is not linear, but rather a "journey toward individuation" (Chickering and Reisser 1993, in Evans et al. 2010). The seven vectors are: (1) developing competence, (2) managing emotion, (3) moving through autonomy toward independence, (4) developing mature interpersonal relationships, (5) establishing identity, (6) developing purpose, and (7) developing integrity. Chickering emphasized the power that environments exert on student development, underscoring the importance of establishing educationally influential environments (Evans et al. 2010). Chickering's theory can be especially useful for education abroad as we examine how our programming and interventions can influence student development in all phases of study abroad, and how advisers can be more intentional in the environments we create in order to foster development.

In addition to psychosocial theories, William Perry's theory of intellectual and ethical development, Lawrence Kohlberg's theory of moral development, and Carol Gilligan's theory of women's moral development are relevant to education abroad professionals, as these theories examine how students construct meaning and develop worldviews. Perry's model includes a continuum of development of "positions" (rather than stages) from duality to evolving commitments. Kohlberg's theory focuses on the process of how students make moral judgments. Gilligan's theory of women's moral development acknowledges that previous theories had set men as the standard of normal and specifically analyzes women's moral development (Evans et al. 2010). These theories have important implications for education abroad, when we support students abroad as they confront challenges to their values and potential moral dilemmas in the context of different cultural environments.

Cognitive structural theories that examine concepts such as perspectives, self-authorship, and reflective judgments are especially relevant to students studying in a cross-cultural setting. It is also vital that education abroad advisers take into account theories of identity development: social identity development, privilege and oppression, racial identity, gender identity, gay/lesbian/bisexual/transgender identity, national identity, and spiritual identity.[1] Research shows that exposure to different worldviews alters students' identity development—perhaps this is a part of what returnees mean when they profess the life-changing effects of study abroad (Vande Berg, Paige, and Lou 2012). This changing of or disruption to one's identity, or perhaps the

---

[1]There are too many important theorists in these areas to name; a comprehensive resource to learn about these areas of student development is *Student Development in College: Theory, Research, and Practice* by Evans et al., 2010.

anticipation of how one's identity will affect and be affected by study abroad, can evoke anxiety, which is important for advisers to address when preparing students to go abroad.

Further, as advisers facilitate matching students with appropriate programs abroad and prepare students to go abroad it is useful to understand learning theory. For example, David Kolb's experiential learning model examines how individuals learn from primary experience, reflect on that experience, develop abstract concepts, and then apply the learning to new settings (Kolb 1984). Additional theories useful to advising students as they prepare for the changes inherent in crossing cultures include Nancy Schlossberg's transition theory (Evans et al. 2010) and Jack Mezirow's transformational learning (Vande Berg, Paige, and Lou 2012). These theories can help advisers guide students in preparing for challenges to their perspectives, values, and assumptions.

Recent research indicates that individuals are taking longer to recognize themselves as adults, living with and/or being financially dependent on parents longer than in the past, putting off marriage and child-bearing until later in life, and other traditional markers of adulthood being postponed or avoided entirely (Hofer 2012). Further, the concept of autonomy, which is a key aspect of "emerging adulthood," (individuals between the ages of 18 and 25, a coin termed by Jeffrey Arnett, Hofer 2011) is obstructed by the cultural shift in students' reliance on technology as a vehicle to remain attached to parents. Hofer's research indicates this "electronic tether" impedes students' movement toward autonomy and hinders the development of skills of self-regulation, which negatively affects learning, achievement, and success in college (Hofer 2010). Many education abroad advisers recognize the impact these factors and this cultural shift have on all phases of the education abroad experience. Advising and predeparture preparation sessions should encourage students' autonomy and confront the overreliance on technology as a tie to home, which inhibits student autonomy, cultural involvement, and integration.

Many academic disciplines include theories relevant to advising, including education, psychology, neuroscience, human ecology, intercultural communication, and anthropology, to name a few. Vande Berg, Paige, and Lou (2012) shed light on a number of theories from multiple disciplines from which the education abroad field can learn. More research is needed to bring these fields together in order to better understand advising techniques and effectiveness and how best to apply this knowledge to education abroad advising. Nonetheless, advisers who are familiar with the theoretical background are better equipped to assess and address how a student's developmental stage fits into education abroad program selection, planning, and preparation, as well as what issues and challenges the student may face abroad. Advisers can then better guide students in cultivating skills of self-direction and decisionmaking, encouraging them to progress in their growth and maturity, furthering their development.

Advising Models and the Role of Adviser

Several advising models originating in the field of academic advising are applicable and extremely useful to education abroad. A review of the literature shows multiple references to the continuum of "prescriptive" versus "developmental" advising (Alexitch 2002; Barbuto et al. 2011). Prescriptive advising refers to a one-way advising relationship where the adviser imparts knowledge to the advisee and instructs the student on what to do, whereas developmental advising refers to an adviser/advisee relationship that is collaborative and process-oriented. Developmental advising, which is considered the more effective model, includes a progression of steps starting with the exploration of goals, followed by choice making and implementation.

Barbuto et al. (2011) propose a new model of advising derived from the leadership field, which is applicable to education abroad, known as "full range advising." Full range advising is a continuum where the adviser's behavior ranges from least effective to most effective. These behaviors include three groups on the continuum: (1) laissez-faire, (2) transactional, and (3) transformational. Laissez-faire advising is "hands-off" advising (i.e., no intervention). Transactional advisers more passively advise and deal with problems after they occur. By contrast, transformational advising emphasizes assessing individual students' needs and developing educational plans and programs suited to each student's goals. This model also accentuates the importance of encouragement, challenge, and intellectual stimulation. Transformational advising is thought to be the most effective advising model (Barbuto et al. 2011).

Smith and Allen's (2006) research identified five underlying constructs students deemed as most important to advising: integration, referral, information, individuation, and shared responsibility. These concepts can be extremely useful in considering the role of the education abroad adviser. "Integration" specifically refers to students making "connections" between off-campus experiences and academics, which is in fact an objective of education abroad. "Referral" is connecting students to campus resources. "Information" is self-explanatory—giving students the information they need. "Individuation" is advising according to students' unique characteristics. "Shared responsibility" refers to students taking an active role in "planning, problem-solving and decision making," which is a vital component of student learning.

Different Advising for Different Students

Just as there is no one theory that explains all students' development processes, there is no "one size fits all" advising model. Research and experience show that theories and models can apply very differently to students with different identities such as gender, race, ethnicity, and sexual orientation. Education abroad advisers must recognize the importance of adapting advising techniques and processes depending on the needs of different individual students, as well as for different "groups" of students. The issue of "underrepresented groups," generally linked with the discussion of diversity in study abroad, has been a hot topic in the field of education abroad for some time; there are numerous books, articles, conference presentations, online discussions, listservs, and websites dedicated to this subject.

Advisers must not make the mistake of assuming they know anything about an individual just because of knowing his or her group classification (Cunningham 2003). Some research suggests the most effective techniques for advising different underrepresented groups emphasize adopting a multifaceted and proactive approach to advising and humanizing advising (Museus and Ravello 2010). Faculty can be an important link between underrepresented students and study abroad, since many students first hear about study abroad through their faculty and because faculty members play such an influential role in students' decisionmaking (Lewis n.d.). Perhaps the most important factors for advisers to understand in advising different underrepresented groups are the barriers to participation for various groups. Understanding the obstacles students may face helps advisers guide students to the programs that will best suit their needs, as well as encouraging students to deal with the challenges inherent in the process. Barriers to participation in education abroad may include cost, academics, gender, peer pressures, fear, lack of family support, cultural attitudes, and lack of information or misinformation, to name of few. In advising various groups, it is especially important to collaborate with partners, such as faculty, parents, the international student office, financial aid office, and any offices or advisers who work with students of color, first-generation college students, nontraditional students, or students with disabilities.

Advisers should familiarize themselves with resources that address the barriers and needs of specific groups. The following are several underrepresented groups with which advisers should be prepared to work and some helpful resources for each group:

Students of Color

- The Diversity Network, an organization dedicated to "advancing diversity and equity in international education," www.diversitynetwork.org.
- "Advising Students of Color," from the National Academic Advising Association (NACADA) Clearinghouse of Academic Advising Resources, http://www.nacada.ksu.edu/Resources/Clearinghouse/View-Articles/Advising-students-of-color.aspx.

LGBTQ Students

- NAFSA's Rainbow SIG website and bibliography, http://www.rainbowsig.org.
- The U.S. Department of State travel website, http://travel.state.gov/content/passports/english/go/lgbt.html.
- CIEE Knowledge Series, "Identity: Sexual and Gender Expression Abroad," http://www.ciee.org/study-abroad/publications-center/.

International Students

- Work closely with your campus's international student and scholar office to make sure students understand immigration processes and implications and study abroad.
- Explore NAFSA's resources on supporting international students and scholars at http://www.nafsa.org/Find_Resources/Supporting_International_Students_And_Scholars/.

Students with Disabilities

- Mobility International's mission is "to empower people with disabilities to achieve their human rights through international exchange and international development." http://www.miusa.org/.

STEM Students

- "Science and Technology Students DO Study Abroad: Supporting Successful International Experiences in the STEM Majors," NACADA 2012 Region 8 Conference, http://www.slideshare.net/cainefrancis/stem-students-do-study-abroad.
- Fritz, Jennifer Ellis, "Increasing Study Abroad Participation for STEM Students at Bucknell University," NAFSA's 2012 Connecting our World Grassroots Leadership Program, http://www.connectingourworld.org/files/Grassroots_Leadership_J_Fritz.pdf.

First-Generation College Students
- Forum on Education Abroad bibliography, "Engaging First Generation College Students in Education Abroad," http://www.forumea.org/documents/ Bibliography.pdf.
- Browne, Heather, Karyn Sweeney, and Michelle Tolan, "Engaging First Generation College Students in Education Abroad," 2012 Forum on Education Abroad Conference, http://www.forumea.org/documents/ForumFirstGenerationStudents_Mar20KS.pdf.

General Resources on Advising Underrepresented Groups:
- Diversity Abroad articles, http://www.diversitynetwork.org/articles.
- IES Abroad diversity resources, http://www.iesabroad.org/study-abroad/ about/diversity-resources.

Advising Content
Education abroad advising goes far beyond simply providing information to students regarding program options and administrative processes. There are several fundamental components of advising content.

Institutional Mission and Policies
It goes without saying that advisers are expected to be knowledgeable about their institutions' missions and policies, and that their student advising policies and content must be aligned. Furthermore, all of these policies should be available in written form and communicated to students. In many ways, the education abroad office is a microcosm of the university itself, since education abroad offices handle many components of higher education: academics, curriculum, credit transfer, admissions, financial aid, counseling, student affairs, and policy creation and implementation. As such, education abroad advisers must wear many hats, and the content of advising sessions must address many issues, administrative as well as educational.

Student Goals and Expectations
There is currently much discussion in the field about student learning abroad, increasing emphasis on the need for articulated learning outcomes, and how various programs fare in regard to student learning. How does this translate to advising students? It could be asserted that student learning in education abroad begins with the very first advising session. As stated in the models of prescriptive advising (Alexitch 2002) and in full-range advising (Barbuto et al. 2011), one of the most essential components of advising is to help students identify their academic, personal, and professional goals. Only then can

advisers guide the student to an appropriate education abroad program and help the student effectively prepare for the overseas experience. Goal identification is a complex process. Some students may have no idea what their goals are or how to articulate them, or even why they want to study abroad, and some students are more motivated than others to engage in this exploration process. Advisers can use a number of techniques to open this conversation. Perhaps it is more important for advisers to begin by asking the questions, "why do you want to study abroad?" and "what do you want to study abroad?" before asking the question, "where do you want to study abroad?"

Expectations are an important part of the goals discussion as well. Discussing students' expectations of the education abroad experience, as well as expectations of the advising process, can help advisers assess students' needs and manage expectations. In addition, an adviser also must carefully consider how the institution's learning outcomes match with students' goals and expectations, and how to appropriately bring those into alignment. In addition to identifying goals early on in the advising process, goal setting should be an important component of predeparture preparation (see chapter 4).

PRACTICAL TIPS AND BEST PRACTICES

Intake Forms: Education abroad offices can use intake forms, either paper or electronic, which students complete prior to their first advising appointment. Forms can include questions about academic and personal goals and expectations.

Questions to Ask the Student: Ask the "why?" and "what?" questions prior to "where do you want to study abroad?" question.

Academic Planning

Education abroad should not be viewed as a disconnected component of a student's college education; rather, it should be integrated into the whole of students' academic careers. Education abroad advisers are certainly not meant to take the place of academic advisers and faculty advisers; rather, they should be partners in the process. However, education abroad advisers must not neglect the academic component of advising, since it is a key point of education abroad.

As part of discussing goals, education abroad advisers should address with students their academic goals and objectives and those of the education abroad experience as a whole, as well as of particular programs which students may be considering. Some students may know precisely how education abroad fits into their academic focus, whereas other students may be seeking to study abroad as a "break" from their major and an opportunity to explore other academic areas of interest. In any case, it is vital that students plan their education abroad experiences to fit within their degree requirements, for both reasons of curricular integration as well as logistical reasons (e.g., to graduate on schedule, to plan not to be away during the semester a required course is offered).

Advisers should be well-versed in their institutions' degree requirements, as well as in the academic offerings of education abroad programs available to their students. It can be challenging to keep up with such a quantity of information; as such, advisers must frequently consult and direct students to various sources of information, such as websites, handbooks, online course databases, as well as academic advisers, program provider staff, and other campus administrators. Further, advisers must encourage students to prepare academically for education abroad, perhaps by taking relevant language courses and other coursework relevant to the country or region of study, and/or meeting any necessary language or content course prerequisites.

PRACTICAL TIPS AND BEST PRACTICES

Implement Academic Department or Discipline-Specific Advising Documents: The University of Minnesota's Learning Abroad Major Advising Pages (MAPs) are considered a national model for advising and curriculum integration. The web pages include resources for developing MAPs, guidance regarding responsibilities of academic departments and advisers, and detailed templates for creating MAPs. http://www.umabroad.umn.edu/professionals/curriculumintegration/majoradvising/.

Program Selection

Guiding students in program selection is one of the most important components of education abroad advising. While some institutions have an "approved list" of programs, others have an open policy in which students can apply to any program they wish, and there are many variations in between. Similarly, there are numerous variations on program costs and financial aid policies, which can be a key deciding factor for students. Many schools have an application and/or petition process for program approval (see chapter 3). Regardless of the number and type of options available, it is an education abroad adviser's responsibility to guide students in the process of finding the appropriate program match.

As previously suggested, advisers might want to consider avoiding location-based advising ("Where do you want to study abroad?") by instead concentrating on advising students about different types of programs, academic and cultural opportunities, levels of ambiguity and student autonomy on different programs, and the intensity of academic and cultural challenge and immersion in various options. Then advisers can guide students to the program or programs that best fit their interests, goals, comfort with ambiguity, and how much independence, immersion, and challenge they are seeking.

Program Types

There are varying types of programs and different ways of classifying programs (see chapter 14). The Forum on Education Abroad (2011b) published a glossary of terms that includes thorough definitions of program features, types, and subtypes. Engle and Engle (2003, 4) state: "It is nearly as difficult to generalize about program types as it is to generalize about the experience of individual students." Nevertheless, advisers can use these classification systems and terms to help students navigate through the process of program selection.

Engle and Engle (2003) list seven "defining components" of overseas programs which advisers can take into account in guiding students:

1. Length of student sojourn
2. Entry target-language competence
3. Language used in coursework
4. Context of academic work
5. Types of student housing
6. Provisions for guided/structured cultural interaction and experiential learning
7. Guided reflection and cultural experience

According to these defining components, Engle and Engle's (2003, 2013) original research cites five "levels" into which programs could be classified[2]:

1. Study tour/educational tour
2. Short-term study/cross-cultural exposure
3. Cross-cultural contact program
4. Cross-cultural encounter program
5. Cross-cultural immersion program

Setting aside any judgments on program quality or rating different programs based on classification, this categorization can be useful in helping students gauge where they are in terms of their development and preparation—personally, academically, and culturally—and how this fits with various types and levels of programs. Furthermore, this categorization

---

[2]In Engle's new developmental model for student learning abroad, the names of some levels given in the 2003 research have changed slightly; both names are listed here. In addition, a sixth level, cultural integration, was added in 2013.

can help advisers encourage students to consider how they may progress in order to be prepared for a more challenging type of program.

Lilli Engle (2013) recently created a new developmental model for student learning abroad, expanding on the aforementioned levels and adding a sixth level of cultural integration. This new model "addresses the key issue of balancing challenge and support in relationship to identifiable student learning outcomes." Though much of the current discussion of the model is focused on learning outcomes and guided intervention abroad, this model can also be extremely useful to advisers in helping students identify an appropriate program.

Also useful in helping students differentiate between programs, the following are commonly used terms describing different types/models of programs:

- **Branch campus:** Some U.S.-based colleges and universities have their own campuses abroad, which may or may not offer courses and/or degrees to students from the host country as well as to study abroad students.

- **Customized programs:** Often developed and operated by a program provider, customized programs are designed and administered based on a particular university's or college's specifications and requirements. Usually only students from said college/university participate in the program.

- **Direct enrollment:** Sometimes synonymous with "integrated university study," in this type of program students enroll in regularly offered university classes alongside degree-seeking students from the host university, rather than courses only with fellow study abroad students. Students typically live in university housing when directly enrolled and must fluently speak the language of the university/host country. Direct enrollment may be independently arranged by a student or facilitated by a program provider. Some institutions have preferences or requirements regarding applying independently versus using a program provider. Advisers should be knowledgeable and able to advise students about the differences, such as level of independence desired, students' comfort level with ambiguity and autonomy, and sometimes practical concerns such as financial limitations.

- **Exchange:** An exchange program implies a reciprocal arrangement between universities, which may be "bilateral" (one-to-one exchange) or "multilateral" (involving more than three universities exchanging students, not necessarily student-per-student, nor the same two universities in the group trading students). Exchanges are a type of direct enrollment and often involve a special financial arrangement of paying home university tuition and/or fees.

- **Faculty-led program:** This type of program is led by one or more faculty members from the home institution who accompany the group of students overseas and most likely teach one or more of the courses on the program.
- **Field study or field-based program:** Based on experiential learning, this type of program includes extensive hands-on learning and practical application pedagogy, such as field-based research, service learning, internships or volunteer work, or field-based science or environmental programs. This type of program often appeals to a more independent student looking for a different type of learning environment than the typical U.S. university system.
- **Island program:** This type of program typically keeps the study abroad students together as a group for coursework and/or housing and extracurricular activities. As such, the cultural integration on an island program is less than with some other program types. Some education abroad professionals feel that this term has negative connotations, so it is becoming less common.
- **Language institute:** Language institutes may be affiliated with a host university, or they may be freestanding, nondegree-granting institutions. The primary focus is language learning. Some college and universities do not grant credit for language institutes unless they are part of a degree-granting university. Many language institutes offer programs for varying periods of time, and students can register for the desired duration.
- **Study abroad center:** Sometimes based at or affiliated with an in-country university and sometimes operating independently, a study abroad center typically involves teaching by local faculty and courses comprised of study abroad students, sometimes from many different colleges and universities. Courses may be taught in English or in the local language, and sometimes students may take a combination of center-based courses and regular university courses.
- **Study tour:** Study tours are typically short-term programs, sometimes part of academic coursework offered by a home campus. This type of program may have a thematic focus and likely includes travel to multiple locations.
- **Hybrid:** Increasingly, education abroad programs are becoming combinations of these program types and are impossible to singularly classify.

Program Duration

Program duration is another important factor as students consider study options, and their education abroad advisers should guide students toward appropriate programs. Increasingly, students are choosing shorter programs. *Open Doors* data show that the "growth in study abroad over the past 20 years has occurred entirely in mid-length and short-term programs ranging from one semester to eight weeks or less" (IIE 2012, 20). This has been a subject of much discussion in the education abroad field in recent years, and colleges, universities, and program providers have been faced with the challenge of developing programs with sound pedagogy and student learning outcomes, as well as aims of cultural immersion, while students' desire is to study abroad for shorter and shorter periods of time. Many are raising questions about the "more is better" assumption the field has made for many years. Advisers must be equipped to discuss program length with students, while working within constraints of institutional limitations and competing factors such as student academics, finances, extracurricular activities, family support, internships, and other résumé-building endeavors.

The terms most often used in referring to the length of time for which a program operates employ typical academic terminology, such as quarter, semester, and year (academic year or calendar year). The term "short-term" (see above) is usually shorter than the aforementioned terms, typically eight weeks or less (IIE 2012). Short-term programs may be offered during the summer (either northern hemisphere or southern hemisphere summer), or January or May terms.

Financial Planning

Financial considerations are likely to be an important concern for many students in program selection and predeparture planning, and advisers must be able to guide students in all aspects of financial planning, including considerations regarding the costs of the education abroad experience, financial aid, scholarships, and budgeting.

Students must budget for tuition, room, board, and any program or home institution administrative fees, in addition to travel costs, passport, required visas and/or immunizations, books and supplies, cell phone, and other personal expenses.

Financial aid availability and portability is an important issue, and for some students, may be a deciding factor in program selection. Federal law dictates that a student can receive federal financial aid for study abroad if the study abroad is approved by the home college or university (Gliozzo 2009). Colleges and universities, however, have differing policies on the portability of institutional financial aid. Again, collaboration with partners is essential; education abroad advisers must work closely with financial aid offices, bursars, program providers, and outside scholarship programs to ensure financial aspects of the education abroad process are clear-cut and policies are transparent and understandable. Parents are also important partners, as financial questions are one of the primary reasons parents contact advisers.

Education abroad fee structures vary widely from institution to institution (see chapter 21). Some colleges and universities charge "home fees" for study abroad, meaning the home institution tuition and/or fees are charged for study abroad, regardless of the program cost; the institution then pays the program directly. Other institutions do not charge fees at all; the student pays the program directly for the program costs. Yet another structure is one in which institutions charge a study abroad or administrative fee to the student, but the student pays the program for tuition and fees. Some programs charge a comprehensive fee that includes accommodation, and sometimes students pay only tuition to an institution, and pay accommodation and/or meals separately. Navigating these options and administrative processes can be confusing for students, some of whom may be accustomed to their parents overseeing their university financing or financial aid.

Advisers must also be prepared to advise students about competitive and need-based and/or merit-based scholarships offered by organizations or program providers (for example, Gilman, Boren, Fulbright, Rotary, DAAD, and Bridging Foundation scholarships, among others). Students may seek help from the adviser in crafting scholarship application essays. Advisers are encouraged to consult individual scholarship organizations' websites, as they often include webinars and other resources focusing on how to write a competitive application.

PRACTICAL TIPS AND BEST PRACTICES

See the guide, "Budget Estimate Creation and Dissemination for Study Abroad Programs," created by NAFSA's Education Abroad Knowledge Community Subcommittee on Financing Education Abroad, 2012–13. http://www.nafsa.org/Find_Resources/Supporting_Study_Abroad/Budget_Estimate_Creation_and_Dissemination_for_Study_Abroad_Programs/

IIE Passport-supported Study Abroad Funding website is a directory of study abroad scholarships, fellowships, and grants for U.S. students.

Additional Advising Matters

In addition to counseling students about goals, academics, program selection, finances, and other practical aspects of education abroad, many other topics arise during the course of advising, such as cross-cultural adaptation, health and safety, student mental health issues, and many other logistical planning matters. Advisers should cross-reference other chapters in this book for information on these subjects.

Advising Programming and Techniques

Programming

Advisers can utilize different forms of advising, both individual and group. Individual advising can be effective for in-depth discussions about students' goals and expectations, and of course for any discussions about sensitive information, whereas group advising may be effective for content such as informing students about program options. Many offices conduct group advising sessions out of necessity and efficiency, due to the volume of students and/or programs and/or shortage of advising staff.

Research suggests that peer influence has a significant impact on students' choice to study abroad, and peer advising can be used effectively to promote study abroad, as well as to provide a more personal level of advising than that offered by a professional adviser (Lo 2006). Peer advisers can be a valuable supplement to other education abroad advising offered by colleges and universities (Lo 2006). There are numerous examples of effective peer advising programs and much variation regarding peers' responsibilities, qualifications, and training. Many education abroad offices utilize study abroad returnees in advising in a less formal way than peer advising, such as returnees attending study abroad informational or predeparture meetings. This can be extremely effective in both informing students about what to expect from the abroad experience, as well as giving returned students a useful outlet to process their experiences.

Techniques

In addition to knowing the subject matter to discuss with students and possible programming options, education abroad advisers must also develop effective skills and techniques. NACADA offers information on advising session techniques applicable to any advising appointments that includes topics such as opening the advising session, talking with the student, silences in the conversation, admitting your ignorance, avoiding the personal pronoun, delivering bad news to the student, dealing with the frequent visitor advisee, and setting limits and ending the advising appointment (NACADA 1990).

Technology and Social Media

Whether advisers like it or not, the reality is students increasingly seek advising through technology, rather than face-to-face conversations. According to a recent survey from Wakefield Research, 99 percent of students have at least one digital device, and nearly 70 percent use at least three devices each day. Nearly 50 percent of students check these devices every 10 minutes.[3]

Education abroad advisers can use social media to connect with students both individually and through groups and can be used to reach large numbers of students at a time. For example, Facebook groups can be used to generate interest in study abroad and encourage students to attend meetings or make appointments to talk with advisers directly. Some advisers have found student-generated group pages where students have posted questions to each other that may be best answered by an adviser (Traxler 2007). Facebook can also be used to connect study abroad returnees with prospective study abroad students, aiding in the advising process.

In addition to social media such as Facebook, LinkedIn, Twitter, and so on, some offices and programs offer real-time virtual advising for students utilizing instant messaging (e.g., Digsby, Pidgin, Trillian, Zoho) or meeting through technology such as Skype. The possibilities are endless and constantly changing. Advisers should consult students as well as their campus technology departments to keep up with the latest technology.

Evaluating Efficacy

Assessment has been greatly emphasized in higher education in recent years. Education advisers and administrators must also periodically evaluate adviser effectiveness and the effectiveness of advising services and processes. Evaluation varies depending on institutional context (large public university, liberal arts college, community college), size of office (one-person office, multi-staff program provider), student population (traditional age, first-generation college students, nontraditional), education abroad offerings (faculty-led, approved list programs, direct enrollments), and more. Advisers and their managers should assess how advising is meeting the institutional mission and departmental goals, how advisers are meeting student and programmatic needs, and advising processes and procedures. Importantly, advisers and administrators should collect and analyze the results of any evaluations and work together with campus partners to implement changes in order to increase efficacy. Feedback can also be used to assess the training and professional development from which advisers may benefit.

---

[3]Campus Technology, "Students Increasingly Comfortable with E-Texts" (2013) http://campustechnology.com/articles/2013/07/23/research-students-increasingly-comfortable-with-etexts.aspx.

Conclusion

Clearly, the process of education abroad advising is complex and multifarious. Each day in education abroad advising is unlike the next, and every student has different advising needs, goals, and interests. As such, effective education abroad advisers are required to possess a great deal of knowledge and many varied skills. Advisers must develop advising structures and techniques that are comprehensive and holistic, yet individualized to students' needs. Successful education abroad advising encourages students' growth, development, and autonomy, and helps students begin to develop the intercultural competence and cross-cultural skills they will need while abroad.

References

Alexitch, Louise. 2002. "The Role of Help-Seeking Attitudes and Tendencies in Students' Preferences for Academic Advising." *Journal of College Student Development* 43, 1:5-19.

Barbuto, John, Joana Story, Susan Fritz, and Jack Schinstock. 2011. "Full Range Advising: Transforming the Advisor-Advisee Experience." *Journal of College Student Development* 52, 6:656-670.

Cunningham, Leigh. 2003. "Multicultural Awareness Issues for Academic Advisors." NACADA Clearinghouse of Academic Advising Resources. http://www.nacada.ksu.edu/Resources/Clearinghouse/View-Articles/Multicultural-a84.aspx.

Engle, Lilli. 2013. "What Do We Know Now and Where Do We Go From Here?" Opening plenary. Forum on Education Abroad Conference, Chicago, Illinois. April 3, 2013. http://www.forumea.org/documents/LilliEngleKeynotewithslides.pdf.

Engle, Lilli and John Engle. 2003. "Study Abroad Levels: Toward a Classification of Program Types." *Frontiers: The Interdisciplinary Journal of Study Abroad* IX, 1-20.

Evans, Nancy, Deanna Forney, Florence Guido, Lori Patton and Kristen Renn. 2010. *Student Development in College: Theory, Research, and Practice.* San Francisco, California: Jossey-Bass.

Forum on Education Abroad. 2011a. "Code of Ethics for Education Abroad." Carlisle, Pennsylvania: Forum on Education Abroad. http://www.forumea.org/documents/ForumonEducationAbroadCodeofEthics.pdf.

Forum on Education Abroad. 2011b. "Education Abroad Glossary." Carlisle, Pennsylvania: Forum on Education Abroad. http://www.forumea.org/EducationAbroadGlossary2ndEdition2011.cfm.

Forum on Education Abroad. 2011c. "Standards of Good Practice for Education Abroad." Carlisle, Pennsylvania: Forum on Education Abroad. http://www.forumea.org/standards-standards.cfm.

Gliozzo, Charles. 2009. "Financial Aid and Study Abroad: Basic Facts for Students." Washington, D.C.: NAFSA: Association of International Educators. https://www.nafsa.org/findresources/Default.aspx?id = 8329.

Hofer, Barbara and Abigail Sullivan Moore. 2010. *The iConnected Parent: Staying Close to Your Kids in College (and Beyond) While Letting Them Grow Up*. New York, New York: Simon and Schuster/Free Press.

Hofer, Barbara. 2011. "Student-Parent Communication in the College Years: Can Students Grow Up on an Electronic Tether?" *The Bulletin* 79, 2:36-41.

Hofer, Barbara. 2012. "A Parent's Role in the Path to Adulthood." *The New York Times*. May 28, 2012.

Institute of International Education. 2012. "Duration of U.S. Study Abroad, 2000/01-2010/11." *Open Doors Report on International Educational Exchange*. http://www.iie.org/opendoors.

Kolb, David. 1984. *Experiential Learning: Experience as the Source of Learning and Development*. Englewood Cliffs, New Jersey, Prentice-Hall.

Lewis, Nasha. n.d. "Faculty: The Link Between Underrepresented Students and Study Abroad." *Diversity Network: Advancing Diversity & Inclusive Excellence in International Education*. http://www.diversitynetwork.org/articles/faculty-the-link-between-underrepresented-students-and-study-abroad.

Light, Richard. 2001. *Making the Most of College: Students Speak their Minds*. Cambridge, Massachusetts: Harvard University Press.

Lo, Stephanie. 2006. "Defining the Peer Advisor in the U.S. Study Abroad Context." *Journal of Studies in International Education* 10, 2:173-184.

Museus, Samuel and Joanna Ravello. 2010. "Characteristics of Academic Advising that Contribute to Racial and Ethnic Minority Student Success at Predominantly White Institutions." *NACADA Journal,* 30, 1:47-58.

NACADA. 1990. "The Advising Appointment." Originally published in Academic Advising News 12, 3. http://www.nacada.ksu.edu/Resources/Clearinghouse/View-Articles/Advising-session-techniques.aspx.

NAFSA. 2009. "NAFSA's Statement of Professional Competencies for International Educators." Washington, D.C.: NAFSA: Association of International Educators.

Smith, Cathleen and Janine Allen. 2006. "Essential Functions of Academic Advising: What Students Want and Get." *NACADA Journal* 26, 1:56-66.

Traxler, Julie. 2007. "Advising Without Walls: An Introduction to Facebook as an Advising Tool." *Academic Advising Today* 30, 1:9,13.

University of Minnesota. 2012. "Learning Abroad Major Advising." Multiple pages. http://www.umabroad.umn.edu/professionals/ curriculumintegration/majoradvising.php.

Vande Berg, Michael, Michael R. Paige, and Kris Hemming Lou. 2012. *Student Learning Abroad: What Our Students Are Learning, What They're Not, and What We Can Do About It.* Sterling, Virginia: Stylus Publishing.

CHAPTER 3

EDUCATION ABROAD APPLICATIONS:
Balancing Data Collection and Student Preparation

By Joe Sevigny

Introduction

The use of applications in the study abroad experience generates an interesting debate. One camp of thought argues that study abroad applications are an unnecessary additional burden on students and staff. Why require *another* application when the student has already applied for admission to their home institution? Why reinvent the wheel? Just use the information that has already been collected.

Another camp argues that applications provide an opportunity not only to collect valuable additional student and program data, but also to establish guidelines, set expectations, and provide important guidance and direction in the early stages of the predeparture experience. The application can and should be an opportunity for self-reflection on the part of the student so that the right program choice will lead to a successful and rewarding experience abroad.

Exploring the concept of applications in the study abroad experience is important because of the need to determine the scope and tone of this important portion of the predeparture preparation phase of the student's experience. In addition, the benefits to the institution or organization in terms of data collection and consolidation of steps in the predeparture process can be significant.

Initial Assessment: Establishing Goals and Objectives for a Study Abroad Application

Exploring the idea of applications in the study abroad experience casts light on two important concepts to consider: purpose and value. These two key concepts should provide the basic framework around which an application is built that best suits the needs of your students and your institution or organization.

The application can have a number of purposes, but it is essential to determine from the outset the main purpose. This will be derived from the initial assessment and further refined as your plan evolves. It is important to consider the role that the application will play in the early phase of the student's predeparture experience. Will the application be nothing more than a formality to get the student started, or will it help the student make the best program choice possible? Additionally, how will the application fit in to your procedures and what will your office gain from the application? What are you hoping to achieve from the application?

As you ponder these important points, you should begin to formulate a set of goals that the application will be designed to achieve. These goals will apply to both the student and to your institution. Here is where the need to delve into the true purpose of the application becomes crucial.

The primary objectives for instituting an application for study abroad are discovered after an initial thorough and realistic assessment of the goals to be attained and the resources available to meet those goals. The usual questions must be asked:

WHY do we need an application?

WHAT do we hope to accomplish with our application?

WHO are the stakeholders that must be involved?

WHEN is the optimum time for an application in the predeparture phase?

HOW will this improve our process?

WHERE do we begin?

The answers to these questions will help formulate a policy that applies to your application and will assist in giving it initial form and function.

The application can play an important role in a holistic predeparture experience for the student. Indeed, this should be a primary goal. As such, the components of the application should provide value to both the student and your office. We begin to see how purpose and value become dual concerns during the initial development of your application plan.

Program selection in the realm of education abroad is a paramount consideration for both the student and the institution. The application should function as a tool to aid in the program consideration and selection process. The goal should be excellent program fit for the student, and this can be achieved through thorough self-reflection. Incorporating an essay into the application process, for example, is helpful in having the student pause and reflect on his or her program choice.

The applicant's justification for wanting to study abroad should be rooted in a sincere desire to further educational objectives and goals, as well as enhance future employment opportunities. The essay will help the applicant reflect on why his or her program choice makes the best sense from an educational and personal growth perspective. Situational essay topics are a good way to prompt the applicant to offer insight into current global events. Asking students to write about current global conflicts or social trends will gauge their connection to the world around them and their knowledge and interest in current global affairs.

The collection of data is one of the most basic concepts behind having an application. This topic is covered in greater detail toward the end of this chapter, but it is critical to consider exactly what information you want to collect and the value that this information will provide.

From Concept and Design to Development and Deployment

Implementing a study abroad application requires a strategic approach. There are many pieces that must come together to form a coherent and concise experience for the student, while providing the expected results and benefits for the stakeholders.

The initial concept for the application will begin to take shape after considering the answers to the questions why, what, who, when, where, and how. Establishing goals and the realistic assessment of resources available to achieve those goals begins to move the focus from a macro overview to a more narrowly focused view on form and function. The flow of the application and the importance and use of the data collected starts to take priority.

The Stakeholders: It Takes a Village

Determining the various stakeholders in your quest for the best study abroad application may provide a bit of a reality check. Although it may be "your" application, you cannot accomplish this task alone—nor should you. The design and implementation of an application provides an opportunity to develop and foster important partnerships that are crucial to a successful study abroad experience. It is therefore necessary to identify all of the stakeholders that will play a role in this process and include them in each stage of this process.

The list of stakeholders will vary depending on the scope of your institution's study abroad policies. You should consider not only the various players that come into direct contact with your office and your students as they plan their study abroad program, but those players who also have a less direct but equally important role to play.

Application Content

After you have established the purpose and value of your application and identified the goals and aims, it is then important to begin to consider the content. Depending on the goals you have identified, the content of your application should yield the information you deem important to collect, and the application should also satisfy the various goals you want the student to achieve.

Faculty	The role of faculty in helping you formulate an application is significant. Faculty are deeply involved in such areas as program and course approvals, providing recommendations for students, and language assessments. Continually engaging faculty throughout your study abroad process will create a lasting partnership that benefits all parties.
Academic Advisers	Their role in reviewing course selections and degree requirements make these stakeholders a very important addition to your committee.
Registrar	Your registrar is often the main point of contact for transfer of study abroad credit and other aspects related to degree progression and completion. Consulting with the registrar early and often will help create a smoother flow to your application and avoid confusion or contradiction.
Financial Aid	Funding a study abroad experience can be a very difficult puzzle to assemble for a student. Every institution has a different policy on the portability of aid. In addition, there are countless external funding opportunities geared specifically for study abroad. Including a financial aid representative in your application planning group will add an important constituent that may assist your students in considering funding options earlier in the process.
Student Judicial Affairs	Part of your application process should include a check on a student's judicial background at your institution to ensure they are in good standing.
Legal Counsel	Liability, health and safety, and other legal matters are always a consideration in the realm of study abroad. Consulting with your legal counsel office early will help assure that you are proceeding on the correct and legal path.
Information Technology	Your IT department will play a necessary role in the implementation of your application. Working closely with your IT staff will help keep the scope of your application project on a realistic level and will help you understand technical limitations sooner rather than later.
Career Services	Many students believe that studying abroad will be an asset when they begin to search for a job after school, so involving your career services office in the study abroad process is a good idea, and an example of cross-departmental cooperation that benefits the student in every way.

Students	You should consider adding a student presence early in the application planning process. Having student feedback on a product that will be used by students will help assure greater acceptance and satisfaction. Consider including students from various backgrounds in terms of ethnicity, gender, and sexual diversity, Pell Grant recipients, nontraditional learners, and so on.
Parents	Parents play a very visible and important role in the student's study abroad experience. Engaging parents early in the process, and keeping them engaged, will promote a good flow of communication and help eliminate additional calls to your office.
Providers	If your institution utilizes study abroad program providers, they will have their own application process. Consider collecting information on your application that will satisfy the requirements of some providers that are regularly used by your students. This will help speed the completion of provider applications and alleviate duplication.

Ideally, the application should be a component of a thorough predeparture advising program. This program should be designed to help the student create goals for studying abroad by establishing appropriate expectations, helping the student understand approved program options and requirements, assuring academic policies and procedures are followed and completed, and prompting students' in-depth self-reflection. Placing the application near the end of the advising process allows the student to begin the application with a defined sense of purpose and a better understanding of the required tasks ahead.

An important expectation to set with the student is the understanding that your institution's study abroad application may not be the only application required. Students wishing to participate in programs offered by other institutions or providers will more than likely be required to complete a separate application. This concept can sometimes confuse applicants and has the potential to cause missed deadlines if not clarified early in the process.

There are a variety of application types that can be used. The type you select should complement the flow of the predeparture process and should be easy to locate, navigate, and complete. Your selection of an application type will be driven by a number of factors, determined in large part by budget and resources available.

A paper application, downloadable from your website, may meet your requirements. Paper applications offer a low-maintenance, simple option. An important consideration with paper applications is the collection of additional required documents. These will need to be collected and filed manually in a student's application file. In addition, if your office utilizes a database, there will be the need to enter application data into the database. Therefore you should plan on staff time to accomplish the data entry.

Online applications are widely utilized in the study abroad predeparture advising process. If you are considering an online application, the first important decision to make is whether to go with an off-the-shelf application from a reputable vendor or to create an application in-house. Both options require considerable resources.

Purchasing an application from a vendor is a substantial financial undertaking. If your office is well funded, this may be the best option for you. But even after you secure the necessary funding, you will still need your organization's information technology department to assist in the implementation of the application. Staff training is an important consideration.

Building an application in-house allows you to customize the application to your exact specifications. This allows you to build your application based on your current process. You will still need to budget for consultants or IT department staff to build your application, in addition to staff training on how to use the application system.

As you consider your options, one idea that could save time for both you and your students is to model your application and application requirements on those of the organizations/providers with programs most widely used by your students. By dovetailing your process program partners that host a large number of your students, aligning application elements can accomplish most, if not all, of the application requirements for both entities.

As you begin to develop the flow of your application, you will also refine the steps and the data elements that will become the components of your application. By this time you will have determined what data you want to collect above and beyond any student data already in your system. If your students use a variety of programs and dovetailing your application process isn't feasible, you should consider what your office absolutely must collect at the application stage and allow the external organizations and providers to collect what they require. This will greatly streamline your internal application process.

The following list offers some possible options that can be used to create a simple yet effective study abroad application. Ideally, much of this information will populate your application directly from your institution's main student database.

Application Deadlines	Students are deadline challenged, so it is very important to establish solid deadlines that are well advertised. If you are using an online application, ideally it should be impossible to access or submit an application once the deadline has passed.
Personal Information	Basic information about the student, such as home and school address, student ID number, birthdate, citizenship, and ethnicity are basic and necessary pieces of information to collect.
Program Choices	After thorough advising, the applicant should be prompted to choose at least two programs ranked first and second in the event that a back-up choice becomes necessary.
Emergency Contact Information	Collecting this information is important for health and safety considerations. In addition, providing parents with information on their student's program and progress will help create an atmosphere of cooperation and reduce calls and e-mails.
Upload Capability	A well-functioning online application allows the applicant to upload all required supplemental application documents. This aggregates the documents together and aids in the ease and speed with which the application can be completed.
Essay	Requiring an essay as part of the application process allows the student to reflect on their goals for studying abroad and also requires them to justify their program choice.
Letter(s) of Recommendation	This requirement helps build academic support for the student's program choice by requiring them to consult with faculty. It also allows your office to gain a better understanding of the applicant's academic skills.
Language Assessment	For students participating in programs requiring language skills, this important component will help determine the applicant's preparedness and program suitability.
Transcripts	Your policy on the collection of transcripts will determine if the applicant will be required to submit an official or unofficial transcript. Most external program providers will require an official transcript.

Photo	Many applications require the applicant to submit a headshot photo. Ideally, this will be an uploaded, digital headshot. Be very clear and specific regarding the photo requirements. Alert the applicant that this photo could be used for other purposes (ID card abroad, etc.).
Criminal History	This information is important not only to outside study abroad program providers; many student visa applications request this information as well.
Contract or Waiver	This is a very important consideration, and you should consult with your legal department about this requirement. Will you require a parent or guardian to also sign the contract/waiver? Consider a clause allowing for the release of information as required by FERPA.
Passport Copy	A copy of the photo page of the applicant's passport is a common application requirement and reinforces the importance of having a passport that is valid for at least six months past the study abroad program's end date.
Résumé	Requiring a résumé at the point of applying can be very useful, especially for internship or service-learning programs.
Portfolio or Performance Recordings	For arts-related programs, these items are crucial requirements. Consider the use of YouTube or other online video programs for students to submit performance pieces. They can simply submit the links of their performances.
Financial Worksheet	Requiring the applicant to submit a worksheet that details program costs against available funding will set the student on an early path to not only assuring that study abroad is financially feasible, but to investigating scholarships as well.
Application Fee	Many study abroad applications require an application fee. Consider how this fee will be collected (cash, credit card, etc.), and how to ensure your office is credited for the funds collected.
Deposit	Will you require a deposit to confirm the student's place in their program of choice? A confirmation deposit can also help control and manage program size, which is an important consideration for popular programs with capacity concerns.

As your application takes shape and you determine the steps involved, you should also consider the strategies for keeping applicants engaged and moving through the process. It is not uncommon for a student to begin the study abroad application process and get stalled along the way. Students are simultaneously juggling many different priorities and commitments, and can easily become distracted from the application process. It is therefore important to deploy strategies that proactively engage your applicants and prod them toward completing the application.

Regular reminders, sent by e-mail or—more effectively—text messages, are a basic and necessary strategy to help applicants complete their application. As deadlines draw near, your messages should be more frequent and the sense of urgency more prominent.

Depending on the level of technology and support behind your application, offering a portal provides some useful benefits for your applicants and other stakeholders. A portal allows applicants and other stakeholders to log in and view the status of an application or perform other functions related to an application. For applicants, they are able to see the progress of their application and which documents have been received. This allows the applicant to stay better connected to the process and more aware of their status.

Some portals can extend to other players in the application process. For example, offering faculty the ability to give recommendations and language evaluations through a portal helps facilitate their role in the application process by providing a quick and easy-to-use tool.

Data Collection

One of the greatest advantages of having a study abroad application is the ability to collect data. The collection and analysis of data related to study abroad can unveil trends that can help shape your program offerings while contributing important information to the greater field. It is therefore important to carefully consider which data will be necessary to collect during the application process.

If your institution or organization utilizes an existing student database, and if your study abroad application can link directly to this database, your application may not need to request as much data for the applicant. Ideally, much of the basic information on an applicant that already exists in the main database should populate your study abroad application. This will help streamline your application by eliminating unnecessary data fields and even entire application steps.

Listed below are some of the basic data elements that a study abroad application should include. You should consider any other data elements that would provide useful and important information for analysis.

Address and Phone Number	Collect both home and school addresses. Consider formatting issues for international addresses and phone numbers.
Citizenship	The number of international students studying abroad continues to rise. Collecting citizenship allows you to monitor this trend within your own institution. In addition, you are able to identify and flag non-U.S. citizens early in the process for further intervention and advising on the student visa application process.
Ethnicity	A considerable amount of very interesting and useful analysis will result from collecting optional ethnicity data. This question should be required, but you must offer an opt-out for no response.
Gender	Basic data pieces that should feed from your main database, if applicable.
Date of Birth	
Student ID Number	
Grade Point Average	Statistics related to grade point average are an important metric to review.
Major/Minor	Analytics on major and minor in study abroad are critically important to understanding student motivation and program or location choice.
Pell Grant Status; First Generation in College; First Generation to Study Abroad	Collecting this data can help you identify under-represented students who are interested in studying abroad. These populations are often difficult to identify and collecting this data will help with outreach efforts and diversifying your study abroad population.

Reporting and Analysis

As you collect data via your application, you will learn very quickly just how important and powerful some analysis of your data can be.

The more obvious data analysis, such as total number of students studying abroad in a given term or year, or most widely used programs, can help your office gain the attention of your institution's leadership. If your data show a consistent upward trend in study abroad enrollment, this has the potential to provide justification for requesting additional funding or staffing for your office.

Other important analyses that can be performed from data collected during the application process are:

1. **Location.** Performing an analysis on study abroad location choice will help you better understand how this trend compares to the field at large. In addition, the results of your analysis will help you maintain a robust set of program offerings for your students and faculty.

2. **Term Selection.** The choice of term for study abroad could have important implications for other stakeholders. For example, a severe imbalance in study abroad enrollment across semesters or quarters could cause an excess or deficit of available on-campus student housing.

3. **Major/Minor.** Analyzing study abroad enrollment by major or minor is helpful in developing a portfolio of programs that are useful to both your student population and your faculty.

4. **Program Duration.** If your program portfolio consists of many programs of varying lengths, including summer and short-term faculty-led programs, it is important to review the data on program duration to assure that your portfolio is updated to accurately reflect the study abroad trends of your student population.

5. **Underrepresented Populations.** The education abroad field shares a common goal of diversifying the study abroad population and reaching out to underrepresented students. As you begin to collect data on ethnicity, Pell Grant status, first-generation information, and so on, you will be able to identify underrepresented student populations and initiate outreach activities to attract them to study abroad.

Contributing Data to the Field

The collection of data is also important to the greater field of study abroad. Each year, the Institute of International Education (IIE) sponsors *Open Doors*, which is generally considered the preeminent research and analysis document in the field of study abroad. As more and more institutions and organizations contribute their data to the *Open Doors* report, a clearer picture develops of the important trends and changes in our field.

Conclusion

The goal of this chapter is to demonstrate how an application can assist study abroad professionals in better managing part of the predeparture advising process, as well as collect important data for trend analysis. Studying abroad is a potentially life-changing experience, and over time it has become an advantageous component of a solid career path. The predeparture advising phase of a student's study abroad experience is critical to establishing expectations and requiring the student to reflect on and justify their program choice. A well-planned application that fits your process has the potential to save time and help collect important information that can be used to improve study abroad advising and program portfolios.

References

Breakell, Tina and Bradley Titus. 2013. *By Example: Resources for Education Abroad Offices and Advisers.* Washington, DC: NAFSA: Association of International Educators.

Lancaster, Amy. Assistant dean for international programs and academic administration, Wofford College. Personal communication with the author, Joe Sevigny. September 2013.

Trimpe, Julie. 2007. *The Case for a Database—Better Advising, Program Support, Academic Recognition.* Washington, DC: NAFSA: Association of International Educators.

CHAPTER 4

PREPARATION AND ORIENTATION

By Eric A. Canny

Introduction

Preparing students, and their parents, for study abroad requires critical analysis of what appears to be unexceptional information but from a radically different point of view. Preparation and orientation must be thought of as a holistic learning process, with norms and frameworks that can be applied in order to impart key information in a way that stimulates critical thinking about what preparing for study abroad means to students and their parents. A framework to apply to the entire process, which should start well before orientation, is "anchored instruction," defined by Bransford et al. (1990) as:

> The model ... designed to help students develop useful rather than inert knowledge. At the heart of the model is an emphasis on the importance of creating an anchor or focus that generates interest and enables students to identify and define problems and to pay attention to their perception and comprehension of these problems. ... The major goal of anchored instruction is to enable student to notice critical features of problem situations and to experience the changes in their perceptions and understanding of the anchor as they view the situation from new points of view (123).

An example of this is the common refrain heard in the field: "no one believes culture shock will happen to them." Yet, what if this issue were anchored in experiences that the student could relate to and then applied to the entire study abroad experience? For example, ask students about the experience they had when they were new to the home institution: the culture of the academics, the perceptions of the campus, learning their way around physically, understanding the idioms of the campus, and so on. Most students will readily identify with this "shock" process, and can extrapolate it to a conversation about possible analogous experiences abroad. Too often in study abroad preparation, no anchor is laid that can readily allow students or their parents in the process to "identify and define problems and to pay attention to their perception and comprehension of these problems."

It is likewise important for international offices and educators to remember they are not alone in the process of orienting and preparing students and their families for study abroad. Regardless of the size of a campus, there are myriad resources to draw upon for assistance. This preparation process should not only begin post admission to the home campus, or even during advising as a student starts on the campus, but ideally should be part of the entire campus ethos; laying the groundwork for anchored learning to occur more readily during the final stages of preparation and orientation. Rather than thinking of this as "study abroad," it is best to apply the lens of internationalization and understand that such a process requires the active participation of the entire campus community at many stages in the learning cycle.

Partnerships and Programming

"Internationalization is the conscious effort to integrate and infuse international, intercultural, and global dimensions into the ethos and outcomes of postsecondary education."

NAFSA: Association of International Educators, 2010

"[Internationalization is] the process of integrating an international/ intercultural dimension into the teaching, research, and service functions of the institution."

Jane Knight, 2003

These two quotations highlight the fundamental point of how internationalization throughout an institution works in the context of study abroad. Specifically, they demonstrate that study abroad or international offices cannot remain isolated from the rest of the institution. In order to catalyze internationalization effectively, they must instead be integrated into "teaching, research, and service functions," all of which can help students and those who support them better prepare for a study abroad experience and learn from it over the long term. Nor can the field of study abroad any longer be considered a stand-alone at the periphery of the student's academic experience. Equally important to keep in mind is that there is no longer only one type of student to one type of program in a handful of locations, as reflected in the Institute for International Education's *Open Doors* reports. International offices must partner with as many departments of the institution as possible in programming around academic, professional, and personal needs and goals as they relate to study abroad and intercultural understanding. In doing so, at the point of "orientation" these principles are already accomplished at the macro-level, ideally having resulted in the student's decision of where to study abroad and why. Orientation thus becomes like an academic course, and the syllabus is comprised of anchored experiences that break down highly specific material into manageable learning outcomes organized in a logical sequence. By anchoring each of the learning outcomes in this way, it is possible to balance between individualized, program-specific learning objectives and general principles for all students.

This practice of an anchored instruction is intertwined with issues related to (a) required infrastructure, (b) financial aid and cost, and (c) reaching underrepresented students and engaging them, so they are aware not only of the possibility of study abroad and how it applies to them, but also of the unique issues that could inform their decision before they apply. Partnerships are critical as the student moves through advising, post admission, and orientation, and they support the work of the international office through bringing together experts across the campus to convey important information— while also allowing study abroad preparation to be staggered, so that students and parents have the knowledge and skills that they need when they need them, and are not oversaturated with information at the last minute. An additional benefit to the international office, as well as for students and their families, is that spreading out the study abroad preparation process helps other offices, such as financial aid, become equipped to answer questions relating to study abroad from students and parents in alignment with the professional practices and legal requirements of their particular areas.

Essential Learning Outcomes

Another holistic lens to consider when developing a study abroad preparation model is the Association of American Colleges and Universities' (AAC&U) Liberal Education and America's Promise (LEAP) campaign. The LEAP campaign is organized around a robust set of essential learning outcomes. Described in *College Learning for the New Global Century,* the learning outcomes and a set of "Principles of Excellence" provide a framework to guide students' cumulative progress through college; they are also directly applicable to the preparation for study abroad. Through AAC&U's Valid Assessment of Learning in Undergraduate Education (VALUE) initiative, a set of rubrics has been developed to assess the learning outcomes listed below. This process begins as students enter the institution, and continues at successively higher levels across their college studies. Such a model, when extrapolated across the internationalization of an institution as defined earlier by NAFSA and the American Council on Education (ACE), allows the students' preparation to infuse their entire academic career, reinforcing students' advising and selection of courses that directly link to their program selection, linking these to their academic plan, and better preparing them to move through the orientation and preparation process within a framework of critical thinking and writing for the "new global century."

Guided by LEAP essential learning outcomes, students are prepared for twenty-first-century challenges by gaining:

1. **Knowledge of human cultures and the physical and natural world**
   * Through study in the sciences and mathematics, social sciences, humanities, histories, languages, and the arts

   Focused by engagement with big questions, both contemporary and enduring

2. **Intellectual and practical skills,** including
   * Inquiry and analysis
   * Critical and creative thinking
   * Written and oral communication
   * Quantitative literacy
   * Information literacy
   * Teamwork and problem solving

   Practiced extensively, across the curriculum, in the context of progressively more challenging problems, projects, and standards for performance

3. **Personal and social responsibility,** including
   * Civic knowledge and engagement—local and global
   * Intercultural knowledge and competence
   * Ethical reasoning and action
   * Foundations and skills for lifelong learning

   Anchored through active involvement with diverse communities and real-world challenges

4. **Integrative and applied learning,** including
   * Synthesis and advanced accomplishment across general and specialized studies

   Demonstrated through the application of knowledge, skills, and responsibilities to new settings and complex problems (Association of American Colleges and Universities 2007)

Additional relevant resources from AAC&U include:
- What is a Twenty-First Century Liberal Education?
- Liberal Education and America's Promise (LEAP)
- Transforming the Study Abroad Experience into a Collective Priority
- Assessing Global Learning: Matching Good Intentions with Good Practice
- Global Learning Inventory Framework— A Smart Grid for Global Learning

ACE likewise provides frameworks for internationalization and global competencies from which any institution could draw to expand the preparation process across academic learning outcomes and personal and professional goals.

Some resources from ACE include:
- ACE Higher Education Topics: Campus Internationalization
- ACE Center for Internationalization and Global Engagement (CIGE)
- ACE Higher Education Topics: Global Higher Education

Background and Infrastructure

The development of an infrastructure for study abroad preparation and orientation will vary greatly from one institution to another. To guide its design, as well as address learning outcomes, including academic, professional, and personal needs and goals, one would be well-advised to start by asking a series of questions specifically tailored to each campus, and the types of study abroad programs offered (e.g., faculty-led, exchange, affiliate). From the answers to these questions, one can then work backward to create an integrated infrastructure and planned approach that systemically integrates the outcomes with partners on, and possibly off, campus, in addition to the institutional partners and offices who must be included in the anchored learning process.

Possible questions to consider in a review of the development of an infrastructure could include, but are not limited to:
- Who must be involved?
  - Institutional partners
  - Students
  - Parents
  - Faculty and staff advisers
  - Academic departments
  - Student life and student support offices
- Why do we need to prepare our students, parents, and those supporting them?
- When is the optimum time for the preparation and orientation phase(s)?
  - Prior to applying
  - At time of application
  - Post application
- What do we hope to accomplish with our process of preparation?
- How do we combine the questions above to define an optimum process?
- How do we build assessment into the process as we design it?

The Forum on Education Abroad supports this comprehensive approach to preparation for study abroad in its Education Abroad Glossary (2011), stating that "orientation programming in education abroad ideally is ongoing and designed to support students throughout the study abroad experience, highlighting ways to transform experiences into academic, personal, and professional growth."

Specifically, the Education Abroad Glossary defines predeparture orientation as:

> Programming intended to prepare students for a meaningful, successful, and educational experience abroad. Predeparture orientation addresses everything from practical concerns with passports and student visas, health and safety, and academics, to cultural adjustment, intercultural learning, and diversity awareness. [It] includes information on what to expect in the education abroad program, including such matters as housing, finances, transportation, and emergency contacts. Orientation may consist of written materials, in-person meetings, webinars, online training modules, e-mail correspondence, phone conversations, or (typically) some combination of these elements. (2011)

An example of such an ongoing holistic high-impact program to support students throughout the study abroad experience is Stetson University's Global Leadership Program. The program is a 7-semester (3.5 year) program aimed at transforming students into inspired, significant global leaders. Students in the program gain global leadership competencies to help foster positive global change. The program requires a 2-hour weekly colloquium, held each semester, paired with opportunities for students to grow as campus leaders. This includes mentoring and service-learning experiences, as well as requiring participants to study abroad during the spring semester of their second year at Stetson. Each fall semester, students take a course that compliments the colloquium and meets a specific global leadership requirement. Finally, students are provided with several course options each semester that include international components to reinforce and anchor their experience in academic as well as other growth areas.

Two other resources that focus on the importance of high-impact practices are *High-Impact Educational Practices: What They Are, Who Has Access to Them, and Why They Matter* by George Kuh (2008) and *Global Learning: Aligning Student Learning Outcomes with Study Abroad* by Kevin Hovland (2010). Kuh's work identifies several high-impact learning activities and describes the characteristics that make them so, while the latter examines high-impact activities in the implementation and preparation of study abroad programs.

According to Kuh, high-impact activities are effective because they:

1. Demand that "students devote considerable time and effort to purposeful tasks" (14).

2. Locate "students in circumstances that essentially demand they interact with faculty and peers about substantive matters, typically over extended periods of time" (14).
3. Increase the "likelihood that students will experience diversity through contact with people who are different from themselves" (15).
4. Ensure students "typically get frequent feedback about their performance" (17).
5. Provide "opportunities for students to see how what they are learning works in different settings, on and off campus" (17).

An international office's ability—in collaboration with others—to move into high-impact and innovative practices is nearly limitless. It is important as part of the background and structural development, however, to define learner characteristics and outcomes as part of the strategies invoked to design those practices. In particular, international offices are not only preparing students for their experiences abroad, but preparing entire families.

The following is a sample list of *possible* learner characteristics to consider when defining learning outcomes and the demographics to be reached.

1. Students:
   - Will be studying abroad, either by choice or by encouragement or even pressure from parents or others
   - Can be freshmen to graduate students, representing many ages and all schools/colleges/departments of the institution
   - May be internal students, those from other institutions, or international students
   - Different academic and cultural backgrounds
   - Often self-identify their experience unique to the study abroad location, potentially rejecting commonalities of experience across locations
   - May have lived/traveled extensively, or never have been abroad
   - Come from diverse backgrounds, including in terms of ethnicity, socio-economics, gender, etc.
     - Learning and physical disabilities
     - Non-English as the first/primary language
   - Varying degrees of knowledge/use of information technology for communication
2. Parents/guardians of students:
   - May not want child to be abroad
     - Student may be first child to attend college and/or first generation
     - Student may be only child

- May represent internal constituencies, and possibly external as well, i.e., from other institutions
  - May reflect different academic and cultural backgrounds
- May be U.S. or international citizens
- May have lived/traveled extensively with family, or have never been abroad
  - Very diverse, including in terms of ethnicity, socioeconomic background, gender, etc.
  - Non-English as the first/primary language
  - None to extensive knowledge/experience with information technology for communication

The above examples, and more based upon specific institutional demographics, can then be applied to analysis of the content in any preparation and orientation program stream.

- Sample areas to consider at this stage may include: Presentation of materials students/parents need to know
- Access to forms, applications, data for completion of processes and decision making (students and parents)
- Venues for students/parents to share experiences (cognitive and emotional)
- Administrative data (individualized) allowing access to predefined materials
- Feedback mechanisms

In building a robust infrastructure, as stated in the introduction, international offices should be preparing students to study abroad in partnership with other entities on campus, both as part of orientation as well as through ongoing programs and events. Below is a partial list of potential partners, which, as with other examples, is not exhaustive and will vary upon the organizational structure and resources of any given institution.

Potential Partners
- Offices of academic affairs and student success
- Administrators
  - International learning committee
  - International staff
- Alumni
  - Students
  - Parents of returning students
- Ambassador programs (returning and departing students, international students, mixed)

- Athletics
- Bursar
- Campus life
  - Diversity
  - Housing and residence life
  - Leadership programs
  - Greek life
- Counseling
- Faculty
  - Leaders (current and past)
  - International learning committee
  - International faculty
- Financial aid
- Funders/donors
- Information technology
- Institutional research
- International student organizations
- Language, political science, history, gender/race, international studies, international business programs
- Learning technologies
- Local resources (e.g., world affairs councils, local ethnic/nationality organizations, chambers of commerce, Rotary clubs, etc.)
- Marketing
- Student accommodations office
- Public safety
- Registrar
- Rotating series of predeparture "global," regional, local programs
- Staff
  - International learning committee
  - International staff
- Third party (study abroad, crisis management, insurance)
- Wellness (if distinct from counseling)

Examples of programming and events to support the infrastructure development stage may include:
- Academic and student success
- Campus life (diversity)
- Counseling
- Faculty (if preparing for faculty-led programs) as well as foreign faculty
- Financial aid presentations
- Fulbright presentations/funding

- International education week(s)
- Learning technologies (capstone modeling, online storytelling, documentation)
- Office of student accommodations
- Returning student panels
- Third party (study abroad, crisis management, insurance)
- Rotating series of predeparture "global," regional, programs
- Virtual presentations (site directors, students abroad, parents)
- Wellness (if distinct from counseling)

Technology and Social Media

Permeating any discussion of how to communicate in study abroad preparation and orientation is the question of how to most effectively understand and use new communications technology and social media, as they continue to affect almost every aspect of how institutions teach and communicate. Given the global reach of many international offices, this can be magnified in how we must adapt to meaningfully connect with students and parents, as well as faculty and staff on our campuses, to make them aware of our program options. The best practices for effective use of these tools will be in part determined by any given campus culture, the specific goals of each type of technology/social media as it relates to learning outcomes, and most importantly, grounding practices in cognitive theory. The latter is critical, as international offices too often forget that students as well as their families are indeed learning during this process, and that we are not imparting lists of information but rather key concepts, ideas, and material to be processed; this in order for students and those who support them to be better able to engage in the process, learn, and move through the orientation process and all the tasks required to prepare to study abroad, as well as best experience their time abroad. It should also be noted that these tools must be examined in terms of security, confidentiality, and privacy to ensure they are used appropriately and per best practices regarding information that may be shared in the public domain.

A potential ally in this is your college of education or education department, or those who have resources on cognitive theory and multimedia learning. Turn to and engage experts in these fields. As in the development of an academic course, they could share perspectives from other classes and assist in creating a comprehensive study abroad preparation program with a logical sequence of learning objectives. If a holistic model is implemented, such as those previously referenced, the constraint of the "brief time" one tends to have in conducting a formal orientation session may be decreased—though of course will not be completely alleviated. Moreover, how information is imparted to students, parents, or those supporting students could require novel ways of using technology, social media, print, and in-person communication.

Two articles that highlight the ways in which multimedia learning can quickly overload learners—which also dispel some common myths about today's learners—are:

Mayer, Richard, and Roxana Moreno. 2003. "Nine Ways to Reduce Cognitive Load in Multimedia Learning." *Educational Psychologist* 38, 1: 43–52.

Spiro, Rand, and Jihn-Chang Jehng. 1990. "Cognitive Flexibility and Hypertext: Theory and Technology for the Nonlinear and Multidimensional Traversal of Complex Subject Matter." In *Cognition, Education, and Multimedia: Exploring Ideas in High Technology.* Edited by Don Nix and Rand Spiro. Hillsdale, N.J.: Erlbaum Associates.

Both articles reinforce the concept that with the definition of learner characteristics, learning outcomes, and strategies, one must first define the pedagogical approaches that will be most effective for the target audience. Based upon these, one can select from the resources available to best communicate the information using technology, avoiding cognitive overload, and reinforcing the concept of anchored instruction.

The following are some points to consider when providing an online system or multimedia tools that enable students and parents to access information (in conjunction with in-person experiences):

- Self-select from a variety of mediums based upon skills and learning styles.
- Provide seamless movement (via administrative and design means) between information on predeparture, arrival, the on-site experience, and return to the home campus.
- Layer thematic schema moving from simple tasks (process) to complex theoretical models (diversity, cultural awareness, etc.).
- Provide mechanisms for users to submit, comment, and process the experiences they are going through (ending isolation, learning from each other as well as staff, etc.), layering the cognitive with the emotional.

Possible ways to assist in the development of such a wide-ranging model may include:

- Student, faculty, staff surveys of how current resources are utilized, including both institutional and noninstitutional resources
- Technology norms and resources available at the institution
- Comfort with the technology, as well as access issues (e.g., firewalls and parents' access to secured systems)
- Samples of technology to convey information may include:
  - Web applications, or "apps"

* Blackboard
* Custom-built systems
* Existing enterprise information systems
* Sharepoint
* Prezi
* Podcasts
* Third-party provider software
* Web forms

■ Link existing software from various parts of the institution to overlap with the themes and information that need to be conveyed, thus reinforcing collaboration and an anchored approach.

Below is one sample schematic outlining possible ways in which learners will access your systems and information, and options of specific technologies to be deployed and integrated to achieve goals based upon the prior decisions of learner characteristics, learning outcomes, etc. It is important to consider the ways in which social media can expose, connect, share, and provide feedback—of course highlighting how different froms of social media have defined purposes and outcomes.

Working with institutional allies such as university marketing, the academic marketing department, the digital media program, and so on, is critical to developing a social media integration theory-model that meets the needs of your learners, especially given the particulars of existing use, infrastructure, and cohesion in messaging.

FIGURE 1. Social Media Integration Theory Model[1]

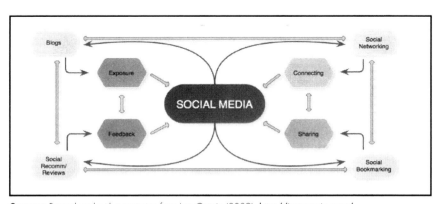

Source: Reproduced with permission from Isra García (2009), http://isragarcia.com/.

[1]A updated integration model can also be found at http://isragarcia.com/strategic-human-media-integration-model.

As stated previously, any model should be based upon the norms on your campus (e.g., is Twitter popular or not; Facebook; Instagram, etc.), and based upon the prior examples of learner charteristics—elements to consider in evaluating technology use and resouces available. Likewise, it is important to diagram the overall social media landscape at your institution, and apply it to your:

- Learning outcomes
- Learning characteristics
- Campus norms
- Consistency (e.g., use WordPress if that is the institutional norm)
- Types of devices used by your learners
- Security of data
- Tracking of data (e.g., indication of whether or not a student read a document, or just said that they did)
- Ability for students abroad to engage in this process (e.g., is Facebook the norm in a particular country, and if not, are you able to link to what is)

A more detailed visual example of social media, how it is accessed, and the primary goals that could be of use is shown in figure 2 below.

FIGURE 2. Social Media Landscape

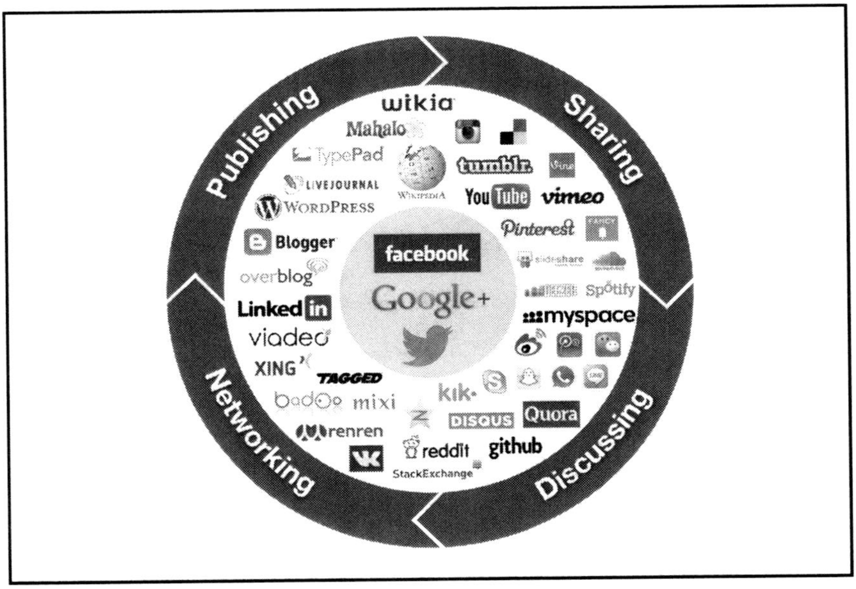

Source: Reproduced with permission from Frédéric Cavazza (2013), www.fredcavazza.net.

Finally, additional factors to consider related to the integration of social media and technology in preparation and orientation include:

- Staying ahead of the curve
- News and other information dissemination (crisis response)
- Privacy and "control" of information
- New technology, which changes expectations and operations
- Limitations on your infrastructure based upon norms/conditions where the program is operating

Education Abroad Preparation Content

Following are selected examples of, and resources for, preparation content. As the content must be specific to each institution, the mission and vision (institutional and international), as well as learning outcomes and goals in each area, there will be great variance from one institution to another. One is encouraged to develop a framework for the prior themes and then build the content around the answers to these issues, questions, and ideas as they relate to each institution.

Examples and Resources

Academic (Goal Setting and Success Strategies)

- NAFSA
  Orientation/reentry programming resources
- Michigan State University
  Office of Study Abroad learning goals
- The Forum on Education Abroad
  Education Abroad Glossary Standards of Good Practice for Education Abroad
- Butler University
  Study abroad information for parents

Professional Goal Setting and Networking

- Michigan State University
  Professional development
- The British Council
  Culture at Work: The Value of Intercultural Skills in the Workplace
- The National Career Development Association
  "Maximizing the Career Development of Students Who Study Abroad"
- IES Abroad
  "How Study Abroad Shapes Global Careers"
- American Institute for Foreign Study
  Impact of Education Abroad on Career Development

Personal Considerations (Identity, Culture Shock, and Managing a Personal Network)

- College Student Journal
  "Studying Abroad: The Role of College Students' Goals on the Development of Cross-Cultural Skills and Global Understanding"
- Kalamazoo College
  "Culture Shock and American Students Abroad: Building a Better Orientation Program"
- Fulbright Commission
  Culture shock

Financial Planning

When considering financial planning, it is critical to know your institutional processes and procedures (e.g., if institutional aid applies, and on which types of programs) and availability and limits of internal resources such as study abroad scholarships. Partnering with the financial aid office is essential so that students and anyone who supports them financially are aware of these critical factors as they select their programs. By the time of orientation, they should have made their decision regarding what program to attend based on academic, personal, and financial outcomes that align with overall study abroad advising.

Preliminary budgets should have been developed ahead of time, so that when orientation arrives the information imparted can be highly specific on topics such as common spending traps and means of moving funds regularly, as well as in crisis, among other issues.

Scholarship advising requires advance planning and action, with many deadlines for scholarships occurring a term or more in advance of the application process. While students might be moving through these processes simultaneously, the advising—and conversations about what will and will not happen should scholarships be awarded late in the process—ought be discussed and planned for in advance.

Some sources of funding planning information and preparation include:

- U.S. Department of Education
  U.S. Network for Education Information (USNEI)
- Institute of International Education
  IIEPassport Study Abroad Funding
- University of Missouri
  Study Abroad Financial Planning Worksheet
- Grand Valley State University
  Study Abroad Funding Packet

Health and Safety

Some examples sources of health and safety information include:

- U.S. Department of State
  Students Abroad: Health
- The Center for Global Education
  International Resource Center information

Passports and Visas

Some examples sources of passport and visa information include:

- U.S. Department of State
  Students Abroad: Travel Docs
- NAFSA
  Visas for Education Abroad
- University of Colorado-Boulder
  Passports and Visas

Institutional Partners

Three primary institutional partners will likely help an international office keep abreast of student demographics, assessment, and trends: the offices of institutional research, admissions, and campus life.

Admissions

From admissions, one can secure data early on of the potential interest in study abroad, and from what specific demographic groups and academic areas, along with other information. While this data is preliminary, it helps to plan for infrastructure, staffing, and other needs. Additionally, admissions can often provide similar feedback on parents, their interests, concerns, and so forth, which are often voiced at events, open houses, and other interactions. When possible, international offices should be present at admissions events, to showcase study abroad, describe the process, and answer questions, which provides a feedback loop on current resources and changes in incoming demographics.

Institutional Research

Institutional research can provide and reconfirm data (e.g., census data and diversity, etc.) as well as provide critical information on numbers of students in certain majors, allowing international offices to cross-correlate this to national data (e.g., *Open Doors*) or internal data such as surveys and events. Since learning outcomes—from preparation and orientation, to study abroad program, to reintegration back to the home institution—should align to your institution's learning outcomes and reporting methods, institutional research is likewise an important partner in assessment, feedback, and surveying of students.

Campus Life

Finally, campus life and its often myriad interconnecting departments, including such functions as counseling, student activities, and health and well-being, is often one of the largest entities on campus, with immediate access to and close knowledge of students. As stated above, there are often strong relationships between the international office and many of the offices within student life. These connections are especially important during the preparation stage.

The marketing funnel provides a visual example of information flow to and from these various learners during study abroad preparation, and can be used in the development of a holistic anchored learning approach.

FIGURE 3. Marketing Funnel Reconsidered

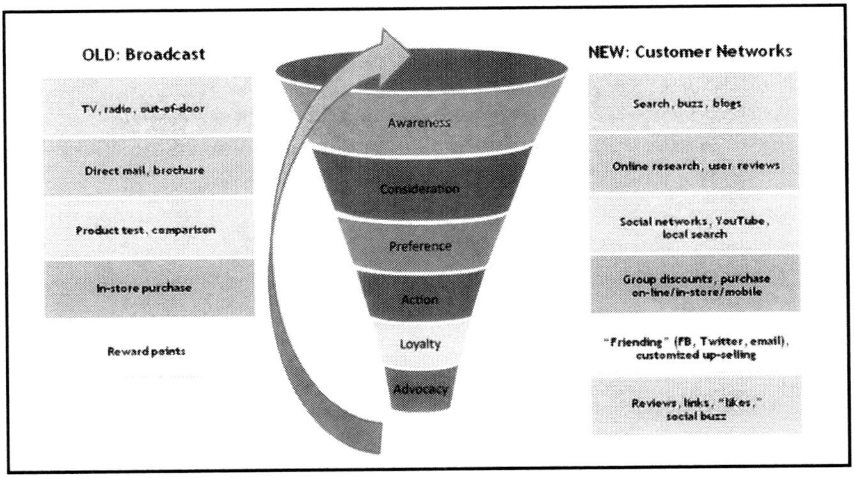

Source: Reproduced with permission from David Rogers, *The Network is Your Customer: Five Strategies to Thrive in a Digital Age* (New Haven, Conn: Yale University Press, 2011).

Underrepresented Student Groups

Preparing underrepresented groups involves much more than orientation, since in many cases the work must begin to engage them in such a way that they perceive study abroad as an option in the first place. Connecting back to many points previously mentioned—from a holistic approach across their academic career; to partnerships on-campus across academic, support, and other divisions; to programming that supports their needs that is perhaps best done in conjunction with other offices—an integrated process is critical to assisting students who are underrepresented in study abroad. Though not exhaustive, sample groups and resources are listed below.

LGBTQ

- NAFSA Rainbow Special Interest Group (SIG)
- IES Abroad: LGBTQ Support
- Smith College: Sexual Orientation and Identity
- The Education Abroad Network: Study Abroad for LGBTQ Students
- Global New York University LGBTQ Resources
- NYU Student-to-Student Guide: LGBT
- GlobalGayz
- International Lesbian, Gay, Bisexual, Trans and Intersex Association
- University of South Florida: LGBT Student Guide for Education Abroad
- Michigan State University: Study Abroad for Gay, Lesbian, Bisexual, and Transgendered Students

Minority Students

- Diversity Abroad: Diversity and Inclusion Abroad
- Indiana University: Minority Issues
- Carnegie Mellon University: Scholarships for Minority Students
- Karin Fischer, "Colleges are Urged to Try New Approaches to Diversify Study Abroad" (*The Chronicle of Higher Education*, 2012)
- Karen Shih, "Study Abroad Participation Up, Except Among Minority Students" (*Diverse: Issues in Higher Education*, 2009)
- Connie Perdreau, "Building Diversity Into Education Abroad Programs" (American Institute for Foreign Study Foundation, n.d.)

STEM

- Jennifer Ellis Fritz, "Increasing Study Abroad Participation for STEM Students at Bucknell University" (*Connecting Our World Grassroots Leadership Program*, 2012)
- Boren Awards for International Study: Special Initiative for STEM Majors
- Lynn Anderson, *Science, Technology, Engineering, and Math (STEM) Students and Education Abroad* (NAFSA, 2009)
- NAFSA *International Educator* Archives

First Generation

- George Sanchez, "Intensive Study Abroad for First-Generation College Students" (*Peer Review*, 2012)
- Supporting Diversity through First-Generation College Students in Study Abroad: A Comprehensive Approach (*Forum on Education Abroad conference*, 2013)
- Engaging First Generation College Students in Education Abroad (*Forum on Education Abroad conference*, 2012)
- NAFSA, Engaging First-Generation College Students in Study Abroad
- Teresa Heinz Housel, "How to Figure Out Study Abroad as a First-Gen College Student" (*First Generation Student blog*, 2013)
- Bryan Andriano, "Study Abroad Participation and Engagement Practices of First-Generation Undergraduate Students" (EdD Dissertation, The George Washington University, 2010)
- Teresa Heinz Housel, "First Generation Focus" (*Inside Higher Ed*, 2012)
- Jessica Greenbaum, "A Diversity Initiative in Global Education for First-Generation Students" (*Capstone Collection*, 2012)

Disability

- Mobility International USA
- Eve Katz, "Students with Disabilities Studying Abroad" (*International Educator*, 2007) University of Pittsburgh: Disabilities
- Baldwin Wallace University Study Abroad: Disability Services for Students Information Sheet

Music

- Studyabroad.com: Music Study Abroad Programs
- Brandeis University School of the Creative Arts

Law

- American Bar Association: Foreign Study
- The International Law Students Association
- Stetson University Center for Excellence in International Law

Graduate

- U.S. Department of Education
- Institute of International Education Fulbright Programs
- Idealist.org: Benefits for a U.S. National Getting a Degree Abroad
- Diversity Abroad: Graduate Study Abroad

- Christopher Gearon, "More Graduate Students Consider Study Abroad" (*U.S. News and World Report,* 2011)
- Erin Sullivan, "Study Abroad: Ten Reasons to Do Grad School Abroad" (Education.com, 2011)

International
- The International Education Financial Aid website
- InternationalStudent.com
- The Ohio State University: Study Abroad for International Students

Veterans
- Post 9/11 GI Bill: Study Abroad Programs
- GI Bill Benefits for Study Abroad
- Steven Maieli, "Study Abroad Offers Many Advantages—and GI Bill Can Cover It" (*Army Times* 2013)

Conclusion

As international educators, our goal is to teach. What tools and means you elect to do this will depend upon your institution, scope and scale of programs, the populations you serve, and you. However, the ideas that we attempt to impart can vary from the very complex to the mundane. One must always be aware, as Bransford et al. (1990, 123) says, our goals are to help students "develop useful rather than inert knowledge," in addition to:

> ...[providing] an emphasis on the importance of creating an anchor or focus that generates interest and enables students to identify and define problems and to pay attention to their perception and comprehension of these problems.
> ...[enabling] student to notice critical features of problem situations and to experience the changes in their perceptions and understanding of the anchor as they view the situation from new points of view.

Only through this can we hope to anchor students' preparation solidly, so that it not only prepares them for their time abroad, but lays the groundwork for reflection and introspection while abroad and upon their return.

References

Association of American Colleges and Universities. 2007. Liberal Education and America's Promise (LEAP) Essential Learning Outcomes. Washington, D.C.: AAC&U. http://www.aacu.org/leap/vision.cfm.

Association of American Colleges and Universities. 2007. *College Learning for the New Global Century*. Washington, D.C.: AAC&U. http://www.aacu.org/leap/documents/GlobalCentury_final.pdf.

Bransford, John, Robert Sherwood, Ted Hasselbring, Charles Kinzer, and Susan Williams. 1990. "Anchored Instruction: Why We Need It and How Technology Can Help." *In Cognition, Education and Multimedia: Exploring Ideas in High Technology*. Edited by Don Nix and Rand Spiro. Hillsdale, N.J.: Erlbaum Associates.

Forum on Education Abroad. 2011. *Education Abroad Glossary*. Second Edition. Section 2.6. Carlisle, Pa.: Forum on Education Abroad. http://www.forumea.org/EducationAbroadProgramFeaturesandTypes.cfm

Hovland, Kevin. 2010. *Global Learning: Aligning Student Learning Outcomes with Study Abroad*. Washington, D.C.: NAFSA: Association of International Educators. https://www.nafsa.org/uploadedFiles/NAFSA_Home/Resource_Library_Assets/Networks/CCB/AligningLearningOutcomes.pdf.

Kuh, George. 2008. *High-Impact Educational Practices: What They Are, Who Has Access to Them, and Why They Matter*. Washington, D.C.: Association of American Colleges and Universities.

Knight, Jane. 2003. "Updating the Definition of Internationalisation." Boston, Mass.: *International Higher Education*.

Mayer, Richard, and Roxana Moreno. 2003. "Nine Ways to Reduce Cognitive Load in Multimedia Learning." *Educational Psychologist* 38, 1: 43–52.

NAFSA. 2010. *The Changing Landscape of Global Higher Education*. Brochure. Washington, D.C.: NAFSA: Association of International Educators. http://www.nafsa.org/_/File/_/positioning_brochure.pdf

Rogers, David L. 2011. *The Network is Your Customer: Five Strategies to Thrive in a Digital Age*. New Haven, Conn.: Yale University Press.

Spiro, Rand, and Jihn-Chang Jehng. 1990. "Cognitive Flexibility and Hypertext: Theory and Technology for the Nonlinear and Multidimensional Traversal of Complex Subject Matter." In *Cognition, Education, and Multimedia: Exploring Ideas in High Technology*. Edited by Don Nix and Rand Spiro. Hillsdale, N.J.: Erlbaum Associates.

CHAPTER 5

WHILE ABROAD

By Thomas Teague

Background and Infrastructure

The importance of considering all elements of the education abroad experience—including predeparture, program abroad, and reentry—as components of a process has been echoed throughout the profession for some time now. Authors of the second edition of *NAFSA's Guide to Education Abroad for Advisers and Administrators* (1997) proposed as much when they mentioned that " ...education abroad programming cannot be limited to the actual time spent in another country, but represents a three-phase, inclusive learning process." Bruce La Brack also advocated for this holistic view of student learning when, using as a case study the University of the Pacific, he discussed the "almost symbiotic linkage" of predeparture and reentry, along with the time abroad, as a "relatively unbroken learning process" (La Brack 1993).

However, much focus has been placed on the pre- and post-elements of education abroad with the assumption that student learning and development abroad would occur on its own without guidance and assistance from faculty or staff. Now, as education abroad research has become more sophisticated and garnered greater visibility, scholars have found that active, purposeful and strategic guidance and interventions are necessary in order to cultivate growth and progress toward the achievement of targeted student learning outcomes (Vande Berg, Paige, and Lou 2012). This chapter focuses on the considerations inherent in providing adequate support and structure for students during their program abroad, within the spirit of linking predeparture to reentry. Topics discussed include the value of partnerships, strategies to support students in this phase of the process, technology, content to emphasize, and information related to student groups.

With the increased reliance on accountability by administration, government, and other constituents to ensure that education abroad does what many tout it can do, advisers and administrators cannot simply sit by while their students are abroad and expect them to simply absorb, perhaps by osmosis, knowledge, growth, and understanding of the world around them. Intention, strategy, and adherence to goals should be employed. First and foremost, underlying any program abroad should be some sort of student learning outcomes. What do we want our students to be able to do, acquire, and learn while they are abroad? Specific outcomes may vary depending on the type and structure of a program. Some outcomes may be extremely discipline-specific, while others may be quite general, something that would pertain to any and all students regardless of major or program of study. Some general outcomes that tend to be commonly supported on most education abroad programs include increasing intercultural development, including intercultural sensitivity and competence, acquiring a sense of global-minded-ness, and encountering personal growth.

Another outcome that many education abroad advocates envision in their program is interaction with the host community for the development of cross-cultural learning. Anthony Ogden, in his article, "The View from the Veranda: Understanding Today's Colonial Student," emphasizes the importance of host-community interaction to student learning and development. He calls for practitioners to move students away from the "veranda" mentality, where they encounter host cultures and issues from a place of comfort, and where they only interact with the host culture "as needed." Ogden argues for educators and administrators to rethink how they design education abroad programs. Programs should be developed where it is impossible for students to "avoid direct and meaningful contact with the host culture, to learn with and from them, to explore new values, assumptions and beliefs" (Ogden 2007–08). Ogden provides an example of one such way he has tried to encourage increased interaction within the host community by providing a letter to students describing ways they can maximize their time abroad and get involved on site.

Whatever our goals or learning outcomes are for students, it is important to integrate the education abroad experience into the curriculum, thereby fortifying its value to outside constituents and communicating with students the necessity of incorporating this opportunity in their degree plan and overall college experience. There are several resources related to curriculum integration, many of which can be found via the NAFSA website.[1] The idea of curriculum integration is perhaps most key while the student is abroad, as this is the time where the practice unfolds and the proverbial rubber meets the road.

Strategies

When considering predeparture orientation or reentry programming, it is important to think about the structure of that programming and the method in which it is delivered and facilitated. The while-abroad component should be no different, and practitioners should think carefully about how to best serve their own students.

---

[1]Curriculum integration resources can be found on the NAFSA website at http://www.nafsa. org/Find_Resources/Supporting_Study_Abroad/Network_Resources/Education_Abroad/ Curriculum_Integration__Best_Practices/.

Comparing In-Person and Distance/Online Learning

During all phases of the education abroad process, certain information must be conveyed to students involving topics such as health, safety, logistical considerations, culture, academic content, and so on. Practitioners must consider whether they should deliver this information in-person, on site, or through some sort of online vehicle. What works for one organization or institution may not work for another. What are the learning objectives of providing the information? Who will convey the information: expert speakers/staff or international or home-institution student peers? Will the information be delivered in a group setting via lecture or in a more intimate, one-on-one setting? How can material be delivered effectively online? Where can technology assist, either in-person, on site, or online? These are just a few questions to ponder when determining a model of information sharing and teaching for your own students. You may even find that what works for one of your programs may not be best for another program.

Type of Program

The type of program must be considered when determining how to support and guide students abroad. There are a myriad of structures that an experience abroad can take. Who's directing the program? Perhaps the students are participating in a direct-enrollment program, one with a third-party provider organization, or a faculty member? The needs of the students should be assessed prior to designing how the information should be developed and facilitated. Who might be on site with the students? For example, if you know that some students are participating on a third-party provider program that touches on information you plan to deliver, how can you work with that partner to convey it instead of doing it yourself? What efficiencies can be uncovered and relationships developed in the process? If a faculty member is directing a program abroad, might he or she have suggestions on how to deliver the content in a more appropriate way to further integrate that information into the experience while on site? Finally, if you have students participating in independent experiences abroad, how do you effectively facilitate information delivery and learning in an online format? Might there be any software or organizations that can provide such services?

Interventions

Much of Engle and Engle's research concludes that "program intervention brings results" (Vande Berg, Paige, and Lou 2012, 41), at least when discussing intercultural learning and competence. Their findings indicate that the mere provision of program elements such as homestays, direct enrollment courses, and cultural activities do not necessarily further increase intercultural learning. Reflection and guidance is important to the learning process. How might you be able to strategically intervene to help further the growth and development of your students abroad? Might it be through structured reflection prompts and careful feedback? Could it be through providing homestay families who will actively engage with your students, or perhaps including a buddy program with local students? How will students be given the opportunity to debrief and reflect on these experiences, as per the type of program, partnerships, and resources available, in addition to the vehicle of delivery?

Content Delivery: Examples and Variations

Institutions and organizations across the world have developed various strategies to deliver important content in unique ways to students abroad.

Bellarmine and Willamette Universities

Bellarmine and Willamette Universities use an intentional, targeted intervention model to convey important intercultural concepts and facilitate intercultural learning among their students. While this model includes a pre- and post-program component, the while abroad component is unique in that it involves students corresponding electronically with one another and instructors in small groups. Each week, students participate in specific activities in their host community, reflect on prompts that accompany the activities, and then post their responses for group members and the instructor to see. Each group member must provide feedback to others in the group. This exercise helps students develop the process of reflecting, generating explanations or generalizations, and testing those generalizations, which provides new experiences for students to reflect upon. It helps students to hear different points of view as they engage in this process (Vande Berg, Paige, and Lou 2012).

Global Scholar: Online Learning for Study Abroad

Created by The Center for Global Education, the Global Scholar website houses three online courses that guide students through the education abroad experience, from before the program, while abroad, and after the program. The "while abroad" course discusses topics such as logistical issues abroad, diversity abroad, culture and language, and preparing to return home. At the completion of all three courses, students can receive a global scholar certificate.

ISA Prague

Many third-party program organizations provide essential on-site orientation services as well as continued assistance to students while abroad. One such on-site staff, associated with International Studies Abroad (ISA) in Prague, Czech Republic, attempts to challenge their students in order to cultivate the learning process. For example, instead of lecturing to students the proper etiquette involved in many Czech activities, such as grocery shopping, the staff role plays a scene and asks the students to choose what is proper or improper. Then everyone debriefs the scene and the staff discusses the correct behavior. Another activity that the on-site staff conducts is a city scavenger hunt, where students go out on their own to complete certain tasks, within a time limit, in a race-type format. This activity engages students in the local community, requiring them to interact with locals, navigate transportation, operate in a foreign language, and more. At the end of the experience a debriefing is conducted once more and students are given a chance to discuss, in a structured environment, their thoughts and feelings.

Leader for a Day

On Leadership Lessons from Prague, a faculty-directed program operated via the University of Kentucky, the faculty director organizes students on site into groups of 4–5 and tags one student each day to be the leader of his/her respective group. The night before, the faculty director meets with all group leaders for the upcoming day and debriefs them on where they need to be and by what time(s), and what items all students need to bring. Each day's leaders are to make sure the groups are prepared and on time. Students are required to create blog entries for each day and discuss how their experiences relate to the concepts of leadership discussed during class time. The director also provides in-person opportunities for discussion as well. Students report that by participating in this activity, they feel much more knowledgeable about the material and can apply it to any context, foreign or familiar.

Partnerships

Staffing for support while abroad can be a challenge. Who will do what and how? With such questions, it is important to determine who your partners are and how they may be able to help support your students abroad. When exploring and identifying potential partners, think about how they can help (1) accommodate your students' needs, (2) fit in to and accommodate your mission/strategic goals, and (3) incorporate your learning outcomes through their services. With the right partners, not only can you hopefully increase efficiency, but provide consistent and appropriate support on site, thereby furthering the concept of a holistic education abroad process.

There are many groups that can partner with education abroad staff and administrators to support student learning while abroad:

- **Faculty:** These individuals tend to direct many programs abroad and are consistently people who students look up to and listen to for suggestions and advice.
- **On-site staff:** These individuals, such as those associated with a third-party program provider, host institution, or domestic institution branch campus, are on site and have easier access to interact and communicate with students. They also likely have more knowledge of the host community and can help identify and implement strategies for information sharing, intervention, and student learning.
- **Campus programs:** These programs can act as partners in that they offer avenues through which students can seek support and engagement. Whether on the home campus or an international campus, the programs that may be offered—such as counseling services, community service office, tutoring, and so on—can help students have a more successful experience.
- **Student peers:** The old adage says that students tend to learn best from their peers, those who've experienced what current students are going through. Study abroad returnees, international students, and other program participants can all provide a strong peer group that can be leveraged to support student learning while abroad.

Technology

When supporting and informing students abroad, think about how technology can be utilized in order to be more effective and efficient. In an environment that requires education abroad practitioners to do more with less, we must all turn to technology for assistance. Some options include:

- **E-mail and/or telephone:** Sometimes nothing is more reliable than picking up a telephone to reach a student or sending them an e-mail. Most students abroad today carry a cell phone with them, making it much easier to reach them than in years past. Also, with the advent of Wi-Fi, students seem to always stay connected to the Internet.
- **Video conferencing:** Do you need to deliver particular information "in-person" but cannot afford to travel abroad to deliver it? Conduct a video conference with students (via Skype, ooVoo, etc.) while they are abroad, if able. If working with an on-site partner or host institution, perhaps they can help arrange for the conference on their end while you do the same on yours.

- **Social media:** We live in a world of hashtags, handles, status updates, and tweets. Education abroad offices and organizations across the world are getting involved with various social media such as Facebook, Twitter, Instagram, Vine, YouTube, etc. to reach students in ways that other forms of technology fall short of doing. Why not put health and safety reminders on social media? Or perhaps post a message to one of your program's Facebook pages.
- **The "app" generation:** Provide your students with examples of web applications they can download to use abroad, if they have a smart phone. There are literally thousands of apps, many for free, that can help students, including but not limited to currency converters, language translators, photography aids, budgeting assistants, maps, guidebooks, and travel apps.
- **Ask an adviser:** Given the advance of technology, students today tend to want things on their time and in real time as much as possible. Some offices are accommodating this trend by developing real-time chat software, where a student can simple click a button and enter into an instant message-type conversation with someone in their home country or at their institution. The University of Kentucky Libraries is one such institutional entity with their LibAnswers "Live Chat" function. Education abroad third-party provider Cultural Experiences Abroad (CEA) is also utilizing similar software where students can chat live to ask adviser-specific questions or review important items related to their program.

Programming and Events

Just as education abroad practitioners develop programmatic elements to support and inform their students prior to and after the program abroad, they must also do so during the program abroad itself in order to help promote a streamlined, coherent, and holistic experience. There are a variety of ways in which students can be supported and engaged while abroad. Below are a few that can be employed regardless of the duration or type of the program. Think about how your partners might be able to help facilitate each one.

- **Community engagement and integration activities:** This includes activities, such as scavenger hunts or having students meet and talk to at least one host-country national in a given time frame. Visit resources such as the NAFSA Intercultural Activity Toolkit or the Education Abroad Faculty Toolkit to learn more about other activities that can be used to engage students abroad.

- **Peer-to-peer interactions:** Provides students opportunities to engage with their host-country or international peers while abroad, via structured program social events, tutoring partners, buddy programs, etc. Students' international peers may be able to support them in ways that program staff or faculty cannot due to the nature of their relationship and generation.
- **Advising:** Either formally, informally, or both, it is important to check in with students to see how they are doing academically, personally, and so on. This strategy could be in the form of an e-mail from the home university or organization or via on-site meetings that occur periodically throughout the program. Such time can allow for students' needs to be addressed as well as time for feedback and reflection.
- **Guided reflection:** Students cannot merely grow and learn via exposure alone, but must be given opportunities to interact and unpack what they've experienced in those interactions. Cultural mentors, whether staff, faculty, peers, or others, can provide useful feedback to help students learn more deeply and make connections.
- **Maximization tips:** Provide ways that students can maximize their time abroad and get the most out of their experience. In his article, "The View From the Veranda" (2007–08), Anthony Ogden provides such examples for students.
- **Develop work, internship, or volunteer abroad (WIVA) experiences:** Typically these types of experiences further engage and integrate students into the host community. They can often also require them to apply the information they've learned in order to successfully navigate their environment and responsibilities, contributing to their overall growth in the process. More resources regarding WIVA experiences can be found via NAFSA's online resource library.

Content While Abroad

What content do students need to be apprised of abroad and how can that information be facilitated so as to support them? While some information is dependent on the program itself, some general topics should certainly be discussed, as they can affect the abroad experience for every individual. In the spirit of ongoing orientation and a holistic education abroad process, keep in mind the pieces of information that students need to know specifically while they're abroad, as this is when they'll likely pay attention to it most—when they're in the moment. Think about the following topics and what your students would need to know while abroad to help them be successful.

Academic Content

First and foremost, students should remember that they're abroad participating on an educational program and should remain focused on the academic nature of the opportunity. As such, understanding the etiquette and culture of the local community towards academic study is important. Students should be aware of the expectations held by those directing their program, whether faculty, staff, or administrators. Students should be made aware of resources available to them on site as well as at the home institution, such as tutoring services, study spaces, library, research resources, and so on. Academic orientations are a great way to share this information, starting with a tour of the academic facilities and the relevant resources so that students can actually see what is open to them. Engaging host country students to lead parts of this orientation can be an effective peer-to-peer model that allows visiting students to make connections with others beyond their program group.

Since the academic environment—and even everyday life—around the world can be very different from students' experiences in the United States, students may require guidance during their program to successfully navigate the transition. Interacting with students, whether through some form of technology or via on-site faculty or staff, is a good way to gauge where they are in their studies as well as in their growth and development. Doing so can help you to support students as needed, but also challenge them. Talk to your education abroad counterparts in the host community to learn what they do to support students academically. How might they be able to assist you?

Professional Experiences

While students often set academic goals for their education abroad experience, many also set professional goals. Thus it is important to provide them with some guidance and support to help them explore themselves professionally. Many programs offer some sort of engaging element beyond straight courses, such as internships, research opportunities, service learning placements, field study, community service, etc. These types of experiences simultaneously afford students the opportunity to meet local community members, explore their professional interests, test their cultural assumptions, and reevaluate their goals and values. If interested in incorporating such an element into your program, peruse the WIVA resources found on the NAFSA website.

Having a program with a formal WIVA component is not the only way that you can support your students in exploring professional interests and opportunities. If you have students studying at a foreign institution or on a similar type of program abroad, encourage them to explore whether or not there are professionally relevant clubs and organizations present on campus. Buddy programs may also serve a similar purpose. Work with on-site partners to find opportunities for students to interact with local professionals in some way, whether by attending a lecture, setting up informational interviews, or shadowing opportunities. Not only can cultural mentoring be valuable, but professional mentoring is as well. These types of experiences can supply students with the chance to network and begin building connections that may serve them well in the future.

Personal Considerations

Personal considerations can vary and span a wide range of topics. Sharing information with students about identity—what it means to be "you" abroad—and cultural adjustment is key. Simply sharing information with students before they depart for their program is not sufficient, as in many instances they will have not truly experienced much of what they're being told from an education abroad practitioner. When students arrive abroad and spend time in the host community, they will likely begin to understand how their view of themselves and their experiences in the host culture are important to how well they do on site. During predeparture orientation, students may not recognize the importance of topics such as race and ethnicity, gender, sexuality, socioeconomic status, religion, and ability. Discussing these topics while abroad can be more effective because students are experiencing the environment firsthand.

Because students often encounter experiences that challenge their identity or affect their transition to the host community, it is important to provide them with opportunities to reflect on those experiences. This could be offered through informal conversation, through requiring they keep a blog or journal, or group discussion, whether formally or informally. In their book, *The Global Classroom: An Essential Guide to Study Abroad* (2010), authors Jeffrey Lantis and Jessica DuPlaga provide a worksheet with questions designed to help students explore their experience abroad from a variety of angles, including through the lens of their personal and cultural identities. Additionally, *Maximizing Study Abroad: A Students' Guide to Strategies for Language and Culture Learning and Use* (Paige et al. 2002) provides resources to help support and challenge students while abroad, as they navigate interactions that involve cultural understanding, communications, host families, and adjustment to the host culture.

Other strategies that some institutions and organizations have used to help direct students' reflections include gathering education abroad students and host community students together to discuss seemingly similar topics, such as dating, making friends, gender, race and ethnicity, sexuality, and religion, in a safe, structured format. Third-party program provider, AMIDEAST, organizes this type of activity with their Egypt program students. Activity participants report finding it intriguing and beneficial, as they learn the extent of differences in views and etiquette around these topics. Hearing from people their own age who are from the host culture enlivens topics and allows students to question perceptions and values undergirding certain practices.

Budget Management

When preparing for education abroad, many students find themselves concerned about the cost of the experience and how much money they should carry with them for the duration of their program. Students often struggle to manage their budget abroad and fall short of funds. Therefore, teaching budget management while abroad is extremely important. Showing students what the host country currency looks like and its exchange rate to U.S. currency is key, as students will use this information for the rest of the program. Also, demonstrating the correct way to use automatic teller machines (ATMs) in the host country, and discussing which ATMs are safe to use, could potentially save students from trouble later, as identity theft and other dangers can arise in many international locales. Furthermore, reviewing proper ways to store money is also important. On-site staff or faculty directors, and even international peers, can demonstrate strategies to help students keep their money safe and away from petty theft and pickpockets. Complementing this idea is advising on how many funds to obtain at one time, due to theft threat as well as international exchange and bank fees.

Providing a guided experience or structured activity involving interaction in a local store or market could be a useful exercise as it helps students better understand the local shopping culture and currency, as well as make observations about how much particular items might cost. Technology can be a useful tool to help encourage budget management abroad. For example, if students have a smart phone, they can download budgeting apps to help them keep track of their spending. Regardless of the information conveyed to students and the vehicles through which it is distributed, students should take time to reflect on how they are spending their money and the context in which they're doing it. Doing so may help them notice trends or bad habits, and help them make observations about their behaviors, particularly regarding how they might be considered in comparison with the host culture.

Health and Safety

Students are provided with a wealth of health and safety information prior to their program's departure. Still, health and safety topics need to be reinforced while students are abroad through the on-site orientation and ongoing training. Providing health and safety information in both written and other forms is important, as not all students may be able to follow and remember a lecture presentation. Again, on-site staff, such as with a host institution or third-party program provider, can assist in facilitating health and safety information. Understanding how any of your partners approach health and safety issues, though, is essential so you can determine if their systems mesh with your own policies and procedures.

In addition to the nuts and bolts of health and safety, such as how to use your insurance, who to call in the event of an emergency, what to do if you're ill, and so on (see this guide's relevant section on health, safety, and risk management), students need to understand how to stay healthy and safe within the context of their host culture. Culture contains so many nuances that it can be easy to place oneself in a harmful situation unknowingly. However, once students are living in the host culture, they have the opportunity to observe up close the nuances that can affect their health and safety—nuances such as proper social etiquette, proxemics or nonverbal communication, behavior, dress, and so on. Inviting guest speakers or facilitating workshops on this topic could be a strategy to help facilitate this information. As many education abroad locations provide access to the Internet in some form, it is always wise to provide Internet links to health and safety-related websites, so students can view this information on demand and in private.

Sometimes students may not feel comfortable discussing some matters related to health and safety, particularly if they do not wish to disclose sensitive information or have others know about certain aspects of their identity such as race and ethnicity, gender, sexuality, religion, body image, and health or ability. These students will need access to information on such issues, as well as a safe space and a supportive environment. There are a variety of online resources available to students regarding health, safety and culture. The NAFSA website contains a variety of resources for practitioners, from mental health concerns to security issues, and even information about recommended practices. Other health and safety resources that may be helpful include the U.S. State Department and the Center for Global Education's SAFETI website. Many institutions and third-party provider organizations also have a wealth of resources for students— particularly those regarding various diversity considerations that could affect student health and safety abroad— such as IES Abroad and Indiana University.

Passports and Visa

Providing information and support for students regarding travel documents should not end once they land in the host country. In some countries, students must obtain appropriate documentation or residence permits in order to remain for study. Students should be advised and guided on site about how to obtain such documentation; taking students to complete these transactions is additionally helpful as students can look to you or on-site staff for assistance.

Also, keep in mind that travel, particularly to other countries, is one of the most common activities students participate in abroad. Many students may not realize, however, that they need a visa to enter some places. If you partner with on-site staff or faculty directors, require that your students inform them of such travel arrangements. Properly notifying students of these issues and rules ahead of time can help decrease potential health and safety hazards in the end. In addition, reviewing with students how to properly carry and store their essential travel documents, such as passports and visas, is important. Along the same vein, remember to provide information for students about what to do if a travel document gets lost or stolen, and if possible, encourage them to contact on-site support or the home institution emergency contact for assistance.

Student Groups

Data Collection and Use

For many education abroad offices and organizations, data tends to be collected at the end of an experience, such as the predeparture orientation or perhaps when students return from their program abroad. Collecting data from your students while they are abroad is also essential, as noted in chapter 20. Capturing such information while students are in the middle of their program can potentially prove useful for benchmarking, program development, learning outcome purposes, student support, and more. Use technology or partnerships to help maximize the opportunities for data collection. Think about sending simple, short electronic surveys to students, or see if faculty directors or on-site staff can conduct focus groups. Data collection doesn't have to be formal to be useful. Informal interactions with students, such as those which occur while on an excursion or in passing in a classroom space, can provide very rich information. If you happen to use a Facebook page or other social media outlet for your students, think about checking in with them in that space and asking questions to obtain feedback.

Consider also trying to collect feedback at multiple points during students' programs abroad. Doing so may help you identify particular trends and obtain a more holistic view of their experience, as well as indicate areas for greater support and improvement. Check with institutional or organizational peers to see how they might be collecting data on their students. Also, visit the Forum on Education Abroad's website to view resources relating to outcomes assessment and other research endeavors. Work with your partners to see how they may be able to assist in achieving any assessment or evaluation goals you have. Having data about your students' experiences abroad will prove useful as the profession continues to interact in a higher education environment of increasing accountability. For more information on data collection, see chapter 20.

Underrepresented Student Groups

Education abroad attracts students from all backgrounds and walks of life, some more than others. As such there are a myriad of student groups that can be considered underrepresented, such as first-generation college students, students of color, students with disabilities, male students, graduate students, international students, and others. With such diversity represented, those who identify with one or more groups may require additional support and information to ensure a positive experience abroad. As mentioned in the health and safety section of this chapter, it is important to provide resources, websites, and safe spaces for discussion to allow students multiple ways to access information on these sensitive topics. In addition to the resources listed at the end of the health and safety section of this chapter, other resources for underrepresented student groups include:

- Diversity Network
- ALLAbroad
- Mobility International
- NAFSA Rainbow SIG International Educators Resources

Even if you provide these resources for private perusal, it is important to also provide a safe space for students to ask questions and explore and discuss issues and observations that are salient to them. Working with international and home-campus partners is crucial. On-site partners can help to create and develop that safe space, even if it is simply a staff member's office. They can also assist in helping students explore issues as they arise and provide guidance. Home-campus colleagues can collaborate with the home education abroad office to ensure a consistency in messaging, should they too be working with many of the same students who are abroad. This consistency helps to reinforce familiarity and support, which can be a powerful feeling when in a foreign environment where things are different and perhaps somewhat disconcerting.

Another resource that may prove beneficial to students includes personal stories and anecdotes from education abroad alumni with whom they can relate. Online magazines and websites such as Transitions Abroad, Glimpse, and Verge contain articles that students can read and even potentially contribute to as they live out their experience abroad. Again, technology can prove useful as students with smart phones can download apps to help them navigate their time abroad and connect with the population with whom they identify, such as the LGBTQ community or individuals with disabilities. Nonetheless, while all students should be supported while abroad, students who identify as part of an underrepresented group may required additional support, whether they ask for it or not.

References

Hoffa, William, and John Pearson, eds. 1997. *NAFSA's Guide to Education Abroad for Advisers and Administrators.* Washington, D.C.: NAFSA: Association of International Educators.

Vande Berg, Michael, R. Michael Paige, and Kris Hemming Lou, eds. 2012. *Student Learning Abroad: What Our Students Are Learning, What They're Not, and What We Can Do About It.* Sterling, Va.: Stylus Publishing.

La Brack, Bruce. 1993. "The Missing Linkage: The Process of Integrating Orientation and Reentry." In *Education for the Intercultural Experience.* Edited by R. Michael Paige. Yarmouth, Ma.: Intercultural Press.

Lantis, Jeffrey and Jessica DuPlaga. 2010. *The Global Classroom: An Essential Guide to Study Abroad.* Boulder, Colo.: Paradigm Publishers.

Ogden, Anthony. 2007–08. "The View from the Veranda: Understanding Today's Colonial Student." *Frontiers: the Interdisciplinary Journal of Study Abroad* 15 (Fall/Winter).

Paige, R. Michael, Andrew Cohen, Barbara Kappler Mikk, Julie Chi, and James Lassegard. 2002. *Maximizing Study Abroad: A Students' Guide to Strategies for Language and Culture Learning and Use.* Minneapolis, Minn.: Center for Advanced Research on Language Acquisition, University Of Minnesota.

CHAPTER 6

POST STUDY ABROAD

By Chelsea Kindred

As international educators, we commit to supporting a student's study abroad learning trajectory including predeparture, on-site, and post-study abroad. This chapter explores the reasoning behind reentry programming, the various ways in which we can aid alumni in building a vocabulary with which to articulate their international experience, and cites examples of structures in place to help alumni reflect on and integrate their study abroad experience into their academic, professional, and personal lives.

Background and Infrastructure

To frame the context of the post-study abroad discussion, we must first answer the following questions:

Why is the period after a study abroad experience important to student learning?

As students return to the comfort of a familiar campus culture and pace of life stateside, it is integral for education abroad facilitators and practitioners to continue intentional structured reflection and engagement. Students can quickly become immersed in their primary culture upon return home and lose touch with their experience abroad. In his online tool, "What's Up With Culture?" Bruce La Brack (2003) uses a shoebox metaphor to encourage students not to pack away their study abroad experience alongside photos and mementos in a shoebox. Instead, La Brack suggests students view their study abroad experience as an integral part of their daily personal, academic, and professional lives.

Study abroad returnees impact the campus community, local and state communities, and the national populace as they apply a deeper understanding of cross-cultural engagement to the challenges of our time, be it as large as national discourse on public policy and immigration reform or as small as accompanying a grandparent to apply for a passport. Longitudinal studies show that alumni are daily utilizing skills they strengthened or enhanced during their time abroad. By nurturing this process, international educators can cultivate an informed alumni base eager to share their experience with prospective students and the world.

What are the desired outcomes of a post-study abroad program?

The Forum on Education Abroad (2013) succinctly summarizes successful reentry programming as structured to meet three objectives: (1) reflection, (2) articulation, and (3) integration.

Reentry programming should:

1. Encourage deeper engagement and understanding of the study abroad experience, the cultural complexities introduced, and the personal impact on the student.
2. Provide students with useful vocabulary to articulate the content of their study abroad experience (without resorting to over-used adjectives such as "life-changing" or "awesome").
3. Outline ways in which students can apply their newfound understanding to different facets of their lives, from a micro to macro level.

The discussion of outcomes of the study abroad experience and reentry programming in particular would be incomplete without the addition of the findings from multiple longitudinal studies completed within recent years. While the student experience is variable and there is no conclusive study, scholarship within the field in recent years has examined the outcomes of the study abroad experience. Studies such as the IES Abroad alumni survey (2002) and the American Institute for Foreign Study (AIFS) alumni survey (2013) outline a crucial platform of support for the long-term impact of the study abroad experience. The SAGE research project (2010) and the GLOSSARI Project (2004) were both conducted by university systems and closely measured both academic and civic outcomes of the study abroad experience.

What are the benefits of investing in student learning outcomes post-study abroad?

By providing resources to encourage reflection and engagement in returnees, we invest in international education as a field and increase the complexity of dialogue about the study abroad experience. Students who are more informed and articulate regarding the ways they interacted with a foreign cultural environment become more informed advocates for international education and engagement. This nets a greater return for the field of study abroad, as our best marketers of the experience are these highly enthusiastic and articulate returnees. With crucial preparation, these students can seamlessly weave the outcomes from the study abroad experience into their professional paths and potentially engender additional internationalization of diverse fields and applications.

By investing in the entirety of the student learning process, education abroad facilitators and educators can provide structured intervention in the crucial phase of reentry.

Common Reentry Programming Models

After we begin to understand the "why" of reentry programming and establish outcomes that are best suited for one's specific student population, we can turn to the "how" of reentry programming.

REENTRY PROGRAMMING MODELS

Single Reentry Session or Event	Many institutions host a reentry orientation, whether a half-day event filled with cultural understanding activities or résumé review, or a few hours in the afternoon or evening to reconnect with the study abroad office, vocalize and share the student experience, and provide a space for students to formalize the next steps in their academic careers. Food is typically provided to encourage attendance. **Example:** The University of Cincinnati Reentry Night includes a dinner. Oklahoma State University hosts a photo contest and displays finalists at the study abroad fair.
Peer-to-Peer Program	Models of peer-to-peer advocacy vary widely. Some peer advising programs on university campuses have students apply to work for a term or a year within the study abroad office advising students and orienting them to the study abroad process. Peer advisers can also visit classrooms, volunteer at international education events, and conduct strategic outreach to student groups. Peer mentorship programs can also encourage one-on-one study abroad advocacy after extensive training by the study abroad office or partnering international education organization (IEO). **Example:** Colorado State University's Peer Advisor Program includes extensive training. Peer mentors serve as first-round advisers in the study abroad office. They also conduct information sessions, classroom visits, and participate in predeparture orientation.

Reentry Course (For-Credit and Noncredit Models)	To encourage structured reflection, students on many campuses are encouraged or required to take a study abroad course that includes predeparture, on-site, and reentry components. **Example:** Wake Forest University offers INS 152, "Cross-Cultural Engagement and Re-entry." This is the third one-credit course in a series of cross-cultural engagement courses completed by the student throughout their study abroad experience. The course gives students a chance to reflect both on their experience abroad and their reentry into life back in the United States. It also provides an opportunity to learn ways to leverage the international experience—be it for jobs, careers, or international experiences in the future.
Student-Led Programming	Many institutions with fewer resources and dedicated staff rely upon student initiative to initiate the reentry process. Student organizations such as study abroad clubs and international education organizations have sprouted where institutions have less-specific reentry programming. To found a student-run organization, many campuses require as few as 4–5 students. **Example:** Lincoln's Globetrotters, a student-run organization at the University of Nebraska-Lincoln.
Regional Reentry Conferences	As the field grows in its understanding of the importance of this final piece of intentional study abroad programming, the popularity and attendance of regional reentry conferences has grown significantly. **Example:** New England Returnee Conference; Minnesota Returnee Conference; and Lessons From Abroad Reentry Conferences are some of the many models of these programs. For these conferences, international educators serve as facilitators and collaborators with a network of institutions to deliver quality reentry programming. As an independent nonprofit organization, Lessons from Abroad provides a curriculum and other resources to make it easy for regional university partnerships to execute a conference and provide this important service to returned students when resources and budgets are stretched thin.

Stakeholders and the Importance of Collaboration

Partnerships and collaboration are necessary when approaching the feasibility of producing any of the reentry programming models above. Who are the stakeholders when approaching reentry programming? How can your collaborations strengthen the quality of your programming?

FIGURE 2. Resources for Study Abroad Alumni

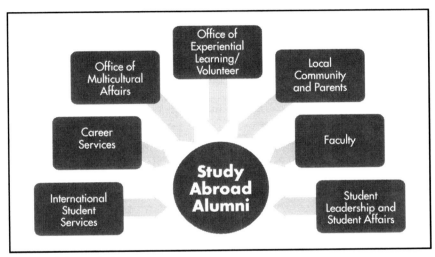

Source: Chelsea Kindred

As you consider the objectives and desired outcomes for the post-study abroad experience on your campus, take a moment to consider the best possible resources for students. The following examples and questions can be used as a guide.

International Student Services

What types of support exist on campus for international students? How can international students and scholars on campus engage a recently returned, culturally sensitive study abroad returnee? How could international students and scholars help cross-market international education to students on campus by utilizing international and returned study abroad students to continue to encourage cross-cultural engagement and competency? Moreover, how can study abroad students apply their knowledge and experience from abroad to help international students succeed?

Career Services

How does the career services office define the outcomes of study abroad? Students often visit career services for résumé review, mock interviews, and professional career advice. What collaboration is possible? How could the study abroad office partner with the career services office to provide an essential professional development context to the study abroad experience? What types of international job opportunities does the career services office promote?

Office of Multicultural Affairs

It is important for students to understand that the study abroad experience of living within another culture and deftly navigating cultural conflicts does not have to be reserved for times that they are outside of the borders of the United States. Consider what events the office of multicultural affairs provides for students on campus, which would be of benefit to study abroad returnees. How can multicultural affairs help returned study abroad students reflect on their experience? What types of programming is offered by the office of multicultural affairs to encourage continued student engagement in multicultural opportunities? Students may also have new questions about their own identity related to race, gender, sexuality, ability, religion, or socioeconomic status. These offices have resources to help students as they negotiate their intersecting identities.

Office of Experiential Learning / Volunteer

Many returned students focus on getting abroad again, but do not have the resources to identify other opportunities outside of the traditional credit-bearing experience. How does your office of experiential learning or volunteer opportunities advise students on international destinations? What nearby populations or communities represent your international opportunities? How can returned study abroad students engage with that population?

Local Community and Parents

How can returnees engage with the community? What underrepresented cultural groups within your community can speak to motivated returnees about current issues that need a culturally sensitive perspective? What festivals or celebrations occur throughout the year that highlight or mirror your study abroad program offerings? For example, if your city hosted an international festival, returned students from that year's selected country could volunteer and reconnect with their study abroad experience in a new way. How do students articulate the outcomes of the study abroad experience to their parents? How does your office engage parents to understand the benefits and value of the study abroad experience? Why do we need informed parents to advocate for study abroad?

Faculty

How do students engage with faculty upon return from their study abroad program? How do faculty perceive the goals of the study abroad office? How do faculty understand the modern study abroad experience? How do faculty engage study abroad returnees in their teaching? Why is it important to engage faculty on your campus? What are the benefits of faculty support?

Student Leadership and Student Affairs

How can your office connect returned study abroad students to leadership positions on campus? What opportunities do these offices offer that would benefit from an international perspective? Why do returned study abroad students make great student leaders?

Programming and Events to Facilitate Reentry

After considering the types of events and potential partners for collaboration, a diverse variety of events are possible. In lieu of listing all types of events that one could collaborate with and facilitate at any given institution, please consider this chart as an outline of scaled events, ranging from formal events to informal events, and in-person events to online events.

FIGURE 2. Examples of Reentry Programming and Events

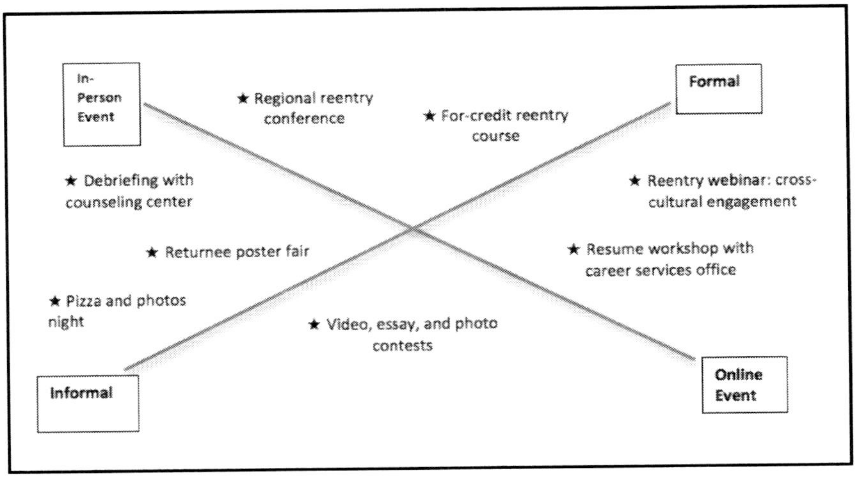

Source: Chelsea Kindred

Consider the needs of your students and the structure of your institution when determining the type of event that works best. Each event could be executed in a number of ways with a variety of outcomes. Determine what your goals and learning objectives are prior to the event and construct the event to meet those goals. Some examples of reentry programming goals include: promote community among returnees, market to prospective students, and generate engagement and investment from faculty and staff.

Reentry Conference Programming Models
Included below are successful models for reentry programming that encourage reflection, articulation, and integration of the study abroad experience.

New England Study Abroad Returnee Conference
Originally conceived by the Boston Area Study Abroad Advisors group in 2002 (renamed BASAA: New England Education Abroad Community in 2006) this conference offers opportunities for returned students to network, reflect, and engage with their study abroad experience. The conference agenda includes concurrent sessions with topics ranging from study abroad in a job interview to leadership skills for returnees. The *International Educator* article, "Bringing It Home: Multifaceted Support for Returning Education Abroad Students" by Mendelson and Citron (2006), explores the impact on the students within the region.

Minnesota Study Abroad Returnee Conference
Started in 2006, the Minnesota statewide returnee conference offers another regional opportunity for returned students. This conference actively utilizes a variety of media, including reentry webinars throughout the year, to reach students outside of the official day of the conference. Sample session content and more information can be found on their website.

Lessons From Abroad
Lessons From Abroad, an established nonprofit organization, held its first conference in February 2008 at the University of California-Berkeley.
  Lessons From Abroad conferences' objectives include helping students:
- Process their emotions from the experience
- Learn to articulate their experience for résumés, job interviews, and graduate school applications
- Discover additional opportunities for going abroad again
- Acquire tips for how to live an internationally focused life (Lessons From Abroad 2013)

Using Technology and Social Media for Reentry Programming

The current generation of students is adept at navigating different types of technology and avenues for communicating information. By providing various outlets for students to access reentry information, the field can better reach students where they are and deliver valuable information in a palatable way.

Innovative Ideas for Technology in Reentry Programming

Digital stories

Some institutions have capitalized on student enthusiasm for digital media, including songs, photos, and videos, by requiring students to compile them in a compelling way. Austin College's Center for Global Learning requires a similar digital storytelling assignment in a cross-cultural interaction course that runs alongside students' study abroad program. Such assignments provide a structured environment for students to reflect on their international experience by engaging with media they produced themselves.

Blog or Vlog Opportunities

Thoughtful prompts and intentional structure can coax student writing to meet the objectives of reflection, articulation, and integration. By advertising these reflective pieces on your institution or organization's blog, student reflection serves as marketing material for prospective study abroad students as well as reentry programming. Organizations such as the Matador Network provide opportunities for students to share and earn feedback on their writing in an academic setting.

Student Profiles

Published profiles of alumni students on your website or utilized during orientation are helpful tools to encourage alumni reflection and successfully market to prospective students. The Institute of International Education (IIE) Gilman scholarship program has a number of student alumni profiles showcased on their website.

Webinars or Online Content

As students readjust to life stateside, their reentry concerns may not appear in a linear timeline within the first three weeks or months of reentry. Online content that is available for access at any time during a student's academic career (as well as any time of day!) works well for student who needs flexibility in when they access reentry information. Webinars can also facilitate collaboration (résumé webinars, for example, can integrate content from career services, etc.). Websites such as Small Planet Studio offer free reentry webinars online.

Innovative Ideas for Social Media in Reentry Programming

Major Social Media Platforms

Social media outlets provide online forums for student/institution communication throughout the study abroad experience, including reentry.[2]

LinkedIn

As students begin to utilize their study abroad experience as professional preparation, social networking site LinkedIn allows students to keep in contact with various parts of the study abroad experience (e.g., host institution or partner, foreign internships, home institution). LinkedIn community groups can serve a number of purposes, including:

- Highlighting job opportunities applicable to students with study abroad experience
- Interacting with students interested in professional career opportunities
- Highlighting returned student blogs and accomplishments

Facebook

Facebook is the epitome of student social networking usage and the media outlet that allows for the most customizable content and audience distribution. Students use Facebook more often than e-mail; it proves to be a great outlet for disseminating reentry information. Other uses include:

- Connecting students to reentry opportunities
- Connecting alumni to one another
- Connecting alumni to other pieces of media that encourage reentry reflection

Instagram

The photo sharing service Instagram is a great platform to showcase student photos and give prospective students a glimpse into daily life abroad. Consider hosting photo contests via social media by creating a tag that students can use on their photos and that you can easily search for and add to the stream, such as #TUabroad or #WildcatsAbroad. Students can easily share photos using a hashtag on-site and after. Popular trends such as #tbt (i.e., "throwback Thursday") can also be appropriated with a study abroad twist when returned students post photos of their experience to reconnect with it.

- Connect prospective students with photo representation of alumni experiences
- Engender alumni reflection and continued community by sharing pieces of the experience

---

[2]For examples of social media interaction from one international education organization, see Kindred, Chelsea, "API Social Media Examples" at http://www.nafsa.org/_/File/_/gea_api_socialmedia_supp.pdf.

Building Community Through Technology

Facilitators can compile a variety of content, and there are various modes for delivery of the content. Returned students are generally eager to share their experience. Below are suggested ways of delivery, depending on the goals of your office.

FIGURE 3. Modes of Content Delivery

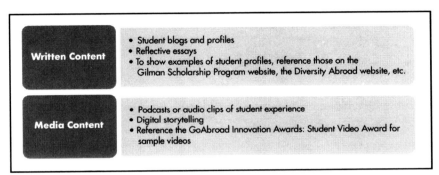

Written Content
- Student blogs and profiles
- Reflective essays
- To show examples of student profiles, reference those on the Gilman Scholarship Program website, the Diversity Abroad website, etc.

Media Content
- Podcasts or audio clips of student experience
- Digital storytelling
- Reference the GoAbroad Innovation Awards: Student Video Award for sample videos

Source: Chelsea Kindred

Returnee Content

We have discussed in this chapter why reentry programming is important and the different ways you can facilitate programming, whether through events in-person or through alternative media sources. We will now delve into the ideal concepts and strategies to incorporate into reentry programming, keeping in mind our main objectives of reflection, articulation, and integration of the experience.

To narrow the scope of the discussion, let's focus on the three main communities within the student's realm of influence that will benefit from the student's improved understanding of their study abroad experience and the content specific to each.

Academic Community

What opportunities exist on campus for returned students to continue to connect to their international experience?

The first natural pairing would be international student services. Many institutions offer opportunities for students to volunteer with international student events and one-on-one mentorship. Students can continue to navigate the cultural differences they explored during their study abroad program in an intentional and structured environment.

How do returned students impact the home campus academic experience?

Students often return to their coursework with a renewed international perspective. Many students alter course degree plans to include additional foreign language or international and cross-cultural study.

What types of communication can the institution facilitate to encourage more in-depth study of global issues?

Collaborate with academic advisers on campus to provide the tools necessary to advise a returned student with these interests in mind. Challenge the students to maintain a connection with their study abroad experience through their required coursework within their discipline of study.

Professional Community

Kimberly Franklin writes in *Frontiers: The Interdisciplinary Journal of Study Abroad* (2010, 169) about long-term career impact and professional applicability of the study abroad experience.

> Study abroad outcomes assessments are routinely conducted immediately following a participant's return from abroad, or shortly after graduation. The majority of research focuses on the impact of study abroad in the areas of language acquisition, knowledge gained, and changes in personal values, attitudes, and interests. The Georgetown Consortium Project is a comprehensive example of such. The central question that drove the research was, "What is it that our students are learning while abroad?" With a wide-ranging scope of focus, student learning was evaluated in three areas: gains in second-language oral proficiency, gains in intercultural sensitivity, and learning within a disciplinary context.

What are the most effective strategies for leveraging study abroad in a job search? How can a student integrate study abroad into a professional career?

Connect students to former alumni who are currently employed in a variety of career paths. Longitudinal studies can also be helpful resources for students striving to apply their study abroad experience to their professional trajectory. By providing students with options and a variety of applications, we can go beyond the common misnomer that a job utilizing a student's abroad experience must happen abroad. A cultivated alumni list with diverse examples and alumni willing to reach out and connect to recently returned alumni strengthen this approach.

Many structured activities exist to engender deeper discussion of the skills a student earned or enhanced during their time abroad. The objective of these activities is to correlate specific instances and examples from the student's time abroad to specific job skills and desirable traits. In the *AIFS Student*

Guide to Study Abroad and Career Development (Tillman 2011, 2), the Duke University Career Center is quoted referencing a College Placement Council Foundation study that surveyed 32 international employers and colleges to find out what international employers looked for in potential employees. "The three most important skills [employers looked for in a job applicant] were cognitive skills, social skills, and 'personal traits.' Problem-solving ability, decision-making, and knowing how to learn are highly prized cognitive skills. Social skills were described as the ability to work effectively in group settings, particularly with diverse populations. Personal traits mentioned frequently included flexibility, adaptability, and the capacity to be innovative."

We can ensure successful professional articulation of the study abroad experience by keeping these categories in mind and giving students tools to unite experiences abroad with tangible job skills.

Two example activities are listed below.

FIGURE 4. Exercise 1

This activity helps link skills to tangible event examples during the student's time abroad, for unique interview or cover letter contributions. See the first entry for an example.

SKILL	EVENT
Improved communication skills	*Dinner every night at host family's home, challenge to keep engaged in the daily dialogue*
SKILL	EVENT

SKILL	EVENT

Source: Chelsea Kindred

FIGURE 5. Exercise 2

SOUNDBYTING:
REFLECTING ON YOUR STUDY ABROAD EXPERIENCE
Note your top memory in each area.

Biggest Cultural Mistake:
Funniest moment:
Scariest experience:
Most thrilling memory:
Most moving experience:
An important relationship:
A trip I took:
Other:

Choose One Memory and Give the Highlights. *Focusing on one memory from above, write down the top 3–4 highlights or points you want to make.*

1.	2.
3.	4.

Summarize and Generalize. Summarize and generalize about the experience. Explain what you took away from the experience and what you learned about yourself, human nature, and/or interacting across cultures.

Source: Activity adapted from Berardo, Kate, **Culturosity.com**. (Lessons from Abroad Study Abroad Returnee Conference, 2008). Used with permission.

Personal Community

"Simple exchanges can break down walls between us, for when people come together and speak to one another and share a common experience, then their common humanity is revealed."

—President Barack Obama,
Istanbul, Turkey (April 7, 2009)[3]

We must remind students who return from an experience abroad that they are now imbued with a unique perspective in which to view the world. This valuable voice is crucial in an expanding global community, and can make a difference in the decisions that affect our nation's future relationships with other nations. Study abroad returnees, with their enthusiasm for intercultural experience, are shared not just with entities on campus, but with family, friends, and a community beyond one's borders. According to the 2013 *Open Doors* report, returned study abroad students have an experience that less than 3 percent of their peers have. It is the student's responsibility to apply that unique voice to their personal community, and our responsibility as educators to give them the tools to be successful in doing so (IIE 2013).

In what ways can we shape the conversation that these students are having about international education and in which directions can we point them to apply a newfound passion?

Our hope is that students will come home more intellectually curious and more culturally sensitive, but how can we parlay these new traits to make the world a better place? Ralph Waldo Emerson wrote, "Nothing great was ever achieved without enthusiasm." How can your students most effectively advocate for international education?

To capitalize on student enthusiasm, consider the following courses of action:

- Share motivating statistics with returnees, such as:
  - A public opinion poll from Connecting Our World (NAFSA 2012b) that found:
    - 73 percent of U.S. citizens believe that colleges need to do a better job of teaching students about the world, or they won't be prepared for the global economy.
    - 65 percent believe that if students don't learn foreign languages, they will be at a competitive disadvantage in their careers.
    - 57 percent believe international education is essential to the educational experience.
    - But only slightly more than 1 percent of all U.S. college students study abroad!
- Draw clear correlations between study abroad and current issues. For example: How does immigration reform relate to study abroad?
  - International students in the United States are affected by immigration policy.
  - Our immigration policies can influence the policies of other nations.
  - Our immigration policy affects how the rest of the world views us and how we see ourselves as a nation.
- Share the Mapping The Nation resource to motivate students to make clear connections between international industry in your area and personal cross-cultural competency.
- Motivate students by reminding them that collective action starts with individual initiative. Give them clear tools to do something impactful within a small period of time. For example:
  - Require students to sign up for action alerts on NAFSA's Connecting Our World homepage.
  - Encourage students to contact local and state legislators regarding issues they feel passionately about.

---

[3]From "Remarks of President Barack Obama at Student Roundtable in Istanbul," 2009. http://www.whitehouse.gov/the_press_office/Remarks-Of-President-Barack-Obama-At-Student-Roundtable-In-Istanbul.

- Use social media outlets to spread the word about a cause students are interested in.
- Research groups within the community with a similar focus.
- Engage parents in a reentry discussion about how their student's international experience impacted the parents or their family life.
- Discuss the "horizontal root" theory, as described in "Coming Home: Relationships, Roots, and Unpacking." Mendelson and Citron (2005) write:

> When you go abroad, you deliberately "uproot" yourself from the environment where you have always lived and, in the process, lose a lot of familiar reference points and distance yourself from your familiar support networks ... We think of people who have lived in more than one place as being more "horizontally-rooted," a trait that may be accompanied by a feeling of wanderlust as you realize how eager you are to explore new places. People who have had the experience of adapting to different ways of living develop skills that can enable them to adjust—plant their roots, if you will—in other new environments with increasing ease. This ability to feel almost at home anywhere—but not quite as totally rooted anywhere as you once did—can be at once exhilarating and frustrating. This is not to say you forfeit your home connections, your "vertical roots," by choosing to embrace new experiences and expand your network of relationships. But it is a common experience for people returning home after time abroad to have a confused sense of self and conflicting loyalties about how they fit back into their home culture. Some of the functions of those vertical roots that served you well for so long were replaced by your horizontal roots while you were gone. Where are you going to plant your roots now? Are you exactly the same person you were before you studied abroad? Do your parents or friends think so? Odds are that you have changed, and you will need to think about these changes in order to come to terms with the "new" you and appreciate the rich hybrid that you have become as a result of blending your home and host culture perspectives and experiences.

- Advise students during the reentry phase on opportunities within the local community for international engagement and outreach.
- Invite community members to your study abroad fair to promote interaction between local businesses and extracurricular opportunities with international components for students.

Promoting Continued International Engagement

There are plenty of options for students who wish to study abroad again. Reentry programming should include a basic overview of work, volunteer, and internship opportunities abroad for students. As we empower students to vocalize and affect change within their communities, we can provide additional resources and tools for them to go abroad again and refuel their passion. Adding these opportunities to your existing study abroad or global opportunities fair and resource library provide an additional level of engagement between your office and your returned student population.

Creating Access to Study Abroad For Different Student Groups

As the most recent *Open Doors* report numbers show (2013), the field of international education is reaching many students with the message of the importance of international education. There are still crucial populations that traditional marketing efforts are not reaching, whether these are underrepresented majors, ethnic minorities, or LGBTQ students.

The study abroad experience in itself involves the renegotiation of a student's identity, and there are many underrepresented populations that may require alternative strategic framework to the discussion of identity abroad. The traditional approach may not connect with specific populations. For example, many predeparture orientations approach students as if they have never navigated a secondary culture, yet many are proficient at navigating different cultures. First-generation college students navigate the college experience in a similar way to a student arriving in South America for the first time. Many students are second or third culture students who are already navigating an American identity and cultural framework, and come with skills that should be acknowledged and integrated into preparation curriculum.

In the same way, we can utilize underrepresented student experiences to explore identity and connect students to deeper engagement and reflection during their post-study abroad experience.

Your alumni can reach these groups with targeted marketing in ways that your office may currently be unable to. Students can:

- Generate content to appeal to specific groups and dispel myths and misconceptions about the study abroad experience. Former API Study Abroad peer mentor and University of Ohio student Lo Martinez (2012) made a great video showcasing a variety of students from diverse backgrounds speaking about their study abroad experience.
- Share alumni and other student reflections with underrepresented groups. Blogs and student stories are a compelling way to introduce the discussion of the value of the study abroad experience, and can appeal

to students in a way that traditional classroom presentations cannot. Blog resources include:

- Diversity Abroad Network
  http://diversitynetwork.org/Diversity-Network-Blog/Latest
- NAFSA Rainbow SIG
  http://www.rainbowsig.org/
- Benjamin A. Gilman Scholarship Program's YouTube channel (featuring stories and videos from Gilman scholarship recipients) http://www.youtube.com/playlist?list = PLD8275B7E9040E447& feature = plcp
- Mobility International USA blog (on student experiences and access to experiences abroad)
  http://www.miusablog.org/
- All Abroad resources (advice from mentors)
  http://allabroad.us/advice.php

Thinking about these diverse student experiences is essential to creating opportunities for discussion and interaction. Just as the student experience stateside is variable, so too is the study abroad experience, and the impact it has on students' return stateside.

Conclusion

In sum, reentry programming is paramount to the continuation of student learning during the study abroad process. By providing students with the tools and resources for successful engagement with their community, international educators can create a more enthusiastic and articulate alumni base. This alumni base can have implications on local, state, and national communities for years to come as these students continue to apply the lens of their cross-cultural experience abroad to their everyday lives.

As education abroad professionals, our commitment to student learning extends past the student's return to the home campus, and continues to their continued contributions to their community, with personal, academic, and professional applications.

Additional Web Resources

Austin College Digital Stories
http://www.austincollege.edu/academics/centers-and-institutes/center-for-global-learning/digital-stories/

Benjamin A. Gilman International Scholarship Profiles
http://www.iie.org/programs/gilman-scholarship-program/about-the-program

Colorado State University Returning Student Resources
http://educationabroad.colostate.edu/students/returning-home/

Lessons From Abroad
http://www.lessonsfromabroad.org/

Mapping the Nation
http://mappingthenation.net/

Matador Network
http://matadornetwork.com/

Minnesota Study Abroad Returnee Conference
http://www.mnreturneeconference.org/

New England Study Abroad Reentry Conference
http://nestudyabroadreentryconference.wordpress.com/

Oklahoma State University Returning Student Resources
http://ieo.okstate.edu/ieo.aspx?page = 183

Small Planet Studio Reentry Webinars
http://www.smallplanetstudio.com/products/rr-webinar/

University of Cincinnati Returning Student Resources
http://www.uc.edu/international/study-abroad/returning-to-uc.html

Wake Forest University Cross-Cultural Engagement Courses
http://bit.ly/1nQPTLv

References

American Institute for Foreign Study. 2013. "AIFS Study Abroad Outcomes: A View From Our Alumni 1990–2010." Stamford, Conn.: American Institute for Foreign Study. http://www.aifsabroad.com/advisors/pdf/AIFS_Study_Abroad_Outcomes.pdf.

Center for Global Education. N.d. "Impact of Study Abroad on Retention and Success." UCLA Graduate School of Education and Information Studies. Los Angeles, Calif.: University of California-Los Angeles. http://globaledresearch.com/study-abroad-impact.asp

Dwyer, Mary. 2004. "Charting the Impact of Studying Abroad." *International Educator* (Winter 2004): 14–20.

Forum on Education Abroad. 2013. "Best Practices, Resources, and Programming for Returned Students: Supporting, Reflecting, Articulation, and

Integration." Forum on Education Abroad Standards Committee working group. Presented by Lorien Romito, Katie Roller, and Frank Serna. Chicago, Ill.: Ninth Annual Forum on Education Abroad Conference. http://www.forumea.org/documents/BestPracticesforReturnedStudents-handout.pdf.

Franklin, Kimberly. 2010. "Long-Term Career Impact and Professional Applicability of the Study Abroad Experience." In *Frontiers: The Interdisciplinary Journal of Study Abroad* 19 (Fall/Winter). Carlisle, Pa.: The Forum on Education Abroad.

IES Abroad. 2002. "Alumni Survey Results." Chicago, Ill.: Institute for the International Education of Students. http://www.iesabroad.org/study-abroad/why/alumni-survey-results.

Institute of International Education. *Open Doors 2013.* New York, N.Y.: Institute of International Education. http://www.iie.org/Research-and-Publications/Open-Doors/Data.

La Brack, Bruce. 2003. "What's Up With Culture?" Online cultural training resource. University of the Pacific School of International Studies/U.S. Department of Education. http://www2.pacific.edu/sis/culture/.

Lessons From Abroad. 2013. "How To Host an LFA Conference." Lessons from Abroad. http://www.lessonsfromabroad.org/wp-content/uploads/2013/06/How-to-Host-LFA-Conference-FINAL.pdf.

Martinez, Lo. 2012. "Experiencing Diversity Abroad." Academic Programs International/Ohio University. YouTube video, 5:56. Posted July 25, 2012. http://www.youtube.com/watch?v = gAzSkewzAuw&feature = youtu.be.

Mendelson, Vija and James Citron. 2005. "Coming Home: Relationships, Roots, and Unpacking." *Transitions Abroad* 29, 1 (July/August). http://www.transitionsabroad.com/publications/magazine/0507/coming_home_from_study_abroad.shtml.

Mendelson, Vija and James Citron. 2006. "Bringing It Home: Multifaceted Support for Returning Education Abroad Students," *International Educator* 15, 3 (May/June). http://www.nafsa.org/_/File/_/education_abroad_inted_2006.pdf.

NAFSA. 2012a. "Measuring the Impact of Study Abroad." Washington, D.C.: NAFSA: Association of International Educators. https://www.nafsa.org/Resource_Library_Assets/Public_Policy/Measuring_the_Impact_of_Study_Abroad/.

NAFSA. 2012b. "Public Opinion Supports International Education." Washington, D.C.: NAFSA: Association of International Educators. http://www.nafsa.org/_/File/_/2012_edstudentsglobaleconomy.pdf.

Paige, R. Michael, Elizabeth M. Stallman, Jae-Eun Jon, Bruce La Brack. 2009. "Study Abroad for Global Engagement: The Long-Term Impact of International Experiences." Los Angeles, Calif.: NAFSA Annual Conference &

Expo. https://wiki.wooster.edu/download/attachments/45711608/Study +
Abroad + for + Global + Engagement + - + The + Long-term + Impact + of +
International + Experiences.pdf

Paige, R. Michael, Gerald W. Fry, Elizabeth Stallman, Jae-Eun Jon, Jasmina
Josi. 2010. "Beyond Immediate Impact: Study Abroad for Global Engagement (SAGE)." The SAGE research project report. Minneapolis, Minn.:
University of Minnesota. http://www.calstate.edu/engage/documents/
study-abroad-for-global-engagement.pdf.

Peterson, Julia. 2012. "Study Abroad? There's a Club for That." UNL
Announce. Lincoln, Nebr.: University of Nebraska-Lincoln.
http://newsroom.unl.edu/announce/todayatunl/1782/9978.

Sutton, Richard and Donald L. Rubin. 2004. "The GLOSSARI Project: Initial
Findings from a System-wide Research Initiative on Study Abroad Learning
Outcomes." In *Frontiers: The Interdisciplinary Journal of Study Abroad* 10.
http://www.frontiersjournal.com/issues/vol10/vol10-04_suttonrubin.pdf.

Tillman, Martin. 2011. *AIFS Student Guide to Study Abroad and Career Development.* Stamford, Conn.: American Institute for Foreign Study. http://www.
aifsabroad.com/advisors/pdf/Tillman_AIFS_Student_Guide_Career.pdf.

PART II

EDUCATION ABROAD RESEARCH

CHAPTER 7

GETTING ACQUAINTED WITH COMPREHENSIVE INTERNATIONALIZATION: U.S. and Abroad

By Kati Bell

Introduction

Over the past two decades, higher education institutions in the United States and around the world have transformed to respond to the demands of an increasingly globalizing world. One response in higher education to the pressure of worldwide globalization is the development and implementation of comprehensive internationalization plans.

What exactly is "comprehensive internationalization?" Many education abroad administrators have probably heard and used this mouth-mangling, 12-syllable phrase, but they may be unclear about what comprehensive internationalization really refers to and how it may be similar to or different from globalization. Education abroad professionals may also inquire: How does comprehensive internationalization impact my work in education abroad? What is my role in a campuswide internationalization strategy?

This chapter will provide an understanding of how comprehensive internationalization in higher education is defined, discuss some of the motivations and drivers of comprehensive internationalization, and introduce recent critiques of comprehensive internationalization at universities in the United States and around the world. More importantly, this chapter will provide a framework for understanding whom we serve through education abroad and how we can work toward a critical culture shift in supporting education abroad programs that promote equity and diversity.

Understanding Comprehensive Internationalization: Definitions from International Education Research

Jane Knight, a prominent international educator and recognized authority on comprehensive internationalization, was among the first to develop a definition that is still quite commonly used. Knight's definition understands comprehensive internationalization as a series of policies developed around the common campus goal of creating a more globally connected student and faculty body (Knight 2004). Similarly, John Hudzik, author of the NAFSA publication, *Comprehensive Internationalization: From Concept to Action* (2011) and current NAFSA Senior Scholar for Internationalization, describes comprehensive internationalization in more detail, defining it as the development and implementation of multifaceted campus programs and activities that have a recognizable international dimension, including: international recruitment of students and faculty, study abroad programs, and developing an international dimension to the academic curriculum through foreign language studies, international, and area studies majors (Hudzik 2011). By developing these ambitious, campuswide, and internationally focused policies, many universities seek to reach a goal of creating a more globally aware campus community.

Two concepts that are frequently treated as synonyms are "internationalization" and "globalization." Despite the inconsistency in usage, there is general agreement in research literature regarding differentiation between the terms. Globalization is understood as the increasing interconnectedness of the world community. It is a phenomenon fueled by economic, political, and societal changes resulting from recent innovations such as information technology, mass air travel, and the growing dominance of English as the common language of business and education. Internationalization, by comparison, is recognized as the reaction of higher education to the recent globalization phenomenon. Internationalization in higher education manifests itself in the drive to develop comprehensive internationalization policy at individual universities with the goal to move the university toward being part of this increasingly interconnected world landscape. To recap, globalization has impacted higher education institutions in such a way that many universities around the world are compelled to develop policy that leads to a more globally connected and globally literate university community. Comprehensive internationalization describes the policies and programs developed at higher education institutions to bring about the goal of a more globally aware campus community.

Brief History of Internationalization in Higher Education

Historically, universities have always been internationalized in various forms. European universities established in the fifteenth and sixteenth centuries taught in a common language—Latin—and placed a high value on transnational scholarship that was sustained throughout the medieval and Renaissance periods. Between the eighteenth century and World War I, universities' international efforts were focused on export of education, primarily through colonization and also through an emphasis in the production and dissemination of research publications. Most scholars agree that the modern international education movement stems from the post World War II and cold war period. In this era, governments from Western and communist countries took an active effort to recruit and finance students from developing countries for both political means as well as for idealistic endeavors.

This was the climate in which the doctrine of peace through educational exchange, as visualized by Senator William J. Fulbright in the late 1940s, was developed and realized. Under the federally funded Fulbright Program, more than 300,000 scholars have researched and studied in the United States and around the world (CIES n.d.). In the decade leading up to the turn of the millennium and the one that has followed, higher education has felt the impact of the growing connectedness or globalization of the world community. Due to this increasing interconnectedness, international education has risen in prominence and importance in higher education. Globalization is impacting higher education in many ways and will continue to impact the decisions made by leaders at institutions of higher education around the world.

Motivations and Rationales for Comprehensive Internationalization

Understanding the definitions and background goes a long way in demystifying comprehensive internationalization. It is also very useful to understand the many motivations and rationales driving an increase in the development of comprehensive internationalization plans at higher education institutions around the world. Research reveals that several motivations to internationalize are prevalent in higher education today. Two of the most prevalent motivations are (1) the perceived increased commodification of higher education and an increased competition among universities for international rankings, and (2) internationalization as a means for developing global connections for the benefit of students and faculty.

A review of recent research on tertiary education trends reveals a movement in higher education away from a culture traditionally separated from business toward one with increasing focus on entrepreneurial activities (Mok 2007). While it is in some ways admirable to see higher education as seeking out innovative solutions to address current issues in higher education—such as reduced government support and the dramatic increase in demand for higher education worldwide—some innovations may serve to perpetuate social and economic inequities. One such example is the assertion that higher education has used its transition into internationalization as a justification to increase international student recruitment and enrollment (Stromquist 2007).

It is a common practice for universities, especially in developed countries, to recruit noncitizens, i.e., international students, as a mechanism for increasing university revenue through additional tuition and fees not charged domestic students. In this respect, internationalization in higher education can be seen as a response, in some instances, to declining public funding for universities (Mok 2007). Commodification of higher education may pose a threat to educational equity by reducing access to students who are less able to pay a free market rate for higher education (Cantwell and Maldonado-Maldonado 2009). Restricting access to increasingly costly higher education perpetuates social reproduction of inequity by insuring that only the upper classes benefit from the better earning potential afforded by a university education (Stromquist 2007). In this scenario, students from lower socioeconomic classes compete for access not only with wealthier students in their own state, but also wealthier students abroad who represent a greater source of revenue for universities (Taylor 2004).

A second motivation for comprehensive internationalization involves a change in how universities perceive themselves and other institutions of higher education. Universities have moved from a traditionally isolated position in society to becoming increasingly more interconnected and reactive to external world events, while also becoming more competitive with one another (Mok 2007). The popularity and importance of global university rankings, such as those published annually by *U.S. News & World Report,* the *Times Higher Education,* and Shanghai Jiao Tong University has seen a dramatic increase over the past decade. Data from the recently published *Measuring and Assessing Internationalization* (Green 2012) reports that international rankings have increased in influence as an indicator of university performance. Thus this shows a growing trend for rankings to be the basis for the development of new policy, priorities, and resources in higher education (Green 2012). Marginson's (2007) review of global university ranking systems noted that the number of enrolled international students and the number of foreign-born faculty are now included as ranking factors for a growing number of universities, especially outside of the United States. The inclusion of internationalization elements in ranking systems leads universities to focus on policies that will result in increased numbers of enrolled international students as well as students participating in study abroad programs (Marginson 2007). Knight's (2010) research also recognized this trend, and points to the increased competition among universities for prestige and rankings as a strong external pressure for universities to adopt comprehensive internationalization plans.

Comprehensive Internationalization
Outside of the United States

The development of comprehensive internationalization plans is a phenomenon occurring in both the United States and universities around the world. There are some specific differences between how comprehensive internationalization is embodied at U.S. universities and at institutions of higher education around the world. One of the biggest differences in the United States is the influence of external organizations on the impetus to develop comprehensive internationalization plans at institutions of higher education (Trondal 2009). Outside the United States, the central government, usually through a ministry of education, plays much a bigger role in the development of curricula and the general operation of publicly funded universities. These universities have, in many cases, been mandated by the central government to develop and adapt internationalization strategies such as comprehensive internationalization. U.S. universities tend to be driven by more intrinsic motivators, such as the desire to be more competitive among peer institutions through the promotion of a more international perspective, and increasing revenue and diversity through international student enrollments. U.S. universities tend to emphasize the international student enrollment and study abroad aspects of internationalization, while universities abroad tend to be more focused on the internationalization of the faculty body and increasing international research collaborations.

Though internationalization has, in general, enjoyed a relatively accepting place in higher education, it has more recently been the focus of some critique from researchers within the international education field. Critique is primarily focused on the overwhelming lack of critical analysis and research on the impact of internationalization on higher education. More specific critique has recently been applied toward the increased fervor of international student enrollments. In the education abroad area, critique is focused on access and availability of study abroad programs for student populations that do not traditionally participate in education abroad, such as first-generation students, racially and ethnically underrepresented students, and students from STEM and health science fields. Additionally, critique has been applied to education abroad due to the lack of quantitative assessment of study abroad program outcomes. As a result, there has recently been a strong push to assess and quantify the outcomes of education abroad. (For more on assessment, please see chapter 24.)

Connecting Education Abroad with Campus Comprehensive Internationalization Goals

Depending on the size of the campus, education abroad professionals may or may not be aware of all the various programs and departments devoted to comprehensive internationalization. In today's university setting, it is not uncommon for university departments to be siloed. This isolation of offices can lead to an unintentional ignorance of programs with similar international goals (but different student populations), in addition to a reproduction of effort and a lack of focused communication on shared objectives (Bell 2013). The following is a short list of some of the most common manifestations of comprehensive internationalization plans at universities outside and within the United States:

Student Mobility
The inbound and outbound movement of students earning degrees at the university, student mobility is an umbrella term that refers primarily to international student recruitment (inbound) and education abroad programs (outbound). In many cases, international student enrollment shares an organizational structure with education abroad. But it is not uncommon for education abroad and international student enrollment to be in separate organizational structures at the same university.

Curriculum Internationalization
Curriculum internationalization is a purposeful redesign of university curriculum to include multicultural awareness and language competency in already existing curricular goals. This includes adding requirements for study abroad and language learning, creating new international or global studies majors, promoting faculty-led programs, and encouraging service learning and internships (both domestic and abroad).

Overseas Branch and/or Satellite Campuses
These include university developed and funded academic programs taught in another country. Faculty at overseas satellite campuses can be from the home university and/or hired host nationals. Enrolled students may be either host country students or students from the home university.

Twinning Agreements
Twinning agreements are affiliations between two or more overseas universities that seek to combine curriculum in order to produce either a dual/joint degree (one diploma from two universities) or a double degree (a diploma

from each university). Twinning agreements are also referred to by the number of years at each university, e.g., 2 + 2, 3 + 1, 2 + 1 + 1.

Faculty Overseas Engagement

Programs developed to encourage and track the collaboration of faculty in overseas research, teaching, and publishing.

In many instances, especially in U.S. universities, education abroad is considered a key component to nearly every comprehensive internationalization plan. Dutschke's (2009) research on campus internationalization initiatives and study abroad indicates that, "although they [international educators] have endeavored to broaden the scope of internationalization...study abroad remains the primary indicator of internationalization." Education abroad finds itself under an umbrella term of "student mobility," a designation more commonly employed by international educators outside of the United States, and simply understood as the movement of students inbound and outbound of the university.

Education abroad has many different types of programs with varying organizational structures that support it (see chapter 14). Common education abroad program types in the United States are bilateral exchanges and programs through study abroad organizations. Non-U.S. universities tend to focus more on direct exchanges and consortium-bound exchanges to accommodate education abroad students, and are less dependent on study abroad organizations to place their outbound students overseas.

Ownership and responsibility of educational abroad programs at the university fall under different models. As mentioned earlier, many universities use a centralized model to house both international student services and education abroad in a single office or center. When these two areas are in separate areas, it is not uncommon for education abroad to reside in academic affairs, due to the academic nature of the programs. International student enrollment is often located in student affairs, extended learning, or combined with the multicultural office. At larger campuses there sometimes exists both a centralized education abroad office and school/college specific offices. This is model is used for many graduate programs with highly specialized education abroad affiliations, such as law, business, and health sciences.

Critical to the continued growth and development of international education and education abroad is the collection and reporting of data (see chapter 20). Education abroad data should be collected and reported on in regular intervals. In the United States, the Institute for International Education (IIE) maintains the annual *Open Doors* report, which tracks education abroad and international student activity for U.S. universities. A more extensive review of educational activity comes from the Organisation for Economic Co-Operation and Development (OECD). The supranational organization publishes *Education at a Glance*. This extensive report provides in-depth information on structure, finances, and access to educational programs, including education abroad, for all member countries.

Education abroad has a large and very supportive professional community, both in the United States and around the world. National and international professional organizations established to support both education abroad and international education are a tremendous resource to international education professionals at all levels. Some professional organizations specific to education abroad include the Forum on Education Abroad, the American Institute for Foreign Study, the Council on International Educational Exchange (CIEE), and the European Association for International Education.

Comprehensive Internationalization, Education Abroad, and Equity

This chapter has introduced a standard definition for comprehensive internationalization, highlighted campus motivations for developing comprehensive internationalization plans, provided an overview of how education abroad connects with larger comprehensive internationalization plans, and touched on some recent critiques of comprehensive internationalization from within the international educational field.

It is important to emphasize a lesser-known role that education abroad professionals have in disrupting the reproduction of inequity within their own student populations through the adaption of comprehensive internationalization policy. As education abroad professionals, we recognize that student participation in overseas academic programs provides a significant opportunity for personal transformation and academic growth. These opportunities should be developed in a way so that they are available to all students at the university, regardless of the students' course of study or financial situation.

As international educators, we share an obligation to strive toward universal access to overseas programs, and we should not be complacent about groups of students turned away from an education abroad opportunity due to their course of study (major) or lack of financial means. Therefore, through the development of comprehensive internationalization plans, we should endeavor to encourage university administrators toward a commitment to the following:

- Equity of access to all educational abroad programs for 100 percent of the student population (i.e., an education abroad opportunity for every major)
- Active recruitment of marginalized and nontraditional students to overseas activities and relevant support throughout the study abroad process

- Provision of financial support to ensure 100 percent accessibility to education abroad

It is unlikely that education abroad professionals came to this field to simply serve a very small portion of the campus student population (a student population that already possessed the social capital to seek out an overseas experience and had the income level to afford the program's cost). Education abroad programs should not divide the campus into have and have not. If a university commits to endorsing education abroad programs as a viable and recommended activity, the university also needs to commit to the equal access to these opportunities for the entire student population by developing programs that fit with every major and developing funding mechanisms that provide access to every student interested in pursuing the opportunity.

It is our responsibility to work toward generating this important paradigm shift. Many university administrators have not thought about education abroad in these terms, and may be comfortable with the unfortunate status quo that allows for only a small part of the student body to participate in education abroad. The development of comprehensive internationalization is a ripe opportunity to educate campus administrators about equity and accessibility in international education.

References

Bell, Kathrina A. 2013. *"Similar Goals and Dueling Agendas: Perceptions of Campus Internationalization and Equity Policies."* Doctoral dissertation. Retrievedfrom ProQuest Dissertations and Theses.

Cantwell, Brendan, and Alma Maldonado-Maldonado. "Four Stories: Confronting Contemporary Ideas about Globalisation and Internationalisation in Higher Education." *Globalisation, Societies and Education* 7, 3 (2009): 289–306.

Council for International Exchange of Scholars (CIES). N.d. "History." Fulbright Scholar Program. Washington, D.C.: CIES. http://www.cies.org/history.

Dutschke, Dennis. 2009. "Campus Internationalization Initiatives and Study Abroad." *College and University* 84, 3: 67–73.

Green, Madeleine F. 2012. *Measuring and Assessing Internationalization* Washington, D.C.: NAFSA: Association of International Educators.

Hudzik, John K. 2011. *Comprehensive Internationalization: From Concept to Action.* Washington, D.C.: NAFSA: National Association of International Education.

Knight, Jane. 2010. *Higher Education in Turmoil: The Changing World of Internationalization.* Rotterdam, The Netherlands: Sense Publishers.

Knight, Jane. 2004. "Internationalization Remodeled: Definition, Approaches, and Rationales." *Journal of Studies in International Education* 8, 1: 5–31.

Marginson, Simon. 2007. "Global University Rankings: Where to From Here?" Proceedings of Asia-Pacific Association for International Education. Singapore: National University of Singapore.

Mok, Ka Ho. 2007. "Questing for Internationalization of Universities in Asia: Critical Reflections." *Journal of Studies in International Education* 11: 433–454.

Stromquist, Nelly. 2007. "Internationalization as a Response to Globalization: Radical Shifts in University Environments." *Higher Education* 53: 81–105

Taylor, John. 2004. "Toward a Strategy for Internationalization: Lessons and Practice from Four Universities." *Journal of Studies in International Education* 8, 2: 149–171.

Trondal, Jarle. 2010. "Two World of Change: On the Internationalization of Universities." *Globalisation, Societies and Education* 8, 3: 351–368.

CHAPTER 8

EDUCATION ABROAD RESEARCH

By Eduardo Contreras Jr.

Introduction

More than 20 years ago, NAFSA published its first *Guide to Education Abroad for Advisers and Administrators.* That same year, Whitney Houston was atop the Billboard charts with her version of "I Will Always Love You," the movie Jurassic Park was a hit at the box office, and the former governor of Arkansas began his first term as president of the United States. Although much has changed in pop culture, politics, and education abroad since 1993, there were several pearls of wisdom in that NAFSA guide that still influence the latest itera- tion of this publication. William W. Hoffa's introductory words are especially relevant for this chapter. Hoffa explained that NAFSA selected the term "educa- tion abroad" rather than "study abroad" as a "...recognition of the earliest and broadest principles in the field, namely support for all varieties of living and learning abroad that have genuine and lasting educational value" (Hoffa, Pear- son, and Slind 1993, xvii). It is precisely that search for educational value that is at the core of this chapter on education abroad research.

Research on education abroad is not new. Scholars have been studying and writing about this endeavor since the 1920s.[1] Today, any reliable academic search engine will generate at least a thousand articles, books, and editorials that have been published since the turn of the twenty-first century on this subject.[2] The old and new research on education abroad represents a wide array of academic disciplines that utilize qualitative and quantitative data to reflect a vast assortment of perspectives on this endeavor. Just as there is a diversity of disciplinary perspectives on education abroad, there is also a range in the quality of research. Although much of the research on study abroad is based on verifiable evidence, carefully substantiated arguments, and fundamental research practices, other research is based on suspicious data,

---

[1] Although the following articles would not be considered rigorous by today's research standards, these early reports contain illuminating details on the first junior year abroad programs to Europe: David Allan Robertson, "The Junior Year Abroad," *The Educational Record* 7, no. 2 (1926); Walter Hullihen, "Present Status of the 'Junior Year Abroad,'" *The French Review* 1, no. 2 (1928); Edwin C. Byam and Marine Leland, "American Undergraduates in France," The French Review 3, no. 4 (1930); Horatio Smith, "The Junior Year Abroad, " World Affairs 96, no. 1 (1933).

[2] For an extensive review of education abroad literature published between 2004 and 2011 see: Albert Biscarra, David Comp, Gary Rhodes, "Research on U.S. Students Study Abroad: An Update, 2004–2011. A Bibliography with Abstracts," UCLA Center for International and Development Education and UCLA Center for Global Education, http://globaledresearch.com/book_research_comp_update.asp?year=2004.

biased assumptions, or is poorly argued. This chapter highlights examples from the former category with the aim of providing practitioners with a foundational base of knowledge about education abroad research. This chapter should benefit both those with little or no experience in the field and those who are now savvy veterans of the education abroad community.

Raw Data And Research Portals

The Institute of International Education's annual *Open Doors* report is an essential resource for anyone seeking raw data on student mobility. Published annually in November, the *Open Doors* report contains copious information on both international students and scholars studying in the United States, and U.S. students studying abroad. The report includes rich data that addresses questions such as, "How many American students participated in study abroad programs in the previous academic year? Where did they study? What were their majors? What institution sent the most students abroad? What is the most popular program length?" Although these data could not be considered research on their own, *Open Doors* is an essential place to find detailed quantitative data on outgoing students participating in education abroad programs. Additionally, it is important to note that IIE bases its *Open Doors* report on self-reported data from institutions of higher education and is not a part of U.S. Department of Education data centers such as the Integrated Postsecondary Education Data System (IPEDS). Beyond this resource, individual institutions will often publish their own reports regarding outgoing students on their websites or in formal publications.

Several useful resources have arrived in recent years that provide space for readers to understand education abroad across multiple disciplines and modes of inquiry. The Forum on Education Abroad has more than a decade of work in the field, with established conferences that discuss many issues in study abroad including assessment, standards, health, safety, curriculum integration, and other important topics. The Forum website often publishes reports on standards of good practice in education abroad, the state of the field, curriculum and outcome assessment projects, and glossaries of terms.

Beyond the Forum, *Frontiers: The Interdisciplinary Journal of Study Abroad* publishes a wide range of original research about education abroad. Founded in 1994 at Boston University, *Frontiers* typically publishes two volumes per year. The manuscripts submitted to the journal undergo a double blind international peer review and the editorial board includes faculty and administrators from institutions of higher education around the world (Frontiers n.d.).

Finally, both NAFSA and the Center for Global Education provide regular updates on the current research on education abroad. NAFSA's "Review of Global Studies Literature" publishes short reviews (no more than 1500 words) on current books in the field of international education, with many specific reviews about education abroad research (NAFSA 2010). The Center for Global Education maintains a list of research on education abroad that includes abstracts when available, and the site also curates special collections of research on specific topics such as, "the impact of study abroad on retention and success."[3] Moreover, there are a number of other associations that produce their own research and occasional white papers about education abroad. These include the Association of International Education Administrators (AIEA), the American Institute for Foreign Study (AIFS), the Council on International Educational Exchange (CIEE), the Institute for the International Education of Students (IES), and the School for International Training (SIT).

The History of Education Abroad

This section will be useful for newcomers to the field who want a deeper dive into how education abroad began, spread, developed, and changed over its nearly 100-year history. Those seeking more information on current research should skip ahead to the next section.

Although Indiana University introduced the first faculty-led, short-term study abroad program for undergraduates in 1879, the University of Delaware (UD) launched the first academic-year program for juniors in 1923 and called it the "Foreign Study Plan."[4] Smith College designed a similar program two years later and named it the "Junior Year in France." Both programs employed similar models where a U.S. faculty member traveled abroad to supervise students who had been carefully selected for their advanced French language proficiency. Students began their stays abroad in smaller cities where they took courses designed to ease their transition to life abroad. Upon completing those short preparatory courses on language and culture, U.S. students enrolled in languages courses designed by the Sorbonne in Paris. Similar to many study abroad programs today, the U.S. administrators at UD and Smith planned excursions and cultural visits to regional sites to supplement the classroom education. Students and administrators sought value—educational

---

[3]See The Center for Global Education, "Study Abroad Research Online," http://globaledresearch.com.

[4]For more on Indiana University's first education abroad programs see: Indiana University, "Early History: About Us: Overseas Study: Indiana University," http://overseas.iu.edu/about/history/history_early.shtml. For more on the early years of the University of Delaware Foreign Study Program see: Hullihen, "Present Status of the 'Junior Year Abroad.'" John A. Munroe, *The University of Delaware : A History* (Newark, Del.: The University, 1986). See especially chapter 8: 263–267. Whitney Walton, *Internationalism, National Identities, and Study Abroad: France and the United States,*1890-1970 (Stanford, Calif.: Stanford University Press, 2010). Chapters 3–4.

and otherwise—in their education abroad programs that they defined alongside academic (language training), professional (skills for employment), andniversal (intercultural competence) aims.[5] By the end of the 1920s, many people in higher education considered these programs a success.[6]

While there were very few assessments of education abroad in the early days to see how or what students were learning, IIE sent a questionnaire to students who participated in these junior year abroad programs in 1930 to determine employment outcomes. Most students surveyed went on to careers in education. Specifically, of the 245 students who completed questionnaires, 73 percent took positions in teaching, research, or administration, and only 5 percent listed their occupations as "industry or business" (Hewlett and Connely 1930). Based on the success of these two programs, the junior year abroad became the primary means of overseas study for undergraduates for the first half of the century. In terms of educational value, these two program models were highly influential for much of the history of education abroad. Building on Thomas Kuhn's notion of the "paradigm shift," Michael Vande Berg has argued that the junior year abroad was the first major paradigm in education abroad (2007; 2004). According to Vande Berg, today the field has moved toward a more student-centered model; however, the justifications and assumptions about student learning built into the junior year abroad model still influence many program designs today (Vande Berg, Paige, and Lou 2012).[7] Following the Second World War, the narrative for education abroad became more discursive; therefore, it is worth now turning to other historical research to illuminate the developments for the field in the second half of the twentieth century.

Current Research

Historiography of Education Abroad Literature
There have been numerous changes in study abroad since the middle of the twentieth century that have been chronicled by historians and other academics that are also important for contemporary education abroad students and professionals. Two recent indispensable works in this domain are Hoffa's

---

[5] These aims were explicitly expressed in several places including an official letter from the Institute of International Education entitled: "The Junior Year in France: An Open Letter to Teachers of French and College Faculties," (1928). See also: Eduardo Contreras, "Considering Study Abroad's Past to Prepare for Its Future," *IIE Networker,* Fall 2013.

[6] See for example, Institute of International Education, "Annual Report, " (New York, N.Y.: The Institute of International Education, 1927).

[7] See especially chapter 1, "Student Learning Abroad: Paradigms and Assumptions," of Vande Berg, Paige, and Lou, *Student Learning Abroad* (2012).

A History of U.S. Study Abroad: Beginnings to 1965 (2007) and Hoffa and Stephen C. DePaul's *A History of U.S. Study Abroad: 1965–Present* (2010).

In the latter publication, several authors focus on the dramatic changes in the decades following 1965. These scholars demonstrate how study abroad programing expanded beyond the junior year abroad model to include multiple program types to meet the needs of different historical, institutional, and individual student contexts (DeWinter and Rumbley 2010; Rodman Merrill 2010). Two chapters show how study abroad became slightly more diverse in terms of the students who participated and the international destinations (Stallman et al. 2010; Ogden et al. 2010). Another chapter describes the development of intercultural communication in the twentieth century, while another chapter demonstrates how qualitative standards emerged to assess learning outcomes (Bennett 2010; Comp and Merritt 2010). Finally, the role of education abroad administrators in the field is addressed in one chapter that illustrates how these administrators professionalized and established greater legitimacy within higher education over the latter half of the previous century (Sideli 2010). Collectively, these studies provide useful groundwork for understanding the development of study abroad and the ways in which this growth has created opportunities and challenges for professionals working in the field.

In addition to these two volumes, scholars have studied the interplay between cultural norms about gender and the development of education abroad. Since the second year of overseas study at the University of Delaware in 1924, women have outnumbered men on formalized study abroad programs.[8] The predominance of women on these programs in the twentieth century has been influential in different ways. For example, Joan Gore applied Foucauldian discourse analysis to argue that a dominant narrative has prevailed over the twentieth century regarding education abroad. This narrative considers education abroad an extension of the European grand tour, and suggests that since it is "...pursed predominately by women, it must be academically unimportant" (Gore 2005, 58). Accordingly, Gore contends that this line of thinking has diminished the impact of study abroad in U.S. higher education over the twentieth century. Historian Whitney Walton considers the role that gender played in shaping the study abroad experiences of American women who studied in France in the past century. Walton's work makes deft

---

[8]For more on this from a historical perspective see: Whitney Walton, "American Girls and French 'Jeunes Filles:' Negotiating Identities in Interwar France," *Gender & History* 17, no. 2 (2005). Mark H. Salisbury, Michael B. Paulsen, and Ernest T. Pascarella, "To See the World or Stay at Home: Applying an Integrated Student Choice Model to Explore the Gender Gap in the Intent to Study Abroad," *Research in Higher Education* 51, no. 7 (2010). April H. Stroud, "Who Plans (Not) to Study Abroad? An Examination of U.S. Student Intent," *Journal of Studies in International Education* 14, no. 5 (2010). Steven W Shirley, "The Gender Gap in Post-Secondary Study Abroad: Understanding and Marketing to Male Students" (Dissertation, University of North Dakota, 2006).

use of primary source materials such as diaries, letters, home-stay family comments, and faculty notes to show how gender norms and stereotypes structured identify formation and recognition of national stereotypes in the experiences of women studying on junior year abroad programs in France in the twentieth century. Additionally, initial parental and administrative concerns about the safety and care of women living abroad shaped the structure of education abroad programs at Smith College, and the University of Delaware in the 1920s, and beyond (Contreras 2013b).

Educational Context

Education abroad has come a long way since the days of the junior year abroad. Indeed, by the beginning of the new millennium, there was a call to democratize education abroad on a grand scale. In 2005, the U.S. Congress and President George W. Bush appointed a bipartisan commission of leaders in business, higher education, and government to evaluate the state of education abroad. The Lincoln Commission, which took its name from the sixteenth president of the United States for his efforts to transform higher education in the nineteenth century, made a number of recommendations, including increasing the number of undergraduates studying overseas to 1,000,000 by the 2016–17 academic year (Lincoln Commission 2005). Although the Lincoln Commission justified study abroad in ways similar to the rationales offered in the 1920s, there were also new justifications that reflected twenty-first century concerns. For example, as described in the previous chapter, education abroad is an important aspect of student mobility and contemporary discussions about globalization and economic competitiveness. In the twenty-first century, education abroad is often mentioned as part of campus internationalization strategies and discussions.

Since the 1980s, scholars have described the ways in which education abroad works within the context of higher education broadly, and, more recently, in the context of campus internationalization strategies.[9]

---

[9] For example, see John E. Bowman, "Educating American Undergraduates Abroad: The Development of Study Abroad Programs by American Colleges and Universities," in *Council on International Educational Exchange Occasional Papers No 24* (1987). Craufurd D. W. Goodwin and Michael Nacht, *Abroad and Beyond: Patterns in American Overseas Education* (Cambridge [Cambridgeshire]; New York: Cambridge University Press, 1988); *Missing the Boat: The Failure to Internationalize American Higher Education* (Cambridge [England]; New York: Cambridge University Press, 1991). Richard D. Lambert, *International Studies and the Undergraduate*, ed. American Council on Education (Washington, D.C.: American Council on Education, 1989). Peter N. Stearns, *Educating Global Citizens in Colleges and Universities: Challenges and Opportunities* (New York: Routledge, 2009): 65–96. Council for International Educational Exchange, "Educating for Global Competence: The Report of the Advisory Council for International Educational Exchange," ed. CIEE (1988).

In general, the work done by these scholars includes descriptions of many of the following topics:

- The size and scope of education abroad programing on a national level
- The levels of participation at different institutional types
- The administrative challenges to education abroad
- The structure of education abroad offices
- The level of faculty involvement and curricular integration
- The educational aims and outcome assessments of programs

Some authors also consider the factors limiting further expansion of study abroad. For example, in *Missing the Boat: The Failure to Internationalize American Higher Education,* Craufurd Goodwin and Michael Nacht argue that several factors stand in the way of international experiences, including limited funding, rigid institutional cultures, political divisions on campuses averse to international collaboration, and dangerous or unpredictable conditions overseas (Goodwin and Nacht 1991). Although written in the early '90s, many of the issues outlined by Goodwin and Nacht may still obstruct avenues to new study abroad opportunities for students today. More recently, Joan Gore's work (2005) describes how negative stereotypes and powerful clichés about education abroad as an ornamental "Grand Tour" for wealthy women serve to keep the practice on the margins of higher education.[10]

Critiques of Education Abroad

Collectively, these surveys provide a solid foundation for considering logistical or administrative issues in education abroad today; however, these works infrequently take a critical stance about the field. As part of a comprehensive report on *Study Abroad in a New Global Century* in 2012, the Association for the Study of Higher Education (ASHE) echoed this concern regarding the lack of criticisms about education abroad (Twombly et al. 2012). The ASHE authors suggest that there are three broad areas of critique. First, there are questions about implicit purposes of study abroad, such as the idea that education abroad is a "...political tool" or "instrument of cultural and economic imperialism." Next, there are criticisms of the elitism of education abroad that argue that overseas study only serves affluent white students from elite institutions. Finally, the ASHE report explains that there are general critiques of the "nature of the study abroad experience itself" (Twombly et al. 2012, 95).

In 2003, Lilli and John Engle criticized the field for lacking a nuanced classification system for the large variety of education abroad program types.

---

[10]For policy implications for Gore's argument, see especially chapter 7 (Gore 2005).

In their article, Engle and Engle proposed a classification system that would accurately reflect the components and aims of the entire range of overseas studies programs, thereby increasing transparency and better informing students and others about the types of programs in existence (Engle and Engle 2003). In this way, students, faculty, administrators, and providers would all be on the same page with their objectives, which would also make it easier for evaluations, assessments, and research to consider whether educational goals were being met. Peter Stearns also has written about the shortcomings of education abroad today (2009, 65–96). Like Engle and Engle, Stearns has expressed concerns about the efficacy of educational evaluations of the wide variety of program types. Moreover, Stearns mentions the following areas of concern:

- An inherent U.S. "parochialism" in programs that is defined by English-only instruction, isolation, and student demand for "American amenities" while abroad (66);
- Overburdening of study abroad programs to provide self-contained international experiences without attention to how overall curricular matters can be modified on home campuses;
- A lack of formal assessment programs to evaluate the educational benefits of education abroad to students;
- Excessive costs that mostly appeal to highly motivated students;
- Limited faculty involvement on some campuses;
- Low numbers of student participation from certain fields such as STEM disciplines; and
- Disproportionate representation of study abroad participants based on social and ethnic categories (67).

The critiques of education abroad outlined in this paragraph shed light on areas in need of research and a number of the issues addressed here have been considered in detail by a scholars and practitioners in recent years. Many thoughtful articles on some of these critiques appeared in *The Handbook of Practice and Research in Study Abroad*, edited by Ross Lewin in 2009.[11]

---

[11] The following chapters of *The Handbook of Practice and Research in Study Abroad* (2009) touch upon many of the issues addressed by Stearns: Connie Currier, James Lucas, and Denise Saint Arnault, "Democratizing Study Abroad: Challenges of Open Access, Local Commitments, and Global Competence in Community Colleges," Riall W. Nolan, "Turning Our Back on the World: Study Abroad and the Purpose of U.S. Higher Education," Earl Picard, Farrah Bernardino, and Kike Ehigiator, "Global Citizenship for All: Low Minority Student Participation in Study Abroad—Seeking Strategies for Success," Lisa Chieffo and Lesa Griffiths, "Here to Stay: Increasing Acceptance of Short-Term Study Abroad Programs," Maria D Martinez, Bidya Ranjeet, and Helen A. Marx, "Creating Study Abroad Opportunities for First-Generation College Students," Philip Wainwright et al., "Going Global in the Sciences: A Case Study at Emory University." See also: Twombly et al., *Study Abroad in a New Global Century: Renewing the Promise, Refining the Purpose*, 95–104.

Research on Educational Value and Student Learning in Education Abroad

The value of education abroad is a popular sentiment among students today. Alumni often assess their experiences abroad as the "best thing I ever did in college," while those who did not spend time studying overseas during their undergraduate years say, "my one regret was not studying abroad." These anecdotal bits of evidence have some value, but without systematic inquiry in the form of formal research and assessment, these glowing statements cannot be used to make meaningful decisions. Beyond individual testimonies and assumptions that education abroad is beneficial, what is the evidence for educational value in these experiences? Here, a scan of the emerging field of education abroad research can be most useful. The best examples from this type of research can help administrators and professionals justify the educational benefits of education abroad and guide their decisions about student learning outcomes.

Before moving further, it should be noted that conducting research about education is complicated.[12] The same general problems with education research apply to education abroad research. Namely, due to the variety of study abroad program types, destinations, living situations, disciplines, and individual program aims, there is no universally applicable mode of inquiry to test for learning outcomes. Randomized trials, often the "gold standard" in educational research, are typically not possible or even ethical in this type of research.[13] Additionally, since program sizes and types vary widely across the different colleges and universities, it is difficult to establish sample sizes large enough to generate generalizable results about educational value that apply across all education abroad programming. Moreover, the "golden rule" of education abroad programming—that "one size does *not* fit all,"—means that there are no universal programs or ways of designing overseas study; therefore, there are no one-size-fits-all research models. This variety and the difficulty in producing unified research strategy may be more of a boon than a curse since it necessitates lines of inquiry from a number of academic disciplines, theoretical frameworks, and research methodologies such as quantitative, qualitative, mixed-methods, and action research.

---

[12] For an in-depth look at some of the broad dilemmas in conducting educational research see: Carl F. Kaestle, "The Awful Reputation of Education Research," *Educational Researcher* 22, no. 1 (1993); David F. Labaree, "Educational Researchers: Living with a Lesser Form of Knowledge," *Educational Researcher* 27, no. 8 (1998); D.C. Phillips, "Muddying the Waters: The Many Purposes of Educational Inquiry," in *The SAGE Handbook for Research in Education: Engaging Ideas and Enriching Inquiry*, ed. Clinton Conrad and Ronald Serlin (London: SAGE, 2006).

[13] For more on the issues with utilizing randomized, controlled experiments in education see: "Muddying the Waters: The Many Purposes of Educational Inquiry."

Both researchers and administrators seeking to evaluate their programs have entered this terrain of assessment and evaluation with varying degrees of success. Given the vast array of published work in this area, the remainder of this chapter will focus on work conducted to determine educational value in the following areas.

1. **Academic Outcomes** (e.g. foreign language, discipline-specific knowledge, etc.)
2. **Professional Outcomes** (e.g. career objectives)
3. **Universal Outcomes** (e.g. intercultural competence and student development)

Readers who read the section of this chapter on history will notice the similarity between these three categories and the original objectives mentioned by the first study abroad programs. In many ways, academic, professional, and universal aims of education abroad have always been a part of the objectives of these programs; however, the degrees to which these aims have been articulated and achieved have varied widely over time.

Academic Outcomes

Academic outcomes for education abroad are highly valued by faculty and administration, but notoriously difficult to measure.[14] Over the years, there have been many studies on language acquisition and education abroad.[15] Beyond studies that demonstrate how education abroad may enhance second language acquisition, one of the most compelling arguments for education abroad has been that it "…enriches and diversifies undergraduate education by offering academic learning of a sort not possible on the home campus, yet of a standard worthy of home campus academic credit" (Hoffa and DePaul 2010, 8). This statement has long been assumed to be true among advocates of education abroad; however, only recently have studies shown that there are measurable academic benefits for students who participate in overseas study.

---

[14]For a deeper discussion of the difficulties in measuring outcomes and the methodological shortcomings of education abroad research see: Twombly et al., *Study Abroad in a New Global Century: Renewing the Promise, Refining the Purpose*, 90–93.

[15]On second-language acquisition: Sally Sieloff Magnan and Michele Back, "Social Interaction and Linguistic Gain During Study Abroad," *Foreign Language Annals* 40, no. 1 (2007). Joseph Collentine and Barbara F. Freed, "Learning Context and Its Effects on Second Language Acquisition: Introduction," *Studies in Second Language Acquisition* 26, no. 2 (2004). Richard D. Brecht, Dan E. Davidson, and Ralph B. Ginsberg, "Predictors of Foreign Language Gain During Study Abroad," in *Second Language Acquisition in a Study Abroad Context*, ed. Barbara F. Freed (Amsterdam/Philadelphia: J. Benjamins, 1995). Barbara F. Freed, *Second Language Acquisition in a Study Abroad Context*, Studies in Bilingualism, vol. 9 (Amsterdam/Philadelphia: J. Benjamins, 1995). Additionally, see: Joan Carson and Ana Longhini, "Focusing on Learning Styles and Strategies: A Diary Study in an Immersion Setting." *Language Learning* 52 (2002): 401–438. Sally Magnan and Michele Back, "Social Interaction and Linguistic Gain During Study Abroad." *Foreign Language Annals* 40, 1 (2007): 43–61.

One of the major worries of students and faculty is that students who study abroad will not graduate on time; however, research and administrative efforts to integrate education abroad into the curriculum are challenging this popularly held notion. First, since the late 1980s and 1990s, certain institutions of higher education have implemented curriculum integration projects that broadly aim to identify factors that prevent students from studying abroad, and then design policies to help students overcome these factors.[16] The Forum on Education Abroad and NAFSA have both published online guides and lists of best practices in curriculum integration (NAFSA 2013). Notably, the University of Minnesota has made strides in curriculum integration by partnering with various academic units on campus to meet the needs of specific departments and larger institutional aims toward internationalization (Woodruff 2009). The university developed a plan where departments and faculty take an active role in vetting overseas studies programs. Through this time- and labor-intensive process, faculty must approve programs, while advisers create advising sheets that are unique to each student's degree plan. Through these efforts, the University of Minnesota has increased the number of students who study abroad from 15 percent of the total student population to 30 percent, even though they have yet to meet their goal of 50 percent (Fischer 2010). This successful case study demonstrates the potential for curriculum integration to have an impact on campus. But what has the research shown?

Jodi Malmgren and James Galvin studied graduation rates at the University of Minnesota-Twin Cities and found that study abroad did not harm graduation rates there. Moreover, the study reported that study abroad participation was, "...highly correlated with high graduation rates among under-prepared and at-risk undergraduates as well as students of color" (Malmgren and Galvin 2009, 29). These findings were particularly relevant to the Twin Cities, since Malmgren and Galvin found that students surveyed reported graduating on time was either "somewhat," "very" or "the most important factor" in their decision to study abroad.

Heather Barclay Hamir's research (2011) also supports the claim that students who study abroad will not necessarily have their graduation delayed. In Hamir's research, data gathered from the 2002 entering cohort at the University of Texas-Austin (7,845 students) were analyzed in three groups of students: students who studied abroad (participants), students who applied but did not participate (applicants), and students who did not apply to study abroad (nonparticipants). In the study, Hamir found that students

---

[16]For efforts at curriculum integration at liberal arts colleges in the late 1980s and early 1990s, see: Barbara B. Burn, *Integrating Study Abroad into the Undergraduate Liberal Arts Curriculum: Eight Institutional Case Studies* (New York: Greenwood Press, 1991).

who studied abroad (participants) graduated at higher rates than either the applicants or nonparticipants (2011). Hamir's study is noteworthy for its large sample size and mixed-methods approach (utilizing quantitative and qualitative data analysis). Her research demonstrates how study abroad participation at Texas-Austin promoted student engagement (in participants) in ways consistent with previous theories of student involvement and development in higher education.[17] Malmgren and Galvin's and Hamir's studies are noteworthy for practice since, as Twombly et al. point out, "...it is very important to provide students with data showing that study abroad does not delay or negatively affect graduation but that some careful planning may be necessary to ensure that this does not happen" (Twombly et al. 2012, 84). In addition to these studies, researchers are also finding that students tend to be more engaged in academics following their education abroad experiences (Dolby 2004; Dolby 2007; Hadis 2005).

Professional / Career Outcomes

The impact of education abroad on professional aims and long-term career outcomes is difficult to measure and more research is needed in this area. As Twombly et al. explain (2012), many of the studies on long-term career outcomes are retrospective assessments. Contemporary assessments of long-term professional outcomes, such as the 1930 IIE study mentioned above, generally survey alumni with questions about their current employment and highest degrees obtained.

One notable study from 1990 sent questionnaires to a cohort of alumni who studied abroad from the University of California, the University of Colorado, the University of Massachusetts-Amherst, and Kalamazoo College. Based on responses to the surveys and follow-up phone calls, researchers in this study found that 45 out of 76 alumni had somehow incorporated their education abroad experience into their careers (Carlson et al. 1990). More recently, R. Michael Paige, Gerald Fry, Elizabeth Stallman, Jamina Josi, and Jae-Eun Jon (2009) surveyed 6,391 study abroad alumni and found that 35.2 percent of former students reported that study abroad helped their career to a "large degree," and 39.9 percent indicated that study abroad had helped their career to "some degree." Additionally, 37.7 percent of the participants in the survey reported that their careers were currently or had been "internationally oriented" (Paige et al. 2009, 38).

---

[17]For more on student involvement theory see: George D. Kuh et al., *Student Success in College: Creating Conditions That Matter,* 1st ed. (San Francisco: Jossey-Bass, 2005). Also: Alexander W. Astin, "Student Involvement: A Developmental Theory for Higher Education," *Journal of College Student Personnel* 25 (1984).

Finally, Emily Norris and Joan Gillespie conducted a study of 3,700 alumni from the Institute for the International Education of Students (IES) programs between 1950 and 1999. This longitudinal study revealed differences between cohorts from different eras. For example, students in the cohorts from 1990 to 1999 were almost two times as likely to have been influenced by their IES experience than the students from the 1950s and '60s, and "ten times more likely to have participated in internships while studying abroad" (Norris and Gillespie 2009, 387). Norris and Gillespie also found that 74 percent of the students who self-reported to be working in a "global career" said that their study abroad experience "ignited interest" in their chosen profession. This statistically significant finding suggests that for these students, there was a correlation between their global careers and their education abroad experience (Norris and Gillespie 2009, 390). Additionally, a 2012 survey conducted by IES found that nearly 90 percent of its study abroad alumni were employed within six months of graduation, compared with 49 percent of the respondents of a separate study who found employment within a year of graduation but did not study abroad (Cook-Anderson 2012).

Universal Outcomes

One explicit and implicit outcome of education abroad since its beginning has been the idea that students can develop their own identities and sensitivity to other cultures. Essentially, by spending time in other national contexts, it is believed that students can gain a deeper understanding of cultural norms and differences with the host nation. This outcome has often been described as intercultural competence. Darla Deardorff's work has been especially helpful in defining this term and outlining strategies to assess outcomes in this area (2009). Beyond Deardorff's research, there is a large body of literature on intercultural competence that continues to expand.[18] There are several aspects of intercultural competence that advocates of education abroad suggest students will develop after their

---

[18]See Milton Bennett, "A Short Conceptual History of Intercultural Learning." Philip H. Anderson et al., "Short-Term Study Abroad and Intercultural Sensitivity: A Pilot Study," *International Journal of Intercultural Relations* 30, no. 4 (2006). Dan Landis, Janet Marie Bennett, and Milton J. Bennett, eds., *Handbook of Intercultural Training*, 3rd ed. (Thousand Oaks, Calif.: SAGE Publications, 2004). Philip Anderson, et al., "Short-Term Study Abroad and Intercultural Sensitivity: A Pilot Study." *International Journal of Intercultural Relations* 30, no. 4 (2006): 457-69. Stephanie Shaheen, "The Effect of Pre-Departure Preparation on Student Intercultural Development During Study Abroad Programs" (Dissertation, Ohio State University, 2004). Tracy Rundstrom Williams, "Exploring the Impact of Study Abroad on Students' Intercultural Communication Skills: Adaptability and Sensitivity," *Journal of Studies in International Education* 9, no. 4 (2005). Richard C. Sutton and Donald Rubin, "The Glossari Project: Initial Findings from a System-Wide Research Initiative on Study Abroad Learning Outcomes," *Frontiers: The Interdisciplinary Journal of Study Abroad* 10(2004). Hadis, "Gauging the Impact of Study Abroad: How to Overcome the Limitations of a Single-Cell Design." Mell Bolen, ed. *A Guide to Outcomes and Assessment in Education Abroad* (Austin, TX: 2007). Joshua S. McKeown, *The First Time Effect: The Impact of Study Abroad on College Student Intellectual Development* (Albany, NY: SUNY Press, 2009). Most recently see: Vande Berg et al., *Student Learning Abroad: What Our Students Are Learning, What They're Not, and What We Can Do About It.*

overseas study experiences. For the most part, research has found that students who study abroad demonstrate positive elements of intercultural competence upon returning home. A recent literature review of this research categorized studies that looked at each of the following aspects of intercultural competence (Twombly et al. 2012, 72–76):

- Study abroad participant's view of host culture or country
- Study abroad participant's global perspective or world mindedness
- Study abroad participant's intercultural awareness or sensitivity

To cite just a few studies that are emblematic of larger trends in research in these three areas, Kenneth Cushner and Ata Karim's research indicates that students develop a more positive view of their host culture after studying abroad (2004). Patricia Golay surveyed students at Florida State University and found that there was a statistically significant difference in attitudes toward global mindedness between students who studied abroad and those who did not. Additionally, of the students she surveyed, there was a significant difference in global mindedness among the study abroad participants in their post-survey results (Golay 2006). Finally, a multiyear study at Georgetown University's Office of International Programs found that "students enrolled in study abroad programs averaged more progress in intercultural learning and oral proficiency in their target languages than control students studying in these same languages" (Vande Berg, Connor-Linton, and Paige 2009, 2).[19] Additionally, the project found that on average, woman made greater gains in intercultural learning than their male study abroad counterparts.

Finally, it should be noted that gains in intercultural learning do not occur by osmosis. As Milton Bennett has written, "…the mere experience of being immersed in another culture does not necessarily translate into either specific knowledge about that culture or transferable principles about intercultural relations" (2010, 419). This belief that intercultural learning automatically occurs in students who study abroad has had a dominant rhetorical hold on practitioners for many years. Very recently, Michael Vande Berg, R. Michael Paige, and Kris Hemming Lou (2012) have argued for the emergence of a new paradigm of thought in education abroad that moves beyond the existing epistemological frames that may have been responsible for these notions of cultural osmosis.

According to Vande Berg, Paige, and Lou, there are three "master narratives" for ways in which people have conceptualized learning in education

---

[19]Findings from research on a short-term sociology program provide additional insights on this topic: Dennis Poole and Tamara Davis, "Concept Mapping to Measure Outcomes in Study Abroad Programs," *Social Work Education* 25, no. 1 (2006).

abroad: the positivist, the relativist, and the experiential/constructivist (Vande Berg, Paige, and Lou 2012, 15–19). Briefly, the positivist narrative was most common during the early part of the twentieth century on programs such as the junior year abroad. This narrative assumes that students learn through experiences and observations in the world. The relativist ideology is a more recent narrative, which suggests that all cultures are equal and that students learn best through immersion. These narratives have proven insufficient when it comes to student learning, however, and are being replaced by the experiential/constructivist narrative that does not consider students passive receptors of knowledge. Instead, the narrative argues that students learn by constant interactions with their environment and self-reflection of their own understanding of the world around them. In an extensive review of recent research on intercultural learning, Paige and Vande Berg have found several studies that demonstrate how active and thoughtful interventions in student study abroad experiences have positive associations, with increased intercultural awareness.[20] The research reviewed by Paige and Vande Berg shows that intervention at different points of the entire study abroad process (predeparture to reentry) is beneficial for student learning. Moreover, Paige and Vande Berg suggest that the modes of instruction more commonly associated with the positivist and relativist narratives may be less effective that those associated with the experiential/constructivist narrative.

Although the studies cited by Paige and Vande Berg demonstrate the positive impact of certain types of interventions in a student's education abroad experience (e.g., cultural mentoring, exercises to stimulate self-reflection, and explicit programming designed to help the student become more culturally self-aware), there is little attention given to the needs of specific underrepresented student groups. As mentioned above, the students studying abroad have diversified slightly over the twentieth century, particularly in their majors—but in terms of race and socioeconomic status (SES), the numbers are modest.[21] These numbers lag behind the enrollment data for higher education more broadly and have prompted some scholars to study the reasons for underrepresentation in education abroad. Notably, in 2011, Mark Salisbury, Michael Paulsen and Ernest Pascarella applied an adapted version of an integrated student choice model to identify differences between white and minority students' decisions to study abroad. This student choice model claims that students make decisions about college

[20]See chapter 2 (R. Michael Paige and Michael Vande Berg, "Why Students Are and Are Not Learning Abroad: A Review of Recent Research") in *Student Learning Abroad: What Our Students Are Learning, What They're Not, and What We Can Do About It.*

[21]For a more detailed assessment of this history see: Stallman, "The Diversification of the Student Profile."

enrollment that are within "situated" contexts that are "...uniquely shaped by the combination of an individual's accumulated values, attitudes, beliefs, obligations, limitations and opportunities" (125). The authors applied this model to study abroad decisions made by 6,828 students at 53 two- and four-year institutions.

Some notable findings include the following:

1. White students with higher levels of SES had higher odds of intending to study abroad.
2. Arguments that studying abroad will increase a student's opportunities for cross-cultural development "...appear to have no affect on increasing study abroad intent among most minority students" (144).
3. Asian-American and Hispanic students were more likely to intend to study abroad if they received a financial grant. Conversely, white students were less likely to intend to study abroad if they received a grant.

This study demonstrates that there is not a one-size-fits-all model for education abroad programming for students from different groups. As Salisbury et al., point out (2011), there are complex differences between racial groups, and within those racial groups there are heterogeneous factors that further complicate each individual student's decision to study abroad. Even with myriad issues to consider, administrators can use research like this to make thoughtful decisions about recruitment and programming to meet the learning needs of a diverse array of students.

Conclusion

As this chapter has shown, the field for education abroad research is rich and has room for debate and growth. Research has shown that the quest for educational value in overseas study is ongoing and highly contextual. Including a chapter on this developing body of research in the newest iteration of the *Guide to Education Abroad* is a testament to the good work of professionals in the field, and the growing number of researchers who have focused their analytic gaze on education abroad. Like the popular culture and political references in the introduction to this chapter, some of the studies mentioned here might have resonance 20 years from now, while others may seem as anachronistic as computer-generated dinosaurs from late twentieth century Hollywood films. Regardless of how the accumulated knowledge about this field evolves, the focus on upholding educational value in education abroad will endure as a central aspect of this endeavor.

References

Anderson, Philip H., Leigh Lawton, Richard J. Rexeisen, and Ann C. Hubbard. 2006. "Short-Term Study Abroad and Intercultural Sensitivity: A Pilot Study." *International Journal of Intercultural Relations* 30, 4: 457–69.

Astin, Alexander W. 1984. "Student Involvement: A Developmental Theory for Higher Education." *Journal of College Student Personnel* 25: 297–308.

Bennett, Milton J. 2010. "A Short Conceptual History of Intercultural Learning." In *A History of U.S. Study Abroad: 1965–Present*. Carlisle, PA: Frontiers: The Interdisciplinary Journal of Study Abroad.

Biscarra, Albert, David Comp, and Gary Rhodes. n.d. "Research on U.S. Students Study Abroad: An Update, 2004–2011." A Bibliography with Abstracts. UCLA Center for International and Development Education and UCLA Center for Global Education, http://globaledresearch.com/book_research_comp_update.asp?year = 2004.

Bolen, Mell, ed. 2007. *A Guide to Outcomes and Assessment in Education Abroad*. Austin, Tex.: The Forum on Education Abroad.

Bowman, John E. 1987. "Educating American Undergraduates Abroad: The Development of Study Abroad Programs by American Colleges and Universities." In *Council on International Educational Exchange Occasional Papers* No 24.

Brecht, Richard D., Dan E. Davidson, and Ralph B. Ginsberg. 1995. "Predictors of Foreign Language Gain During Study Abroad." In *Second Language Acquisition in a Study Abroad Context*. Edited by Barbara F. Freed. Amsterdam/Philadelphia: J. Benjamins.

Burn, Barbara B. 1991. *Integrating Study Abroad into the Undergraduate Liberal Arts Curriculum: Eight Institutional Case Studies*. New York: Greenwood Press.

Byam, Edwin C., and Marine Leland. 1930. "American Undergraduates in France." *The French Review* 3, 4: 261–69.

Carlson, Jerry S., Barbara B. Burn, John Useem, and David Yachimowicz. 1990. *Study Abroad: The Experience of American Undergraduates*. New York: Greenwood Press.

The Center for Global Education. "Study Abroad Research Online." http://globaledresearch.com.

Chieffo, Lisa, and Lesa Griffiths. 2009. "Here to Stay: Increasing Acceptance of Shot-Term Study Abroad Programs." In *The Handbook of Practice and Research in Study Abroad: Higher Education and the Quest for Global Citizenship*. Edited by Ross Lewin. New York: Routledge.

Collentine, Joseph, and Barbara F. Freed. 2004. "Learning Context and Its Effects on Second Language Acquisition: Introduction." *Studies in Second Language Acquisition* 26, 2: 153–71.

Lincoln Commission. 2005. "Global Competence & National Needs: One Million Americans Studying Abroad." Washington, D.C.: Commission on the Abraham Lincoln Study Abroad Fellowship Program.

Comp, David, and Martha Merritt. 2010. "The Development of Qualitative Standards and Learning Outcomes for Study Abroad." In *A History of U.S. Study Abroad: 1965–Present.* Carlisle, PA: Frontiers: The Interdisciplinary Journal of Study Abroad.

Contreras, Eduardo. 2013a. "Considering Study Abroad's Past to Prepare for Its Future." *IIE Networker* (Fall): 15–17.

Contreras, Eduardo. 2013b. "International Experiments in American Higher Education at the University of Delaware and Smith College: Study Abroad in the 1920s." Qualifying Paper, Harvard Graduate School of Education.

Cook-Anderson, Gretchen. 2012. "Studying Abroad in College Helps Graduates Make More Money and Land Jobs Faster." *Diversity Employers:* 11–13.

Council for International Educational Exchange. 1988. "Educating for Global Competence: The Report of the Advisory Council for International Educational Exchange." Porland, Maine.: Council for International Educational Exchange.

Currier, Connie, James Lucas, and Denise Saint Arnault. 2009. "Democratizing Study Abroad: Challenges of Open Access, Local Commitments, and Global Competence in Community Colleges." In *The Handbook of Practice and Research in Study Abroad: Higher Education and the Quest for Global Citizenship.* Edited by Ross Lewin. New York: Routledge.

Cushner, Kenneth, and Ata Karim. 2004. "Study Abroad at the University Level." In *Handbook of Intercultural Training.* Edited by Dan Landis, Janet M. Bennett and Milton J. Bennett. Thousand Oaks, Calif.: SAGE Publications.

Deardorff, Darla K. 2009. *The SAGE Handbook of Intercultural Competence.* Thousand Oaks, Calif.: SAGE Publications.

DeWinter, Urbain J., Laura E. Rumbley. 2010. "The Diversification of Education Abroad across the Curriculum." In *A History of U.S. Study Abroad: 1965–Present.* Carlisle, PA: Frontiers: The Interdisciplinary Journal of Study Abroad.

Dolby, Nadine. 2004. "Encountering an American Self: Study Abroad and National Identity." *Comparative Education Review* 48, 2 (2004): 150–73.

Dolby, Nadine. 2007. "Reflections on Nation: American Undergraduates and Education Abroad." *Journal of Studies in International Education* 11, 2: 141–56.

Engle, Lilli, and John Engle. 2003. "Study Abroad Levels: Toward a Classification of Program Types." *Frontiers: The Interdisciplinary Journal of Study Abroad* 9: 1–20.

Fischer, Karin. 2010. "U. Of Minnesota Integrates Study Abroad into the Curriculum." *The Chronicle of Higher Education:* March 28. http://chronicle.com/article/U-of-Minnesota-Integrates/64859/

Forum on Education Abroad. "Home." Carlisle, Pa.: Forum on Education Abroad. http://www.forumea.org.

Forum on EducationAbroad. "Toolkit Resources for Curriculum Integration of Education Abroad." http://www.forumea.org/documents/InnovationsinCurriculumIntegration-toolkit.pdf.

Freed, Barbara F. 1995. *Second Language Acquisition in a Study Abroad Context.* Amsterdam/Philadelphia: J. Benjamins.

Frontiers. n.d. "Frontiers: The Interdisciplinary Journal of Study Abroad." http://www.frontiersjournal.com/.

Golay, Patricia A. 2006. "The Effects of Study Abroad on the Development of Global-Mindedness among Students Enrolled in International Programs at Florida State University." Dissertation, Florida State University.

Goodwin, Craufurd D. W., and Michael Nacht. 1988. *Abroad and Beyond: Patterns in American Overseas Education.* Cambridge [Cambridgeshire]; New York: Cambridge University Press.

Goodwin, Craufurd D. W., and Michael Nacht. 1991. *Missing the Boat: The Failure to Internationalize American Higher Education.* Cambridge [England]; New York: Cambridge University Press.

Gore, Joan Elias. 2005. *Dominant Beliefs and Alternative Voices: Discourses, Belief and Gender in American Study Abroad.* Edited by Philip G. Altbach. New York: Routledge.

Hadis, Benjamin. 2005. "Gauging the Impact of Study Abroad: How to Overcome the Limitations of a Single-Cell Design." *Assessment & Evaluation in Higher Education* 30, 1: 3–19.

Hamir, Heather Barclay. 2011. "Go Abroad and Graduate On-Time: Study Abroad Participation, Degree Completion, and Time-to-Degree." Dissertation, University of Nebraska.

Hewlett, Theodosia, and Willard Connely. 1930. *A Decade of International Fellowships: A Survey of the Impressions of American and Foreign Ex-Fellows.* New York: The Institute of International Education.

Hoffa, William W. 2007. *A History of U.S. Study Abroad: Beginnings to 1965.* Carlisle, PA: Frontiers: The Interdisciplinary Journal of Study Abroad.

Hoffa, William W., and Stephen C. DePaul. 2010. *A History of U.S. Study Abroad: 1965–Present.* Carlisle, PA: Frontiers: The Interdisciplinary Journal of Study Abroad.

Hoffa, William W., John Pearson, Marvin Slind, eds. 1993. *NAFSA's Guide to Education Abroad for Advisers and Administrators.* Washington, D.C.: NAFSA: Association of International Educators.

Hullihen, Walter. 1928. "Present Status of the 'Junior Year Abroad.'" *The French Review* 1, 2: 25–37.

Indiana University. "Early History: About Us: Overseas Study: Indiana University." http://overseas.iu.edu/about/history/history_early.shtml.

Institute of International Education. 1927. "Annual Report." New York, N.Y.: The Institute of International Education.

Institute of International Education. 1928. "The Junior Year in France: An Open Letter to Teachers of French and College Faculties." New York, N.Y.: The Institute of International Education.

Institute of International Education. *Open Doors Report on International Educational Exchange.* http://www.iie.org/Research-and-Publications/Open-Doors.

Kaestle, Carl F. 1993. "The Awful Reputation of Education Research." *Educational Researcher* 22, 1: 23, 26–31.

Kuh, George D., Jillian Kinzie, John H. Schuh, and Elizabeth J Whitt. 2005. *Student Success in College: Creating Conditions That Matter.* San Francisco: Jossey-Bass.

Labaree, David F. 1998. "Educational Researchers: Living with a Lesser Form of Knowledge." *Educational Researcher* 27, 8: 4–12.

Lambert, Richard D. 1989. *International Studies and the Undergraduate.* Washington, D.C.: American Council on Education.

Landis, Dan, Janet Marie Bennett, and Milton J. Bennett, eds. 2004. *Handbook of Intercultural Training.* 3rd ed. Thousand Oaks, Calif.: SAGE Publications.

Lewin, Ross, ed. 2009. *The Handbook of Practice and Research in Study Abroad: Higher Education and the Quest for Global Citizenship.* New York: Routledge.

Magnan, Sally Sieloff, and Michele Back. 2007. "Social Interaction and Linguistic Gain During Study Abroad." *Foreign Language Annals* 40, 1: 43–61.

Malmgren, Jodi, and James Galvin. 2009. "Effects of Study Abroad Participation on Student Graduation Rates: A Study of Three Incoming Freshman Cohorts at the University of Minnesota, Twin Cities." *NACADA Journal* 28, 1: 29–42.

Martinez, Maria D, Bidya Ranjeet, and Helen A Marx. 2009. "Creating Study Abroad Opportunities for First-Generation College Students." In *The Handbook of Practice and Research in Study Abroad: Higher Education and the Quest for Global Citizenship.* Edited by Ross Lewin. New York: Routledge.

McKeown, Joshua S. 2009. *The First Time Effect: The Impact of Study Abroad on College Student Intellectual Development*. Albany, NY: SUNY Press.

Munroe, John A. 1986. *The University of Delaware : A History*. Newark, Del.: The University of Delaware.

NAFSA. 2010. "Review of Global Studies Literature." Washington, D.C.: NAFSA:Association of International Educators. http://www.nafsa.org/resourcelibrary/default.aspx?id = 19338.

NAFSA. 2013. "Curriculum Integration: Best Practices." Washington, D.C.: NAFSA:Association of International Educators. http://www.nafsa. org/Find_Resources/Supporting_Study_Abroad/Network_Resources/Education_Abroad/Curriculum_Integration__Best_Practices/.

Nolan, Riall W. 2009. "Turning Our Back on the World: Study Abroad and the Purpose of U.S. Higher Education." In *The Handbook of Practice and Research in Study Abroad: Higher Education and the Quest for Global Citizenship*. Edited by Ross Lewin. New York: Routledge.

Norris, Emily Mohajeri, and Joan Gillespie. 2009. "How Study Abroad Shapes Global Careers: Evidence from the United States." *Journal of Studies in International Education* 13, 3: 382–97.

Odgen, Anthony C., Heidi M. Soneson, and Paige Weting. 2010. "The Diversification of Geographic Locations. " In *A History of U.S. Study Abroad: 1965–Present*. Carlisle, PA: Frontiers: The Interdisciplinary Journal of Study Abroad.

Paige, R. Michael, Gerald W Fry, Elizabeth M. Stallman, Jasmina Josi , and Jae-Eun Jon. 2009. "Study Abroad for Global Engagement: The Long-Term Impact of Mobility Experiences." *Intercultural Education* 20: 29–44.

Phillips, D.C. 2006. "Muddying the Waters: The Many Purposes of Educational Inquiry." In *The SAGE Handbook for Research in Education: Engaging Ideas and Enriching Inquiry*. Edited by Clinton Conrad and Ronald Serlin. London: SAGE Publications.

Picard, Earl, Farrah Bernardino, and Kike Ehigiator. 2009. "Global Citizenship for All: Low Minority Student Participation in Study Abroad—Seeking Strategies for Success." In *The Handbook of Practice and Research in Study Abroad: Higher Education and the Quest for Global Citizenship*. Edited by Ross Lewin. New York: Routledge.

Poole, Dennis, and Tamara Davis. 2006. "Concept Mapping to Measure Outcomes in Study Abroad Programs." *Social Work Education* 25, 1: 61–77.

Robertson, David Allan. 1926. "The Junior Year Abroad." *The Educational Record* 7, 2: 98–113.

Rodman, Richard, Martha Merrill. 2010. "Unlocking Study Abroad Potential: Design Models, Methods an Masters." In *A History of U.S. Study Abroad:*

1965–Present. Carlisle, PA: Frontiers: The Interdisciplinary Journal of Study Abroad.

Salisbury, Mark, Michael Paulsen, and Ernest Pascarella. 2010. "To See the World or Stay at Home: Applying an Integrated Student Choice Model to Explore the Gender Gap in the Intent to Study Abroad." *Research in Higher Education* 51, 7: 615–40.

Salisbury, Mark, Michael Paulsen, and Ernest Pascarella. 2011. "Why Do All the Study Abroad Students Look Alike? Applying an Integrated Student Choice Model to Explore Differences in the Factors That Influence White and Minority Students' Intent to Study Abroad." *Research in Higher Education* 52, 2: 123–50.

Shaheen, Stephanie. 2004. "The Effect of Pre-Departure Preparation on Student Intercultural Development During Study Abroad Programs." Dissertation, Ohio State University.

Shirley, Steven W. 2006. "The Gender Gap in Post-Secondary Study Abroad: Understanding and Marketing to Male Students." Dissertation, University of North Dakota.

Sideli, Kathleen. 2010. "The Professionalization of the Field of Education Abroad." In *A History of U.S. Study Abroad: 1965–Present.* Carlisle, PA: Frontiers: The Interdisciplinary Journal of Study Abroad.

Smith, Horatio. 1933. "The Junior Year Abroad." *World Affairs* 96, 1: 30–32.

Stallman, Elizabeth, Gayle A. Woodruff, Jinous Kasravi, David Comp. 2010. "The Diversification of the Student Profile." In A *History of U.S. Study Abroad: 1965–Present.* Carlisle, PA: Frontiers: The Interdisciplinary Journal of Study Abroad.

Stearns, Peter N. 2009. *Educating Global Citizens in Colleges and Universities: Challenges and Opportunities.* New York: Routledge.

Stroud, April H. 2010. "Who Plans (Not) to Study Abroad? An Examination of U.S. Student Intent." *Journal of Studies in International Education* 14, 5: 491–507.

Sutton, Richard C, and Donald Rubin. 2004. "The Glossari Project: Initial Findings from a System-Wide Research Initiative on Study Abroad Learning Outcomes." *Frontiers: The Interdisciplinary Journal of Study Abroad* 10 (Fall): 65–82.

Twombly, Susan, Mark Salisbury, Shannon Tumanut, and Paul Klute. 2012. *Study Abroad in a New Global Century: Renewing the Promise, Refining the Purpose.* ASHE Higher Education Report 38, 4. Hoboken, NJ: Wiley Periodicals.

Vande Berg, Michael. 2007. "Intervening in the Learning of U.S. Students Abroad." *Journal of Studies in International Education* 11, 3/4: 392–99.

Vande Berg, Michael. 2004. "Introduction." *Frontiers: The Interdisciplinary Journal of Study Abroad* 10: xii–xiii.

Vande Berg, Michael, Jeffrey Connor-Linton, and R. Michael Paige. 2009. "The Georgetown Consortium Project: Interventions for Student Learning Abroad." *Frontiers: The Interdisciplinary Journal of Study Abroad* 18: 1–75.

Vande Berg, Michael; R. Michael Paige, and Kris Hemming Lou, eds. 2012. *Student Learning Abroad: What Our Students Are Learning, What They're Not, and What We Can Do About It.* Sterling, Virginia: Stylus Publishing.

Wainwright, Philip, Preetha Ram, Daniel Teodorescu, and Dana Tottenham. 2009. "Going Global in the Sciences: A Case Study at Emory University." In *The Handbook of Practice and Research in Study Abroad: Higher Education and the Quest for Global Citizenship.* Edited by Ross Lewin. New York: Routledge.

Walton, Whitney. 2005. "American Girls and French 'Jeunes Filles:' Negotiating Identities in Interwar France." *Gender & History* 17, 2: 325–53.

Walton, Whitney. 2010. *Internationalism, National Identities, and Study Abroad: France and the United States, 1890–1970.* Stanford, Calif.: Stanford University Press.

Williams, Tracy Rundstrom. 2005. "Exploring the Impact of Study Abroad on Students' Intercultural Communication Skills: Adaptability and Sensitivity." *Journal of Studies in International Education* 9, 4: 356–71.

Woodruff, Gayle A. 2009. "Curriculum Integration: Where We Have Been and Where We Are Going." University of Minnesota: Board of Regents.

Wynveen, Christopher J., Gerard T. Kyle, and Michael A. Tarrant. 2012. "Study Abroad Experiences and Global Citizenship: Fostering Proenvironmental Behavior." *Journal of Studies in International Education* 16, 4: 334–52.

PART III
HEALTH, SAFETY, AND
RISK MANAGEMENT

Kiribati • Korea, North • Korea, South • Kosovo • Kuwait • Kyrgyzstan • Laos • Latvia • Lebanon • Lesotho •

Liberia • Libya • Liechtenstein • Lithuania • Luxembourg • Macau • Macedonia • Madagascar • Malawi •

Malaysia • Maldives • Mali • Malta • Marshall Islands • Mauritania • Mauritius • Mexico • Micronesia • Moldova

• Monaco • Mongolia • Montenegro • Morocco • Mozambique • Namibia • Nauru • Nepal • Netherlands •

Netherlands Antilles • New Zealand • Nicaragua • Niger • Nigeria • Norway • Oman • Pakistan •

Palau • Palestinian Territories • Panama • Papua New Guinea • Paraguay • Peru • Philippines • Poland •

Portugal • Qatar • Romania • Russia • Rwanda • Saint Kitts and Nevis • Saint Lucia • Saint Vincent and the

Grenadines • Samoa • San Marino • Sao Tome and Principe • Saudi Arabia • Senegal • Serbia • Seychelles •

Sierra Leone • Singapore • Sint Maarten • Slovakia • Slovenia • Solomon Islands • Somalia • South Africa •

South Korea • South Sudan • Spain • Sri Lanka • Sudan • Suriname • Swaziland • Sweden • Switzerland • Syria

• Taiwan • Tajikistan • Tanzania • Thailand • Timor-Leste • Togo • Tonga • Trinidad and Tobago • Tunisia •

Turkey • Turkmenistan • Tuvalu • Uganda • Ukraine • United Arab Emirates • United Kingdom • Uruguay •

Uzbekistan • Vanuatu • Venezuela • Vietnam • Yemen • Zambia • Zimbabwe • Afghanistan • Albania • Algeria •

CHAPTER 9

PHYSICAL AND MENTAL HEALTH OF STUDENTS

By Jennifer White

Introduction

One of the most significant, and most challenging, aspects of education abroad advising and international program management is advising students on health and safety concerns abroad. While students and their families often seek assurances that the student will remain "safe" while abroad, education abroad professionals should refrain from providing guarantees of students' safety and well-being, since there are many factors beyond the institution's and adviser's control that can influence the navigation of health and safety issues abroad. Not least among these issues are the choices made by each individual student whether to follow advice given in predeparture and on-site orientations regarding health and safety issues.

Education abroad advisers and institutions need to provide as much thorough, accurate, and up-to-date advising as possible to help students make informed choices, but cannot control student behavior abroad any more than on campus. This fact should be emphasized in the waiver and assumption of risk documents that students sign in advance of participation in a given education abroad program. Parents often want to know whether a given location abroad is "safe" or not, and whether their student will remain healthy throughout the duration of the program. Such concerns take on a heightened level of importance since the perception of risk increases with the unknown (Schmidt 2004).

Common Types of Mental Health Issues Among Study Abroad Students

Major Depression, Dysthymia, and Bipolar Disorder

Students with major depression can exhibit symptoms such as feeling hopeless or worthless, fatigue, difficulty concentrating, or excessive crying, which persist over a period of months or years. Dysthymia is a less intense form of major depression with similar symptoms, so students are often unaware they are coping with a form of mental illness. Bipolar disorder is characterized by mood swings or alternating cycles of depression followed by elation or increased activity called mania (Lindeman 2009, 13). Education abroad professionals observing students with these symptoms should refer them to a mental health professional for evaluation and treatment.

Anxiety: Generalized Anxiety Disorder, Phobias, Panic Disorder, OCD, and PTSD

Anxiety is part of everyday life, but when it "becomes persistent and overwhelming to the point that it interferes with an individual's day-to-day functioning" (Lindeman 2009, 18) it is considered a mental health issue. Treatment includes cognitive behavior therapy, medication, and self-care modalities. Generalized anxiety disorder is chronic and often does not carry a specific source for the individual's anxious feelings. Phobias are linked to specific situations and bring on intense feelings of anxiety, sometimes even when the activity is considered but not actually occurring. Panic disorder involves intense onset and short duration of symptoms such as rapid heartbeat, shortness of breath, and excessive fear. Obsessive-compulsive disorder, or OCD, involves ritualized patterns of behavior developed to cope with obsessive fear and anxiety. Posttraumatic stress disorder, or PTSD, can follow a traumatic event and involves the reliving of the trauma in the form of flashbacks or nightmares and symptoms such as hypervigilance, emotional numbness, and anger (Lindeman 2009, 19–20).

Eating Disorders

Eating disorders are increasingly common among both female and male college students, and can sometimes become exacerbated by the study abroad experience. Whether anorexia nervosa, in which the individual's weight is typically less than 85 percent of normal range, or bulimia nervosa, with its recurrent binge and purge cycle, these disorders pose serious concerns to a student's health and should be referred to a health professional for counseling and ongoing care. It is important to be aware of past history of these disorders, even if currently under control, because of the possibility for recurrence during the sojourn abroad.

Attention Deficit Hyperactivity Disorder (ADHD)

Students with ADHD have difficulty concentrating and often manage their symptoms with a combination of medication and accommodations for learning differences, such as extra time on examinations. Frequently, ADHD medications are among those that cannot be brought legally into the host country, so early advising of students with this condition is crucial.

Sources of Stress Abroad: Culture Shock

Even for students in good mental and physical health, the transitions involved with study abroad can pose significant challenges. Despite thorough predeparture orientations designed to prepare students for the rigors of living abroad, students may be "unprepared for the impact that this experience can have on their emotional well-being, including mood, stress level, behavior patterns, or identity development. In addition, the process of adjusting to a new culture can exacerbate preexisting concerns or developmental challenges that the student may have been managing quite well at home" (Lindeman 2009, 4).

Medical Information Form as an Advising Tool

An important tool in advising students regarding health concerns abroad is the education abroad office's medical information form. Following established best practices in the field of education abroad is essential in this highly sensitive area. First, the medical information form should be collected after the application stage, and not during it. Secondly, it needs to be reviewed in a comprehensive way by both the campus health administration and legal counsel for compliance with institutional, state, and federal rules and regulations. Lastly, the tone of communications with students when requesting this highly confidential information is extremely important. Carefully communicating that the information is requested in order to help the office assist the student in obtaining necessary medical care and support abroad will encourage students to be accurate and fully disclose any current or prior medical or mental health concerns.

Medical information forms need to be designed to comprehensively assess a student's physical and mental well-being, and should contain questions regarding both current and prior conditions from the past 5 years. Clinician verification forms should be provided by those professionals most directly involved in the management of a present condition. In other words, the campus student health staff should not be signing off on a student's readiness to study abroad if that student is being treated for anxiety and depression by an off-campus psychiatrist and/or psychologist. Students need to be informed that they must seek the clearance of those clinicians most directly involved in their care so that an accurate assessment can be made of their current physical and mental health.

Predeparture Orientation

Predeparture orientation can often occur too late in the preparation cycle for issues such as securing adequate supply of medications. Students need to be advised of these processes and necessities early on, whether through individual advising, information presented on a medical information form collected earlier in the semester before departure, or by other means. Predeparture orientation should include a thorough briefing for students. It should, for example, advise students to carry prescription medications in their original containers, with a copy of the prescription when possible, and adhere to their regular schedule of medications while abroad. Ideally, the predeparture orientation program will be of sufficient length to allow for guest speakers from student health and counseling services on campus to attend and present their expert knowledge on this topic.

Successful Support and Response Begins at Home

Developing Your On-Campus Network

Cross-training and collaboration with campus health and counseling services on the home campus proves extremely valuable to the education abroad office. At some institutions, clinicians are willing to consult with students in crisis abroad, while at others concerns over distance treatment will result in reluctance to directly communicate with students experiencing a crisis while abroad. It is crucial for education abroad staff to understand the dynamics of their campus in this regard before being faced with a crisis situation.

Creating and Revising Medical Information Forms

Collaborating with student health personnel on campus is key to developing an accurate and useful medical information form. Clinicians can suggest appropriate terminology that education abroad staff may be unaware of, and can provide important information on what services—such as required vaccinations—are available on campus in addition to off-campus resources for less common vaccines. Campus legal counsel should review all forms, including the medical information form, prior to distribution to students.

Best Practices and Protocols Working with Students with Significant Physical or Mental Health Conditions

Student Consultations

As soon as practicable after the collection of medical information forms, individual meetings should be arranged with students who have disclosed significant physical or mental health conditions. Timing of these consultations is important. In order to comply with Americans with Disabilities Act (ADA) regulations, it is vital that consultations occur after a student has been accepted to a study abroad program; however, there should also be sufficient time for students to address any issues prior to departure. Some students may wish their families to be involved in these discussions, while others will prefer to meet independently. Families may be consulted by phone or video conference to address their concerns if in-person meetings are impractical.

On-Campus and Community Assessments

Psychological assessments conducted either on campus or in the community may be indicated in order to determine whether or not a student's current state of mental health is stable enough to participate in study abroad. Unfortunately, the view still prevails among certain clinicians that study abroad will provide a much-needed break from stressors at home, and that the experience will have a positive effect on a student's self-confidence. Unfortunately, the reverse is often true. Students may have an extremely difficult time adapting to their new environments without the support system of family, friends, and clinicians close by to assist them when circumstances warrant. For example, students with mild anxiety or eating disorder issues on the home campus may experience significant worsening of their symptoms due to the effects of dislocation, culture shock, and distance from significant sources of support. Unfortunately for the students and colleagues abroad, the stress often becomes too much for the student to process, and suicidal ideations may begin to be expressed. It is at this point that the student should be encouraged to return home and seek the mental health care that he or she needs prior to returning to campus for the following semester.

Establishing Partners on Campus and Contacts Overseas to Support Students

Negotiating Accommodations Abroad

Depending on the student's choice of study abroad location, accommodations may or may not be available abroad to assist students with learning disabilities, mobility issues, and other concerns. For example, institutions in the United Kingdom generally have extensive support services in place, with accommodations offices similar to those in the United States. However, not all international sites will have the same services in place, and it is incumbent on the home institution to verify availability of support and accommodations for those students with learning differences or medical conditions requiring accommodation. These communications and negotiations with international partners should begin as soon as the home institution becomes aware of student need.

Ensuring Contact from Host Institution

If the home institution wishes to be contacted in the event of a medical or other emergency involving their students, such communications and agreements should be mutually arrived at either by inclusion in a memorandum of understanding or by a more informal means, such as e-mail exchange. Some countries and host institutions may hold divergent views from many U.S. institutions on the desirability of such communications, so it is important to avoid making the assumption that emergency notifications will automatically take place.

Best Practices in Information Sharing

Once medical information forms have been collected and reviewed, and student consultations are completed, decisions must be made about what information should be shared with which parties, and what the best means of communication will be.

Standard good practice includes:

- Providing information on medical and mental health conditions to program directors from the institution's faculty or institution abroad;
- Ensuring, in the case of third-party program providers, that the partner organization has the same documentation as the home institution;
- Ensuring that a student's signed release has been obtained, authorizing the disclosure of this sensitive information; and
- Promptly destroying and disposing of such records at the end of the student's study abroad experience.

Medication: Establishing Availability and Accessibility Abroad

The process—occasionally lengthy and convoluted—of ensuring that medications can be brought into a given country legally and/or obtained on site is best addressed by the institution's international insurance coverage team. A list of students, countries to be visited, and medications required can be shared with the insurance provider, who will then vet the list and inform the adviser of any issues. If a medication cannot be legally brought into the country where a student plans to study abroad, that information must be communicated promptly so that the student and his or her health provider can determine the best course of action. If the medication will not be available on site, the student must begin a sometimes lengthy process of consultation with health providers and insurance companies in order to obtain a sufficient supply of medication to cover the entire duration of the student's time abroad.

Additional Web Resources

Active Minds on Campus
Provides information related to addressing the stigma surrounding mental illness among college students.

Campus Blues
Online resource for student mental health.

Mental Health America
Includes mental health, alcohol, and drug abuse information geared toward college students.

Mobility International USA—Americans Going Abroad
Created by a nonprofit organization dedicated to helping advance opportunities for those with disabilities to travel abroad, this website presents a wealth of information on finding exchange programs, funding resources, disability disclosures, and more.

University of Minnesota's Access Abroad Resource
An online resource for administrators and students, with extensive resources and advice for students with disabilities who plan to study abroad.

References

Forum on Education Abroad. 2011. *Standards of Good Practice for Education Abroad, 4th Edition.* Carlisle, Pa.: Forum on Education Abroad.

Lindeman, Barbara, ed. 2009. *Best Practices in Addressing Mental Health Issues Affecting Education Abroad Participants.* Washington, D.C.: NAFSA: Association of International Educators.

NAFSA. 2003. *Responsible Study Abroad: Good Practices for Health and Safety.* Washington, D.C.: Association of International Educators.

Rogers, John and David Larsen. 2002. *Optimizing Health Care in International Educational Exchange.* Washington, D.C.: NAFSA: Association of International Educators.

Schmidt, Markus. 2004. "Investigating Risk Perception: A Short Introduction." In *Loss of Agro-Biodiversity in Vavilov Centers, With a Special Focus on the Risks of Genetically Modified Organisms (GMOs).* PhD dissertation, University of Vienna.

Sygall, Susan and Michele Scheib, eds. 2005. *Rights and Responsibilities: A Guide to National and International Disability-Related Laws for International Exchange Organizations and Participants,* Eugene, Ore.: Mobility International USA.

CHAPTER 10

RISK MANAGEMENT PLANNING FOR EDUCATION ABROAD:
Issues, Challenges, and Resources

By Gary Rhodes

Background Information

Education abroad programs can provide universities with a significant opportunity to add international learning as a part of campus internationalization strategies. It can be a life-changing experience for students, while providing international learning, supporting retention and success, and having a positive impact on potential career opportunities. However, health and safety challenges have also resulted in the injury and death of students, faculty, and staff participating in study abroad programs. Environmental challenges, transportation accidents, political unrest, and other incidents have resulted in program interruptions, requiring institutions to support student safety in the area during a crisis, and in some cases providing emergency group or individual evacuation support to a safer location. Content in this chapter will support institutional planning activities to: help faculty and staff recognize potential health and safety risks; develop planning activities to support decisionmaking when risks are determined to be too high to implement programs; limit known risks; implement crisis management planning; prepare response activities in case known risks result in low-level, medium-level, or high-level crises; and to inform faculty, staff, and students regarding risk avoidance and response in the case of a crisis abroad.

Risk Management

To effectively manage potential risks for study abroad, it is necessary to first identify those potential risks. Education abroad programs include all the aspects of university academic and student service issues. To begin thinking about what risks may impact programs, it is important to think through both the typical challenges one finds on a home campus in the United States, and those that may exist abroad. The following list of 23 health and safety issues (Rhodes n.d.) provides a place to start when thinking about what potential issues might be faced abroad that could impact program implementation, as well as the health and safety of students, faculty, and staff:

1. Alcohol and drug use and abuse
2. Conflict between students or between students and program faculty/staff
3. Crime and violence
4. Crisis management
5. Emergency communication
6. Environmental challenges/disaster response
7. Faculty and staff leaders with limited knowledge and skills to support effective decision making for health and safety support
8. Fire safety
9. Kidnapping and terrorism
10. Legal issues abroad
11. Medical/physical health response
12. Mental health support
13. Political instability challenges/response
14. Responding to discrimination abroad
15. Responding to guidance of the U.S. Centers for Disease Control and Prevention abroad
16. Responding to guidance by U.S. Department of State abroad
17. Science laboratory hazards
18. Sexual harassment and assault
19. Supporting students with special needs and disabilities
20. Transportation safety
21. Tropical diseases/special health issues in the developing world
22. Water safety
23. Other health and safety challenges

An important place for faculty and staff to start is to review all existing education abroad programs and consider the level of risk to faculty, staff, and students based on each of the issues above, and consider how those risks manifest themselves in the countries and cities where programs are implemented. After this review, the next step is to determine if those risks are being managed at an appropriate level, or whether it is necessary to change implementation practices, move program or housing or other implementation sites, or even discontinue a program.

Once the institution decides that implementation methods limit risk to an appropriate level, the next step is to decide how to manage the risks that have been recognized. Once an effective method for managing risks is implemented, faculty, staff, and students in the United States and abroad should be informed about the risks that are known and to provide orientation resources to help them effectively avoid and manage them. Following this, it is important to prepare faculty, staff, and students to respond when known or other risks result in health or safety incidents, in order to effectively manage low-level to high-level crises or emergencies abroad. Once those incidents are managed and programs move forward, it is crucial to evaluate how the response was implemented and then to revise policies, procedures, orientation, and information management, and begin the process again. Education abroad program staff should not review and implement risk management practices alone. Staff should work with a team of experts in the United States and abroad to better understand potential risks, and develop methods to manage risks and respond to health and safety incidents.

Methods to Evaluate Potential Risks

Friend (2011) suggests using a risk matrix, where risks can be analyzed and labeled as: "insignificant," "low," "medium," "high," or "extreme" to help in evaluating and managing risks. The crisis management team can create a framework to support decisionmaking for potential health and safety challenges, which allows them to make decisions on when to offer a program and when the risks and challenges are too high to allow for that program to take place. In the past, many institutions used U.S. Department of State Travel Warnings as one determining factor in deciding when to cancel a program abroad. In recent years, State Department Travel Warnings have added regional definition, noting that it may only be specific parts of a country where safety concerns are problematic. Thus an increasing number of colleges and universities have allowed for programs in countries with a Travel Warning after analyzing which parts of a country may allow for a level of safety and security they are comfortable with. In the same way, the education abroad staff—in coordination with its risk management team—can develop a checklist of potential health and safety challenges that can be used to create a risk matrix for evaluating risks, in addition to implementing support processes and services that limit risk based on the level of risk and realities on the ground in the country and city abroad. An institution can consider the list of 23 health and safety issues on page 160 as a starting point for evaluating levels of risk, identifying ways to limit those risks, and preparing to respond to them abroad.

To develop appropriate policies and procedures, it is important to be aware of U.S. government laws as well as education abroad and higher education guidelines, standards, and good practices that inform risk and crisis management for study abroad. These regulations and good practices can limit institution liability. If a college, university, or study abroad provider is sued based on the death or injury of a student, they will generally point to good practices or standards that were not met by the institution implementing the program. Effective risk management requires that there is collaboration across a campus to develop policies and procedures that are developed and supported by faculty, staff, and students across campus.

Putting Together a Risk/Crisis Management Team

On a U.S. college or university campus, managing potential risks involves collaboration across campus, including with those who have relevant expertise in evaluating and responding to potential risks. Education abroad faculty and staff can't be expected to be experts on each of the potential health and safety challenges that could take place in all the countries and cities where programs occur. One of the critical elements in analyzing risks, limiting risks, and managing risks is to put together a risk/crisis management team in the United States and abroad. The campus risk/crisis management team will typically include a variety of staff members with a variety of responsibilities, including:

1. Campus police/security/24-hour crisis hotline
2. Counseling center
3. Fire safety
4. Government relations
5. Health center director/medical staff
6. Lab safety
7. Legal counsel
8. President's office
9. Public relations
10. Residence hall management
11. Risk manager/insurance
12. Student affairs/services staff
13. Student representative

These and other campus-based staff should be engaged in risk management for study abroad. As education abroad programs are implemented in countries and cities outside the United States, it is important to include international faculty and staff in the risk/crisis management team. Depending on the type of programs abroad, the following offices should also be involved:

1. Campus travel
2. Campus study abroad office(s)
3. International/on-site faculty and staff
4. International insurance/24-hour emergency assistance support
5. Liaison with U.S. embassy or consulate
6. On-site counseling support
7. On-site facilities support

8. On-site health providers
9. On-site legal counsel
10. On-site security/local police
11. On-site travel providers
12. Study abroad provider representative(s)

It is important to engage the members of the risk/crisis management team in activities that enable them to identify potential risks, make decisions about which risks are too large to effectively manage, limit risks where identified, and collaborate in response to crises and emergencies that take place, regardless of how effective risk management strategies have been. According to Rhodes and Ludeman (2012), it is important to understand that approaches to risk and risk tolerance vary from institution to institution and from country to country. Upon recognition of those differences, education may be necessary to have on-site practices mirror the needs of the U.S. institution implementing programs.

Developing Education Abroad Case Studies

Although most education abroad programs are implemented with only limited health and safety challenges, more than 270,000 students participate in education abroad programs for credit each year, in addition to 45,000 U.S. students studying for degrees abroad, and many other faculty, staff, and students that go abroad on international campus programs (athletics, internships, research projects, development projects, community service, field studies, campus ministry, etc.). Incidents that have taken place can provide real case studies to help a risk management team consider what they would do to avoid that type of incident and respond effectively. Samples of such incidents include:

1. **Natural disaster:** Students in Japan during earthquake, tsunami, and nuclear power plant leak. On March 11, 2011, a magnitude 9.0 earthquake struck northern Japan, followed by a tsunami with waves topping 70 feet. The tsunami resulted in instant destruction of property and the death of tens of thousands of citizens. The Japanese earthquake and tsunami then resulted in nuclear power plant safety issues.

2. **Political unrest:** Since the beginning of 2011, many countries in the Middle East have experienced a significant amount of political and social unrest, leading to peaceful protests in some countries and violent clashes between the protesters, police, and army in others. In a number of instances, the unrest has spawned violence and the death of protesters, resulting in the evacuation of study abroad students from those countries.

3. **Murder:** In Italy in November 2007, an international student from Great Britain was murdered. A study abroad student from the United States and her Italian boyfriend were charged and convicted of the British student's murder. After nearly 4 years in prison, the student's verdict was reversed and she was released. In 2013, the Italian government decided to hear the case again, but the U.S. student refused to return to Italy for the hearing.

4. **Transportation:** In July 2011, three U.S. study abroad students were killed in New Zealand when a van one of the students was driving crashed and overturned after the driver lost control. Students had organized the excursion independently from the study abroad program.

5. **Apartment fire:** In April 2011 in Paris, four international students— two from Sweden, one study abroad student from the United States, and one from Australia—were among five who died in an apartment fire after attempting to escape out of the fourth-story windows. There were no smoke detectors in the building and no fire escape. Another U.S. study abroad student suffered severe burns.

6. **Transportation:** In July 2011, one student was killed and three were injured when a van driven by a U.S. university faculty member went over the side of a ravine in Costa Rica.

7. **Drowning death:** In March 2011, the body of an American student studying at a Spanish university was found at the bottom of a river in Madrid. The student had been last seen at a Madrid nightclub.

8. **Mental health issues:** In 2005, a U.S. student committed suicide by jumping from the top of the Arc de Triomphe in Paris. The student had left a note, and other students and a professor arrived just as he jumped to his death. According to news reports, he had not shown earlier signs of depression or other mental health issues.

9. **Health care/supervision/sexual assault incident:** In 2001, a study-abroad student on a faculty-led program in Peru fell ill. There was only one faculty member leading the program. They left the student at a local medical clinic alone. The student was subjected to an unnecessary medical procedure and was sexually assaulted while under anaesthesia.

10. **Robbery and sexual assault:** Some students were sexually assaulted, and all 16 people in their group were robbed, when a group of armed bandits flagged down a bus at gunpoint during an anthropological tour of Guatemala. The student group was held captive in a field for an hour and a half before being released.

Developing a case study based on these incidents closer to home can help in working through potential issues and challenges.

Resources to Provide Standards and Good Practices to Inform Risk Management and Program Administration

The U.S. higher education community has developed a certain set of shared good practices and minimum standards on issues such as safety, sexual harassment and assault, crime, and recordkeeping on campus that may be very similar or very different to the policies and procedures that take place abroad. At this time, each institution is responsible for developing appropriate policies and procedures and implementing a protocol for health and safety to support quality programs and limit institutional liability.

The following documents represent some of those available that provide lists of issues, good practices, and standards that can help institutions develop effective risk management policies and procedures for study abroad. It is expected that in the case of a serious injury or death where a legal claim is made against a college or university, the plaintiff's attorney will obtain access to these documents and review the institution's policies and practices against the good practices and standards referenced in them. As a result, using these documents to support quality practice serves both the development and implementation of good practice, and also limits potential institutional liability.

Resources to support institutional review of good practices for study abroad health and safety are referenced below. Faculty, staff, and students can refer to the full documents to help develop appropriate policies and procedures for their programs.

Effective Tools for Education Abroad Risk Management

There are a number of documents that provide standards, good practices, and checklists of issues supporting effective implementation of health and safety practices for education abroad. Statements about good practices include legal implications, as a plaintiff's attorney could use them as a checklist of practices that an institution should have followed to operate programs effectively. Unless institutions aggressively train faculty and staff to understand these documents and connect them to resources, there is the potential for institutions and their staff to appear ineffective and unaware of best practices, resulting in liability.

Although not an exhaustive list, most successful program administration and health and safety experts would agree that the following documents and resources should be recognized in the field.

The Interassociational Advisory Committee on Safety and Responsibility in Study Abroad

Responsible Study Abroad: Good Practices for Health and Safety

In 1996, there were a number of highly publicized health and safety incidents that resulted in the death and injury of study abroad students. In response, representatives from a broad range of institutions in the education abroad field—originally known as the Interorganizational Task Force on Safety and Responsibility in Study Abroad—developed a set of best practices for health and safety. The task force requested that colleges, universities, and study abroad providers send letters of support to sign off on these guidelines, which were published in 1998. As the field moved to make these best practices more widely disseminated, concerns were raised by the legal higher education community that the term "guidelines" raised too high the level of responsibility. Hence, the language for the document was revised to "good practices," and an update was published in 2002. The basic language of the document is similar to that in the original version and begins with the following statement of purpose:

> Because the health and safety of study abroad participants are primary concerns, these statements of good practice have been developed to provide guidance to institutions, participants (including faculty and staff), and parents/guardians/families. These statements are intended to be aspirational in nature. They address issues that merit attention and thoughtful consideration by everyone involved with study abroad. They are intentionally general; they are not intended to account for all the many variations in study abroad programs and actual health, safety, and security cases that will inevitably occur. In dealing with any specific situation, those responsible must also rely upon their collective experience and judgment while considering their specific circumstances (Interassociational Advisory Committee 2002).

The language describing the good practices seems to only provide some general ideas, and includes the modifier "should," as in a list of things that institutions should do. The content in the document does not include enforcement procedures, or language that necessarily mandates what an institution has to do, nor is there an organization verifying how institutions respond to the good practices. However, the use of the term "should" does pass along a stronger statement, which could provide a plaintiff's attorney with the contention that the field has suggested that institutions using "good practices" aren't just thinking about these concepts, but should implement them. The language provides a strong instrument for a plaintiff's attorney if they were to review and evaluate institutional policies and procedures since 1998, when the first document was published.

Along with providing the list of things an institution "should" do, it also includes a list of things an institution "cannot do," many of those related to the adult age and independent nature of university students, continuing with responsibilities of participants, and recommendations to parents, families, and guardians. This is an important tool for institutions to use as a method to: review current health and safety practices, pass along responsibilities to students, and inform parents/families/guardians. Reviewing the list of good practices is an important step to take to both improve institutional practices and limit liability.

The Forum on Education Abroad

The Standards of Good Practice for Education Abroad
Standards for Short-Term Programs
Code of Ethics
Quality Improvement Program (QUIP) Review
Critical Incident Database

The Forum on Education Abroad was created in 2001 in response to the call for an increase in the amount of resources and information available to support the study abroad field. In January 2005, the U.S. Department of Justice Antitrust Division and Federal Trade Commission designated the Forum as the Standards Development Organization (SDO) for the field of education abroad. The Forum's *Standards of Good Practice for Education Abroad* have been updated a number of times and were developed by and relate to many different types of education abroad program providers, including colleges, universities, and nonprofit and for-profit institutions.

Although institutions have been evaluated through the Forum's Quality Improvement Program (QUIP) based on the standards, it has not created a list of "approved" or "failed" global study abroad programs. All standards information and documents can be found on the Forum on Education Abroad's website at forumea.org/standards.cfm. As the Forum on Education Abroad has been recognized as a standards organization, and their standards and "Code of Ethics for Education Abroad" include implications for education abroad program health and safety practice, it is important that institutions use them in a review of institutional policies and procedures. Plaintiff's attorneys would have a stronger case for applying content in the Forum's *Standards of Good Practice for Education Abroad* and its "Code of Ethics for Education Abroad" for institutions that are members of the Forum on Education Abroad, and at an even higher level for institutions that have gone through a QUIP review.

U.S. Government

U.S. Department of State Travel Warnings, Travel Alerts, and
   Country-Specific Information
U.S. Department of State Overseas Security Advisory Council
   (OSAC) Resources
U.S. Centers for Disease Control and Prevention Country-Specific
   Health Information
Clarification on Clery Act Requirements for Study Abroad

The U.S. Department of State provides safety guidance for every country around the world, including information on crime and transportation. For countries with special safety challenges, a U.S. Department of State Travel Alert or Travel Warning may be issued. These alerts and warnings should be considered when reviewing program safety, and provided to faculty, staff, and students. Staff can obtain regular updates on safety issues around the world by having their institution join the Overseas Security Advisory Council (OSAC). The council's constituents can obtain site-specific feedback from OSAC staff, and have on-site staff join OSAC "country councils" to share country-specific safety and security information. The U.S. Centers for Disease Control and Prevention also provides health information for every country in the world. That information should be used in evaluating health issues, and be provided to faculty, staff, and students.

The Jeanne Clery Disclosure of Campus Security Policy and Campus Crime Statistics Act (20 USC § 1092(f)) requires U.S. colleges and universities who participate in Title IV federal student financial aid programs to disclose information about crime on and around their campuses, or in off-campus facilities as described by the Act. In 2011, the U.S. government published an update to *The Handbook for Campus Safety and Security Reporting*, which provides guidelines for colleges and universities on what information to collect, publish, and disseminate related to crime and safety incidents that occur abroad. Institutions could be fined by the U.S. government for not collecting and disseminating the data, and a plaintiff's attorney could claim that institutions are operating below government standards and not providing sufficient information to students and families about incidents and potential health and safety risks abroad.

Council for the Advancement of Standards in Higher Education

CAS Standards for Education Abroad Programs

The Council for the Advancement of Standards in Higher Education (CAS) develops standards in higher education. CAS is a consortium of associations in higher education whose representatives achieve consensus on the nature and application of standards that guide the work of practitioners. The standards and guidelines are developed for the use of practitioners and educational leaders. Based upon professional judgment and societal expectations, they include principles that are fundamental to student learning and development, and guidelines for practice for particular functional areas. CAS has developed a set of standards for education abroad programs.

United Educators

A Checklist for Campus Administrators Managing Short-Term
    International Programs
A Checklist for Leaders of Short-Term International Programs
Managing the Risks of Short-Term International Programs: A UE Roundtable
Minors on Study Abroad Trips
Risk Management Guide for Study Abroad
Short-Term International Programs: A UE Online Course
Travel Alerts, Warnings, and Advisories
Understanding and Managing the Risks of Short-Term International Programs

United Educators is one of the largest liability insurance companies used by U.S. colleges and universities. Along with providing liability insurance, United Educators has created a set of publications that provide background information about good practices for education abroad, checklists, and an online course to inform institutional faculty and staff about short-term international program good practices. This content can inform good practice for any organization implementing education abroad programs.

NAFSA: Association of International Educators

Health and Safety Resources for the Education Abroad Knowledge Community

NAFSA's Education Abroad Knowledge Community is focused on supporting faculty and staff involved in the implementation of education abroad programs. NAFSA has developed a broad range of publications, training programs, webinars, and conference sessions focused on issues related to health and safety for education abroad. The range of topics covered by NAFSA Publications with health and safety content range from mental health, crisis management, and orientation issues. Plaintiff's attorneys could point to NAFSA materials as those widely disseminated to education abroad program faculty and staff. A higher level of responsibility could be pointed to institutions that have faculty and staff who are members of NAFSA, and at an even higher level if program leaders were members of NAFSA and had been involved in creating publications or presenting at conferences on relevant issues.

Center for Global Education at UCLA

Safety Abroad First - Educational Travel Information (SAFETI) Safety Audit
  Checklist for Study Abroad
Legal Audit of Study Abroad
SAFETI Adaptation of Peace Corps Resources
Alcohol Awareness for Study Abroad Video and Faculty and Student Guides
Student Study Abroad Handbook
GlobalScholar.us Online Courses for Study Abroad

The SAFETI Clearinghouse of the Center for Global Education at the
Graduate School of Education and Information Studies at the University of
California-Los Angeles (UCLA) has developed a broad range of resources
for faculty, staff, and students to support effective health and safety practices. This includes a checklist of health and safety issues with background
information on a wide variety of issues along with sample forms and policy
documents to inform good practice by colleges, universities, and program
providers implementing education abroad programs. The legal audit document for study abroad provides a checklist of issues with legal and health and
safety implications. There are also a set of documents taken from U.S. Peace
Corps Health and Safety content on issues like risk and crisis management,
which have been edited to be relevant for the education abroad field. Other
resources developed by the center include an alcohol awareness video with
faculty and student guides as well as student-centered resources including
an online study abroad handbook and online courses with health and safety
content for direct use by students. These resources can be used to inform
administrative practice and to inform students about issues and help them
prepare for health and safety challenges abroad.

Terra Dotta

Signature Documents
Community Library
Faculty, Staff, and Student Tracking and Communication

Terra Dotta software includes signature documents that can be used not only
to deliver content to students, but also to have students confirm that they have
read through the documents. It can also include tests to confirm understanding
of specific health and safety issues. The Terra Dotta Community Library (TDCL)
includes many documents that have specific health and safety implications.
This content can be revised by institutions and delivered by students through
the enrollment management software, and can be used by institutions to
confirm that students were informed and prepared about specific health and
safety issues or circumstances. Terra Dotta Software also connects enrollment

management information and travel data to enable institutions to better track faculty, staff and students. This enables institutions to quickly find and provide information and support with the knowledge of their locations and contact information. When immediate communication is required, that can be provided through sending relevant messages through cell phone, e-mail, and text.

A Critical Tool: Insurance and Emergency Assistance Coverage

No matter how comprehensive your analysis of potential issues abroad, the risk-limiting efforts you put in place, or the level of security you integrate into program activities, unfortunate incidents may still occur. To be able to effectively respond to health and safety challenges abroad, it is critical that institutions and individual students have insurance to cover various costs, including major medical needs, mental health support, medications, transportation insurance, 24-hour assistance, emergency evacuation, and repatriation insurance. Institutions should also have insurance to respond to potential liability concerns.

Institutions vary in their insurance and emergency assistance requirements for students. Some require that all students have insurance and emergency assistance coverage that the institution obtains, manages, and charges students for directly, with no opportunity to waive out of the requirement. Others may have insurance and emergency assistance coverage that students can waive out of if they can show proof of sufficient other coverage. Others may have a list of potential insurance options, but do not require any insurance or emergency assistance coverage for their students.

As study abroad participation by students with high financial need increases, it is important that comprehensive insurance and emergency assistance be considered as a requirement for students. Students with limited means may not have enough funding to cover medical and emergency assistance care when they really need it. Students may or may not fully understand the insurance coverage for routine and major medical and emergency needs in the United States. As most students have limited experience in the countries where they study abroad, it is likely they will not have much expertise about the medical care system. This underscores the importance of providing the support they may need for major medical and emergency assistance and insurance while abroad.

It is critical that institutions provide information about what support is available abroad, and consider providing specialized insurance to cover costs as well as costs for responding to potential emergencies. If institutions do not provide the coverage, they should consider providing information to students about what additional coverage is available to them.

Having sufficient insurance is a critical part of effective risk management. Following is a brief background about different types of insurance coverage that students should have during study abroad:

1. **Major Medical:** Students should be informed about how to get medical care in the countries where they will study and travel during their study abroad experience, and how the potential cost of minor and major medical care will be supported. Some international insurance companies have agreements in hospitals outside the United States and can arrange for advance payment for the cost of medical care. In others cases, students may need to pay in advance and then ask for reimbursement.

2. **Evacuation:** If special transportation support is needed for medical care outside of the education abroad location, or a location where a student travels during personal time, it is important to have insurance coverage to help them get to where they can receive appropriate medical care. In the case of environmental challenges, political uprising, or special mental health breakdowns, there may also be the need for specialized transportation, which could be very expensive and not affordable for a student without insurance.

3. **Repatriation of Remains:** If a student dies while abroad, repatriation of remains insurance can cover the cost of bringing his or her body back home.

4. **24-Hour/Emergency Assistance:** Students may need help at any time while abroad. Some insurance policies integrate 24-hour emergency assistance support, while others have one company provide medical insurance coverage and another company provide 24-hour emergency assistance. 24-hour assistance can be as simple as a phone line available at any time to provide advice to students on medical care or safety issues.

5. **Liability:** Institutions, faculty, staff, and students can require additional financial support if they are charged with a crime or sued by another individual. Liability insurance can help cover those costs. For faculty, staff, and students, an umbrella policy offered through your auto or home insurance may suffice.

6. **Other:** There are many other forms of insurance coverage that can support special program needs, from transportation insurance to athletics, and scuba diving air embolism support as well as support for other high-risk activities that may be excluded from a general insurance policy. In some cases, it may be helpful to purchase insurance issued in the country where programs take place.

Most universities have an office that is responsible for insurance coverage on campus. At many universities, this falls under the office of risk management. Collaboration between the education abroad and risk management offices is important when determining policies related to insurance coverage.

Risk Reduction Strategies for Students

It is important to emphasize that students should be involved in all aspects of the risk management process. Including students in the risk management team allows them to provide feedback on risks as students see them and provide guidance on ways to better inform students about challenges. Institutions should develop ways to inform students about health and safety issues: before they apply for a program, after they are accepted, prior to leaving the United States, after they arrive abroad, at regular times while they are abroad, and after they return to the United States.

Methods that institutions use to inform students include:

- Print documents (paper and saved to computer hard drives or a flash drive);
- Website content (open access and password protected);
- Apps for Smart Phones and Tablets/iPads;
- Documents delivered through enrollment management software (where institutions can confirm both delivery and students' statements that they've read the documents, in addition to providing a quiz to confirm students have understood the content);
- In-class and online courses that integrate health and safety content; and
- Live presentations in the United States and abroad.

To enable students to act as informed adults abroad, institutions should find ways to confirm students have received: information about health and safety issues and challenges; the support that is available; the limitations of that support, which is not equal to what they would find on the home campus; and how students are expected to be part of the effective response to crises and emergencies abroad. According to Rhodes, DeRomaña, and Ebner (2014), a pretravel health consultation is also an important part of student planning for education abroad.

Conclusion

Education abroad programs can be the highlight of a college or university experience. However, any form of international travel has its inherent health and safety risks and challenges. It is critical that colleges and universities access field-based resources, guidelines, standards, and good practices and government resources and bring together a risk management team that can effectively evaluate potential challenges, decide whether or not to offer a program, effectively manage the challenges, and prepare to respond to low-level incidents as well as worst-case scenarios abroad as a part of their effective administrative practices for education abroad.

References

Council for the Advancement of Standards in Higher Education (n.d.). "Applying CAS Standards." Washington D.C.: Council for the Advancement of Standards in Higher Education.

Friend, Julie. 2011. "Danger Ahead!" Health and Insurance Supplement to *International Educator* 20, 6:1–8.

Interassociational Advisory Committee on Safety and Responsibility in Study Abroad. 2002. "Responsible Study Abroad: Good Practices for Health and Safety." Washington, D.C.: NAFSA: Association of International Educators. Retrieved on October 23, 2013 from http://www.nafsa.org/uploadedFiles/responsible_study_abroad.pdf.

Rhodes, Gary (n.d.). "Analyzing Risks and Capabilities." SAFETI Program Audit Checklist. Los Angeles, Calif.: Center for Global Education at UCLA. Retrieved October 25, 2013 from http://globaled.us/safeti/crisis_and_management/analyze_risk_and_capabilities.asp.

Rhodes, Gary (n.d.). "Crisis Management Handbook," SAFETI Adaptation of Peace Corps Resources. Los Angeles, Calif.: Center for Global Education at UCLA. Retrieved October 23, 2013 from http://globaled.us/peacecorps/crisis-management-handbook.asp.

Rhodes, Gary and Roger Ludeman. 2012. "Legal, Health, and Safety Issues: Crisis Management and Student Services in International Higher Education." In *The SAGE Handbook of International Higher Education.* Thousand Oaks, Calif.: SAGE Publications.

Rhodes, Gary, Inés DeRomaña, and Jodi Ebner. 2014. "Study Abroad and Other International Student Travel." In *CDC Health Information for International Travel 2014.* Atlanta, Georgia: U.S. Centers for Disease Control and Prevention.

Forum on Education Abroad. 2011. *Standards of Good Practice for Education Abroad,* 4th Edition, Carlisle, Pa.: The Forum on Education Abroad.

U.S. Department of Education Office of Postsecondary Education. 2011. *The Handbook for Campus Safety and Security Reporting.* Washington, D.C.: U.S. Department of Education.

CHAPTER 11

INSURANCE FOR EDUCATION ABROAD

By Joseph L. Brockington

Introduction

Insurance is one of the most common forms of risk management in general and for education abroad in particular. As the recent *Open Doors* report from the Institute for International Education (IIE) notes, more and more students are participating in education abroad programs in all corners of the world, and for shorter durations (many participating in multiple programs), while others still are engaged in nonstudy abroad independent international travel projects. As locations have expanded, participation has increased. Along with a growth in independent opportunities for students abroad, there is an increasing need for risk management, and thus, for insurance.

At its simplest, insurance is used to protect financial resources of individuals, institutions, or both. Through the purchase of insurance, individuals and institutions can expand their activities abroad, without placing either individual or institutional finances at risk. Insurance gives people and universities the leave to operate in situations and/or locales where neither have much local information or many—if any—local contacts. Insurance can provide for: routine or emergency medical care; natural disaster, medical, or political turmoil evacuation; even "concierge service" for missed or rerouted flights, lost documents, and emergency loans for individuals. Institutions rely on insurance to indemnify them in the case of potential liability exposure, negligence of directors and officers, kidnap and ransom, workers' compensation, the operation of motor vehicles, and so on.

Organizations offering guidance and standards for education abroad program development and administration typically recommend that participants be insured. In its standards for long- and short-term programs, the Council on Standards for International Educational Travel (CSIET) notes "the organization shall guarantee that every student is covered with adequate health and accident insurance. Such insurance shall: (a) protect students for the duration of their program; and (b) provide for the return of the student to his/her home in the event of serious illness, accident, or death during the program" (CSIET Long-Term Standards 2006).

"Responsible Study Abroad: Good Practices for Health and Safety" (2002) from the Interassociational Advisory Committee on Safety and Responsibility in Study Abroad (formerly the Interorganizational Advisory Committee on Health and Safety), notes that program sponsors should, "require that participants be insured. Either provide health and travel accident (emergency evacuation, repatriation) insurance to participants, or provide information about how to obtain such coverage." The Forum on Education Abroad also included insurance in both the "Standards of Good Practice for Education Abroad" (2011) and the "Standards of Good Practice for Short-Term Education Abroad Programs" (2009). The third edition of *NAFSA's Guide to Education Abroad for Advisers and Administrators* offers some limited guidance concerning insurance (2005, 492–493). The *Guide* recommends health insurance coverage as one mode of risk management and points to the possibility that certain "high risk" activities may be excluded from the coverage. While providing participants with a list of program-vetted, on-site health care providers may be a good idea in theory, institutions and programs will want to talk with their legal council to determine if the identification of health care providers might impose additional duty and/or risk exposure (2005, 493).

The following offers a discussion of considerations for insurance for individuals and institutions, thoughts on minimum benefits, issuing a "request for proposal" (RFP) to insurance underwriters and brokers, and finally some thoughts about how to discuss insurance issues with stakeholders on- and off-campus.

Insurance for Individuals
Even though students (and faculty or staff) may be covered under a "group" policy, ultimately insurance (especially coverage and benefits) accrues to the individual.

Trip Cancellation/Interruption Insurance
Discussion of insurance for education abroad students often begins with "travel insurance"—often called "trip cancellation insurance"—and may include coverage for trip interruption. This type of policy can be purchased by an individual or as a "blanket" policy by the institution or program provider. Specifically, trip cancellation/interruption insurance covers things ranging from illness of the traveler to bankruptcy of the travel provider, and includes weather or natural disaster disruptions, terrorist attacks, a U.S. Department of State Travel Warning, strikes, or personal injury. The benefits provided by trip cancellation insurance in the higher education market often include not only refunds of unused transportation expenses but sometimes also tuition expenses not refunded by the educational institution or program provider. Such policies also include "travel delay" insurance and provide for lost or delayed baggage as well as travel assistance services, such as rebooking of

flights or accommodation. (Note: Travel assistance services often require that individuals register with the service's website to access information.)

Health and Medical Insurance

Much of the discussion of health and medical insurance in various insurance supplements to *International Educator* magazine over the last 10 years has included both outbound education abroad participants as well as inbound international students and scholars. Writing in the 2009 supplement, Joanna Holvey-Bowles of the Institute for Study Abroad at Butler University (IFSA-Butler) notes a number of reasons, here limited to those regarding education abroad, for requiring insurance.

- Students who are studying in, or who may be medically evacuated to, countries with privatized medical systems cannot afford the high cost of medical care.
- While abroad, many students experience a greater sense of freedom than they do at home. They sometimes take unaccustomed risks and engage in unfamiliar behaviors.
- Once an illness or injury has occurred, it is not possible to purchase insurance to cover it. Such a condition is "preexisting" and excluded by almost all student policies.
- Students and their families cannot make reasoned decisions about medical evacuation and/or repatriation of remains during medical crises (Holvey-Bowles, 2009).

"Requiring a vetted insurance plan for education abroad participants as well as international students and scholars makes good policy sense," Holvey-Bowles writes.

—*Relying on a U.S. Health and Medical Insurance Policy in Contrast to a Special Policy for Education Abroad*

Health and medical insurance coverage for education abroad participants can be arranged in two basic ways. A U.S. student or permanent resident may have insurance through a parent or guardian, and expects to use this overseas, or the individual may decide to purchase a policy especially designed for education abroad. Each of these choices has benefits and liabilities. (We will discuss the matter of institution required, recommended, or provided health and medical insurance below.)

Chief among the benefits of wanting to use a U.S. health plan overseas is that someone else will pay the premiums for the time the covered person is abroad. U.S. health plans, however, present substantial liabilities. Many U.S. plans do not cover illnesses contracted or injuries received abroad, or don't cover them in every country, or for longer than the standard two-week tourist visit. U.S. plans may not cover follow-up treatment or rehabilitation in the

United States for patients who became sick or were injured outside the United States, as these may be excluded as preexisting conditions.

A further issue regarding the use of U.S. health insurance overseas concerns how claims are paid. When an individual in the United States goes to a physician for a routine office visit or to the hospital, one presents their insurance card, and the physician, hospital, lab, or pharmacy bills the insurance company directly, charging the covered person a copay, often collected at the point of service, or in the case of hospitalization, perhaps months after the stay. When U.S. insurance plans are used abroad, they typically have no arrangements for paying any medical bills directly. Thus, individuals are asked to provide a credit card *in advance* of receiving services (doctor's office, hospital, lab, pharmacy, etc.). The covered person then submits the invoice for this service to the claims office of the U.S. health plan and receives a reimbursement. In the case of hospitalization overseas for severe illness or injury, the education abroad participant's credit card may be charged for thousands, or tens of thousands, of dollars. This could exceed the credit limit on the card.

Some specialized insurance plans for education abroad function like the U.S. plans, in that the individual pays in advance and then submits the invoices to a U.S. office for reimbursement. More recently, some specialized education abroad insurance plans purchased in the United States have established networks of in-country physicians, hospitals, labs, pharmacies, and so on, so that payments are requested directly from the insurance company and the insured individual is responsible for only a copay at the time of service.

A third way for students to obtain health insurance comes through the student visa process. Certain countries have requirements for student visas whereby the participant must purchase national health insurance. Two examples are Italy and Australia. When students buy national health insurance, they typically take a coupon to the physician or hospital which serves as payment for the medical service. Many of these countries also offer private health insurance in addition to the public options. If national health insurance is used by the participant, individual should check the policy to see where the insurance is valid. In many cases, it is only valid within that country and cannot be used when traveling outside the country or flying to or from the United States.

Health and Medical Insurance: Coverage

A review of literature on insurance for education abroad did not reveal any current recommendations on recommended dollar coverage minimums for policies. The last publication to recommend such minimums was in an insurance supplement article in *International Educator* by Harald Braun and Jürgen Gemmeke (2005), who based their recommendations on standards from CSIET. These are now more than 7 years old, and are in need of updating. In addition to dollar minimums, coverage also includes the types of services the insurance will pay for.

In its most basic form, a health and medical insurance policy for an individual should cover hospitalization in cases of illness, accident, or injury. However, when considering such a basic policy, individuals should think about what comes before and after the hospital stay and whether these are covered by the policy.

Coverage Versus Exclusions

An insurance "exclusion" refers to an event not covered by the policy. Exclusions in insurance policies most often refer to preexisting health or medical conditions. Such exclusions must be listed in the insurance policy. Pregnancy is common among preexisting conditions, as are certain illnesses. Certain activities (such as whitewater rafting, bungee jumping, SCUBA diving, or hang gliding) may also be excluded from insurance coverage. If an individual is hospitalized by accident or injury stemming from such excluded activities, the costs of the hospitalization resulting from such injuries (and the costs of any post hospitalization rehabilitation) would not be paid for under the insurance policy. Insurance policies for education abroad often exclude mental illness, eating disorders, drug, and/or alcohol abuse. Thus it is particularly important that individuals carefully read the insurance policy to determine what is covered and what is excluded. With insurance, however, most everything is negotiable; thus, excluded items can be covered for an additional premium.

In addition to coverage for exclusions noted above, individuals engaged in education abroad may also want to seek coverage for translation services (in those instances where the in-country medical personnel don't speak English), medical evacuation either back to the United States or to a third country (some policies also offer "all the way home" transportation back to the United States when the medical emergency is over), family visit to the sick or injured person in the hospital overseas, repatriation of mortal remains in the case of death overseas, coverage for travel during the program abroad and travel to and from the program from the United States, and coverage for additional treatment in the United States following the program.

Evacuation Insurance

Medical evacuation insurance has long been a recommendation for education abroad activities in countries with developing economies, where hospitalization and health care may not be considered up to U.S. or western European standards. In a typical medication evacuation, when there is a covered illness or injury occurs overseas, generally the individual, the program, the host university, or the home university contacts the insurance or evacuation logistics provider who then takes over the process. Typically all medical and evacuation decisions are made by a panel of physicians working for the evacuation provider. In an evacuation situation, the insured individual is stabilized in a local hospital, then, if deemed appropriate, evacuated to the United States or a third country for treatment. Evacuation can be made via scheduled airlines (with or without a medical assistant) or by a private flight, often accompanied by a physician or nurse.

Since the natural disasters of 2011, including the earthquakes in New Zealand and the earthquake and tsunami in Japan, insurance companies have offered more policies that include evacuation in case of natural disaster. When such evacuation is included in an education abroad insurance policy, benefits may include not only transportation back to the United States, but also a tuition refund. With the events of the Arab Spring beginning in December 2010 and also considering the aftermath of the Kenyan elections of 2007–8, another type of evacuation insurance, for "political turmoil," came on the market. With political turmoil evacuation insurance, it is important for the individual to note what activates it. In some cases, coverage is triggered with a U.S. Department of State Travel Warning. Tuition refunds may also be a part of political turmoil insurance, although they may have different triggers than the physical evacuations of individuals. In both natural disaster and political turmoil evacuations, individuals may be removed to a third country, rather than to the United States. This type of coverage can probably be included for additional premium.

Travel Assistance
Travel assistance (concierge services) is often bundled with health and medical or evacuation insurance. This sometimes includes personal travel assistance, medical travel assistance, security travel assistance, and general travel assistance. Some examples of general travel services include:

World Wide Travel Assistance
- Lost baggage search; stolen luggage replacement assistance
- Lost passport/travel documents assistance
- ATM locator
- Emergency cash transfer assistance
- Travel information including visa/passport requirements
- Emergency telephone interpretation assistance
- Urgent message relay to family, friends, or business associates
- Up-to-the-minute travel delay reports
- Inoculation information
- Embassy or consulate referral

- Currency conversion or purchase
- Up-to-the-minute information on local medical advisories, epidemics, required immunizations, and available preventive measures
- Up-to-the-minute travel supplier strike information
- Legal referrals/bail bond assistance
- Flight and hotel rebooking
- Rental vehicle booking and vehicle return
- Guaranteed hotel check-in

Travel Medical Assistance
- Emergency medical evacuation transportation assistance
- Physician/hospital/dental/vision referrals
- Repatriation of mortal remains
- Return travel arrangements
- Emergency prescription replacement
- Dispatch of doctor or specialist
- In-patient and out-patient medical case management
- Qualified liaison for relaying medical information to family members
- Arrangements of visitor to bedside of hospitalized insured
- Eyeglasses and corrective lens replacement assistance
- Medical payment arrangements
- Medical cost containment/expense recovery and overseas investigation
- Medical bill audits
- Shipment of medical records
- Medical equipment rental/replacement

Security Assistance
- Security evacuation assistance with immediate on-the-ground physical response to help travelers in life threatening security situations, anywhere in the world
- 24-hour response services to assist employees and their families during an incident
- Security and safety advisories
- Global risk analysis
- Consultant referrals to extract client to safety
- Consultation with security specialists to discuss any safety concerns for your travel location or if you need immediate assistance while you are away
- Confidential storage of personal and medical profile for emergencies
- Up-to-the-minute information on current world situations
- Language translation support and services

Personal Services

- Restaurant referrals and reservations
- Event ticketing
- Ground transportation coordination
- Golf tee time reservations and referrals
- Wireless device assistance
- Latest worldwide weather and ski reports
- Floral services
- Private air charter assistance
- Cruise charter assistance
- Latest sports scores
- Find, wrap, and deliver one-of-a-kind gifts
- Movie and theater information
- Latest stock quotes
- Special occasion reminders and gift ideas
- Lottery results
- Local activity recommendations

(AIG/Chartis n.d.)

Personal Liability and Personal Property Insurance

Beyond purchasing medical and evacuation insurance, individuals may also want to consider two additional coverage areas, personal liability and personal property insurance. Personal liability insurance is often required for education abroad participants engaging in internships (corporate or non-profit), particularly in western Europe and Australia, and by subsidiaries of U.S. companies. Personal liability insurance protects the individual (and the internship provider) from claims arising from mistakes or negligence on the part of the internship participant.

When one looks at the general behavior of U.S. students, particularly on smaller campuses, the reason for personal property insurance is clear. Many students leave personal belongings (backpacks, laptops, cameras, phones, and more) unattended. Backpacks are piled up outside the cafeteria or the bookstore, left on tables in the library, or in study cubicles, while owners run to the restroom. Dorm rooms are frequently left unlocked or even open—with no one in the room. This habit is particularly hard to break while the students are overseas, and consequently, students are often surprised and disappointed when they return to collect their belongings and find them gone. Although students are generally advised to take only older items overseas—things that they won't miss as much if stolen, such as particular laptops, cameras, and phones—thefts do happen. Personal property insurance can make the cost of replacement easier to bear. Again it is good to note any exclusion for personal property insurance, especially if certain security measures are required.

Insurance for Programs and Institutions

Foreign Liability

When institutions and programs first think of using insurance as a means of risk management, it typically pertains to foreign liability. Through this type of insurance, institutions (or programs) seek to limit their exposure to claims related to the operation or organization of activities abroad, including the actions of vendors, particularly transportation companies. Without getting into the details of tort and contract law or the legal definitions of negligence, the foreign liability policy is often the basic form of insurance used to protect the institution from the payment of claims resulting from the operation and activities of staff overseas. Some foreign liability insurance policies seem to contain more exclusions than items covered. Thus it is very important that education abroad professionals read all insurance policies—especially these foreign liability policies—very carefully, noting the exclusions, and where appropriate, considering how to convert them into covered items. One particularly common exclusion in these policies states that the institution or program will not be covered by insurance in the event that the overseas location is the subject of a U.S. Department of State Travel Warning. NAFSA's Education Abroad Knowledge Community (EA KC) offers several documents discussing this situation. See also Julie Friend, "Travel Warnings: Developing Effective Response Procedures" (2011).

Trip Cancellation/Interruption Insurance

As education abroad programs and activities expand into less commonly visited locations, insurance companies have started to offer "blanket" trip cancellation or interruption policies. One example of such a policy that was reviewed for this writing offers greater coverage and more benefits than a policy for individuals underwritten by the same company. Among the benefits of the blanket policy are tuition refunds. If a program, particularly a short-term, faculty-led program, is canceled or suspended midway through its expected duration (perhaps as the result of a U.S. Department of State Travel Warning), students will be unable to earn their credits. If the program runs during the academic year, students will be equally unable to enroll for any courses on campus. Tuition refund insurance could easily become a part of a risk management strategy.

Health and Medical Insurance

As part of their risk management response, many institutions and education abroad programs have chosen either to provide all participants with medical and health insurance, or require them to all purchase the same policy. (See Julie Friend, "Why Insurance Providers Matter," in the 2007 *International Educator* insurance supplement.) This practice guarantees that all participants have the same coverage and cases will be handled in the same way in the event of an emergency.

In "Why Insurance Providers Matter," Friend (2007) notes several advantages of a specific overseas institutional health policy, including (a) the ability to use the quantity of an institutional purchase to eliminate exclusions (such as mental health) or to provide coverage for a modest increase in premium; and (b) a 24/7 assistance line, medical translation services, and experienced and professional evacuation and emergency management staff, among other benefits. Moreover, an institutional provider allows the education abroad staff to develop a professional relationship with provider representatives, who will respond in cases of emergency.

More than 90 percent of institutions responding to a risk management survey undertaken by the NAFSA EA KC Health and Safety Subcommittee (2013) agreed that health insurance should be required of all undergraduate education abroad participants. The respondents were equally divided, roughly, between institutions or programs which purchase insurance for participants and those which require students to purchase insurance.

At some institutions (or programs) where students are required to have insurance, they may be permitted to seek what is often referred to as a "hard waiver." Individual students must demonstrate that the insurance they (most often) bring from home meets or exceeds the coverage provided by the institutional plan, including coverage outside the United States. Those participants who cannot satisfy the waiver requirements must purchase the institutionally approved policy. While the "hard waiver" policy may represent a premium cost savings for the participants, institutions/programs will have to bear the cost of staff time to review policies and provide the necessary waivers.

Relying on a U.S. Health and Medical Insurance Policy Compared with a Special Policy for Education Abroad

The discussion of individuals using U.S. insurance abroad or purchasing a special policy for education abroad holds when it comes to institutions or programs. As with individuals, two issues predominate: (1) is the insurance valid outside the United States, and (2) how will claims be paid and/or reimbursed (e.g., will claims have to be submitted to a U.S. office for reimbursement after payment to the health service provider)?

Coverage and Exclusions

Again, the items raised in the discussion of coverage and exclusions for individuals pertain when institutions and/or programs pay for or determine the insurance coverage. It is important that professionals carefully read the insurance policy and be in full agreement about what is covered and what is excluded from coverage. If something, such as a high risk sports activity, is excluded, participants should be notified in advance, in writing. An exclusion might also show up in the policy as a dollar limit to benefits. Likewise, if mental health issues, the effects of alcohol, or drug abuse are excluded, participants need to know in advance. As institutions learn from actual cases, insurance policies need to be reviewed and coverage modified accordingly. Health insurance policies often include ground/air ambulance service, dental repairs or treatment, prescription drugs, family bedside visits, repatriation of mortal remains, accidental death and dismemberment benefits, travel assistance, among other items (Friend 2009).

Evacuation Coverage

Many institutions and programs include medical evacuation in the health insurance required of education abroad participants. The events of the recent years have also led providers to offer evacuation coverage for natural disasters and political turmoil, in addition to medical evacuation. The evacuation of education abroad participants by a professional evacuation logistics provider might be covered by insurance, meaning the costs of such an evacuation will be covered by premiums paid. On the other hand, the institution and/or program can contract with an evacuation logistics provider to remove participants from an affected area. After the participants have been removed, the logistics provider will send the institution/provider an invoice. In either case, once the institution/provider turns the evacuation over to the logistics provider, they take over service. In the agreement or policy with the provider, institutions/providers will want to be certain they understand what happens to the participants once they have been removed from the affected area. Will they be returned to the United States, or left in a third country? How much and how often will the provider communicate with the institution/program?

Directors, Officers, and Workers' Compensation Insurance

While more common in business and industry, most general and/or liability policies for institutions and programs contain coverage for directors and officers as an indemnification for alleged wrongful acts in their official capacities. In some instances the coverage may also include negligence. Education abroad professionals should ask for clarification from the insurance officer at the institution/program. They will also want to clarify what constitutes worker's compensation, and the benefits for which they are eligible. Worker's compensation and other insurance coverage/benefits are of particular interest to overseas staff, whether they are U.S. or foreign. Because these issues are so institutionally specific and fraught with extraterritoriality, education abroad professionals should direct questions to the human resources and risk management offices at their institutions.

Personal Liability and Personal Property Insurance

The issues of personal liability and personal property insurance were discussed as pertaining to individuals. When considered in light of institutions particularly (and of some programs), faculty leaders of short-term programs will want to inquire with human resources and risk management offices as to what is covered, and what the benefits and limits of the coverage are. Exclusions are also very important for the faculty leader to note. Personal negligence on the part of the faculty member may not be covered under institutional policies and could be something that a faculty member may want to cover for him/herself. The personal property of faculty short-term program leaders is rarely covered, unless this is negotiated in advance in the appointment document as short-term leader. While all education abroad participants, including faculty, are typically advised not to take expensive items, tools, or computers overseas, even older or cheaper models are expensive to replace when stolen. Personal property insurance will help in this area. But again it is very important to note benefits and limits of coverage as well as exclusions and security requirements.

Selecting Insurance for Institutions: What to Consider During the RFP and Implementation Process

The process of selecting insurance will differ depending on whether the institution is public or private, large or small, and whether the insurance will be (a) required and paid for by the institution, (b) required and paid for by the participants, or (c) required with participants given the opportunity to provide a hard waiver. Programs may have similar differences. Insurance wishes from education abroad programs at large public universities are most likely required as part of the general university bidding process and will probably be put out as a request for proposals (RFPs). Regardless of whether negotiating education abroad insurance coverage is part of an RFP process or the matter of having a conversation with an insurance broker or agent, education abroad professionals will want to carefully consider how the proposed policy will deal with the items and issues discussed above. By way of summary, let us consider the list once more, however noting that while individual RFPs often include minimum dollar limits for the different benefit areas, there was nothing found in the literature (or on the web) that made public general recommendations concerning coverage limits.

When considering purchasing insurance for education abroad activities, institutions and programs are encouraged to seek coverage, in suggested order of priority, for:

- **Medical and Health Insurance**
  - Coverage for:
    - Hospitalization
    - Medical evacuation (to a third country, to the United States including "all the way home" transportation when a crisis is over, even possibly a foreign student's home country)
    - Routine office visits
    - Prescriptions
    - Translation services
    - Repatriation
    - Family visits
    - Validity in United States on return/outside of host country, or while traveling on academic breaks
  - How payment will be made
  - Be cognizant of possible exclusions in the case of:
    - Mental health/alcohol/drugs/eating disorders
    - Preexisting conditions
    - Other items
- **Evacuation Insurance**
  - Coverage for
    - Medical (if not included in the health and medical coverage)
    - Natural disaster
    - Political turmoil
  - Be cognizant of possible exclusions and/or benefit limitations in the case of:
    - Mental health/alcohol/drugs/eating disorders
    - Evacuation to a third country or return to the United States
    - Other items
- **Travel assistance** (unless included with other coverage)
- **Directors and officers liability** and workers' compensation insurance
- **Personal liability** and personal property insurance
- **Trip cancellation** and interruption insurance

Conclusion

There are some things to keep in mind when discussing insurance for education abroad with administrators, students, and/or parents. With few exceptions, no one voluntarily reads insurance policies. This is a skill and attitude that must be taught to all insurance stakeholders. As important as covered benefits are, a thorough knowledge of exclusions (and the consequences for the insured education abroad participant) are equally important. Institutions and programs providing education abroad experiences should not rely on the waiver/release agreement to inform students of these exclusions. Informing everyone involved about what is covered and what is not in a targeted manner keeps everyone on the same page.

Most institutions and programs rely on a designated risk manager to negotiate all insurance coverage, including that for education abroad. However, as Julie Friend (2009) notes, "she is probably not involved in coordinating medical care abroad, and she certainly does not have time to review past claims in detail." Friend also encourages education abroad professionals to "make a brief record of the medical incidents your students experience abroad each year, and be prepared to discuss the most serious cases. Be frank about what worked and what did not. Your risk manager needs such details to determine whether or not your coverage is adequate." Like most parts of education abroad program management, insurance coverage will benefit from a yearly review, preferably from a number of perspectives (program director, risk manager, attorney, insurance broker, emergency responders from the program, institutional health and safety officers, and so on). Because insurance for education abroad touches all stakeholders, insurance should be everyone's business.

References

Braun, Harald and Jürgen Gemmeke. 2005. "Beyond Duty: Insurance Management in Education Abroad Programs." *International Educator* 14, 2:52 (Mar/April). http://www.nafsa.org/_/File/_/InternationalEducator/EAMarApr05SITE.pdf.

Brockington, Joseph L., Patricia Martin, and William Hoffa, eds. 2005. *NAFSA's Guide to Education Abroad for Advisers and Administrators.* 3rd Edition. Washington, D.C.: NAFSA: Association of International Educators.

Chartis/WorldRisk (n.d). *Emergency Information Card.* New York, N.Y.: American International Group, Inc. Find similar information at "Travel Protector

Assistance Services," http://www.aig.com/Travel-Protector-Assistance-Services_3171_482726.html.

Council on Standards for International Educational Travel. 2006. "CSIET Standards for Long-Term International Educational Travel Programs." Alexandria, Va.: Council on Standards for International Educational Travel. http://csiet.org/about/docs/LT_Standards_-_April_2006.pdf.

Council on Standards for International Educational Travel. 2006. "CSIET Standards for Short-Term International Educational Travel Programs." Alexandria, Va.: Council on Standards for International Educational Travel. http://csiet.org/about/documents/Short-termStandardsApril2006.pdf.

Council on Standards for International Educational Travel. 2010. "Model School Policy on Outbound Student Exchange Programs." Alexandria, Va.: Council on Standards for International Educational Travel. http://www.csiet.org/documents/OutboundMSP-Final-Sep2010.pdf.

Forum on Education Abroad. 2009. "Standards of Good Practice for Short-Term Education Abroad Programs." Carlisle, Pa.: Forum on Education Abroad. http://www.forumea.org/documents/ForumEAStandardsShortTermProg.pdf.

Forum on Education Abroad. 2011. *Standards of Good Practice for Education Abroad.* Carlisle, Pa.: Forum on Education Abroad. http://forumea.org/standards-index.cfm.

Friend, Julie. 2006. "Why Insurance Providers Matter." *International Educator/2007 Insurance Supplement.* http://www.nafsa.org/_/File/_/ie_novdec06_insurancematters.pdf.

Friend, Julie. 2009. "What's in Your Policy?" *International Educator/2009 Insurance Supplement.* http://www.nafsa.org/_/File/_/novdec08_yourpolicy.pdf.

Friend, Julie. 2011. "Travel Warnings: Developing Effective Response Procedures." *International Educator/2011 Health and Insurance Supplement.* http://www.nafsa.org/_/File/_/novdec10_supplement.pdf September 17.

Green, Judith. 2006. Insurance: Not Just a Good Idea. *International Educator/2007 Insurance Supplement.* http://www.nafsa.org/_/File/_/ie_novdec06_insurance_goodidea.pdf.

Holvey-Bowles, Joanna. 2009. "Why Insurance?" *International Educator/2009 Insurance Supplement.* http://www.nafsa.org/_/File/_/novdec08_whyinsurance.pdf

Interassociational Advisory Committee on Education Abroad. 2002. "Responsible Study Abroad: Good Practices for Health & Safety." Washington, D.C.: NAFSA: Association of International Educators. http://www.nafsa.org/uploadedFiles/responsible_study_abroad.pdf.

NAFSA. 2013. "Risk Management Survey Results: Fall 2012." NAFSA EA KC Health and Safety Subcommittee. Washington, D.C.: NAFSA: Association of International Educators. http://www.nafsa.org/Find_Resources/ Supporting_Study_Abroad/Network_Resources/Education_Abroad/ Risk_Management_Survey_Results_-_Fall_2012/.

CHAPTER 12

CRISIS MANAGEMENT

By Gail Gilbert

All organizations sending people abroad should be prepared to manage a crisis situation. As the number of students who travel, work, and study abroad increases, the need for a solid emergency management plan becomes critical. When a crisis is managed effectively, it is no longer a crisis, but rather an emergency with a planned response.

Recent news coverage of incidents abroad remind us that that the margin for error is slim when managing a crisis. When planning for and managing a crisis, an organization must adapt based on their respective tolerance for risk, historical experiences, and interpretation of the overall mission and direction.

This chapter will provide guidance on developing a crisis management plan tailored to the organizational culture, outline tools for effective communication response, and highlight resources that may be used when a crisis occurs.

Crisis Management Considerations

Each organization working with international travel will have varying levels of expertise and experience with crisis management. Prior to approaching specific details on plans, procedures, and resources, it is important to understand the various considerations to be made in crisis management.

A **crisis management policy** is an institutional policy that establishes overall authority and rules related to crisis management. This is important to have in place to give a plan "teeth." A policy is what will point constituents toward compliance, especially for a newly developed plan that is adopted at an institutional level. A policy should clearly state who is mandated to follow the crisis management plan. For some organizations this may be solely study abroad students, while for others it may include faculty or staff travel, noncredit program travel (e.g., through student organizations, volunteer programs, ministry trips), research abroad, or internships. The most effective crisis management policy is overarching and includes all constituents traveling internationally under the auspices of the institution. This is the catch-all approach that will protect all travelers and the organization from undue liability.

The **crisis management plan** outlines procedures for emergencies abroad. A crisis management plan will never be able to detail an exact response to every type of emergency, so it should be general enough to be applied in various situations, but also provide a level of specificity that would allow any responder detailed guidance. Organizations often have policies and procedures in place for domestic crisis response that can be used as a baseline for international plans. Further details about developing crisis management plans will be discussed later in this chapter.

Every organization should identify **a crisis response team** who will serve as a committee for developing and revising plans as needed. They will also be the people who will work directly with emergency response and serve as the front line for the organization in a crisis.

An established **emergency phone number** allows for 24-hour response through a streamlined communication system. There are several ways to approach establishing an emergency phone number, and the approach will vary based on organizational size, job responsibility, and budget. Some offices have an assigned emergency responder who is always on call. This person carries the cell phone attached to the emergency phone number and is the front-line responder in all situations. Back-up responders are established for periods when the primary responder is unavailable. Another approach is to work through the university-established emergency phone number. This is typically routed through the department of public safety, university police, or campus security, serving as dispatchers to reach an on-call member of the crisis response team. This approach allows for a guaranteed response to every call but also adds another link in the chain that may cause delays in response. A newer option is to use a service that establishes an emergency number and a call forwarding service. Calls are forwarded on a rotating basis to the established emergency responders and are sent to the next person in the chain if there is no answer. This is a convenient option if there is an established team of responders, but additional costs for this service should be considered. Finally, there is the option of physically passing the cell phone attached to the emergency number through the team of responders on a rotating basis.

The crisis response plan, procedures, and team are only as good as the **training** that is provided. Training and formal practice exercises should be run on a regular basis to ensure that the team is educated and prepared to respond. Additionally, a review of the response to each crisis incident should take place with the team to identify successes and challenges as well as address any gaps in the plan.

When training for the crisis response team, it is also critical to provide **training to faculty directors,** who serve as the front line or first responder in the case of emergencies on faculty-led programs. These trainings should be mandated at the intuitional level and can take many different forms (e.g., workshop, one-on-one meetings, orientation). When responding to an emergency, one of the first calls to be made is to the emergency contact on file. **Emergency contact information** should be gathered for any student, faculty, or staff member traveling internationally on a university program. Generally, most organizations have established procedures for collecting this information from students, but this step can easily be overlooked when working outside of the realm of study abroad. There are various methods for collecting and storing this information, but the procedures the organization uses should be outlined in both the crisis management policy and plan. It is also important to remember that even if the gathering of this information for faculty and staff does not take place within an international education or study abroad office, it should happen somewhere within the organization, and the office responsible for this information should be represented on the crisis management team.

Moreover, an organization should keep the 24-hour **contact information for any in-country providers** or partner institutions. This is particularly salient for programs that do not have an accompanying faculty or staff member, as the institution will be relying on in-country contacts to assist and coordinate on the ground response. Immediate access to this information becomes critical.

While we all may keep up with the news on a regular basis, there is a deeper responsibility to monitor the in-country events in locations where you are sending constituents. This requires at least one person to be responsible for **regular reviews of country events.** There are many resources listed in this chapter that provide these services to organizations in a digest format. Additionally, in-country contacts can be particularly helpful in providing real-time, on the ground information.

As we have seen with several recent cases, there has been an increased need for nonmedical evacuation. Organizations should ensure that travelers have access to these services either through an organizational or individual **subscription to an emergency evacuation provider.** Some providers include this in a standard policy for medical coverage while others are blanket subscriptions for any travelers with a specific organization. The best way to ensure 100 percent coverage of this nature would be through a blanket coverage plan.

To ensure that travelers have access to medical care, **comprehensive health insurance with medical evacuation coverage** should be mandated. This is another case where an organization can choose to provide this coverage through an institutional plan or require that proof of coverage be submitted for each traveler. Chapter 11 of this publication provides in-depth information on insurance considerations.

As a proactive measure, it is helpful for organizations to have information related to **traveler medical information and history.** The organization can use this to address any ongoing care needs and inform a traveler of potential increased health risks based on the location or nature of a program. This would also be the case with faculty and staff travelers.

An emerging trend in the field of international education is the designation of an institutional **health and safety officer.** This staff member is dedicated to health, safety, and crisis management issues for an organization. A designated health and safety officer can serve as a centralized resource for all health and safety issues and particularly address compliance needs.

A comprehensive **predeparture orientation** is critical to informing travelers proactively on health and safety risks as well as resources. This orientation should provide information about the health and safety landscape of the particular location, supply emergency procedures, and review any insurance or emergency assistance plans that are in place. The organization should also consider how they want to manage the participation of parents in these particular orientations. Some will restrict participation to actual travelers; others will encourage parent participation, while some have separate parent-specific orientations. This should be determined based on the culture of the institution, the needs of the students, and staff capacity.

One piece of information that can be challenging to gather but is essential to have in emergency situations is the **in-country contact information** (cell phones and addresses) for students, faculty, and staff. This can be gathered various ways: through online student management systems, via e-mail, or in an online survey. However the information is gathered, it should be stored in a centralized system that is accessible to all emergency responders.

Organizations can also consider using a **text or e-mail alert system** to account for travelers during an emergency. This can be used to inform relevant parties of a security issues or natural disasters. Additionally, an alert system can be used to solicit responses or check-ins in the case that travelers need to be located and identified as safe.

Often, international activities are seen as separate and apart from the umbrella campus emergency procedures. Full **inclusion in campus emergency procedures** increases the awareness of international activities and its associated risks as well as lends support to the international response team from the wider campus community.

Finally, there are times when **access to immediate funds** is necessary. These funds may cover expenses associated with unexpected airfare, transportation or hotel stays, medical treatments, lawyers, and so on. These funds may be kept in the form of an organizational credit card, bank account, or third-party service. While we always try to plan for every expense, access to these types of funds can become critical in an emergency situation.

Every organization will approach crisis management in a different way, but all of the above considerations should be taken into account at an institutional level. To be truly successful in emergency response, procedures should align with best practices but also be relevant and customized to fit the organization.

Developing Plans and Protocols to Respond to Emergencies Overseas

Crisis Response Teams

Crisis response teams should be established to create, manage, and facilitate crisis response plans. The team is a representation of the organization as a whole and should provide a range of perspectives as well as expertise. Representatives of the crisis response team may include the following:

- **On site/in country:**
  - Embassy official
  - Resident director
  - Partner institution
- **On campus:**
  - Student affairs
  - Risk management
  - Legal representative
  - Campus police
  - Media relations
  - On-site staff
  - Academic affairs (dean, provost, faculty)
  - Health services
  - Counseling services
  - Campus ministry
- **Universal:**
  - Emergency assistance provider
  - Insurance provider

Each member of the crisis response team should have an identified back-up representative in case they are unreachable. If there is not an international crisis response team already in place at an organization, the campus emergency response procedures typically indicate who is involved with that team. Often, especially on campuses, there is an emergency response official who oversees campus response. This individual should be identified early in the process of creating the crisis response team and used as close consultant throughout the process. Additionally, there are external services that can be contracted to work with institutions in the development and training of a crisis response team.

Crisis Response Plan Content

Crisis response plans are not designed to be a step-by-step guide to every emergency case; rather they provide a consistent framework for procedures and communication. The most important elements of a crisis management plan reflect distinct phases: awareness, assessment, communication, decision, action, resolution, and return to normalcy (Friend 2012). Most organizations, particularly U.S. campuses, have overall emergency response plans already in place. These existing plans serve as a base for developing international crisis management plans. The following content should be considered for inclusion within an organization's crisis management plan.

- **Contact phone numbers**
  - Traveler in country
  - Traveler-identified emergency contact
  - In-country providers and partners
- **Insurance**
  - Emergency assistance
  - Crisis response team home/mobile
  - U.S. government
  - Student/faculty emergency contacts
  - Student/faculty in-county information
  - Resident directors' home/mobile
- **Procedures for emergencies affecting an entire program/region** (e.g., natural disaster, political uprising)
- **Procedures for emergencies affecting individuals** (e.g., student death, accident, injury)
- **Communication plan**
- **Questions for responding to specific scenarios** (see appendix A)

The American Red Cross maintains a "Disaster and Safety Library" that can be helpful in planning responses to specific incidents.[1] Although this information is generally centered on events in United States, the principles and safety procedures can be applied universally.

Training

Training for crisis management increases preparation, relieves anxiety, and helps to identify weaknesses in emergency situations. Tabletop exercises are an effective technique that allows the crisis response team to work together to practice emergency response. The Federal Emergency Management Agency (FEMA) provides a training unit on conducting tabletop exercises.[2] Tabletop

---

[1] American Red Cross. "Disaster and Safety Library." Washington, D.C.: American Red Cross. Accessed April 18, 2013. : http://www.redcross.org/prepare/disaster-safety-library.

exercises include all members of the crisis response team as well as representatives who will serve as back-up.[3]

Members of the crisis management team may be new to working with international cases, so it is important that nuances are discussed in training exercises. Additionally, the more educational resources and opportunities that can be supplied to this team, the better they will be prepared to respond. Attending conferences or workshops fosters preparation and understanding.

It is also helpful to include members of upper-level administration in these training exercises, even if they will not ultimately be core members of the emergency response team. This will help to garner organizational support and trust that emergencies can be effectively handled.

Debriefing After a Crisis

Once a crisis situation has been stabilized, a formal debrief with the crisis response team serves as an evaluation of the response, as well as identifies any loose ends that need to be resolved. During the debrief, the team analyzes each step of the response and determines if appropriate procedures were followed. Additionally, members are assigned for follow-up of outstanding issues.

The debriefing can sometimes serve as the most important part of a crisis response. This is where a plan will be refined, evaluated, and practiced. It is most likely that the plan will not work perfectly and that is to be expected. This is an opportunity to ensure that the response will be better next time.

Communication Response Planning

A communication plan is one of the most critical components of crisis management. As a crisis unfolds, an organization will appear to be the most effective if they can clearly communicate with all appropriate constituencies in a timely manner. At U.S.-based institutions, it is likely that there is an institutional communication plan already in place. The best approach is to work with the parties responsible for the institutional plan to ensure that international crisis response is included or reflects the procedures already in place.

Communication Channels and Delivery

When communicating within an organization, it is important to set expectations and involve the appropriate parties. At minimum, the organization's crisis response team should be included in incident-specific updates and

---

[2]To download the FEMA training unit on tabletop exercises (Microsoft Word document), see http://bit.ly/1elgTtm.

[3]For more information, visit http://www.ready.gov/business/testing/exercises.

communication. There may be additional communication channels established based on the nature of the incident and impact of any potential outcomes.

Crisis response will almost always require some degree of communication outside of an organization. This may include communication between a university and program provider, with insurance providers, media, parents, or any number of outside entities. Communication with parties outside of an organization should be centralized with one person, to ensure that the same message is being delivered and all information is being received. This designated person would then be responsible for communicating about these interactions within the organization.

Student Contact

Communication with students while abroad can be a challenge. Students may not feel the need to maintain the connection with their home institution or organization while abroad, even in crisis situations. Prior to departure, students should be made aware of expectations for communication while they are abroad. The home organization should collect in-country contact information for all students, which may include cell phone numbers, international landlines, Skype names, e-mails, and so forth. Many organizations now require students to obtain and carry a local cell phone that can serve as a critical tool during a crisis. According to a 2012 survey conducted by the NAFSA Education Abroad Knowledge Community (EA KC) Health and Safety Subcommittee, 87 percent of organizations will communicate with students via cell phone during a natural disaster or political unrest.

FIGURE 1. Form of Communication Used During Crisis Situations

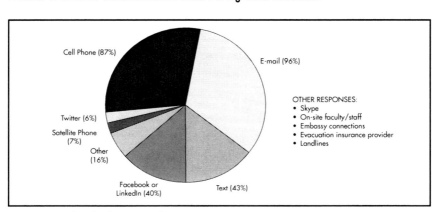

Source: Reproduced with permission from Stacey Tsantir (2012)

WHEN A REPORTER CALLS

*by Mickey Slind, University of Minnesota and Butler University,
former NAFSA EA KC (SECUSSA) chair*

▶ Take control; don't answer questions until you're ready.
▶ Note the reporter's name, affiliation, and phone number.
▶ Ask what the story is about.
▶ Find out the reporter's deadline.
▶ Define the role you'll play in the story.
▶ Suggest other sources.
▶ Set ground rules for the interview: subject area, time, place, duration.
▶ Pick an interview site that is convenient and comfortable for you.
▶ Regard the interview as an opportunity to tell your story or to make your points.
▶ Remember your audience is the public, not the reporter.
▶ Decide what you want the public to understand about the subject.
▶ Pick one or two points you want to make.
▶ Keep your language simple, as though you were explaining to a neighbor.
▶ Avoid jargon.
▶ Prepare relevant examples and analogies.
▶ Make notes for easy reference.
▶ Prepare a list of probable questions and short, concise answers.
▶ Collect material that will help the reporter understand the story.
▶ Rehearse with someone you trust.
▶ If possible, tape the interview so you can catch your own errors before they're part of the permanent print or broadcast record.

▶ If a reporter asks you to comment off the record, decline. Assume everything you say in an interview will appear in the story.
▶ Don't wait for the reporter to ask the "right question." Make your main point early and often.
▶ Be concise; you will be less likely to be quoted out of context if you are clear and concise.
▶ Make sure you understand each question.
▶ If a question contains erroneous information, don't let it slide. Correct it.
▶ Don't evade questions. If you don't know the answer, say so.
▶ Never lie.
▶ Beware of hypothetical questions; don't be pressured into speculating.
▶ Don't ask or expect to approve the story before it is printed or broadcast.
▶ Be available for follow up; encourage the reporter to call back with other questions or for clarifications.
▶ Ask others what they thought of the story. If the story has major errors, don't let anger or embarrassment rule your response.
▶ Call the reporter to correct errors in the story; uncorrected errors get repeated as fact in follow-up stories.
▶ If other reporters call you, use the new contact as an opportunity to correct any errors or misperception.

Reproduced with permission from Mickey Slind (1997)

Even greater numbers of organizations will communication with students via e-mail. Template e-mails prepared to send in the case of a crisis can save time and establish a quick link with students abroad. These templates can address situations that would require a check-in or response from students, an update to inform them that an incident is being monitored, or instructions to remind them of established emergency action procedures.

Finally, as demonstrated by the above subcommittee survey results, students may also be connected through social media tools such as Facebook and LinkedIn. It may also be helpful to maintain an organizational account to communicate with students through these channels in a crisis.

Parental Contact

Parents and guardians make up one of the most important communication channels in crisis management. Parents may be involved if their son or daughter is directly or indirectly affected by a crisis. When communicating with parents, it is important to be supportive and reassuring while setting clear expectations for response. Each organization will have a different approach to working with parents, and the organization's ethos should be carried through these interactions. Parents will find it helpful to have a centralized communication channel, generally one person or office that they will work with. This person should be appointed immediately once a crisis occurs to establish the initial contact and maintain this relationship throughout the crisis response.

Media Interaction

When a crisis situation arises, there is always the potential for media interaction. If there is an institutional media relations procedure (often through the office of communication or public relations) this should be followed. If it is necessary to talk to the media, see the sidebar on page 199, "When a Reporter Calls."

Effective communication during a crisis can promote a truly effective response. Often, constituencies outside of the crisis response team will use communication as the gauge of how the team performed. A communication plan that is appropriate for the organization and accounts for any gaps in the crisis management plan can be a base for effective response.

Resources for When a Crisis Occurs

When a crisis occurs, it is helpful to have resources at your fingertips to address any number of situations. In addition to the resources listed below, it is beneficial to have a list of contacts at organizations that are similar to yours in terms of scope of activities and level of risk tolerance. You can use these contacts as external support (as much as confidentiality will allow) and resources, as it is likely that at least one other organization has been through or is going through a similar crisis. In the field of international education, we are fortunate to have several networks to rely on and experts in all areas of emergencies.

Health, Safety, and Security:
Resources for Monitoring Conditions Abroad

by Les McCabe and Michael Steinberg

As an education abroad professional, you need the most current and accurate information available to make decisions about your programs, faculty, and students. The online resources below offer information from various sources to help you make decisions about safety and security. The U.S. Department of State is considered an essential resource by many education abroad professionals, with the Overseas Security Advisory Council (OSAC) and the Centers for Disease Control and Prevention (CDC) providing excellent supplemental information. The additional resources listed are also used in some offices.

U.S. Government Sources
U.S. State Department

These country-by-country safety and health assessments by the U.S. State Department are updated frequently. Free subscription allows receipt of announcements via e-mail as they are issued. Three types of announcements are provided. The following wording is from the U.S. State Department Travel Advisories website:

▶ **Travel Warnings** are issued when the State Department decides, based on all relevant information, to recommend that Americans avoid travel to a certain country.

▶ **Public Announcements** are a means to disseminate information about terrorist threats and other relatively short-term and/or transnational conditions posing significant risks to the security of American travelers. In the past, Public Announcements have been issued to deal with short-term coups, bomb threats to airlines, violence by terrorists, and anniversary dates of specific terrorist events.

▶ **Consular Information Sheets** are available for every country of the world. If an unstable condition exists in a country that is not severe enough

(continued)

---

to warrant a Travel Warning, a description of the condition(s) may be included under an optional section titled "Safety/Security."

Overseas Security Advisory Council (OSAC)

OSAC is a division of the U.S. State Department that fosters the exchange of security information between the government and the private sector operating abroad. The general website provides information regarding recent events as well as links to current public announcements and consular information. Detailed reports that are country-specific are available to OSAC members, who need a password to conduct a site search. The password can be requested on the website at no charge. (Note that only one person at a given institution may register.)

Smart Traveler Enrollment Program (STEP)

Registration at the U.S. Embassy or Consulate makes the presence and whereabouts of your staff, faculty, and students known in case it is necessary for a consular officer to contact the group/individual in an emergency. During a disaster overseas, U.S. consular officers can assist in evacuations, if that becomes necessary. In order to do this, they need to know the whereabouts of your faculty, staff, and/or students. Registration is voluntary and free, but it should be a big part of travel planning and security.

Local U.S. Embassy and/or Consulate

U.S. Embassies and Consulates overseas traditionally use warden systems to transmit important public announcements and travel warnings to U.S. citizens abroad. These messages may have a direct impact on students' safety and security. U.S. students and staff should register with the embassy. Registration will make their presence and whereabouts known in case it is necessary to contact them in an emergency. However, in accordance with the Privacy Act, information on their welfare and whereabouts may not be released without their express authorization. Registration will also include students and staff in the U.S. Department of State (DOS) warden system, which is used to keep U.S. citizens advised of what to do in case of an emergency (students and staff will be included only if they give their permission).

Federal Aviation Administration

This FAA site contains up-to-date information about which airports (domestic and foreign) meet current aviation security requirements. It also includes an FAQ section that is updated frequently.

(continued)

Transportation Security Administration
This site contains information on aviation security.

Sources from Governments of Other Countries

Australian Department of Foreign Affairs and Trade, Consular Travel Advice
Travel advisories provided by the Australian government.

Foreign Affairs Canada
Travel advisories provided by the Canadian government.

United Kingdom Foreign and Commonwealth Office, Consular Division Travel Advice
Travel advisories provided by the British government.

United Kingdom M15 Security Service
Provides information on the current major threats to UK security and practical advice to help businesses and organisations to protect against them.

French Foreign Ministry (in French)
Travel advisories provided by the French government.

Swiss Government (in French, German, and Italian)
Travel advisories provided by the Swiss government.

New Zealand Ministry of Foreign Affairs and Trade
Travel information provided by the government of New Zealand.

Italian Government (in Italian)
Travel advisories provided by the Italian government.

Spanish Government (in Spanish)
Travel advisories provided by the Spanish government.

Japanese Government (in English and Japanese)
Travel advisories provided by the Japanese government.

International Health Agencies

Centers for Disease Control and Prevention, CDC Travel Information (CDC)
Provides official U.S. government information about health conditions worldwide, including recommendations for immunizations.

U.S. Department of Health and Human Services

(continued)

World Health Organization (WHO)
The United Nations specialized agency for health.

Korean Ministry of Health

Victorian Government (Australia) Health Information
Blue book: Guidelines for the control of infectious diseases.

Australian Government Department of Health
Contains information about health alerts.

Private, Pay-for-Service Companies

In addition to the governmental resources available to international educators, a number of private, pay-for-service companies exist to assist in monitoring safety conditions abroad. In addition to the services, briefings, and consultation they provide to their clients, some of these companies also offer some information free of charge on their websites. Several such companies are:

▸ Frontier MEDEX
▸ IJet Travel Intelligence
▸ International SOS
▸ Mayer Nudell
▸ Stratfor Strategic Forecasting
▸ Terrorism Research Center

Source: This information is adapted from McCabe, Les, and Michael Steinberg. 2009. "Health, Safety, and Security: Resources for Monitoring Safety Abroad." Washington, D.C.: NAFSA: Association of International Educators. http://www.nafsa.org/findresources/Default.aspx?id=8294.

The ability to effectively manage a crisis is critical for any organization that has international travelers. Even the biggest organizations with the most detailed plans make continuous improvements and constantly evaluate the procedures that are in place. While this may seem daunting, remember all of the resources available at your organization, in the wider field of international education, and through service providers. Effective crisis management can turn even the worst crises into emergencies with planned responses.

Resources

American Red Cross. 2014. "Home." Washington, D.C.: American Red Cross. Accessed April 18. http://www.redcross.org.

Brockington, Joseph L. 2006. "Effective Crisis Management." *International Educator* 15, 4 (July/August): 47–52. http://www.nafsa.org/_/file/_/ed_abroad_effective_crisis.pdf.

Center for Global Education. 2014. "SAFETI Clearinghouse." Accessed April 18. http://www.globaled.us.

Federal Emergency Management Agency. 2012. "Exercises." Washington, D.C.: FEMA. Last modified September 28, 2012. http://www.ready.gov/business/testing/exercises.

Forum on Education Abroad. 2014. "Home." Carlisle, Pa..: The Forum on Education Abroad. Accessed April 18. http://forumea.org.

Friend, Julie. 2012. "Learning from Recent Challenges in Education Abroad Crisis Management." *International Educator* 21, 1 (January/February): 56–59. https://www.nafsa.org/_/File/_/ie_janfeb12_edabroad.pdf.

NAFSA EA KC Health and Safety Subcommittee. 2012. "Risk Management Survey Results." Unpublished survey results prepared for NAFSA: Association of International Educators.

Overseas Security Advisory Council. 2014. "Home." Washington, D.C: U.S. Department of State. Accessed April 18. https://www.osac.gov.

Slind, Mickey. 1997. "When a Reporter Calls." Prepared For The Foundations of International Education: Education Abroad Advising. NAFSA Region I Conference: Yakima, Wash.

U.S. Department of State.2014. "U.S. Passports and International Travel." Washington, D.C.: U.S. Department of State. Accessed April 18. http://travel.state.gov.

QUESTIONS FOR RESPONDING TO EMERGENCIES

Universal Concerns Assess the Following:	■ What is the current physical and psychological condition of affected participant(s)? ■ Is the lead on-site staff member now in close contact with all affected participants? ■ What is the proximity of the event(s) to all program participants? ■ What is the imminent risk to participant(s) if they remain where they are? ■ Are all program participants, whether directly involved or not, aware of the emergency? How are they responding to the emergency? ■ Are adequate food, water, and medical attention available? ■ Is adequate and secure housing available? How long will this housing be available? What other appropriate housing options are available as a backup, if needed? ■ What information should be given to students about steps to take in the event that the situation worsens? ■ Should students be evacuated?
If a participant(s) has fallen seriously ill or been seriously injured	■ Is the insurance provider involved/aware? ■ What medical treatment has the student received? ■ Does the attending physician speak English? ■ What is the diagnosis? The prescribed treatment? The prognosis? ■ Are other participants at risk from this illness? ■ Is airlift a desirable and viable action? ■ Does the Response Team need to be convened? ■ Have the student's parents been contacted?
If a participant is suffering from consequences related to mental illness	■ Is the insurance provider involved/aware? ■ What medical treatment has the student received? ■ Is counseling available? ■ If the individual chooses to return home, is it safe for them to go alone? ■ Does the Response Team need to be convened? ■ Have the student's parents been contacted?

If a participant has been assaulted or raped	■ What are the details of the incident? ■ What has the on-site response been? ■ Where has the participant been taken? ■ If a rape or sexual assault, is counseling available? Counseling in English? ■ Has the closest U.S. consulate or embassy been contacted for advice regarding reporting the incident? ■ Has appropriate local law enforcement been notified? ■ What is the medical diagnosis? The prescribed treatment? The prognosis? ■ Is the participant interested in returning to the United States? ■ Does the Response Team need to be convened? ■ Have the student's parents been contacted?
If a participant is missing	■ When was the student last seen? ■ Does anyone have any idea where they might have gone? ■ If the student had left and was expected to return at a specific time, when was the date and time of the expected return? ■ Did the participant tell anyone of plans to be absent? ■ Are search and rescue operations available on site? Are these reliable? Have they already been initiated? Should they be initiated? ■ If other students are enlisted to form search parties, have they been adequately briefed on what to do if they find the missing participant and on the various scenarios they may encounter? ■ Is assistance through the health insurance or travel assistance provider needed? ■ Does the Response Team need to be convened? ■ Have the student's parents been contacted? ■ If you have determined that the student is truly likely to be missing, proceed with the following questions: ■ Has a report been filed with the local police? ■ What is the case number? ■ What other locally and culturally appropriate steps are necessary? ■ Has the embassy been contacted?

If a student has died	■ Have the local police been notified? ■ Has the U.S. embassy been notified? ■ Have plans been made to repatriate the body? ■ What coordination is needed to take care of collecting personal belongings, closing a bank account, liaising with the student's host family, etc.? ■ What counseling support is available for other program students? ■ Does the Response Team need to be convened? ■ Have the student's parents been contacted?
If a student has been arrested	■ Has he or she been detained? ■ Has the U.S. embassy been notified? What has their response been? What is their advice? ■ What agency made the arrest and filed the charges? ■ What are the names, addresses, and phone numbers of arresting authorities? ■ What is the case number? ■ What rights have been granted? ■ Is he/she entitled to place a phone call? ■ Has a local attorney been contacted?
If a student has been taken hostage	■ Has the U.S. embassy been notified? ■ What is the embassy's advice? ■ Have the kidnappers made contact? ■ Is negotiation support available on site? ■ Who is the contact person at the embassy, and at the U.S. Department of State in Washington, D.C.? ■ What are their titles and contact numbers? ■ Does the Response Team need to be convened? ■ Have the student's parents been contacted?

If the emergency is political in nature (e.g., terrorist acts), or if a natural or man-made disaster has occurred	<ul><li>Does the Response Team need to be convened?</li><li>Have the students' parents been contacted?</li><li>Has the U.S. embassy advised participants to take appropriate action?</li><li>Have all participants been made aware of these precautions, and in writing?</li><li>Are all participants following these precautions? Have local authorities imposed a curfew?</li><li>Has travel in or out of the country been restricted in any way?</li><li>Is the group in danger?</li><li>Should regular classes and other program activities be suspended?</li><li>Who or what is the target of any unrest?</li><li>Has any particular group or organization been threatened?</li><li>What kind of military or other security or public safety personnel are present? Are they unusually visible? How are they behaving with respect to the civilian population?</li><li>Is airlift a desirable and viable action?</li></ul>

Source: Gail Gilbert

PART IV

DEVELOPING AND MANAGING EDUCATION ABROAD PROGRAMS

CHAPTER 13

STRATEGIC PLANNING FOR EDUCATION ABROAD PROGRAMS

By Joshua McKeown

Education abroad, like all academic programs, should be designed, delivered, and evaluated within the context of the institution. While starting points may vary by institutional type and tradition, any serious attempt at campus internationalization should start with an understanding of institutional mission (Barnes 2011; Hudzik and McCarthy, 2012).

Without this relationship to the campus mission, attempts to achieve institutional consensus, a mindset of shared responsibility and collaboration within an understood leadership structure, and the resulting program development, policies, and mechanics will suffer. A critical review of the institutional mission, matched with an insider's understanding of how much the statement matches organizational reality, should yield to a few key questions vital to successful strategic planning for education abroad.

Five Key Questions on the Institution's Mission:

1. How does the institution define itself in the global context?
2. What does the institution want students to know about the world?
3. What goals does the institution have for the education abroad program in relation to overall student learning objectives?
4. How academically ambitious, geographically expansive, and inclusive of various campus constituencies is the institution?
5. Are campus structures, policies, and personnel ready for more education abroad programming?

A brief review of select mission statements shows a broad range of institutional self-analyses formed by tradition, size, resources, and with an understanding of ambition appropriate for the institution's capacity. The University of California–Davis, a major public research university in the land-grant tradition, describes itself in its mission statement as "being a transformative, world-class university at heart," whose "mission is to generate, apply and share knowledge to improve quality of life throughout our communities and around the globe" (University of California 2013).

The Massachusetts Institute of Technology, a highly selective private research institution, reflects its history as a global leader in science and technology education and discovery by being "committed to generating, disseminating, and preserving knowledge, and to working with others to bring this knowledge to bear on the world's great challenges" (Massachusetts Institute of Technology 2013).

The State University of New York–Oswego, an education abroad leader among Master's institutions, describes its vision for internationalization in student-learner terms, by seeking to instill "world awareness" so that "students will have a deep understanding of themselves and respect for the complex identities of others, their histories and their cultures through a global curriculum and internationalized co-curricular and extracurricular offerings" (SUNY–Oswego 2013).

Juniata College, a recipient of a Simon Award for Comprehensive Internationalization, reflects its character as a leading liberal arts college in its mission to provide "an engaging personalized educational experience empowering our students to develop the skills, knowledge and values that lead to a fulfilling life of service and ethical leadership in the global community" (Juniata College 2013).

The mission of Northern Virginia Community College reflects both its character as a regional institution focused on the people and employers it must serve, while also reflecting the need to do so in ways that situate it within the larger world: "… to deliver world-class in-person and online postsecondary teaching, learning, and workforce development to ensure our region and the Commonwealth of Virginia have an educated population and globally competitive workforce" (Northern Virginia Community College 2013).

Education Abroad and Institutional Academic Purpose

Education abroad has steadily moved from the fringes of the academic life of the institution more toward its core (Lewin 2009). A well-designed and executed campus education abroad portfolio today should be a coherent collection of experiences and programs that reinforce international curricular objectives (NAFSA 2008). Those objectives, while distinct for each institution, will likely have some common characteristics, with particular focus on the five areas below.

1. Teaching and learning within a geographical or global context
2. Language and cultural knowledge
3. Experiential education
4. Research and faculty-led inquiry
5. Major-specific and general education

"Teaching and learning within a geographical or global context" encompasses all disciplines. There is no longer an assumption that education abroad should be focused on any particular major or set of disciplines. Rather, identifying how best students learn and faculty teach in order to accomplish institutional curricular objectives is the key. Examples can include: (a) traditional programs designed to enhance language and cultural knowledge; (b) experiential education programs such as internships and service abroad; (c) research and faculty-led inquiry such as science research programs focused on sustainability in a global context; (d) major-specific and general education programs such as communications or business courses abroad designed to enhance students' understanding of particular international markets; and (e) education programs introducing students to culturally relevant systems and pedagogies. Taken from this perspective, there is no one correct method or formula for designing and delivering an effective education abroad program. Rather, the perspective should be on how a course or discipline can incorporate important knowledge from particular geographical regions, or global perspectives, and what students should learn in order to be educated for a competitive, global world.

Articulating Specific Institutional Goals

Arising from institutional mission and with a firm grasp of the academic purpose of education abroad within the institution, specific institutional goals related to internationalization should be articulated. Doing so should provide the expertise, campus buy-in, and common understanding of the meaning of success that will lead to a good education abroad program on campus (Lamet and Bolen 2005).

Following are five specific institutional goals for education abroad:
1. Expand academic disciplines and involve new faculty
2. Expand and diversify program destinations
3. Increase education abroad student participation
4. Increase underrepresented student participation
5. Identify and mentor students for external awards

Expand Academic Disciplines and Involve New Faculty

One of the best ways an institution can grow and sustain a high level of education abroad achievement is through active, participatory, and intellectual engagement by many of its faculty members. Ideally most or all faculty will be supportive, but as long as a critical mass of faculty are involved it is likely that the institution will move forward well with an ambitious education abroad program. Faculty in other disciplines, such as laboratory-based STEM fields or state-regulated education disciplines, may not recognize that education abroad can be incorporated into a variety of disciplines. For example, STEM faculty can develop joint research projects with colleagues overseas, actively involving their student researchers in international scientific collaboration. Education faculty can develop partnerships with schools abroad to lead their education majors into practicum and student teaching experiences. Business faculty can make site visits to international corporate and governmental centers to better understand international business. These are often the only ways students in certain tightly sequenced majors can participate in education abroad. By involving many faculty, students should receive a unified message that internationalization is part of their curriculum and the institution is willing to build structures to encourage it.

Expand and Diversify Program Destinations

It is now well documented that education abroad is growing proportionally to regions beyond Western Europe. In the decade from 2000 to 2010, the percentage of U.S. students participating in education abroad programs to Africa and Asia nearly doubled, from 8.9 percent to 17.5 percent of the total U.S. student population going abroad, with increases also to programs in Latin America and the Middle East (Institute of International Education 2011).

Some additional considerations as an institution should be addressed when discussing nontraditional destinations. Among them are the institution's commitments to regions of the world that have become more important in economic, political, and strategic terms. While in theory every country in the world is worthy of study, in practice careful choices should be made so as to maximize success, minimize cost and risk, and encourage respectful engagement with others. To accomplish this requires some calculated risk-taking and financial investments, since programs to nontraditional destinations are often expensive when transportation, risk mitigation, and health and safety protocols are included. England, France, Italy, and Spain are still large draws for U.S. students, but Brazil, China, India, Korea and others are where economic growth and strategic priority are shifting, and where U.S. students are studying in growing numbers (Institute of International Education 2011).

Increase Education Abroad Student Participation

The question of participation level is a complex one. Education abroad can be expensive, time-consuming, and intimidating for students, despite its many benefits. Students may acknowledge the need to be globally competitive but may not connect that sentiment to studying abroad for a variety of reasons (Spencer and Tuma 2007).

Percentage rates are an easy measure. Going from 1 percent to 10 percent campus participation rate would be a meaningful increase, for example. But the institution should determine what is feasible and desirable, and it may not be shown in dramatic rises in participation rates. Creating one more course with embedded education abroad per year can be a sign of steadily increasing involvement. Adding new disciplinary courses into established semester programs could be considered evidence of successful participation, regardless of enrollment. Creating the first faculty-led program, or the first program to a previously unvisited country, can constitute success. Those institutions who feel confident based on existing metrics, and whose education abroad participation has been growing, may feel more ready to articulate specific percentage-based goals and set internal challenges to encourage movement to the next level of education abroad achievement.

Increase Underrepresented Student Participation

Determining who is not studying abroad is a crucial question to answer. For the already high-participating institution, identifying which student populations are not participating can be the difference between good and great comprehensive internationalization. For institutions with low participation rates, this answer can be what leads to a successful program. As with participation rates above, careful review of student composition and expectation level should be part of the institution's articulation of its goals. Nontraditional students or executive students might be able to attend only one short-term program abroad during the course of their studies; scholarships and grants may be most important for some students; mentorship and program leadership from caring faculty might be the difference for those who did not receive that encouragement in their lives before. In other words, as Diversity Abroad has defined it: "To ensure that students from diverse economic, educational, ethnic and social backgrounds are aware, have equal access and take advantage of the benefits and opportunities afforded through global education exchanges." (Diversity Abroad 2012).

Identify and Mentor Students For External Awards

Numerous prestigious external awards for education abroad are available for international education, including Boren, Fulbright, Gilman, and Rhodes scholarships. Students typically benefit from mentorship and guidance in becoming aware of, applying for, and winning prestigious awards. Harnessing successful faculty and identifying students early in their time on campus can be helpful and, for those institutions who seek distinction, can be a noteworthy and prideful goal to articulate and achieve.

Institutional Culture: Where is Education Abroad Centered?

Where education abroad fits into the institution's organizational structure can have a great influence over its successful design, delivery, and sustainability.

The difference between stated international missions or agendas and well-executed, self-sustaining programs that are integrated into the institution's purpose, with goals appropriately challenging for that institution, is often the result of deliberate organizational decisions.

The role of senior campus leadership cannot be overemphasized. Presidents, provosts, and boards are the ones who set institutional priorities, allocate resources, set the risk tolerance acceptable to the institution, and articulate the vision for the international presence of the institution. They also are the ones typically interacting with accreditors, state and federal examiners, external reviewers, and evaluators. They should be the ones to place education abroad in the proper context for external consumption, and should marry that to internal decisionmaking and structure (NAFSA 2008).

Depending on the institutional type, deans and department chairs may also exert leadership through academically focused committees, approval structures, and advising mechanisms in the academic units that can encourage optimal education abroad inclusion. At the operational level, therefore, the education abroad office (however it is structured) needs to be aware of and work in concert with stated and actual institutional goals and priorities as voiced by campus leadership.

The degree to which campus committees such as curriculum approval committees or program oversight committees play a role is likely a function of how the campus views that need. Some campuses employ a high degree of shared governance in education abroad administration, while others will place this responsibility largely in the international office. Where campus culture is enhanced by and demands collegial approaches to program development and administration, the education abroad office should be mindful.

Two other campus administrative entities play a role in a program's success: the finance/business operations office and the risk management office (or function) on campus. Education abroad programming is likely unique on campus due to regular foreign currency transactions and fluctuations, contingency planning for unexpected situations abroad, high levels of emergency planning and security analysis, and sourcing vendors (including third-party program providers) who may not fit into the institution's normal business affairs. The need for safe and secure programs abroad through vendors and providers that adhere to the institution's practice, as well as the need for financial agility in the face of unpredictability, should require a careful and well-coordinated financial planning process. Indeed some well-conceived, "innovative financial models" (Hudzik and McCarthy 2012, 20) are necessary and useful for sustained success of the program.

As a uniquely situated unit on campus with nuanced administrative needs, the education abroad office should have the maximum amount of autonomy and flexibility possible while reporting to campus leaders to ensure expertise and accountability. Overly stringent financial policies that may work well for other units on campus can result in an education abroad program that cannot meet demands from overseas vendors, or cannot manage its spending decisions in the sophisticated ways necessary for sustained success.

In a comparable way, how the institution manages risk is key to a well-executed and sustained program abroad. As stated previously in this chapter, program locations and structures are diversifying, and there are concomitant increases in risks associated with that growth. Some campuses have a risk management office, while others will place the function in the president's or senior leader's office. The need for institutional legal protection, as well as an honest and candid assessment of how much risk the university is comfortable with, should be an ongoing process. The education abroad office should pay special attention when developing programs in countries with U.S. State Department travel warnings, or in parts of the world with known risks of crime, disease, or war, and should be in communication with risk management well before any expenses are incurred or programs are deployed. Whether through a formal approval process or on a basis of inform and consent through dialogue, education abroad program management should work closely with risk management to be sure the institution as a whole, and the individuals working in it, are protected and that students are safe.

Ideally, risk management and education abroad are both seen as campus priorities of equal value. Decisions about program design and delivery should be made by informed international educators trained in the best practice of their profession, who attend conferences by professional organizations regularly, and work in harmony with those responsible for managing institutional risk.

Partners and Portfolio Management

One of the chief considerations for program development, and the one probably most important for the success or failure of programs abroad, is the decision and selection process for program partners abroad. Some specific issues to consider when developing partnerships abroad include:

- program demand
- student demographics
- academic objectives
- financial and political considerations

Determining program demand can be a tricky calculus on any campus, particularly if the education abroad program is new or largely undeveloped. For most institutions, studying abroad is not a requirement, and little financial support is provided, making the opportunity just one of many options students have during their college careers. Determining demand is an attempt to know what students want to study and learn abroad, where they want to go, what they are willing to pay for, and whether or not their parents or guardians will permit it. These are not easy things to determine. Flowing from the concepts described earlier in this chapter—knowing institutional culture and how education abroad is situated within the larger organization—should help in determining what kind of program will fit at the institution and how the program can be optimally structured.

Student demographics play an enormous role in program development. Some factors to consider are whether or not students come from families where international travel and study are explicitly encouraged, whether or not the students themselves have been abroad before for any meaningful length of time, what ability to pay the extra costs incurred by studying abroad students might have, and what other responsibilities students have for work, family, military, sports, or other commitments that may make studying abroad possible or impossible. Knowing these, and possibly other characteristics of the campus student body, will help determine the optimal program structures that will be successful.

A good place to start developing an education abroad portfolio and determining your program partners abroad is identifying within the institution's academic program what disciplines, courses, and particular faculty members will be crucial to program success. Support in these areas is key to forming the structures and policies needed to have successful programs. Emerging from the earlier description of academic purpose of the institution, what are the **academic objectives** for the program? For most institutions today, some recognition of the need for global understanding or world awareness is embedded into the academic program. Pushing past that necessary, albeit superficial, statement, it is important to seek out those particular disciplines, majors, and faculty members who are active abroad and bring that knowledge into the classroom. Such faculty members may be perfect to lead programs abroad, and such majors may include study abroad programs into their curricular options for students, and so on. Knowing this group of faculty and what their goals for education abroad are can help determine which partners are best suited to the type of program you want to develop.

Lastly, understanding **financial and political considerations** on campus will set the parameters when negotiating with program partners abroad. As discussed earlier in this chapter, the location and culture of the management of education abroad on campus is important, as well as the institution's approach to financial and risk management. For some campuses, working with U.S.-based, nonuniversity study abroad organizations (third-party providers, or TPPs) will be most appropriate so that bills can be paid in U.S.

---

dollars, financial uncertainties are minimal, and there are ample U.S.-based personnel to answer questions and resolve problems. For others, relationships abroad that are built and managed directly by the university are preferable because they provide more opportunity for faculty collaboration, more direct enrollment experiences for students, and opportunities for authentic engagement. These are considerations and assumptions based within the institutional approach. They should be discussed in principle with key leaders (president, provost, deans) so that operationally programs abroad are structured in concert with how the institution manages an international portfolio. Ideally, education abroad will be a part of an ongoing, strategic discussion of campus internationalization overall.

Program Location, Design, and Academic Structure

Broadly defined, education abroad can be grouped into two categories: traditional and nontraditional. In reality it has always been more complex, but it is worth discussing in these terms so that campus conversations and policies can be crafted in ways that are understandable and acceptable culturally within the institution. The traditional semester- or year-length programs to Western Europe are still popular and important in most university program portfolios. Many campus leaders and parents still consider this to be what study abroad is, and many in the international education field took part in this type of program. When considering strategic planning for education abroad, it is important to note that there are numerous options for such programs, a largely settled market for them, and considerable overlap in providers' options there. Still, for many students and parents, it is the only realistic option for education abroad they may undertake, owing to a host of factors ranging from personal safety and security to lifelong dreams. Much has already been written on the traditional program to Western Europe, but we should add that even though it does not attract as much attention today, it is still the most popular region of study for U.S. students abroad. Students still go there, the faculty still incorporates it into the curriculum, and parents still support it. Including semester programs to Western European destinations in your program portfolio is still a smart move.

Outside of Western Europe and the semester model, program destinations and structures have largely come to mean faculty-led short-term programs and programs in Africa, Latin America, and developing Asia. Without doubt this is the growth area in education abroad today. Several key points should be made here from a strategic planning perspective which, if addressed early on and in a sustained way, can lead to long-term success. First, faculty-led short-term programs are typically more complicated to organize and provide less financial room to maneuver than semester-length programs. As an institution, a commitment to faculty-led short-term programs should mean a sustained commitment to a professionally managed education abroad operation whose staff is connected to the larger profession, who meet regularly at conferences, who share best practices and knowledgeable connections, and who are empowered to make decisions with that knowledge. Second, faculty expertise in content and teaching should be harnessed well for that expertise, with an understanding that their knowledge of a local destination abroad may or may not be useful for ensuring the program's long-term success.

Programs of bilateral exchange between the university and a counterpart institution abroad are another worthy education abroad model. A thorough review, preferably with site visits, of not just the curriculum but housing and support services should coincide with direct university-to-university exchanges. Infrastructure and conditions on the ground, as well as assumptions about student services and instructional methods, can vary widely around the world. In order for U.S. students to succeed abroad on exchange programs they will need thorough and guided mentorship from trained staff at home on how to succeed there.

Another structure is the study abroad center. These centers, often run by a U.S. university or affiliated with one through a TPP, are organizations designed to offer college courses abroad that are more easily transferable to U.S. institutions and whose services more closely align with what U.S. students expect. There are many benefits to this approach, including predictability of the experience, management of costs and risks, trained staff at home and abroad who speak English and have an investment in a sustained relationship with the institution, and good safety and emergency protocols. In nontraditional destinations abroad there are numerous options, but the world is a big place—there may not be good choices in study center providers where the institution seeks to establish a program. International educators are in a unique position to stay informed and share that information with campus colleagues at key moments, be critical at times of what program offerings exist in many parts of the world, and to be open-minded toward developing new but sustainable structures abroad if deemed a priority on campus.

Regardless of the program model chosen or the destination abroad, ensuring students receive academic credit properly (Forum on Education Abroad 2011) is a perhaps less glamorous but still essential program component without which the integrity of the program will suffer. As discussed earlier, education abroad should be firmly rooted in the mission and academic purpose of the university. Flowing from this should be the deliberate articulation of it into the curriculum. Whether as major credit, elective credit, experiential education, or general education, education abroad is first and foremost education. A proper academic authority, such as faculty oversight committee, reporting line to a dean or provost, or a faculty credentialed international education director, needs to be in place. This is relevant for exchange university courses taken abroad at partner universities, for study center courses taken at TPP-managed centers, and for faculty-led programs taught and led by professors at the institution. A continual and professional oversight of academic content and integrity is essential if the education abroad program portfolio is to have ongoing support on campus.

Determining Program Success

Elsewhere in this book and in international education literature (Bolen 2007) are chapters on outcome assessment, student and faculty feedback and satisfaction, and similar areas of postprogram review. The discussion here of optimal strategic planning is not meant to duplicate that, but rather to identify some key areas to anticipate when designing programs. From an international educator's point of view, a fundamental question should be always: How do we know that program partnerships abroad are working well? Here is where the institution's strategic planning process for education abroad becomes relevant. To put program review into the context of the questions on institutional mission and culture presented earlier:

1. Does the education abroad program fit with the institution's definition of international engagement?
2. Does the program contribute to institutional learning goals for student engagement and global knowledge?
3. Does this program reinforce overall student learning objectives? Which ones, and how?
4. Do the programs represent the ambitions of the campus in terms of location and degree of faculty involvement?
5. Are the campus structures and policies, and the personnel assigned to carry them out, functioning at a sufficient level for sustained success?

Similarly, apply a critical analysis of the academic purpose, structure, and goals of the education abroad program portfolio. The earlier discussion of academic purpose, structure, and goals for education abroad can be viewed more contextually:

1. Do the programs abroad provide faculty and students opportunities for quality teaching and learning within certain geographical or global contexts that are important to the institution?
2. Do the programs provide opportunities for language and cultural knowledge-building that the institution defines as required for a global education?

3. If experiential education is an institutional value, are there internships or other such opportunities abroad? If not, what are the constraints and risks necessary for consideration?
4. Do faculty and students have the opportunity to pursue meaningful and important research projects abroad as part of the institution's education abroad portfolio?
5. Can students in all majors who want to include education abroad do so in a feasible time frame, within an understandable structure, and in a cost-manageable way?

The office or person responsible for education abroad should be able to articulate a response to these or similar questions on a regular basis. At times important to the institution, such as reaccreditation or formulation of institutional strategic plans, this may be a formal process, but it should occur in an ongoing manner as part of effective and sustained management of the portfolio of programs.

There are two other important ways of determining whether or not the program is working which, while less lofty and mission-driven, are often ones that on a day-to-day basis are emphasized. Being explicit about these at the outset of program planning should help to explain what success means to the campus, and also prevent unanticipated setbacks. They are: **participation rates** and **financial sustainability.** The best-designed experience with the most enriching content is not a program unless students enroll in it. Related to that is the question of financial sustainability. While every effort should be made to incentivize faculty to develop innovative programs and reduce costs to students as much as possible with creative use of institutional and other resources, in the end the sustained health of an education abroad program is strongly tied to its financial viability. Optimally, programs should be designed with realistic and achievable program participation rates, combined with a financial structure anticipating realistic costs and expenses. How many students need to take part in order to run? What institutional investments are going to be made and for how long? Which staffing trade-offs have to be made on campus with regard to faculty teaching load if faculty involvement with education abroad is a goal? Who makes that decision and how?

Answers to those questions will no doubt be considered in the context of the situation, but some forethought during the planning process and statements from campus leadership on it should guide program development so that it stays grounded in institutional realities and priorities from the beginning, and so that decisions made later are done so within a reasonably known context. Developing even one new effective education abroad program can be challenging and time consuming, and designing a series of programs that compose a coherent institutional portfolio can be the work of one's career. The elements of this chapter set the foundation for the necessary building blocks toward a robust, sound, and engaging education abroad experience for any institution seeking to enhance its offerings abroad.

References

Barnes, Tim. 2011. "Intentionality in International Engagement: Identifying Potential Strategic International Partnerships." In *Developing Strategic International Partnerships: Models for Initiating and Sustaining Innovative Institutional Linkages.* Institute of International Education.

Bolen, Mell, ed. 2007. *A Guide to Outcomes Assessment in Education Abroad.* Forum on Education Abroad.

Diversity Abroad. 2012. "Mission." Oakland, Calif.: Diversity Abroad. http://www.diversityabroad.com/mission.

Forum on Education Abroad. 2011. *Standards of Good Practice for Education Abroad, Fourth Edition.* Carlisle, Pa.: Forum on Education Abroad.

Hudzik, John and JoAnn McCarthy. 2012. *Leading Comprehensive Internationalization: Strategy and Tactics for Action.* Washington, D.C.: NAFSA: Association of International Educators.

Juniata College. 2013. "Mission." Juniata College. http://www.juniata.edu/about/mission.html.

Lamet, Maryelise and Mell Bolen. 2005. "Education Abroad in the Campus Context." In *NAFSA's Guide to Education Abroad for Advisers and Administrators.* Washington, D.C.: NAFSA: Association of International Educators.

Lewin, Ross, ed. 2009. "The Quest for Global Citizenship through Study Abroad." In *The Handbook of Practice and Research in Study Abroad.* New York: Routledge.

Massachusetts Institute of Technology. 2013. "Mission." MIT Facts. Massachusetts Institute of Technology. http://web.mit.edu/facts/mission.html.

NAFSA. 2008. "Strengthening Study Abroad: Recommendations for Effective Institutional Management for Presidents, Senior Administrators, and Study Abroad Professionals." Washington, D.C.: NAFSA: Association of International Educators.

Northern Virginia Community College. 2013. "Mission, Vision, and Goals." Northern Virginia Community College. http://www.nvcc.edu/about-nova/mission-vision/.

Institute of International Education. 2011. *Open Doors Report on International Education Exchange.* Washington, D.C.: Institute of International Education.

Spencer, Sarah and Kathy Tuma. 2007. *The Guide to Successful Short-Term Programs Abroad.* Washington, D.C.: NAFSA: Association of International Educators.

The State University of New York–Oswego. 2013. "Engaging Challenge: Sesquicentennial Plan." Mission, Vision, and Views. The State University of New York–Oswego. http://www.oswego.edu/about/leadership/sesquicentennial-plan/mission.html

University of California-Davis. 2013. "Mission Statement." General Catalog, 2012–14. University of California-Davis. http://catalog.ucdavis.edu/mission.html.

CHAPTER 14

EDUCATION ABROAD MODELS

By Jason Sanderson

University administrators and faculty consider multiple factors and program characteristics as they prepare new study abroad programs or review portfolios. Among those are program location, duration (e.g. single semester, full academic year, summer or May term, January term, or spring break) and finances; however, before delving into particular details, university administrators and faculty should consider the primary objectives of the new program as they will inform the decision on the program model best suited to meet these objectives. For instance, is the new program intended to assist in furthering an institutional or departmental mission to internationalize the institution? Does a dean want a program that will supplement or complement a specific curricular need on campus? Is the program intended to serve as the first step of new widespread cooperation with a foreign institution? Is enrollment in the program intended to alleviate strain on campus facilities in a given term? Is the program responding to a desire or need expressed by faculty or students? Once staff or faculty have developed and prioritized program goals and objectives and identified institutional resources and budget, the next step is to determine the most appropriate program model.

There is no one-size-fits-all approach to study abroad. There are four primary program models, each with its inherent benefits and challenges. In order to best discuss the advantages and disadvantages of these models, it is useful to define the nature of each program model, as well as identify some of the other names that may be used by colleagues when discussing study abroad. Based on Engle and Engle (2003), the program models discussed in this chapter are: faculty-led programs, exchange programs, island programs, and hybrid programs, as well as a discussion of collaboration with study abroad organizations.

Model 1: Faculty-Led Programs

The structure of a faculty-led program is perhaps the simplest model to conceptualize, but it is deceptively so since the term is used to describe a variety of study abroad programs involving on-site faculty involvement. A faculty-led program can be an alternative spring break travel seminar that is part of an on-campus course or a semester-long experience whereby the faculty leader does not actually teach, but rather serves as a program manager or mentor. These are just two examples that illustrate the great variety of programs that fall into this category. Therefore, when administrators approach or are approached by colleagues to discuss the potential for starting a faculty-led program, all players need to understand the intended role of the faculty member in the execution of the program. It is also important to clarify the level of support that the study abroad office is able to provide during both predeparture and on-site phases of the program. Given the course-based nature of this program model, overall enrollment is typically low, especially if the number of faculty is limited.

Faculty-Led Program Strengths

The advantages of this program model correspond with two fundamental elements of a program where a faculty member of the institution is directly involved with the on-site operation of the program. The first is related to curriculum. If the program has been proposed by a faculty member or academic unit on campus, the course(s) abroad should integrate seamlessly with the curriculum back on campus. The second element is related to student life and campus culture. A seasoned faculty member will likely be familiar with the student body and what potential participants are accustomed to on campus, and the reduced size of the program will lend to a high level of interaction between the faculty member and the program participants. The combination of both can lead to a great level of synergy and an enriching living and learning experience.

Faculty-Led Program Challenges

The greatest potential challenge with this program model is the faculty member. While faculty are familiar with students in the academic setting, they may be less familiar with the pastoral elements required of a faculty leader abroad, namely logistical matters, housing issues, personality conflicts, and other complications that may develop in an intimate group setting. A faculty member may not anticipate the impact these issues can have on the group dynamic or on him or her personally, particularly if he or she is only focused on the in-class teaching and learning component. Model practice requires predeparture training for the faculty leader for this reason.

Faculty-Led Program Development

Generally speaking, the catalyst for a faculty-led program will be a research interest of a professor or a curricular need of a given department. Institutions should develop and follow a proposal and approval process whereby all program elements (e.g., academic, pastoral, logistical, financial, health and safety, etc.) are presented and discussed in committee before moving forward. If the aim is to draw in students from multiple disciplines, other faculty members or departments need to be consulted at this time.

Shortly after the approval of the proposal, stakeholders must also establish a clear timeline of deliverables for the faculty member and the study abroad office, including a plan for student recruitment. Given the need to promote new course options, the syllabi and budgets should be finalized no less than six months before the opening of the registration period for the launch term. Depending on the mechanisms in place at the home institution, getting syllabi and budgets approved may take up to an additional six months; therefore, an ideal timeline would begin roughly one year before full implementation. The registrar should also be consulted if any courses are to be offered by faculty abroad that are already taught on campus to discuss whether the section taught abroad should carry any special notation on the transcript.

Faculty-Led Program: Key Players

The faculty member is of course central to the execution of a faculty-led program. Faculty and administrators (in this case, the study abroad office) should be part of the selection process, either appointing an instructor to the leader position or reviewing faculty applications. The selection criteria should be in writing and available to all stakeholders. The same holds for any additional on-site support staff (e.g., resident or teaching assistants) that may be deemed necessary depending on the size and scope of the participant pool.

Faculty-Led Program: Staffing

As discussed above, the roles of the faculty member and the study abroad office should be clear from the beginning, ideally prior to developing the proposal. Of particular importance are logistics and finances. The size of the group will dictate how many others, if any, should be recruited to assist with the on-site phase of the program. Once the size of a group reaches double digits, model practice suggests additional support should be considered. This is not only important from a practical, logistical standpoint, but also if a problem arises where the faculty leader needs to take time away from the group, someone else would be present to temporarily assume that role.

Faculty-Led Program: Budgeting

Understanding program finances is essential for a sustainable program. Most faculty-led programs are expected to be self-funding. As such, the program proposal must indicate where the breakeven point stands, and should enrollments fall under that number, whether any program elements including faculty remuneration could be modified to make the program viable. If a faculty member will be teaching one course abroad, but would normally teach two courses on campus in that same term, it is important to understand whether there needs to be compensation for the missing course, and, if so, whether the program costs need to cover any course waivers for his or her home department.

Faculty-Led Program: Risk Management

The health and safety environment of a new program proposal should be included in the program development phase. Political stability and natural disasters come quickly to mind, but there are other programming elements, such as community engagement and excursions—which also present potential risks—that should be considered. Even after it has been determined that the location is acceptable, a designated staff member is needed to monitor current events, including in neighboring countries. Also, the faculty leader as well as any other assistants he or she may have on site need to understand the potential for liability of all on-site activities, especially the protocol for organizing an impromptu excursion to a site of cultural significance, in particular if this site is in another region or country.

Faculty-Led Program: Logistics

Even if the study abroad office is able to provide logistical support during the planning and predeparture phases, the bulk of the responsibility will fall on the faculty member while on site. Housing and transportation present perhaps the greatest potential for unforeseeable problems. To minimize the possibility of such problems and after consulting with the study abroad office, the faculty leader should conduct a site visit during the planning phase, with the sole goal of investigating the logistical needs of the program and considering possible alternatives.

Model 2: Exchange Programs

Exchange programs have served as the traditional backbone of study abroad for many years. They involve students from a U.S.-based institution studying at another for a specified length of time (typically one or two semesters) while, in turn, students from the other institution come to the United States to study. Exchange agreements may be restricted to certain departments or academic units or may grant full access to the institution's academic offerings. Some colleagues, in particular those who do not work directly in education abroad, may refer to these programs as direct enrollment or direct matriculation programs, indicating that students register for normally offered coursework which they take alongside local degree-seeking students. While exchange programs most certainly are based on this principle, these terms are not necessarily the same thing, because not all direct enrollment or direct matriculation programs involve bilateral student exchange. Because of these multiple meanings, the first point of discussion for the possibility of establishing an exchange program with an institution is that all key players intend for there to be a bilateral flow of students.

Exchange Program Strengths

Exchange programs have the advantage of requiring few resources to establish once an appropriate exchange partner has been identified. In general, one only needs to agree to the terms (e.g., ratio, services offered, related fees, etc.) of the exchange of students and sign an exchange agreement.

The primary advantage of this program model, however, is perhaps that it can quickly increase the amount of international students on campus, thereby internationalizing the campus with little effort. This program model also affords students the possibility to truly assume the life of a local student, and therefore to become intimately familiar with the nuances presented in terms of local culture and, when applicable, language. Some institutions, particularly public institutions, may find this model attractive as it provides a reasonably economical way for students to be able to study abroad, since they pay their normal tuition and the only variable costs are transportation and living expenses.

Exchange Program Weaknesses

One of the potential disadvantages of this program model is its deceptive simplicity. Entering into an exchange agreement with a foreign institution can quickly raise the status of the U.S.-based institution as well as offer opportunities for further collaboration; however, the support offered on site may be found to be insufficient with regard to student needs or expectations.

Few institutions abroad have as developed systems of pastoral care for their students as are generally found in the United States. While this may seem insignificant to some, comprehensive academic advising and after-hours emergency contacts are an essential component of successful study abroad programs, and most public institutions abroad are not able to offer these services. Additionally, exchange programs are restricted by the exchange partners' academic calendars. Summer programs are seldom possible and discrete fall semester options may be challenging if the host institution's first semester runs into January. Finally, exchange programs are prone to the consequences of local university strikes.

Exchange Program Development

The single most important element of program development with regard to establishing an exchange program is identifying a suitable exchange partner. Faculty and administrators will undoubtedly have connections to various institutions abroad, but that seldom suffices for a sustainable and success-ful exchange program. If the exchange is intended to be restricted to certain departments or academic units, limited faculty contacts may be a good indication of academic fit, but other services, such as those mentioned above, should still be considered. On the other hand, if the exchange is intended to be wide-reaching, then support from multiple academic units will be needed.

In some fields, it may be necessary to research whether the foreign curriculum is compatible with that on the home campus. This is particularly the case in the social sciences where stress on qualitative and quantitative approaches is prevalent. The study abroad office should also be consulted to see whether they may know others with experience working with the intended host institution. The bulk of the time investment with this program model is finding the appropriate partner abroad and negotiating the terms of the exchange. Each of these elements may take several months before the institutions can expect to see each other's students on their campus. A minimum of six months should be planned before the new program is promoted. The registrar should be consulted to discuss how credit earned at the host institution will be transcribed (e.g., should there be something to denote that the credits were taken at another institution?) and whether the grades will be factored into students' overall GPAs. Furthermore, students' on-campus status while on an exchange program should also be discussed (e.g., will they remain registered?) and, in particular, how their status could impact students' access to external financial aid.

Exchange Programs: Key Players

As discussed above, support from various academic units is important if it is hoped that the exchange program will draw from a wide range of disciplines. The other important campus unit which should be consulted in the early stages of establishing an exchange program is the budget and finance office, particularly if this is the institution's first exchange program.

Exchange Programs: Staffing

If the new program is projected to draw high levels of enrollment, administrators may consider hiring someone to serve as a full-time on-site director. Even if projected enrollments are not high, however, having a local liaison to address the shortcomings of the program model discussed above should be considered. Whenever seeking someone to provide services abroad, legal counsel should be consulted about contracts and whether the institution should or needs to take measures to become a legal entity in the host country. If the program is intended to be restricted to a single department on campus, it should be discussed whether it makes sense for that academic unit or the study abroad office to provide predeparture advising.

Exchange Programs: Budgeting

Exchange programs may involve complicated financial models. These models are generally rooted in the U.S.-based institution's tuition structure. The simplest scenario is a 1:1 exchange, whereby tuition is paid by the outgoing student and therefore waived on the other side; however, if that is not the case, it is imperative to project the incoming tuition revenue before establishing the ratio used to allocate exchange places. If the sending institution collects any supplemental fees (e.g., technology, gym access, student clubs, etc.), that should also be taken into consideration. Finally, given the perennial tuition increases on U.S. campuses, it is important to establish timelines by which any unused allocations must be used.

Exchange Programs: Risk Management

Aside from the location of the future exchange partner, which should be considered carefully if in an area of recent instability, the potential disadvantages of the program model with regard to student support should be discussed thoroughly, especially if it has been suggested that no on-site oversight is necessary.

Exchange Programs: Logistics

The logistics of exchange programs can be both simple and complicated. Administrators should discuss matters such as access to housing, particularly in systems where state-run housing cannot be guaranteed, and other basic necessities both with colleagues who have experience in the host country, as well as—whenever possible—with the future exchange partner.

Model 3: Island Programs

Island programs are self-contained programs which have been developed exclusively for U.S. college students. They may be open to students from multiple institutions or completely intended for one sending institution. Overseas branch campuses and study centers are other terms that are sometimes used to describe this program model, but those terms may offer greater academic options than the traditional island program.

Island Program Strengths

The primary advantage of this program model is that the content is at the discretion of the program sponsor or institution; the curriculum can be designed to meet the needs of students. Island programs are generally based on U.S. academic structure, pedagogies, and culture, and as such, program participants rarely experience difficulty in adapting to the academic environment of the program. Even when a foreign language is present, this model allows for substantive coursework to be delivered in English. The program calendar can also be synced with that of the home campus, thus allowing for seamless transition from one location to another. Short-term programs over breaks are also feasible under this model.

Island Program Weaknesses

As can be surmised from the name of this category of program, participants are often isolated and shielded from interaction with the local population. Consequently, it can be a great challenge for them to integrate into the host culture, especially if they are not proficient in the local language. Another potential disadvantage is related to student recruitment and faculty support. Students may be attracted to such programs for reasons that are not entirely academic in nature, and as a result, some faculty may doubt the academic rigor of the program. Additionally, the financial commitment for such programs tends to be higher than other models.

Island Program Development

If administrators are considering establishing an island program for their campus, they will first need to select a location. This location should be in a politically stable country and would ideally be accessible for students with varying levels of mobility, and would be adaptable to meet evolving enrollment needs. Business operations and contractual obligations related to the property where the program will be held should be reviewed carefully, especially if the building or facilities are intended to play a central role in any marketing campaigns.

If faculty from the home campus is expected to teach courses on site, administrators should determine whether there is sufficient interest among the faculty to serve in this role. A steering committee, including study abroad staff and faculty, should be instituted to serve as the body that decides how to best serve the evolving needs of the campus abroad. This program model is perhaps the most involved, and as such, requires the greatest amount of lead time. In addition to the elements discussed for faculty-led programs, more time is needed to see to all of the additional logistical concerns of an island program. The minimum timeframe to establish an island program would therefore be 18 months. As with faculty-led programs, the registrar should be consulted about courses that are also offered on campus. Also, if there is intent to open this program to students enrolled at other institutions in the future, the format in which their grades will be conveyed and submitted to their home institutions should also be discussed.

Island Programs: Key Players

Support from faculty from a variety of academic units is essential to integrating successfully the new program into the home campus ethos. Legal counsel as well as the budget and finance office should be consulted at the very beginning of the planning phase to consider fully the implications of such a potentially costly endeavor.

Island Programs: Staffing

Establishing an island program requires seeking faculty to teach on site, which could involve hiring local instructors in addition to support staff for housing, cultural programming, and support. Depending on the local language and labor laws, it may or may not be appropriate to hire locals for these roles. Given the specific nature of U.S. academic and student life, if locals are hired, home campus staff must provide training in the potential differences with the local university culture. In such cases, it should also be clear whether local hires are expected to conform to American norms. A local attorney should be placed on retainer at least during the initial implementation phase. Also, individual medical personnel should be available for consultation beyond the scope of local medical facilities.

Island Programs: Budgeting

From the beginning, accurate financial budget models as well as cost projections will need to be determined in order to establish a breakeven point. As indicated above, even a small island program is the equivalent of a miniature campus, with the implication for extracurricular activities and support. These services can often come at a premium abroad, especially where proficiency in English among the local population is not common.

Island Programs: Risk Management

Starting an island program abroad inherently implicates the home institution in a greater degree of liability, and as such, every aspect of risk management and health and safety considered for campus operations should be replicated when initially establishing the program. As discussed above for exchange programs, any local hires should be thoroughly trained in the expectations of the home campus with regard to student welfare. Campus risk management officials should travel to the proposed site of the island program during the planning phase and then again before the first students arrive. Even in previously stable locations, evacuation plans need to be drawn up and revised regularly.

Island Programs: Logistics

The logistics of an island program can be complex. Even if projected enrollments are low, full consideration before execution must be given regarding facilities for housing (and possibly dining), student activities, and other extracurricular needs. If any of these aspects involve outsourcing, the facilities should be inspected by a third party, and if possible, by campus officials during their initial site visit. In addition to evacuation discussed above, contingency plans should be put in place for all essential functions of the program. At the very minimum this should include displacement due to unforeseeable circumstances such as flooding, structural integrity issues, propagation of contagious infection or disease, loss of water and/or power, as well as provisions should it be necessary to stay in place during an emergency.

Model 4: Hybrid Programs

Hybrid study abroad programs involve combining aspects of direct matriculation and mediated programming. These programs are sometimes also referred to as mixed programs. In other words, this model integrates elements of exchange programs along with elements of island programs. The courses offered as part of the hybrid program could include local language instruction, a site-specific core course, or, depending on the size of the participant pool, a variety of content courses with relevance to the city or host country which might not be available or accessible at a local university. These programs may be part of an exchange program, or, through special arrangement, may be part of fee-based access to the local university.

Hybrid Program Strengths

As indicated above, hybrid programs combine aspects of both exchange programs and island programs. Consequently, the advantages of this mediated program model are a combination of the advantages of both of these program models, namely the cultural and linguistic integration of direct matriculation programs and the customizable nature of island program curriculum.

Hybrid Program Weaknesses

Since this program model shares advantages with its two component models, it does not do so fully. Therefore, the primary disadvantage of this model is that it does not offer full immersion in the host university system, nor does it afford complete curricular design. Similarly, depending on the intentionality of the program design, the disadvantages of exchange programs such as minimal on-site support, and those of island programs, namely limited interaction with the local population, may still apply.

Hybrid Program Development

While hybrid programs allow for a balance of potential academic short-comings of the future host institution, home university staff selects the host institution following established program goals and outcomes. When determining what types of courses to offer in house, it is important for administrators to consider the academic strengths of the host institution and the needs of their own students. When seeking venues for the in-house courses, the objectives of these courses should be kept in mind. For language or culture courses, conducting them on or near campus to give students the opportunity to practice what they have learned in the classroom makes sense.

On the other hand, if courses are more participatory or experiential, including multimedia and/or excursions throughout the city or surrounding area, a separate location where students would be able to focus on assimilating the subject matter without external distractions would be important. Additionally, administrators will need to decide where program participants should be housed and whether in-house courses should be taught by locally hired instructors. Similar to island programs, administrators should consider establishing a steering committee for the management of the in-house component of the program. Given the hybrid nature of this program model, an implementation timeframe will depend on whether the program more closely resembles an exchange program or an island program. Therefore, administrators should plan on six months to one year to bring a new hybrid program on line.

Hybrid Programs: Key Players

As with exchange programs, faculty and administrators should be consulted early to identify a suitable host institution for the program. Furthermore, faculty from a range of subjects should be invited to discuss what in-house courses should be offered. They should also be part of the discussion whether in-house courses should be taught by home school faculty or local hires. In the case of the latter, faculty will be best poised to evaluate their qualifications for their respective academic disciplines. Much as with the other program models, the registrar will need to be consulted, in particular for hybrid programs, to discuss whether the in-house courses should be transcribed differently from those that students will take directly at the host institution abroad.

Hybrid Programs: Staffing

In addition to hiring instructors for the in-house courses, it may be necessary to hire further on-site support staff. This could include a housing coordinator and a student services counselor. The study abroad office will likely provide program support back on campus, but if there is a given academic focus to the program, the office should consider strengthening ties with that particular academic unit to ensure consistent predeparture preparation.

Hybrid Programs: Budgeting

If the hybrid program is part of an exchange program, the cost of teaching separate courses must be taken into consideration when determining a fair exchange ratio. If it is part of the special fee-paying relationship, the overall costs of both components will need to be calculated well in advance of each semester. While the likelihood of unforeseeable problems will be less than with an island program, contingency plans should still be established in case of major disruption of classes or other essential activities. These plans could include, for instance, expanding course offerings should there be a prolonged strike at the host institution.

Hybrid Programs: Risk Management

Aside from site-specific concerns, there are no particular risks inherent to this program model, beyond those discussed in relation to exchange and island programs. In fact, the hybrid nature of the model allows many of the structural risks of direct matriculation and island program to be potentially mitigated, at least in part by relying more heavily on the complementary component structures. Should the in-house courses rely on excursions, program leaders will want to discuss their plans with university officials during the planning phase.

Hybrid Programs: Logistics

In addition to determining where to hold the separate in-house courses, student housing may need to be included in the logistical plan. In cases where university housing cannot be secured, an on-site liaison may be necessary to ensure that participants' living arrangements are handled quickly and efficiently by people with applicable local knowledge. Finally, in the likely event that the in-house courses will make use of visiting sites that are relevant to the course topics, transportation and possibly temporary lodging will need to be provided. Again, making use of local expertise would probably be the best way to address this need.

Working with Study Abroad Organizations

Study abroad organizations, also commonly referred to as third-party providers, are companies whose primary function is to act as an intermediary between U.S. colleges and universities and institutions abroad. Many of these organizations maintain study centers in various locations around the world, but some are focused on a single geographic area. As such, these organizations may have their headquarters abroad or in the United States. They are generally able to provide U.S.-based institutions with a wide variety of services and programming options, which may include any and all of the study abroad program models discussed above. Furthermore, an increasing number of these organizations offer the option to use their services to set up customized programs when institutions seek to establish a unique opportunity abroad.

Study Abroad Organization Strengths

Working with these organizations is similar to subcontracting, which means that as a fee-paying service, the primary advantage is having experts in local academics and logistics attend to students' needs without having to commit institutional resources for unpredictable enrollments. Using these organizations can instantly offer dozens of study abroad opportunities in a range of countries.

An institution may choose to approve a select number of programs through an organization, but some organizations may offer financial benefits (or discounts) for approving all of their programs as a single programming partner. As mentioned above, another advantage of working with a study abroad organization is the possibility of collaborating to establish a customized program, which would carry the institution's name, but make use of the organization's on-site resources. Finally, nearly all U.S.-based study abroad organizations offer the option of having a U.S.-based school of record issue a transcript with U.S. grades for coursework completed abroad. Having a standardized academic record from abroad can be reassuring for registrars, especially when a campus is in the process of an accreditation review.

Study Abroad Organization Weaknesses

Since these organizations are businesses, their services are fee based, and a high level of service can come at a premium, particularly in settings where local logistics are known to be complicated. The costs of these services must be considered when establishing program fees. Another challenge of working with study abroad organizations is that only a few offers the opportunity to receive international students in exchange for outgoing U.S. students, so campus internationalization is not often connected with study abroad organizations, and as a result, some colleagues on campus, especially faculty, may not embrace a widespread move towards using the services of these organizations. Furthermore, even if the organization is merely facilitating housing and registration into a local university abroad, there may be doubts among the faculty regarding the academic rigor of the courses students will take on site.

Other Considerations

When administrators consider working with a study abroad organization, it is important for them to practice due diligence when seeking out the most appropriate partner. For this process, the study abroad office's expertise and contacts will prove invaluable. When an organization's fees are published widely online and in print, it will be important for administrators to consider their institution's study abroad fee structure. If home school tuition is charged and program costs are significantly lower, talking points should be prepared for inquiries, especially from parents. Finally, working with a study abroad organization can be an effective way to expand a campus' study abroad programming while not having to overburden the study abroad office. That said, however, this convenience does come with a price, and it is up to administrators to determine whether it is worth it given their particular institutional circumstances.

Conclusion

In sum, before undertaking on new study abroad programming, administrators need to be fully aware of their institution's needs and objectives, not to mention the expectations of faculty and students with regard to promoting and accepting new programs. A regular program evaluation process should be implemented to ensure that all programs are relevant to the sending institution's curriculum and culture, which may well translate into changing a program model over time to respond to evolving needs or goals of the home campus.

References

Connell, Christopher. 2009. "Boston University: Choosing to be Great through Internationalization," *International Educator* 18, 6: 38-44.

Connell, Christopher. 2012. "Juniata College Faculty Discovered the World and Students Followed." *International Educator* 21, 6: 34-39.

Connell, Christopher. 2013. "A Well-Coordinated Approach to Internationalization at Saint Benedict and Saint John's." *International Educator* 22, 5: 32-39.

Connell, Christopher. 2009. "Winning Formula in Internationalization Found in a Kansas Corner." *International Educator* 18, 3: 72-87.

Engle, Lilli and John Engle. 2003. "Study Abroad Levels: Toward a Classification of Program Types." *Frontiers: The Interdisciplinary Journal of Study Abroad* 9: 1-20.

Forum on Education Abroad. "Education Abroad Glossary." Last Modified April 2011. Accessed July 19, 2013. http://www.forumea.org/educationabroadglossary2ndedition2011.cfm.

Guess, Andy. "The 'Supply Side' of Study Abroad," Inside Higher Ed. May 19, 2008, Accessed August 12, 2013. http://www.insidehighered.com/news/2008/05/19/iie.

Howard, Kimberley and Brian Kelley. 2010. "Business School Study Tours: A Case Study." *International Educator* 19, 4: 44-47.

Hulstrand, Janet. 2013. "Preparing Faculty to Teach Abroad." *International Educator* 22, 5: 40-43.

Hulstrand, Janet. 2008. "Faculty Abroad: What Do These Innocents Need to Know." *International Educator* 17, 3: 76-79.

Institute of International Education. 2012. *Open Doors 2012 Report on International Educational Exchange.* New York: Institute of International Education.

Johnson, Martha. 2009. "Post-Reciprocity: In Defense of the 'Post' Perspective." *Frontiers: The Interdisciplinary Journal of Study Abroad* 28: 181-186.

Norris, Emily M. and Mary Dwyer. 2005. "Testing Assumptions: The Impact of Two Study Abroad Program Models." *Frontiers: The Interdisciplinary Journal of Study Abroad* 11: 121-142.

Paus, Eva and Michael Robinson. 2008. "Increasing Study Abroad Participation: The Faculty Makes the Difference." *Frontiers: The Interdisciplinary Journal of Study Abroad* 27: 33-49.

Pope, Justin. "American Students Abroad Pushed out of 'Bubbles.'" *USA Today.* September 25, 2011. http://usatoday30.usatoday.com/news/education/story/2011-09-25/study-abroad/50550430/1

Redden, Elizabeth. "The Faculty Role in Study Abroad." Inside Higher Ed. June 3, 2010. Accessed August 12, 2013. http://www.insidehighered.com/news/2010/06/03/nafsa

Redden, Elizabeth. "Faculty Study Abroad Leader Comes under Fire for Decision about Student Health." *Inside Higher Ed.* March 25, 2013. Accessed August 12, 2013. http://www.insidehighered.com/news/2013/03/25/faculty-study-abroad-leader-comes-under-fire-decisions-about-student-health.

Redden, Elizabeth. "The Middlemen of Study Abroad." *Inside Higher Ed.* August 20, 2007. Accessed August 12, 2013. http://www.insidehighered.com/news/2007/08/20/abroad.

Soneson, Heidi M. and Roberta J. Cordano. 2009. "Universal Design and Study Abroad: (Re-) Designing Programs for Effectiveness and Access." *Frontiers: The Interdisciplinary Journal of Study Abroad* 28: 269-288.

Sutton, Richard C. "Expanding Student Choices in Study Abroad." *Inside Higher Ed.* August 22, 2008. Accessed August 12, 2013. http://www.insidehighered.com/views/2008/08/22/sutton.

CHAPTER 15

WORK, INTERNSHIPS, AND VOLUNTEERING ABROAD

By William Nolting

Education abroad programming will probably always be dominated by credit-bearing academic programs, known as "study abroad." But students learn in different ways and have different needs, only some of which can be satisfied by study abroad programs that consist mainly of classroom-based instruction. Programs offering experiential learning through work, internships, volunteering, and service-learning have steadily expanded, as students seek different types of international experiences that have the potential to impact their personal and professional lives.

These newly expanding options include credit-bearing internships while studying abroad; noncredit (cocurricular) full-time internships; credit-bearing service-learning programs; short-term cocurricular volunteer service projects; co-op opportunities; project-based small group projects; student-run groups such as alternative spring breaks; postgraduate teaching abroad fellowships; and research internships abroad in a university, lab, or field site.

This chapter is intended as a guide for advisers in education abroad, career, volunteer, or service-learning offices who consult with students regarding work abroad, internships, service-learning, or volunteer programs. These programs involve special benefits but also special challenges above and beyond that of traditional study abroad programs.

DEFINITIONS

Education abroad includes both classroom instruction and experiential learning. Experiential education, which fuses direct experience with the learning environment and content, may include activities such as field trips, research, or participant observation. The focus of this chapter is on experiential education programs open to students and recent graduates for working, interning, volunteering, and service-learning abroad, described collectively by the acronym WIVA.

(continued)

Work abroad is the umbrella term used to describe various kinds of immersion in an international workplace or community environment with the educational value of the experience itself as the primary purpose, whether for academic credit or not. By design, work abroad programs are temporary, lasting anywhere from a few weeks to two or three years, and they may or may not be related to specific career goals.

An *international internship* typically refers to a short-term (one month to one year) work experience with an organization abroad that allows participants to apply theoretical classroom knowledge in a real-world setting, and gain a better understanding of a given field in a global context. For purposes of this chapter, internships may or may not offer academic credit and may or may not be paid. International cooperative education (co-ops)—similar to but distinct from internships—are paid work programs that are usually integrated into a university-level degree, in which terms of study and degree major-related work are alternated. They tend to be in technical, business, and healthcare fields.

International volunteer service is "an organized period of engagement and contribution to society by individuals who volunteer across an international border" (McBride, Lough, and Sherraden 2010). It seeks to foster international understanding between peoples and nations and to promote global citizenship and intercultural cooperation. *International service-learning* is related to, but according to proponents is quite distinct from, volunteering. Most notably, service learning combines formal instruction with related community service.

When considering international education experiences, the distinction between a work, internship, volunteer, or service-learning experience may appear arbitrary. In this chapter, volunteer service will refer to experiences in which the student participates primarily for altruistic purposes. When discussing work abroad in general, we will use the terms work abroad or WIVA experience.

Demonstrating and Maximizing the Benefits: Research on Learning Outcomes

Studies assessing the impact of internships, volunteering, teaching, and working abroad have been relatively rare until the past two decades. The studies that have been done generally agree in their findings that the benefits of such programs tend to be similar to those of study abroad, only amplified. George

Kuh (2008) describes types of "high impact" learning, including among them internships, service-learning and "global learning." Thus, internships and service-learning taking place abroad represent the intersection of these two types of high-impact learning with that of a third, learning abroad.

There is a significant and growing body of research supporting the conclusion that WIVA programs are high impact. More than two dozen studies were cited in Nolting, Johnson, and Matherly (2005) that examined the impact of work abroad programs. The conclusions are consistent:

> The work [abroad] experience appears to have had a most important influence...the more immersion, the more satisfaction and the more impact...the more a program overseas encourages involvement with the host culture in a variety of roles, with that of worker in the society very important among them, the more we can expect to find enduring [changes in] attitudes and behavior. (Abrams 1979)

More recently, there appears to be a broad consensus developing in education abroad that, in order for experiential learning to be maximized, it must be guided, intentional, and reflective before, during, and after the experience abroad. Three recent studies of the new learning approach focus on the importance of reflection for internships (Pagano and Roselle 2009), for volunteering and service learning (Whitney and Clayton 2011) and on virtual learning combined with internships (Gerken et al., 2012). These techniques are now often utilized by international internship and service-learning programs.

Participation Data

In 2012 the *Open Doors* survey included for the first time a question about Non-Credit Internships and Work Abroad (defined to include work, internships and volunteering). For the pilot year period 2010/11, totals reported were 16,380 for-credit and 8,700 noncredit, giving an overall total of 25,080. In the 2013 *Open Doors*, covering period 2011/12, the combined total increased 33 percent to 33,434 (of which 20,676 were for-credit and 12,758 were noncredit). Adding the noncredit figure of 12,758 to the overall 2013 *Open Doors* for-credit total of 283,332 gives 296,090, meaning that 11.3 percent [33,434] participated in work, internships or volunteering abroad experiences (on a for-credit or noncredit basis).

Anecdotal evidence suggests that, due to underreporting, the actual numbers may be far larger. For example, the University of Michigan, one of the few universities that has a long history of tracking cocurricular education abroad, reported for 2011-12 that 2,060 students studied or interned abroad for credit, while 1,424 students participated in cocurricular, not-for-credit education-abroad experiences such as research, internships, volunteering and student-organized group projects abroad. More than 800 of the cocurricular participants were reported by academic units which provided funding for students to do research, internships, or volunteer projects abroad (University of Michigan International Center 2012).

TABLE 1. Search Results of December 2013 at GoAbroad.com

Type of Education Abroad Experience	Number of Organizations	Number of Programs Offered
Study	873	4764
Internships	790	3485
Volunteer	1024	6228
Teach	181	981

According to The Center for Social Development at Washington University, "Between 800,000 and 1,100,000 individuals in the US reported volunteering internationally each year from 2004 to 2012." Nearly half did so through faith-based organizations. Around 30 percent (240,000 to 330,000) of the total were between 15-24 years old, confirming that the number of high-school through college-age individuals participating in such programs is significant (Lough 2012).

The field of education abroad is still struggling with how best to provide accurate data about participation in WIVA programs. Even with the absence of firm numbers, it is clear that the rates of participation are significant.

Professional Associations

The growth rates of participation in WIVA programs have drawn the attention of professional associations in both international exchange and career services. NAFSA: Association of International Educators, the National Society for Experiential Education (NSEE), and the European Association for International Education (EAIE) each have created standing committees, professional sections, or interest groups devoted to issues in work-, internship-, and volunteer-abroad programs. NAFSA's EA-KC Subcommittee on Work, Internships and Volunteering Abroad (WIVA) was founded in 2002. The International Volunteer Programs Association (IVPA), founded in the mid-1990s, is a network of volunteer-sending organizations that agree to uphold IVPA's standards in order to be admitted as members. The Forum on Education Abroad, established in 2001, chose its name to indicate that its domain encompassed the full range of education abroad programs, including work, internship, and volunteer (Forum on Education Abroad 2011a). Several of these organizations have published statements of good practice for work and volunteer abroad programs, such as NSEE's principles of good practice of experiential education (NSEE 2011) and the Forum's Guidelines for Credit and Non-Credit Volunteer, Internship Experience, and Work (VIEW) Programs Abroad (Forum on Education Abroad 2011b). The Global Internship Conference, while not a professional association, provides a focused forum for exchanges of state-of-the art ideas and publishes presentations on their website (http://www.globalinternshipconference.org). The National Association of Colleges and Employers, the professional association for college career services professionals and human resources/staffing professionals focused on college relations and recruiting, has developed several resources for its members advising students about issues related to the global workplace, including the Global Campus Recruiting Symposium (NACE 2012).

Advising and Administration: Work Abroad Compared with Study Abroad

The growth in WIVA programs and professional associations has resulted in the allocation of added resources for advisers and administrators working with these programs. Advising students for WIVA programs, however, is distinct from study abroad in significant ways. We identify next a few examples to illustrate how advising for work abroad differs.

- **Academic credit and professional development:** Unlike most study abroad, not all work abroad experiences will carry academic credit. The likelihood that a particular experience is linked with academic credit will depend upon the nature of the WIVA program, the traditions for work abroad programs in the host country, the requirements of the sponsoring organization and especially the policies regarding internships and credit at the student's home institution, among many other issues.

- **Institutional control:** One of the most significant ways in which work and study abroad programs differ is with the degree of institutional control. Unlike students who attend study abroad programs sponsored by their home institutions, many students who participate in work abroad programs do so independently, setting up the experience without direct involvement by the institution (of course, students may also choose to study abroad independently, subject to their home institution's policies).

- **Work visas and location:** With a few exceptions, students may in principle study in most countries in the world. Work visa requirements and geopolitical considerations, in contrast, may limit the types of work, internship, or volunteer experiences that are available in a particular country.
- **Financial realities:** Students are often unaware of the great disparities in living standards around the world. They may be surprised that they cannot expect a U.S.-level salary when working in many regions of the world—indeed, the cost of an airplane ticket may exceed a local citizen's annual salary! Moreover, many if not most programs, including volunteer programs, require program fees to cover services ranging from placement to housing arrangement. Even in areas that enjoy a similar standard of living as that in the United States, students participating in paid work programs (most are unpaid) will probably have less to save than they would in a summer job at home, simply because of the additional costs involved in program fees, traveling abroad, paying health insurance, and simply living in a different country.
- **Adjusting to the foreign workplace or community:** In some instances, a student's overall cross-cultural adjustment takes a back seat to simply adapting to holding a job. For students with limited employment histories, adapting to regular work hours, reporting to a boss, or dealing with difficult coworkers can be overwhelming. Even students who have had previous internships may still find it difficult to understand the cultural nuances that shape their workplace or community. These experiences can be further complicated when the organization has little familiarity with working with U.S. students.

Given the above differences in advising and administration of WIVA programs, the allocation of resources by campuses will reflect the type and scope of experiential learning programs that can be effectively designed and maintained. The following chart reflects this continuum, beginning with institutions that make a low commitment of resources (such as staff or money) and rely heavily on programs directed by third-party organizations to those that make a high commitment of institutional resources and direct their own programs. Those seeking to establish their own programs will want to see the NAFSA book, *Internships, Service Learning, and Volunteering Abroad: Successful Models and Best Practices* (Nolting, Donohue, Matherly and Tillman, 2013) from which the following diagram is taken.

FIGURE 1. Models for Institutional Management of WIVA Programs

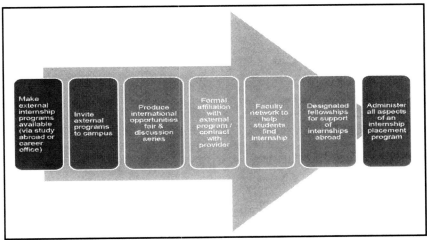

Source: Reproduced from NAFSA, Internships, Service Learning, and Volunteering Abroad: Successful Models and Best Practices (2013)

Advising Considerations

There are many available WIVA options, including some postgraduate opportunities such as Fulbright and Peace Corps, which vary tremendously with respect to duration, location, program structure, and level of on-site support. The advising process should begin with assisting the student to help clarify his or her options and set realistic expectations for the time abroad.

These are questions that are helpful to cover when advising students.

- Get basic information about the student such as year in school and major.
- Where is the student interested in going?
- What are the student's learning goals?
- How important are finances?
- What are the student's foreign language skills?
- Is the student aware of potential health and safety risks?
- How much on-site support does the student want or need?
- How well defined are the student's long-term goals for his or her major or career?

Ultimately the decision about participation in a WIVA program must be that of the student. The adviser can help students evaluate their options, assessing their knowledge about their opportunities and their readiness to pursue them.

When the student has narrowed down the choice to a few specific programs, there are a number of questions the student should keep in mind when reviewing program information. (See Vetting WIVA Program Providers on NAFSA's website for a more detailed checklist to help you select programs to recommend to students.)

- What services does the WIVA program provide: Placement? Housing? What kind of housing? Work permit/visa assistance? Predeparture orientation?
- For study abroad/academic internship programs, is an internship placement guaranteed, or will you find that out only once you're on site?
- What procedures are in place to manage health, safety and security risks (especially in developing regions)? Does the program provide health and evacuation insurance, or is this provided/required by the student's home institution? How is safety addressed in transportation arrangements? Housing arrangements?
- Is there an on-site resident director present? If not, what kind of on-site support does the program provide?
- Will program participants be together on site as a group, or will the student be the only participant at the internship/service site?
- Can they provide contact information for recent participants? If not, there may be better choices.

Types of Work, Internship, and Volunteer-Abroad Programs
For advising purposes, it is useful to categorize WIVA programs into four types: (1) internships, (2) service learning and volunteering, (3) short-term paid work, and (4) teaching. We'll list a sampling of organizations that have (for the most part) been active in NAFSA, but there are hundreds more. Special education abroad web search engines such as IIEPassport.org, GoAbroad.com, Studyabroad.com, and Transitions Abroad.com have the most comprehensive listings. See additional resources at the end of this chapter.

Internships Abroad

Advising Highlights:
- Most direct connection to career tracks.
- Wide range of location and discipline, equaled only by service learning and volunteer options.
- Depending on a student's major and intended destination, paid internships can be challenging to find. Many engineering internships are paid while most liberal arts internships are unpaid.

- May be combined with study for academic credit, or on a cocurricular basis.

Many students seek internships abroad for the same reasons they seek domestic internships. Internships give insight and, occasionally, entry into global careers. Even those who "try out" a career path this way and decide against it feel the experience is valuable. On the other hand, internships abroad are not always like those in the United States. The assignments can be very demanding, leaving little time to explore the local culture.

Alternatively, an internship may lack structure, and the student may be expected to complete a lot of "busy work" at the expense of professional tasks. The intern may have to demonstrate initiative before being given responsible assignments. The selection process for internships tends to be competitive. An excellent command of the relevant foreign language can be required if the internship is in a non-English-speaking country. Prior related work experience is very helpful. Summer internships remain the most popular. Semester and even year-long internships are available. Short-term programs lasting only a month or two are increasingly available. Internship programs have long offered placements in Europe, where there is a tradition of internships in higher education. Increasingly, programs are expanding their placements to other world regions such as Asia (especially China and India), Africa, and Latin America.

There are three main approaches for students to find internship programs:

1. **Study (or academic) internships,** which are study abroad programs that combine a primary focus on courses with an (often optional) internship, are offered by hundreds of colleges, universities, and provider organizations (see listed examples that follow). These usually offer a group experience, either in classes or through organized social activities. Study internships offer courses and academic credit and may be eligible for financial aid.

2. **Specialized internship organizations** offer placements into cocurricular internships, typically without coursework, which may be paid or unpaid. These are usually not-for-credit experiences, though the student's home institution may be able to offer credit through independent study or internship courses. The advising issues for the student will often center around the scope of services provided by the internship organization (the types of internships available, whether housing is included, visa services, etc.).

3. **Internships directly with employers,** such as corporations, governments, and international organizations, without going through a third-party intermediary. Many of these organizations have formal

recruiting processes, and the advising issues arising with these programs have much in common with issues that concern career advising. For example, students will need to learn how to prepare a culturally appropriate résumé, complete a job application, and practice for an interview. And they will be expected to know what to expect in terms of salary (many of these internships are unpaid).

The following represent a small sampling of the types of internship organizations or programs:

- Study/Academic internship programs, both for and nonprofit, open to students at all colleges and universities, such as *AIFS, CAPA, CEA, CET, CIEE, CIS, Foundation for International Education (FIE), ISA, IES Abroad,* as well as numerous colleges and universities including *Arcadia University, Boston University, Butler IFSA, NYU, Michigan State University, SIT, Syracuse University, University of Minnesota, University of Rochester/EPA,* etc.

- Internship provider organizations offering cocurricular internship placements for a fee, open to all students: *Connect-123, CRCC Asia, Cultural Embrace/API, Cultural Vistas, Global Experiences, Intrax/ProWorld.*

- Program internships with a research and/or technical focus such as *RWTH Aachen University, Earthwatch, German Academic Exchange Service RISE (Germany),* and *NanoJapan International Research Experience for Undergraduates.*

- Government, corporations, and international organizations such as *U.S. State Department, U.S. Commercial Services, United Nations, U.S. State Department's Passport to India* program, *InfoSys* corporation's InStep Program (India). Internships with some of these organizations are very competitive, sometimes for graduate students only, and often unpaid.

- Nongovernmental organizations (NGOs) offer internships at their U.S. offices or overseas for the well qualified; most are accessible through programs offering internships or volunteering and/or service-learning—see below.

- Student-run internship programs *Association Internationale des Etudiants en Sciences Economiques et Commerciales (AIESEC)* and *International Association for the Exchange of Students for Technical Experience (IAESTE)* are longstanding organizations that have student chapters at universities worldwide (including many in the United States); the student chapters develop local internship placements and host incoming interns. Student organizations increasingly offer service trips abroad (see next section below).

Service-Learning and Volunteering Abroad

Advising Highlights

- Defined not by pay or lack of it, but by service at the grassroots level.
- Work is with ordinary local people, often with the underprivileged, rather than professionals.
- Excellent career preparation for those interested in careers working on issues related to developing countries or with nongovernmental organizations.

Traditionally, volunteer work abroad has been seen as service work, helping the underprivileged or underresourced and powerless. Though this still may be true in some cases, today most volunteer organizations see their role as one of solidarity with the people in the host community and their goals—the volunteer's role is more that of learner than helper. Sponsoring organizations run the gamut from the U.S. government's Peace Corps to independent nonsectarian volunteer-sending organizations (VSOs). College-based service-learning programs combine volunteering with coursework and provide academic credit, for which tuition is charged. Last but not least, student organizations increasingly organize their own service trips at home and abroad, e.g., alternative spring breaks (www.alternativebreaks.org). All varieties of short-term service programs have experienced rapid growth in the past two decades, with estimates of up to 1,000,000 Americans volunteering abroad annually; of those, 300,000 were of high-school and college age (see Participation Data above).

Volunteer and service-learning opportunities are available in great variety, ranging from the unskilled to the professional, in virtually all areas of the world. Volunteering is frequently one of the few possibilities for work in developing countries, and it can provide essential career preparation for those interested in development or relief work. The very nature of volunteering provides rich opportunities for cultural immersion with local communities.

On the other hand, service work is not for everyone. Idealistic individuals in particular may be frustrated at being able to do little about conditions they would like to see changed; successful volunteers tend to combine idealism with other goals, such as the desire to learn about other cultures. Culture shock can be severe for sojourners to developing countries who may face real poverty for the first time. Health and safety risks may be high, especially in areas that suffer from high crime rates, drug wars, or are recovering from conflicts or natural disasters.

Special note regarding volunteering in medical settings: Volunteers should never perform medical procedures for which they are unqualified! See the essential resource that University of Minnesota has made available for all, Global Ambassadors for Patient Safety.

The application requirements will vary widely depending on the organization, length, and type of assignment. Summer opportunities are most popular. Volunteer and service-learning programs may last from less than a week, to a semester, to two or three years (for postgraduate programs such as Peace Corps). Volunteer and service-learning programs tend to be offered in less-developed countries, though they also exist in traditional study abroad destinations such as Europe.

These represent a small sampling of the types of organizations with volunteer and service-learning programs:

- Government: Peace Corps (postgraduate; assignments last 27 months).
- Academic institutions offering service-learning programs, as well as most third-party study abroad providers: (see study-internships, above); Northwestern University GESI, Augsburg College, Brethren Colleges Abroad, Higher Education Consortium for Urban Affairs (HECUA), International Partnership for Service Learning, Goshen College, Notre Dame, University of Minnesota Studies in International Development.
- Nonsectarian volunteer-sending organizations such as: Child Family Health International, Cross-Cultural Solutions, Amigos de las Americas, Amizade, BUNAC, Earthwatch, Foundation for Sustainable Development, Global Citizens Network, Global Volunteers, ISA/ELAP, Mobility International, Operation Crossroads Africa, Projects Abroad, ProWorld Service Corps/Intrax, United Planet, World Endeavors.
- Religious affiliated organizations such as: American Friends Service Committee, American Jewish World Service Corps, Brethren Volunteer Service, Habitat for Humanity, Jesuit Volunteer Corps, MASA Israel Journey, Mennonite Central Committee.
- Short-term, inexpensive work camps: Volunteers for Peace (VFP).

Short-Term Paid Work Abroad (Work Permit and Placement Programs)

Advising Highlights

- Most work is typical of summer jobs anywhere, such as restaurant or temp work, although enterprising students can find professionally relevant work.
- Wages can make experience relatively affordable, although there will be up-front costs.
- Participants report satisfaction with the degree of self-sufficiency they have achieved.
- Locations primarily in Europe, Canada, Australia, and New Zealand.

In some cases, students are more interested in the experience of living and working abroad, and are seeking experiences that will support their time abroad. Short-term work abroad can be related to a student's career or major, or it may be intended primarily to support a student for a period of time abroad.

The most common approach to secure short-term paid work is to use a work permit program, such as BUNAC, that provides work permits to students and some assistance in finding a job, often already in-country; it is up to the participant to find the job. These programs can procure a short-term work permit (from 4 to 12 months, depending on the country) that allows students or recent graduates to enter a specific country and seek work of any kind.

Work-placement programs, in contrast, find paid job placements for their participants, along with arranging for work permits. Students may also conduct their own job search in advance, using their personal contacts, typically family or alumni, to secure a position. Even in these instances, students still may need the help of a work permit program to secure a visa to work legally. Students should be informed that working for pay without a work permit is nearly always illegal. The student who arrives with the intent to work, but without a work permit, may risk being put on the next flight home.

Work-permit and -placement programs typically charge fees that are relatively low. Work permits can usually be used for any type of work, including professional-type internships—but not always, depending on the country or program. Nearly all jobs involve cultural immersion because work colleagues are usually local citizens. Since students usually find their own jobs, they have control over their employment situation, and credit themselves with success. Application is noncompetitive.

On the other hand, the uncertainty of arriving without a job deters some students (and parents). Even under the best of circumstances, the stress during the job and apartment hunt can be high. It can be difficult to find internship-like positions. Up-front costs include not only the modest program fees but also the cost of airfare and money for expenses before the first paycheck.

Some examples of work permit programs:

- *BUNAC* (work in Australia, Ireland, and New Zealand, plus intern in Great Britain where placement must be prearranged); *Work and Travel Ireland* (USIT), *Cultural Vistas/IAESTE* (Germany, Switzerland, and many more via IAESTE; Cultural Vistas also offers internship placements), *American-Scandinavian Foundation, Australian Embassy's Work and Holiday visa, New Zealand Embassy's Working Holiday visa.*

Examples of work placement programs:

- *Center for Cultural Interchange/Greenheart, Cultural Embrace by API, InterExchange, STA Travel.*

Teaching Abroad

Advising Highlights

- One of the most accessible long-term (one- to two-year) options for recent graduates; some summer opportunities are available to students.
- Many opportunities available in Asia and Latin America, as well as Europe.
- Teaching or tutoring experience before going highly recommended.

Teaching English remains one of the few long-term overseas positions available to new graduates, especially liberal arts majors. Teaching provides considerable opportunities for cultural immersion, especially for those who have some knowledge of the host country language before going abroad. Although teaching English as a foreign language remains one of the most accessible options for postgraduate work abroad, students should know that most positions require a bachelor's degree and some experience teaching or tutoring English, even if only as a volunteer.

Most positions are in East Asia (Japan, Taiwan, Korea, and China) or Europe. Some are also available in Latin America and Africa. Salaries vary greatly depending on the local economy. Positions in relatively affluent countries in East Asia (Japan, Taiwan, Korea) can pay well. In areas with developing economies, such as China, South and Southeast Asia, Africa, and Latin America, the pay may be high by local standards but low by U.S. standards. Most positions are for an academic year; summer- or semester-long placements are available with some organizations.

For all the attractiveness of teaching English, the student should be advised that most of the working day is spent speaking English, which can make learning the host country language difficult. Some programs give only limited training and on-site support; prospective teachers should come prepared. As an adviser, you should be ready to assist the student with their doing due diligence about any teaching opportunities.

The following is a sample list of programs that provide teaching opportunities abroad:

- **Governments:** *U.S. Peace Corps* places teachers of English as a Foreign Language (EFL) in many world regions. The *Japan Exchange and Teaching Program* (JET) recruits EFL teachers through Japanese consulates. Similar programs are administered by the governments of Chile, Czech Republic, France, Spain, South Korea, and Georgia.

- **Exchange programs:** *Fulbright English Teaching Assistantships*—this program has greatly expanded in the past decade, and is currently offered in nearly 70 countries worldwide; future teachers preferred.
- **Universities and education-abroad program providers:** *CIEE Teach Abroad, CCI/Greenheart, Cultural Embrace by API, Princeton-in-Asia, Marshall University, and Western Washington University* offer programs that place teachers into paying positions.
- **Volunteer organizations:** Many nonprofit organizations assist in placing EFL teachers abroad. Teachers will be expected to cover the cost of airfare and a placement fee. Examples include *VIA and WorldTeach*. Many volunteer organizations offer short-term EFL placements (see previous section).
- **Private language schools:** Several chains recruit from the United States for their overseas branches, including *AEON* (Japan) and Hess (Taiwan).

Institutional Context, the Relationship Between Advising and Amount of Administrative Commitment — Before, During, and After the Student Is Abroad

When it comes to specific options, the advice you give may well depend on your institutional context: do you work for a study/education abroad office located in academic affairs; or for an international office, career, or community service office located in student affairs; or perhaps not within a campus environment but for a provider? Does your office administer its own programs, or does it primarily provide advice and resources—or in some cases, both?

Regardless of one's institutional reporting structure, as documented above, a unifying principle for best practice appears to be emerging from outcomes research, namely, that student learning is maximized when there's extensive predeparture orientation combined with reflection while students are abroad, followed by further opportunities for recognition and reflection upon return. In that light, consider the following variations on advising, depending on the institutional context. Note that all these varieties of advising might be possible in the same office: an office that administers study abroad programs might also provide basic information on WIVA opportunities offered by external organizations; an office that administers an internship program may also provide basic advice about academic programs abroad.

Does your office report to academic affairs or student affairs? This may mean that your primary mandate is to provide advice on either credit-bearing or cocurricular options abroad, but perhaps not both.

Amount of Commitment of Resources to Advising or Administration

A very significant factor in your advising work will be the extent to which your office primarily provides information and advising, or primarily administers programs, or a combination anywhere along this continuum. It may even include all of these at the same time.

Low Commitment of Institutional Resources (Primarily Advising Only)

- **Advising:** Typically one-time contact only, consisting mostly of providing basic information and resources rather than in-depth advising and preparation.
- **Providing information on programs:** Referrals to external programs, perhaps via websites of other colleges or universities that offer work, internship, and volunteer abroad programs or sites specifically for program listings.
- **Health and safety:** If there are home campus procedures in place, one's advising will need to be integrated into them; but some campuses may have little health and safety infrastructure. Referrals to external sources (such as U.S. State Department) for information for health and safety, health insurance; no tracking of participants.
- **Funding:** Not offered except via financial aid office, which is available only to educational activities for-credit (study, internships, or service-learning for academic credit).
- **Staffing:** Adviser positions may be divided between several responsibilities, such as advising for study abroad, career services, a community service or service-learning office; or a faculty member doing advising alongside teaching responsibilities.
- **Assessment:** Surveys of past participants; vetting directly with providers and via professional colleagues.

Medium Commitment of Institutional Resources

- **Advising:** Time-intensive and may involve multiple appointments over time.
- **Preparation/orientation:** May involve an internship or service-learning course, or multiple cocurricular workshops.
- **Health and safety, tracking:** Full integration into campus health and safety infrastructure, including tracking of participants while abroad and making emergency assistance available to them. (For an example of a fully-developed, comprehensive health and safety infrastructure, see University of Michigan's Global Michigan site).
- **Heath and Safety, insurance:** Full integration into campus-contracted health insurance for students traveling abroad.

- **Large-scale events:** International opportunities fair and panel presentations about global career tracks and how to get started on them.
- **Learning:** Ideally, structuring of experiential learning takes place before departure (preparatory courses or workshops), while abroad (reflection, blogging, individual guidance, perhaps in-person reflection when possible), and after return to campus (academic work from papers to theses, presentations, peer advising, recognitions, development of portfolio).
- **Assessment of outcomes:** May use instruments such as the GPI or IDI, administered pre- and postexperience, perhaps with control group for comparison.
- **Program referrals:** Referrals to carefully vetted programs for placements into internship and volunteer/service placements; these may sometimes be formally affiliated with the campus via MOUs; programs may be offered by home-campus faculty or departments, or may be offered by external third-party providers.
- **Finances/grants and scholarships for students:** The institution offers competitive grants for students who want to do research, internships, or service abroad; where program is for academic credit, financial aid is made fully available.
- **Staffing:** Adviser positions will usually be devoted to education abroad.

High Commitment of Institutional Resources (Same as Medium, In Addition to the Following)

- **Program advising:** Placements for internships and volunteer/service are developed by a sponsoring campus office; advising would usually direct student toward these programs (perhaps exclusively so, depending on protocol).
- **Placements:** May be individual or group-based.
- **On-site presence:** Often, there will be a faculty director, on-site director, or arranged-for local contact person; home-campus administrators make site visits where possible.
- **Housing:** Housing arrangements will typically be provided, and may range from special group accommodations to family homestays to apartments.
- **Finances (option a)—Grants, fellowships, scholarships:** Full funding that covers all expenses of the student is provided; variations on this are possible, such as funding being need-based or available via competitive application.
- **Finances (option b)—Fees:** Fees are charged to the student to cover all expenses; this will include tuition in cases where the program is

for-credit. Where fees are charged, financial aid and/or scholarships should be available.

- **Finances (option c)—Co-op model:** Most often found in engineering and business, co-op placements are typically paid while also earning academic credit.
- **Staffing:** Adviser positions will also have administrative responsibilities for managing placements abroad, or there may be specialized administrative positions.

Campus Partners

Your campus partners may include some or all of these: study/education abroad office; career services; internship, co-op or service-learning offices; faculty members; academic departments; legal counsel; risk management; health and safety oversight committee; campus health services; institutional research office; alumni association.

External Resources

External resources can include other colleges and universities that advise for WIVA experiences; and professional associations such as NAFSA—especially NAFSA's EA-KC Subcommittee on Work, Internships, and Volunteering Abroad (WIVA), the Forum on Education Abroad, National Association of Colleges and Employers, National Society for Experiential Education, the International Volunteer Programs Association, the Global Internship Conference and others; program providers; health and safety information providers such as the U.S. State Department (http://travel.state.gov) and OSAC (http://www.osac.gov); and health insurance providers.

Conclusion

Research demonstrates that the many benefits to participants of work abroad programs are very similar to the benefits of study abroad—only more pronounced! Campus-based offices, working in tandem with campus partners and external resources, should seek strategies to incorporate work abroad advising into their services so that all students can benefit from the availability of the full spectrum of education abroad options, with the goal of enabling students to take significant steps toward shaping their future in a globalized world.

Further Reading

Brockington, J., W. Hoffa, P. Martin. 2005. *NAFSA's Guide to Education Abroad for Advisers and Administrators, Third Edition.* Washington, DC: NAFSA: Association of International Educators.

Bringle, R. G., J. A. Hatcher, and S. G. Jones. 2011. *International Service Learning: Conceptual Frameworks and Research.* Sterling, VA: Stylus Publishing.

Butin, D. W. 2010. *Service-Learning in Theory and Practice: The Future of Community Engagement in Higher Education.* New York: St. Martin's Press.

Carland, M. and C. Faber. 2008. *Careers in International Affairs.* Washington, DC: Georgetown University Press.

Chisholm, L. 2005. *Knowing and Doing: The Theory and Practice of Service-Learning.* New York: International Partnership for Service Learning.

Collins, J., S. DeZerega, and Z. Heckscher. 2002. *How to Live Your Dream of Volunteering Overseas.* New York: Penguin Publishing.

Damast, A. 2010. "Interns Head Abroad for Work Experience." *Business Week,* March 29, 1-2.

Dorman, S. 2011. *Inside a U.S. Embassy: Diplomacy at Work.* Washington, DC: American Foreign Service Association.

Grandin, J. 2006. Preparing Engineers for the Global Workplace: The University of Rhode Island. *The Online Journal for Global Engineering Education* 1:1, 1-8.

Grandin, J. 1991. Developing Internships in Germany for International Engineering Students. *Die Unterrichtspraxis/Teaching German* 24:2, 209-214.

Griffith, S. 2012. *Teaching English Abroad: Your Expert Guide to Teaching English Around the World. Surrey,* UK: Crimson Publishing.

Hachmyer, C. 2008. *Alternatives to the Peace Corps: A Guide to Global Volunteer Opportunities.* Oakland, CA: Food First Books

Hindle, C. R. Collinson, M. Richard, K. Miller, S. Wintle, N. Cavalieri 2010. *Lonely Planet Volunteer: A Traveller's Guide to Making a Difference Around the World.* Oakland, CA: Lonely Planet Publications.

Hoffa, W. 2006. "A Chronology of the History of Study Abroad in US Higher Education." *Frontiers: The Interdisciplinary Journal of Study Abroad,* 291-304.

Hoffa, W. and J. Pearson. 1997. *NAFSA's Guide to Education Abroad for Advisers and Administrators, Second Edition.* Washington, DC: NAFSA: Association of International Educators.

Hoffa, W., J. Pearson, and M. Slind. 1993. *NAFSA's Guide to Education Abroad for Advisers and Administrators.* Washington, DC: NAFSA: Association of International Educators.

Klingelhofer, W. 1989. *The Harvard Guide to International Experience.* Cambridge, MA: Harvard University Office of Career Services.

Matherly, C. and W. Nolting. March 2007. "Educational Experiences Abroad: Preparation for a Globalized Workplace." *NACE Journal*, 14-20,44.

Matherly, C. and S. Phillips. 2011. "NanoJapan: Preparing Globally Savvy Science and Engineering Researchers." *IIENetworker March*, 39-40.

Mueller, S. and M. Overmann. 2008. *Working World: Careers in International Education, Exchange, and Development*. Washington, DC: Georgetown University Press.

Operation Crossroads Africa. 2012. *What Is Operation Crossroads?* Accessed September 5, 2012, http://operationcrossroadsafrica.org/.

Paige, M. and G. Fry. 2012. *Beyond Immediate Impact: Study Abroad for Global Engagement*. The University of Minnesota. Accessed September 5, 2014, www.calstate.edu/engage/documents/study-abroad-for-global-engagement.pdf

Slimbach, R. 2010. *Becoming World Wise: A Guide to Global Learning*. Sterling, VA: Stylus Publishing.

Stanton, T. G. 1999. *Service-Learning: A Movement's Pioneers Reflect on Its Origins, Practice and Future*. San Francisco, CA: Jossey-Bass.

Stark, R. and B. Bicknell. 2011. *How to Work in Someone Else's Country*. Seattle, WA: University of Washington Press.

Steinberg, M. 2002. "Involve Me and I Will Understand, Academic Quality in Experiential Programs Abroad." *Frontiers: The Interdisciplinary Journal of Study Abroad* VIII:Winter, 207-229.

Tonkin, H. 2004. *Service Learning Across Cultures: Promise and Achievement*. New York: International Partnership for Service Learning.

True, M. 2011. *InternQube: Professional Skills for the Workplace*. Mechanicsburg PA: Intrueition, LLC, www.intrueition.com.

Vandeberg, M. 2009. "Intervening in Student Learning Abroad: A Research-Based Inquiry." *Intercultural Education*, 15-27.

Volunteers in Asia (VIA) 2012. *History of VIA*. Accessed September 5, 2012, www.viaprograms.org.

References

Abrams, I. 1979. "The Impact of Antioch Education Through Experience Abroad." *Alternative Higher Education*, 176-187.

Association of American Colleges and Universities (AACU). 2012. *Liberal Education and America's Promise*. Accessed September 18, 2012: http://www.aacu.org/leap/.

Association Internationale des Etudiants en Sciences Economiques et Commerciales (AIESEC) 2008. *60 Years of Activating Youth Leadership.* Rotterdam: AIESEC International.

American Council on Education. 2008. *College-Bound Students' Interest in Study Abroad and Other International Learning Activities.* Washington, DC: The American Council on Education.

Association for Experiential Education. 2012. *What Is Experiential Education?* Accessed January 20, 2012, www.aee.org/what-is-ee.

BUNAC 2012. *What Is BUNAC.* Accessed January 13, 2012, http://oldwebsite. bunac.org/uk/about/whoIsBUNAC.aspx.

Cultural Vistas. 2012. *CDS About Us.* Accessed January 13, 2012, www.cdsintl. org/aboutus/missionvision.php.

Forum on Education Abroad. 2012. *Education Abroad Glossary.* Accessed September 4, 2012, www.forumea.org/educationabroadglossary2ndedition2011. cfm.

Forum on Education Abroad. 2011a. *A Tenth Anniversary Celebration.* Carlisle, PA: Forum on Education Abroad.

Forum on Education Abroad. 2011b. *Standards of Good Practice for Education Abroad.* Carlisle, PA: Forum on Education Abroad.

Frontiers. 2002. *Frontiers: The Interdisciplinary Journal of Study Abroad* Winter, 2002.

Georgia Institute of Technology. 2005. *Strengthening Global Competence and Research Experiences of Undergraduates.* Atlanta, GA: Georgia Institute of Technology.

Gerken, M., Bart Rienties, Bas Giesbers, and Karen D. Könings. 2012. "Enhancing the Academic Internship Learning Experience for Business Education: A Critical Review and Future Directions." In *Learning at the Crossroads of Theory and Practice.* Dordrecht, The Netherlands: Springer.

International Association for the Exchange of Students for Technical Experience (IAESTE) 2012. Accessed January 13, 2012, www.iaeste.org/about/history.

Institute for International Education. 2012. *Open Doors: Report on International Educational Exchange.* New York: Institute for International Education.

Institute for International Education. 2011. *Open Doors: Report on International Educational Exchange.* New York: Institute for International Education.

Institute for International Education. 2004. *Open Doors: Report on International Educational Exchange.* New York: Institute for International Education.

International Volunteer Programs Association (IVPA). 2012. *Who We Are.* Accessed January 13, 2012, www.volunteerinternational.org/whoweare. html.

Kuh, G. 2008. *High-Impact Educational Practices: What They Are, Who Has Access to Them, and Why They Matter.* Washington, DC: Association of American Colleges and Universities.

Lough, B. 2012. *International Volunteerism in the United States, 2004-2012.* St. Louis, MO: Washington University Center for Social Development.

McBride, A. M., B. J. Lough, and M. S. Sherraden. 2010. *Perceived Impacts of International Service on Volunteers.* Washington, DC: Brookings Institute.

National Association of Colleges and Employers (NACE). 2012. *Global Campus Recruitment Symposium.* Accessed September 1, 2012, http:// www.naceweb.org/uploadedFiles/NACEWeb/Events/2012_Global_Recruit-ment_Campus_Summit/GS_Program_2012.pdf.

National Society of Experiential Education. 2012. *About Us.* Retrieved January 13, 2012, from National Society for Experiential Education: www.nsee.org/about_us.htm.

National Society of Experiential Education. 2011. *Eight Principles of Good Practice for All Experiential Learning Activities.* Accessed August 30, 2012, www.nsee.org/standards-and-practice.

Nolting, W., Donohue, D., Matherly, C. and Tillman, M. 2013. *Internships, Service Learning, and Volunteering Abroad: Successful Models and Best Practices.* NAFSA. (Interactive PDF).

Nolting, W., M. Johnson, and C. Matherly. 2005. "Work Abroad and International Careers." *NAFSA's Guide to Education Abroad for Advisers and Administrators, Third Edition,* 312-339. Washington, DC: NAFSA: Association of International Educators.

Pagano, M. and L. Roselle. 2009. "Beyond Reflection Through an Academic Lens: Refraction and International Experiential Education." *Frontiers: The Journal of Interdisciplinary Research* XVIII:Fall, 217-229.

Peace Corps 2012. *A Proud History, An Ever-Changing World.* Accessed September 14, 2012, www.peacecorps.gov/about/history/.

University of Cincinnati. 2012. *Division of Professional Practice.* Accessed August 30, 2012, http://www.uc.edu/propractice.html.

University of Michigan International Center. 2012. *2011 Statistical Report: International Students, Scholars, Faculty, Staff and Education Abroad.* Ann Arbor: The University of Michigan.

Whitney, B. and Clayton. 2011. "Research on and Thorough Reflection in International Service Learning." *International Service Learning: Conceptional Frameworks and Research,* 145-187. Sterling, VA: Stylus.

CHAPTER 16

PROGRAM ADMINISTRATION

By Angela Shaeffer

Introduction

Each institution's[1] international education opportunities evolve over time, and most offer program portfolios that look much different today than they did 20—or even 10—years ago. Administrators who are considering, or charged with creating, new program avenues, will want to have a firm understanding of their institutions' program history. Making an effort to understand the history of programs at an institution will also help the administrator return to "square one" of program planning: The program's objectives, goals, and institutional fit.

The evolution of an institution's program portfolio is often a result of strategic plans that have shaped the institution. An administrator may be involved in the development of such a strategic plan, or the administrator may enter into a role at an institution that has prioritized internationalization for quite a while. The program provider for which an administrator works may plan to expand to countries newly popular among study abroad students. An administrator may find him or herself working with a program that is already in the planning phase, but has not yet begun, and must see this program through implementation. An understanding of the history of an institution's programming helps contextualize the administrator's role throughout program development and management.

International educators often tell sojourning students that the only certainty is no certainty. "Expect the unexpected" probably appears, in some form or wording, in most predeparture guides. The same notion applies for program administrators. What works one year, may not work as well the next. Institutions continue to adapt to the changing needs of students; study abroad programming must respond to changing demands as well.

Program administration, from the development phase to postprogram, can seem an overwhelming task. This chapter provides information that will help administrators consider their approach to program management, informed by best practices and resources from across the international education field. "Administrators" in this chapter are defined as international educators

---

[1] Institution here includes program providers, schools of higher education, and other organizations offering international learning opportunities.

involved in various phases or processes regarding programming abroad, and includes but is not limited to senior staff, faculty, and education abroad professionals.

Strategic Planning for Successful Programs

An institutional strategic plan that includes internationalization or diversification of international programming catalyzes program development. However, an international office—or, from a provider or organizational perspective, the program development department—does well to create its own strategic plan for program administration. This chapter does not provide a model vision for an office's strategic plan. Rather, this section presents the questions and critical issues that should be addressed—or, in the case of an existing program portfolio being evaluated, questions and issues that deserve revisiting—by program administrators.

Articulating Institutional Vision

Whatever the "why," the first step in moving forward with planning and administering successful programs is the establishment of the institutional vision. The vision for programs should be mission-driven, and should be made transparent to all stakeholders.[2] Margaret Heisel and Robert Stableski (2009) recommend that institutions "conceive and articulate a mission and goal for study abroad" as a first step in building international program capacity (32). As research in international education continues to grow, still "little agreement about what each type of program should achieve" exists (33).

The establishment of learning outcomes and goals for students can help to drive this vision. Tracy Rundstrom Williams (2009) reveals Texas Christian University's determination of desired learning outcomes for study abroad participants as part of its strategic planning process. Desired outcomes at TCU addressed increased understanding of international and cultural issues; increased flexibility; increased open-mindedness and curiosity; and enhanced critical skills. Not only did the outcomes help to drive program development and administration, but they also provided a framework for TCU's post-program assessments and student evaluations.

Centralization and Decentralization:
Impact on Program Administration

Considering a centralized versus a decentralized approach to international program management—and thus development and administration—is a first

---

[2]The term stakeholders, as used throughout this chapter, refers to institutional offices, partners, and on-site staff.

step in designing a strategic plan. The approach may depend on a number of factors as varied as: (1) the capacity of the international programs office, (2) the administrator's role on campus (perhaps they are a faculty member and a study abroad coordinator, or oversee both study abroad and international student services), (3) how program administration has played out over the years on the campus, and (4) the inclusion—or exclusion—of internationalization in the institution's overall strategic plan.

Generally speaking, centralization means that one office oversees all aspects of international program administration. Decentralization tends to mean that academic departments offer their own programs, or students participate in noninstitutional programs and might consult with their registrar offices to process transfer credits. Each approach brings its own benefits and challenges. An administrator's knowledge of her institution's approach (centralization versus decentralization) informs program administration in terms of students' needs, for program approval, transfer of credits, and advising of study abroad (if advising is available). Other departments involved in the study abroad process—financial aid, legal counsel—should also be fully aware of the approach taken, and the administrator may need to keep all relevant parties informed of the processes if a decentralized approach has made communication across the institution sparse in terms of education abroad planning and processes.

Regardless of the approach a campus has instituted in the way of education abroad processes, a program administration office can clearly outline its role, as well as the roles of other offices and individuals, on a website. Clarion University provides a web page titled "Planning and Implementing a Study Abroad Program," for example. On the website, the university's office of international programs specifies its role in program development and walks prospective faculty leaders through the process of proposing study abroad programs (Clarion University 2013).

At the risk of seemingly advocating for centralization, one office or person should update all other stakeholders on campus—including the student body—when changes to the process occur.

Program Models

Without repeating information in previous chapters, this brief section on program models reiterates the basic program models that exist in international education, while also acknowledging that most of these models exist in institutionally created, provider-sponsored, and partnership versions. Generally speaking, three program models exist; these are listed below. For a much more in-depth list of the types of program models that exist, refer to the

Forum for Education Abroad's Education Abroad Glossary, under "Education Abroad Program Features and Types," in addition to chapter 14 of this guide.

- Short-term programs (sometimes called faculty-led programs)
    - These often take place in summer or winter ("mini-mesters")
- Semester and year-long programs, which include:
    - Exchange programs, in which students attend a university abroad
    - Direct enroll, in which students directly enroll in a foreign university
    - Island programs, in which the students attend classes with each other at a center and generally away from a foreign university (and are sometimes faculty-led)
    - Hybrid programs, which combine direct enroll and island program characteristics (and may also be led by faculty)
- WIVA: Work, internship, and volunteer abroad programs
    - May or may not bear credit
    - Often short-term (winter or summer)

A previous edition of the *Guide to Education Abroad* asked, "With so many established programs in place, the first question [when planning a program] is, does your institution need another? ... Setting up a new program means a major investment of human and financial resources." Furthermore, creating new programs: "represents a commitment that has to be sustained, perhaps over a long period of time, often in changing circumstances" (Hoffa, Pearson, and Slind 1993, 157). Clearly, this question remains worth asking when an institution considers adding programs, especially given the increased number of program possibilities and providers since the early 1990s.

A successful strategic plan for building programs should consider various program model options. Most institutions' international program portfolios include various program models. Regardless of the program models an administrator chooses moving forward, it's important to understand the reasons behind those models being chosen, and to revisit the models regularly to make sure they remain the best fit for an institution.

Managing Relationships

Program development and administration go beyond the partnerships that develop programs on the ground abroad. An administrator will need to work with other campus offices dealing with finances and financial aid, legal counsel, academics and transcripts, enrollment management, residence life and housing, and international students. Therefore, as an administrator develops a program, or makes changes to an existing program, efforts should be made to consult with these departments about how the new or revised program might impact what the latter do.

Regardless of the program model(s), an administrator will be creating relationships outside of his or her organization as well. These relationships include partnerships with program providers, and also less-obvious relationships such as transportation companies abroad, or landlords and housing managers, or maintenance companies if the institution has its own facilities abroad. A thorough administrator considers the approach to communication within these relationships.

Successful management of relationships begins with the acknowledgement that an international or program development office is not the only one impacted by the development of new programs. The payoff may be more support from administration and faculty, which is one of Wendy Williamson's "7 Signs of Successful Study-Abroad Programs" (2010). Additionally, when working with partners abroad, an administrator will want to consider how to communicate institutional interests and queries. This acknowledgment should be recognized in some capacity in any strategic plan for building up programs.

Strategic Planning Checklist[1]

Whatever direction an administrator takes in terms of program models, or creating relationships, they should consider the following critical issues moving forward in designing a strategic plan for program administration.

1. Determine need(s) for programs
2. Gauge institutional resources
3. Explore territory/regions of interest (both "old" and "new")
4. Iron out details with stakeholders
5. Plan to publicize and promote both the programs and the processes
6. Ethical Considerations

In its 2011 Code of Ethics, The Forum for Education Abroad suggests six important principals to guide program administration. Successful international educators employ the following ethical considerations throughout program administration.

1. Truthfulness and transparency
2. Responsibility to students
3. Relationships with host societies
4. Observance of best practices
5. Conflicts of interest

---

[3]Adapted from Hoffa et al., "List of Critical Questions to Ask" (167–8) when planning and implementing new programs.

In a previous edition of the *Code of Ethics*, the Forum for Education Abroad also advised administrators to be careful when considering gifts, gratuities, discounts, rebates, and compensation as terms of negotiating programs abroad.

Making a Go of It: Planning for Programs

Successful program administration begins in the program development phase. A clear outline of a program includes administrative and logistical infrastructure (both at the home institution and host site), communication plans, ways of preparing participants (including faculty members), and keeping all stakeholders updated about the program as it is in progress.

Establishing Infrastructure and Finding Balance

Nancy Conrad and George C. Morrison encourage program administrators to consider four "Key Considerations when Implementing, Expanding, or Administering a Study Abroad Program" (2013): Program structure, contractual relationships, immigration and taxation, and student conduct and extraterritorial application of U.S. law. Program administrators do not need to be experts in all or any of these key areas, necessarily; however, educators seeking to establish an international program should be mindful of these aspects and collaborate with offices or departments that can offer further guidance in these matters of importance, such as legal counsel, human resources, or designated school officials (DSOs).

Before establishing programs, administrators should consider two kinds of infrastructure. Administrative infrastructure addresses program coordination at the home institution, and includes (but is not limited to) the following questions:

- **Participant applications:** Who will publicize the program? How will applications be collected, evaluated, and shared with overseas partners (if applicable)? How will students' special needs be addressed and/or accommodated?
- **Logistics:** When will logistical arrangements (airfare, accommodations, excursions, guest lecturers, etc.) be made? Who will make them? How will they be invoiced/paid? Regarding visas and entry documents, what must the home institution provide to students?
- **Academics:** What are the learning goals and objectives of the program? Will the program be limited to certain academic disciplines? What is the academic capacity of the host site (i.e., what disciplines are possible)? How will academic departments be involved in approving or not approving credit and curricula?

- **Cross-campus considerations:** For semester students: When will the registrar be notified of their "absence" from campus and the need for "placeholder" credits? Who will notify residence life of the students who will be leaving campus, or the need for housing for inbound exchange students? With respect to financial aid: When will financial aid packages be released to sojourning students? With respect to human resources: If on-site staff will be hired, how will the hiring process be impacted by hiring policies/practices in the host country? In what currency will these employees be paid? Will benefits remain the same abroad for on-site employees? With respect to information technology: Will students have access to library resources, scholarly databases, and institutional e-mail abroad? Will employees on-site have access to institutional databases, etc.?
- **Preparation/Orientation:** When will this take place? Who will deliver the predeparture orientation(s)? How will sojourning faculty leaders be trained?

The host site infrastructure setup addresses similar questions, but from a different perspective, and includes but is not limited to:

- **Participant needs:** What will be put in place to accommodate students' needs?
- **Logistics:** Who will make on-the-ground arrangements for transportation, excursions, accommodations, orientation, events, etc.? How will these arrangements be paid for? Will the institution have a bank account in-country? Will the institution use wire transfers? Will additional insurance need to be purchased for faculty and/or students? Will students need to have specific documents from the host site in order to get visas/entry documents? Are work-study students eligible for employment on-site?
- **Academics:** What about the site makes it possible or ideal for the study of certain disciplines? Will all activities be for-credit?
- **Cross-campus considerations:** Who will communicate with the home institution when a student drops a course? Withdraws from the program? Breaks the code of conduct?
- **Preparation/orientation:** Who will help students assimilate by getting cell phones, bank accounts, having cultural excursions? What will orientation look like and include? Will faculty and students have on-site support throughout the program? Will they communicate needs to the home institution or to someone on site who acts as a liaison with the home institution? Do on-site coordinators need to help students register with local jurisdictions in order to complete host country entry requirements?

When considering program structure on site, international educators may feel conflicted between decisions. Lilli Engle and John Engle (2003) discuss the different "levels" of cultural exposure and immersion that exist in the world of education abroad programming; in their research, to know and understand the different program levels is to design programs that meet the needs and expectations of students and faculty on-site in the host countries. Balance may not be easy to find in terms of what would create the most culturally engaged program and the program that is most secure or takes less of an administrative toll on the home and/or host institution. Take homestays, for example, as a possibility for accommodations. Host families may offer students once-in-a-lifetime intercultural experiences, an opportunity to see a household in motion in a different cultural context. However, the variability between hosts—in terms of distance to the academic center, Internet access, hospitality of the hosts, and other factors—can contribute to unevenness in the student experience. Consistency is more difficult to control and provide when variability such as this is in play.

Many international educators do not believe that students should study abroad with expectations of consistency—as mentioned earlier in this section, "expect the unexpected" is a common mantra in the world of international education. However, from an administrative perspective, consistency offers legal, financial, and quality assurance benefits. Thus, when considering the building up of local infrastructure, program administrators should determine clear goals that help drive the design of the program and therefore the infrastructure needed on site. Balance is possible, but only when the administrator planning a program has fully considered program infrastructure at home and abroad.

Expectations and Standards of Communication

Clear lines of communication should exist between the institution and host sites abroad as well as other campus offices. Communication plans for successful program administration can include the following:

- How will the home institution be notified when students arrive to the host site? Will this information be communicated to parents as well as stakeholders on campus?
- Who will be notified if a student experiences an emergency abroad? If insurance will be involved in the emergency—e.g., if a student is in the hospital and a parent must travel to be with him/her—who liaises with the insurance company?
- If a student's enrollment changes, how will the home institution be notified?
- Social networking: Will the program have a presence on a social network? Will this presence be overseen by the home institution, or

someone on site with students? What information will be communicated via this social network presence? Who will be invited to be part of the network?

- With traveling programs, will the home institution be updated on programs in progress at regular intervals?
- How will the host site (including traveling faculty leaders) be contacted if the home institution must communicate with them? What is acceptable via e-mail, and what is acceptable via phone call?
- Focus on the positive: Communication strategies can also include positive program or student updates. A partner or on-site coordinator may also want to notify the host institution of interesting projects or experiences

Logistical Preparations

As with infrastructure establishment and communication strategies, logistics depend on the type of program implemented. The answers to the questions listed will change according to the nature of the program. A checklist of logistical preparations might address—but is not limited to—the following:

- **Acceptance notifications:** How will students be notified of their acceptance to the program, and what information will they receive at that time? What information may come later?
- **Accommodations:** Who is making arrangements for accommodations for students and faculty? (Remember, some programs allow or require students to find their own housing.) Do accommodations meet the needs of students and faculty?
- **Transportation:** If housing is not located near the academic program site, who makes transportation arrangements? Is airfare included in the program cost? Are participants traveling alone or as a group? Has transportation (airlines, charter companies) been vetted and considered safe?
- **Academics:** Are participants enrolled in courses? Who enrolls them? Will they know their course schedule before they arrive to the host site? Will the students be receiving credit for the work abroad? What is the credit approval process?
- **Crisis management:** Is a crisis management plan in place? Do people at the home institution and host sites know this plan and understand their roles?
- **Reentry:** Are reentry plans and activities (reentry workshops overseas, or upon arrival back to the United States) in place to help participants reassimilate once returned from their program?

Many offices approach logistical preparation by dividing tasks. Perhaps the office leader—a director, a vice president, an associate dean, or provost—builds program infrastructure and establishes communication strategies, while those that they manage—assistant/associate directors, advisers, coordinators—oversee logistical coordination of programs, further delegating specific tasks such as group flight arrangements, hotel bookings, and invoice payments to their supervisees (program assistants, office managers). Of course, this approach assumes that an office administering programs includes more than one person (or that one or two people are able to take on the roles of many); one-person offices, however, may still find utility in the above-listed considerations.

Preparing Faculty and Staff

Faculty and staff may enter the program arena from a number of corners. Some faculty have run short-term programs for many years, or have been heavily involved in setting up a departmental flagship program; some academic departments have run programs independently, but must then work with an international programs office when an institution's strategic plan includes centralization of international programming. Likewise, an institution may in the past have required students to take a leave of absence for noninstitutional program participation, but then implements a new policy requiring all students to remain enrolled while abroad on credit-bearing programs. Many institutions are moving toward centralizing various aspects of education abroad. A successful administrator understands the perspectives faculty and other institutional staff hold, especially as policies change to accommodate centralized coordination of campus internationalization.

Preparing on-site faculty and staff requires a different approach than preparing faculty and staff at the home institution. Preparation of on-site faculty and staff should include risk assessment and crisis management, and host site–specific logistical and infrastructure information. Preparation of faculty and staff that is not traveling to the host site, but is involved with administrative aspects of the program institutionally—approving credit, distributing financial aid—is less intense, but equally important in planning a successful program abroad.

The program administrator should emphasize the need for risk management planning to education abroad–involved faculty and staff early in the program planning process. By involving institutional offices, such as legal counsel and the dean of students, in risk assessment and program preparation, the administrator ensures that even those not traveling abroad feel as though they have had an opportunity to voice their thoughts throughout the planning process. Engaged stakeholders are more likely to offer support when emergencies arise, or when their input is needed later during the course of a program in progress.

Orientations

Successful programs orient students both in predeparture and on site. Predeparture orientations range from online modules to full-day retreats addressing a variety of topics, including safety and security while abroad, remaining engaged academically, culture shock and difference, currency conversion, identity definition and concerns, dealing with homesickness, and many others. Similarly, on-site orientations vary depending on the type of program. In a direct-enrollment program, a student may take part in a brief orientation geared toward all international students at the host institution, both exchange and full-degree. Other programs may include 2- to 3-day orientations onsite that involve city tours, visits to host campus facilities, and cultural excursions.

Though administrators may not have control over all aspects of the predeparture or on-site orientation, best practice involves an understanding of the type of information that students will receive in both. Once this information is known, the program administrator can make an effort to assist students in understanding where they can find any missing pieces, or can provide it in orientation sessions in which they do have oversight. And though repetition is not necessarily a bad thing, an administrator's awareness of what is covered so that the orientations complement rather than repeat each other will ensure students receive necessary information in various ways.

Successful programs also orient faculty and staff and include them in student orientations. Faculty members may have familiarity with certain host sites and can give more in-depth, site-specific information, or more detailed expectations in terms of academics. Legal counsel can serve to reiterate that when a student breaks the code of conduct, that student poses risk not only to themselves in terms of judicial action, but also to the institution. Residence life may be able to speak about tactfully working through difficult cross-cultural conflicts; no doubt, they see their own fair share of conflicts when students arrive to campus and must learn to live with roommates. Instead of excluding these departments or offices, including other institutional offices in orientation for faculty or students also increases the investment or feeling of involvement in the study abroad process.

Tracking Plans for a Program in Progress (PIP)

Prior to departure, the program administrator should plan how they will manage or oversee the program. Though programs differ in lengths, administrators should set similar benchmarks at regular intervals throughout programs. Benchmarks might include ensuring that all participants have arrived safely;

making sure housing invoices are paid; checking in regularly with site staff and faculty; requiring enrollment reports in order to communicate necessary information to registrar and financial aid offices; and, toward the end of the time abroad, making sure students have communicated any necessary information—housing preferences, enrollment deposits for the following term—to the home institution.

While checking in with programs in progress allows the administrator to remind students and faculty of institutional obligations, it also serves as a reminder that in the world of international education, the concept of "out of sight, out of mind" does not apply. If students and on-site staff or partners feel that a program administrator has remained invested in the program while in progress, they may feel more comfortable coming to the administrator in times of need or with ideas that can help the program improve in the future. Regular check-ins serve as a reminder that the institution is invested in the participants and program and can provide continuity throughout its phases.

Go Time: Implementation and On-site Administration

Orientation On Site

Many variables factor in to the orientation that is delivered in country. A short-term, faculty-led program that will travel to three or four destinations, possibly even different countries, should be organized quite differently from the orientation for a semester-long direct-enrollment program. Regardless of the type of program, on-site orientations should cover the following five topics:

1. Program-specific academic policies
2. Behavioral policies/program code of conduct
3. Site-specific health, safety, and emergency information
4. Cultural introduction to the host region
5. Logistical information (bank accounts, transportation in the region, housing, etc.)

While the best predeparture orientation will address these topics to an extent, having the students both receive and experience this information on site will further realize their study abroad experience.

Housing

Housing should be fully vetted prior to programs taking place. The program administrator, along with legal counsel and possibly staff from residence life at her institution, will need to define what "fully vetted" implies. Additionally, understanding the Clery Act, which requires campuses to report crime incidents that occur on and around campuses will be an important part of this process.[4] Some institutions require that site visits take place before housing can be arranged for students on site for a program; other institutions consider star-rating systems when considering housing options (particularly for hotels and "bed and breakfasts"); still, others rely on the evaluation of housing done by on-site partners. Whatever vetting system used or required to determine housing options for a program, the following should be addressed:

- Convenience to academic coursework site (institution, academic study center)
- Catering options: self-catering (kitchen access), available cafeteria, meal plan, or access to grocery stores
- Safety and security
- Accessibility for students with special needs
- Internet access
- Furniture/room style
- Rooming situation: Will students live with people from the host culture? Each other? Other international students? Will rooms be single or mixed gender?

As is the case on campus, housing plays a significant role in a student's experience abroad. If study abroad staff evaluates housing, this will enable them to be better informed and prepare students accordingly. Staff will also be prepared to answer questions or respond to housing-related concerns from students postarrival.

Staff Support and Communication
Beyond checking in regularly to touch base about on-the-ground happenings, consider informing on-site staff of relevant occurrences and updates from the home institution. The program administrator will have to determine what information is necessary to share with on-site staff. For example, a program provider serving 150 students a semester—of which 10 are from the home institution—may not be interested in hearing that a beloved faculty member is retiring, or that it is time to register for classes for the following semester. However, this information will be important to share with on-site staff if the program is run by the home institution.

Of course, program cycles overlap. Unless programs are offered every other year or so, predeparture planning overlaps with programs in progress. Successful program administrators adhere to the communication plans for each phase of the administrative process, while also remaining flexible and shifting

---

[4]More information about the Clery Act can be found at http://studentaid.ed.gov/about/data-center/school/clery-act, and http://clerycenter.org/summary-jeanne-clery-act.

priorities accordingly. For example, if academic departments on campus want to see current syllabi for courses taught at the host site, the beginning of the semester—when on-site staff are orienting students and likely engaged from sunup to sundown—may not be the best time to attempt to gather this information. If lines of communication are clear and open, the home-based administrator will quickly learn the busiest times of programming for the on-site staff, and vice versa.

Debriefing and Assessment

Every program warrants a formal postprogram debriefing with program staff and administrators. All sides discuss the program from various perspectives, breaking the program into phases and discussing lessons learned. Debriefing is different from assessment, which implies that learning objectives and projected program outcomes are evaluated and analyzed in quantitative and/or qualitative ways. Program debriefings should focus on administrative aspects of the program and lessons learned, and are invaluable to program administrators when the program is next planned.

Lessons Learned: How to Better Administer Programs

The Value of Program Feedback

Feedback from participants is crucial in many ways. Obviously, participants are able to express their opinions on the program, and may provide insightful information regarding programmatic elements of which the institutional program administrator is unaware. (Perhaps housing options have increased, or new disciplines are being offered.) Secondly, if the program administrator doesn't quite know how to request changes to be made on-the-ground, participant feedback can help to influence on-site partners and staff. Third, students might offer constructive feedback that helps update program resources and predeparture orientation. Finally, asking students to evaluate a program helps the administrator to consider through a programming lens the information they want to receive. How are the housing arrangements? What is public transport like from a student's perspective? Is the coursework challenging? What opportunities do students have to interact with the local culture?

While not all feedback necessarily needs to be shared with any or all stakeholders, program administrators should make a habit to address obvious concerns and successes of overseas programs with on-site partners and staff, as well as with other institutional stakeholders. As program administrators, we should hold ourselves to the same standards to which we hold students: Learning does not end when a program ends.

Keeping Resources Up-to-Date

Feedback from participants is just one way to keep resources updated. If program administrators stay in touch with on-site staff and partners proactively, they can update resources fairly easily. Programmatic changes range in scale, and program managers must decide which changes might need to be addressed by other stakeholders. For example, the inclusion of a visit to a museum may not significantly impact the way the program is administered or publicized. However, a significant change to the housing options in a program, or changes in program length—resulting in necessary changes to the type of visa students would need—likely require the administrator to communicate with others, and even possibly revisit the viability of the program.

Expanding Successful Program Models

Two approaches are possible when reviewing the program portfolio. With the "if it's not broke, don't fix it" approach, the program reasonably meets institutional needs, fulfills learning goals and objectives, employs experienced on-site staff, has sustainable infrastructure both institutionally and overseas, offers students a safe, secure, and culturally stimulating experience, and receives positive feedback from all involved. The program is successful and little if any changes are made.

The alternative approach asks, "If it's not broke, can we still make it better?" If the program is short-term, is there the possibility of recreating it as a semester-long model? Could practices employed in the various phases of that program—from planning and publicity to orientation to soliciting postprogram feedback—be applied to other programs? Is the program a model of success and best practice that may be shared with the greater international education community? How can more experiential education—a sort of topic du jour in international education in recent years—be incorporated into the program via internship, service learning, and volunteer opportunities?

Some programs work for what they are: The participant number is ideal, the group dynamic is strong, and the relationship between the institution and the partner involves clear communication and support. Likewise, some programs don't work because group dynamic is weak, not enough or too many students express interest and are accepted into the program, and a line of communication is blurred. In fact, the very same program administered the very same way might suffer different fates throughout its existence.

The successful administrator recognizes when a program needs to continue existing in its present form, when it should be revisited and changed, and when it may be time to recommend that the program be cancelled. The longer the program length, the more difficult these three options may be to consider. For example, many programs need a minimum number of participants in order to meet financial needs, but the administrative timeline for a short-term program may be shorter than the timeline for a semester program, and so the short-term program might get canceled while a semester program may continue to seek out applicants over a longer course of time. In the same respect, as institutions change over time, their program needs shift. Changes to program offerings or administration should reflect institutional changes in priorities and resources. Finally, the successful administrator communicates with other stakeholders when programs are in doubt, and solicits feedback from all those involved in program administration before making decisions that impact a program or others that may be crafted in that program's vision.

The Importance of Site Visits

Regular site visits provide program administrators with invaluable, firsthand documentation of many programmatic aspects and considerations—even if the administrator is not the person conducting the site visit. Many institutions invite faculty, senior and administrative staff, and in some cases alumni to visit prospective or active program sites. Site visits serve not only to inform the home institution of the sites' possibilities or realities as a program host, but also serve to make internationalization a collective effort. Departments may feel more included in program building if they are offered opportunities to participate in site visits. Study abroad returnees often want to talk about their experiences abroad; people on campus who have visited the same site may welcome these students to share their experiences, and may be encouraged to share their own. Senior staff may be more interested in supporting study abroad efforts generally, or in particular regions or with specific academic departments, if afforded the opportunity to visit sites. Firsthand experience is transformative.

Ethical implications should be considered when current or prospective partners offer site visits. The Forum for Education Abroad's Code of Ethics for Education Abroad (2011) offers further insight regarding the ethics of sponsored site visits, and encourages institutions to share in the costs of site visits as an investment in building international programming capacity. Goucher College (2008) offers an example of articulated policy regarding site visits in host countries by members of the college's faculty and staff. Their policy addresses procedures and requirements that site visitors must fulfill, as well as how expenses and honoraria will be handled.

Site visits are most productive when guided by outcomes. The international office and other offices attempting to build or evaluate a program should create a checklist for those conducting site visits. The checklist might include, but should not be limited to, the following programmatic aspects:

- Academics
- Housing
- Transportation
- Engagement with host culture
- Health, safety, and security
- Student identity considerations (gender, religion, etc.)
- Accommodations for students with special needs
- Costs of living
- Support on site
- Crisis management/emergency protocol

The checklist may change depending on the nature of the program for which the visit is taking place (faculty-led vs. direct enrollment vs. provider program, for example). Ultimately, the checklist will guide the visitors in providing a thorough, utilitarian document of great use to program administrators.

Conclusion

Program administrators and managers consider many facets in each stage of program administration. According to a 2008 report from NAFSA's Task Force on Institutional Management of Study Abroad, *Strengthening Study Abroad: Recommendations for Effective Institutional Management for Presidents, Senior Administrators, and Study Abroad Professionals,* successful study abroad programs are characterized by many of the topics identified in this section, including:

- a structured approach to program planning and a faculty-driven process for course approval and credit transfer;
- study abroad options that are regularly updated to respond to academic opportunity and student need;
- clear institutional policies that guide study abroad credit transfer;
- programs that promote the health and safety of students studying abroad, and also manage institutional risk; and
- programs that are regularly evaluated, with the evaluation leading to improvements.

Many of the topics included in program administration warrant their own books, workshops, and conference sessions. As international educators, we continue to incorporate model practices in the development and management of education abroad programs. Our role is critical to supporting the institution's vision of internationalization.

References

Clarion University. "Planning and Implementing a Study Abroad Program." Accessed August 15, 2013. http://www.clarion.edu/53024/.

Conrad, Nancy and George C. Morrison. 2013. "Key Considerations When Implementing, Expanding, or Administering a Study Abroad Program." *White and Williams Education Law News Alert.* Accessed August 2, 2013. http://www.whiteandwilliams.com/resources-alerts-Key-Considerations-When-Implementing-Expanding-Or-Administering-A-Study-Abroad-Program.html.

Engle, Lilli and John Engle. 2003. "Study Abroad Levels: Toward a Classification of Program Types." *Frontiers Journal* 9: 1-20. http://www.frontiersjournal.com/issues/vol9/.

Forum for Education Abroad. *Code of Ethics for Education Abroad.* Carlisle, Pennsylvania: Forum for Education Abroad, 2011.

Forum for Education Abroad. *Education Abroad Glossary.* Accessed September 2, 2013. http://www.forumea.org/EducationAbroadProgramFeaturesandTypes.cfm.

Goucher College. 2008. "Policy on Study Abroad Site Visits by Goucher Employees." Accessed January 7, 2014. http://www.goucher.edu/Documents/Legal/Study_Abroad_Site_Visits_by_Goucher_Employees_policy.pdf.

Heisel, Margaret, and Robert Stableski. 2009. "Expanding Study Abroad: Where There's a Will, There's a Way." *IIE White Paper Series: Expanding Study Abroad Capacity at U.S Colleges and Universities* 6: 28–37. Edited by Peggy Blumenthal and Robert Gutierrez.

Hoffa, William, John Pearson and Marvin Slind, eds. 1993. *NAFSA's Guide to Education Abroad for Advisors and Administrators.* Washington, D.C.: NAFSA: Association of International Educators.

Williams, Tracy Rundstrom. 2009. "The Reflective Model of Intercultural Competency: A Multidimensional, Qualitative Approach to Study Abroad Assessment." *Frontiers Journal* 18: 289–306.

Wendy Williamson. "7 Signs of Successful Study-Abroad Programs." *The Chronicle of Higher Education.* July 25, 2010. Accessed August 1, 2013. http://chronicle.com/article/7-Signs-of-Successful/123657/.

CHAPTER 17

THE EXPERIENCE OF STUDENTS ON SITE

By Heidi Buffington

Most international educators agree that students who go abroad become more independent and mature by experiencing the world away from home. The process of students transforming into global citizens does not happen immediately; students experience cultural adjustment as they cope with life abroad, helping them learn about themselves and others. Because they are at a unique stage developmentally, being abroad can have a transformative effect on the way they think and act in the future. Study abroad helps students "achieve some mastery of skills needed to succeed as an undergraduate and ... to become informed, globally aware citizens" (Ritsema, Knecht, and Kruckemeyer 2011, 98). Throughout this chapter the student experience and the phases of adjustment while abroad will be described.

Gone are the days when study abroad meant full immersion in one country to learn the language for a semester or year. According to the 2012 *Open Doors* report, 38 percent of students who participated in study abroad in 2010/11 were away for one or two quarters or a semester compared to only 3.9 percent who stayed for an academic year (Institute of International Education 2012). Short-term study (eight weeks or less) increased from 56.6 percent in 2009/10 to 58.1 percent in 2010/11 (Institute of International Education 2012; Kehl and Morris 2007–2008, 67).

These shorter stays promote participation, but may not structurally allow for students to go "beyond the surface," rather visiting as if a tourist. Knowing they will be home soon after they arrive, they may not be invested in engaging the local culture. Students who study for a year or semester generally have enough time to experience the ups and downs of cultural adjustment, whereas students who travel on short-term programs or faculty-led programs aren't in-country long enough to have to adjust. With this in mind, this chapter will be written considering semester or year-long sojourners, but most of the concepts could be applied to short-term program participants as well.

Blame it on the "I want it now" commercial culture or technology that promotes and encourages constant contact (although often with no depth): students expect a high-paced study abroad experience. They also view their time abroad as the only chance they have to see the world before settling down and paying back student loans, attending graduate school, and so on. "Students yearn to be abroad, to travel to worlds different from their own, to find excitement, to see new wonders and to have an experience of a lifetime"

(Ogden 2007–2008, 37). Because of a wide variety of programs now available, some of which teach in English, students are not required, or even strongly encouraged, to have foreign language skills, even if the program is in a non-English speaking country.

Another factor affecting students' immersion and adjustment is the amount of faculty and staff contact students have. In faculty-led programs, students rely heavily on the professor for nearly everything, and thus don't always gain valuable skills by doing things on their own. Often students who stay for shorter lengths of time and are coddled by a staff member aren't exposed to as much of the culture as someone who stays longer and has less support.

As with most travel experiences, students tend to look forward to their time away with wanderlust. According to the W-Curve, this is called the honeymoon stage (Hamline University 2013; Pennsylvania State University-Altoona 2013). The W-Curve describes the ups and downs of cultural adjustment, forming a W shape. While students might be nervous about the unknown, in the early part of a semester they tend to feel more enthusiasm for the new adventure. For example, they just can't wait to wander the quaint cobblestoned streets of European cities. Upon arrival, students often see differences, but with rose-colored glasses. Buying food from a busy vendor is novel to them even if they fumble through the language. The beginning is the time when students are open to exploring, making new friends, joining clubs, and finding language partners. The length of this initial honeymoon phase (and all the phases of adjustment) varies depending on the person and their upbringing, social background, open-mindedness, and willingness to learn (Unite for Sight 2012).

Orientation

Shortly after arrival, students participate in orientation, which can vary from short half-day meetings to full-day excursions or longer. Because students are jetlagged, in cognitive overload, or experiencing culture shock, much of the information given in orientation sessions isn't understood or absorbed by the student. Additionally, students are accustomed to being able to access information they missed or need via technology. Students report that small group sessions are more effective than a large auditorium-style orientation. Younger staff or local students sharing personal experiences, especially about safety, alcohol, and drug abuse, tend be received better with more impact than having an older administrator talk to students. Program staff should be mindful of these expectations when the time arrives to update the content and delivery methods of orientation programs.

Given the distractions and disorientation at the beginning of the program, one way to inform students and at the same time help them understand the host culture would be to offer two orientations, one at the beginning of the semester and another at the middle, where students can ask questions about things they've experienced (Harris 2013). "The evidence tells us that when trained cultural mentors intervene in the education of students throughout the study abroad cycle, they learn and develop more effectively and appropriately—much more than those who either stay at home or enroll in programs abroad that do not provide cultural mentoring" (Vande Berg, Paige, and Lou 2012, 418).

Even if students are told useful facts and pertinent information, the most important lesson that can be emphasized during orientation is typically not stressed enough. It seems simple, but students need to be told that they will experience linguistic and cultural challenges and they shouldn't expect everything to be the same as it is at home. Paul Larson from Baylor University says "You have to tell them that it's all going to be different so that they know. Sometimes people sugarcoat the 'things will be different' talk, but you have to just put it out there" (Larson 2013). If they expect differences they'll cope better when confronted with a difficult situation. Students who study in Europe think it will be similar to the United States, but things are quite different. However, students travelling to the global south expect things to be different and they don't have as hard of a time adjusting (Larson 2013). One thing that students do when living abroad is learning to "unlearn" expectations. "Learning to unlearn means setting aside and questioning one's assumptions and preconceived notions" (Ritsema, Knecht, and Kruckemeyer 2011, 89).

Housing

The traditional option of living with a host family can be fundamental for language acquisition and cultural immersion. Students who live in host families tend to adapt better to the change of living abroad and experience more of the host culture, making this housing arrangement one of the best ways to make the most of study abroad. Students tend to be more exposed to the real way of life of a host country, and over time, students gain confidence to function successfully in the host country (Kruse and Brubaker 2007).

Students initially find great difference in their housing abroad from their living situation at home. Insecure students may feel that they have no control in their new foreign environment, so they tend to complain about housing as it is one thing they can change (Chaney 2013). If they switch to live with a different family, often the two families are quite similar (Casado 2013).

Students may avoid host families because they don't want to be part of a family structure or would prefer more independent living options, so they decide to live in a university residence hall, expecting it to be similar to U.S. dorms. And while they live among other university students, providing the benefit of meeting new people and getting an idea of foreign dorm culture, this housing option, as with most things they'll experience, can be quite different. The main issue that will cause students to feel isolated is language and the often cliquey atmosphere. Without sufficient language skills, students may not get involved in certain social situations, and they may start to feel lonely. However, dorms can provide many different activities to create the opportunity for cultural interaction, which all depends on students' motivation. Finding a shared apartment, another alternative to a host family, may also allow for more interaction with locals, if students aren't living with their own countrymen.

Housing has a tremendous effect on how students experience their time abroad. No matter which option students select, the effort to integrate and their ability to navigate this particular aspect of study abroad will impact their understanding of the culture and the language. Students that are housed with others of their same nationality, may have a place to talk about their experiences and a place to vent frustration. This could also be a comfort zone that works to reinforce stereotypes. Students, who live with locals in dorms, apartments, or with host families, have the ability to become more proficient in the language, but they may also feel isolated at times. Program staff should be aware of the different housing environments and how this may encourage or discourage student learning in the local context.

Host Staff Interaction with Students

As students settle into their new environment, they begin to have specific questions and requests for host staff. As even the simplest of tasks can seem confusing and intimidating in a new place, staff can easily become the go-to people for everything. Students expect to receive service as if they were a customer, but administrators need to create a balance of "challenge and support" so that students can learn on their own (Sanford 1967). Staff should be helpful and understanding, while also encouraging students to explore on their own so they become independent. At the end of a semester, students often boast of their accomplishments in successfully navigating the foreign culture. Rye Barcott, a student who studied in rural Kenya, "urges students who do go abroad to get out of their comfort zone and not stay in the American bubble. 'You will get an experience that is enriched beyond your imagination if you go off the beaten path.'" (Leggett 2007, 32)

It's important that students are given the tools to negotiate situations by making information readily available or by having specific informational sessions on gender issues, the dating culture, where and how to buy things, the LGBTQ climate, and even understanding the drinking culture (Harris 2013). By educating students and giving them tools, educators are helping to minimize risk and allow students learn on their own (Martínez 2013). By providing useful links and other advice, students are given initial help. If they are encouraged to do the work themselves (buying tickets online, booking trains, buying a metro pass) they'll learn more and ultimately become more independent and proud of their achievements.

Academic Program

Living in a new culture can be stressful, but also trying to understand how to function in a new academic context can add to students' stress. Many things are different, including professors' expectations, taking tests, or even registration via paper requiring many signatures (Harris 2013). Many students are used to a learner-centered system, and find it hard to understand what is expected of them in a professor-centered classroom where there are no regularly graded assignments and individual guidance from professors is lacking (Brewer 2013, 198). Programs could help students by using the Forum's *Standards of Good Practice for Education Abroad* for on-site academic advising, which lays out guidelines for successful student advising, including helping students get acquainted with their new academic culture and keeping them on track academically (Forum on Education Abroad 2013, 31). The *Standards of Good Practice* were established to "respond to the practical realities of developing, managing, and assessing education abroad programs" and have been used to "shape organizational/institutional policy on education abroad" (Forum on Education Abroad 2013, 3).

Typically students stick together because it's more comfortable to be with people who have a common background. This safety net includes students with differing levels of language comprehension, where the weaker speakers rely on the stronger ones to communicate. Anthony Ogden compares study abroad students to colonials who live in beautiful bungalows and sit comfortably on the veranda observing the local culture from a safe distance (Ogden 2007–2008, 35, 36). Rebecca Solnit says that we need to help students get lost intellectually to facilitate learning; in other words, help them leave the bungalow porch to be among the locals. "Getting lost means giving up some control, but if one knows how to get lost intellectually, it also leads to learning and growth" (Brewer 2011, 199). So taking risks to leave the American bubble can pay off for student learning.

However, breaking free from the bubble can be difficult for some students, as it's easier and less stressful to rely on others in a group. Some programs, such as summer sessions or faculty-led programs, must intentionally design the opportunity for student independence, as a group normally does all activities together and students are herded from place to place. In longer length and larger programs, where students may have more possibilities for contact with locals, there may be more opportunity for freedom; however, only brave, motivated, and curious students may go off the beaten path and try to meet locals and experience the culture. The path of least resistance is often the chosen one, even if before leaving home a student dreamed of immersion in a foreign culture.

Programs should put energy into helping to reduce the boundaries between students and locals caused by the language and culture barrier. In order to help students to spend some time away from their support bubble, programs may need to incorporate cultural activities into the curriculum and organize events that help mix students with locals (e.g., conversation partner meetups, trips, and sports or volunteer work).

If there is a need for language (buying food, making train reservations, or chatting with a language partner), then students are more driven to learn. The old adage "necessity is the mother of invention" could be tweaked to apply to study abroad: necessity is the mother of language learning. While taking classes in an academic setting is what leads students abroad, so much learning takes place outside of the classroom: ordering a coffee, making small talk, or simply observing others. "One common view about studying abroad is that when students travel to and are 'immersed' in a place different from home, they learn many interesting and useful things on their own, and do so rather effortlessly"(Vande Berg, Paige, and Lou 2012, 3). Students need help finding ways to learn, and host institution staff can help by setting up language exchanges, service learning, volunteer opportunities, and even internships.

Community Engagement

Internships can be a great way for a student to get out into the local community and away from other students. If a student arranges an internship through a local organization, the student will have a local contact person in the case that they have questions or concerns. Some internships don't require strong foreign language skills, and students can still observe how office culture is in the host country. "Whether interviewing African villagers to assess the efficacy of a local NGO's efforts, or translating documents in a corporate office in a European city, student interns receive concentrated exposure to a local culture that can result in powerful personal growth"(Rubin 2009, 58).

Certain programs have created other interesting ways to get students learning outside the classroom. Morocco Exchange "offers students not just opportunities to see the sites, but to meet and speak with English-speaking Moroccans. We talk about serious issues: women's rights in a Muslim country, the 'clash of civilizations' and stereotypes, Islam ... and how America is viewed abroad" (Hoppes 2013). The Cities in the 21st Century Program through SIT Study Abroad's International Honors Program (IHP) has a guest lecturer teach students local policies on urban environmental management. So, for example, students visit a landfill and talk with an engineer. Having lunch and talking with locals then helps students discover the problems people face living near a landfill. Afterward, students discuss the varying viewpoints of this one issue to form educated opinions (Ritsema, Knecht, and Kruckemeyer 2011, 90, 95). By getting the students involved in the culture and not just forming ideas from the outside, they are truly learning about the host country.

Although programs can set up amazing opportunities for students to learn, study abroad participants may or may not take advantage of them. The more students move away from their comfort zones during study abroad, the more likely they are to be open-minded and enter other situations involving people of different cultures in the future (Kehl and Morris 2007–2008, 70). What prevents students from stepping off the virtual veranda? Perhaps it's shyness and the fear of being uncomfortable in strange situations. "Stress and anxiety ... are conditions the normal, healthy person tries to avoid, whether at home or abroad. It's only natural, therefore, that if we find our encounters with the local culture stressful and otherwise unpleasant, we begin to pull back from it. And by withdrawing and isolating ourselves from the culture, we seriously undermine any possibility of meaningful adjustment; we can hardly adjust to that which we decline to experience" (Lucas 2009, 201).

Culture Shock and Stress

While students may still be exited by new things as they begin to settle in, they also may cope with a certain level of anxiety on a daily basis. Every student has a different threshold for stress, and some students may only feel a bit of culture shock, while others may suffer greatly. Depression and anxiety are ranked "among the most common psychological problems experienced by students and are only exacerbated by the challenges of cross-cultural adjustment" (Lucas 2009, 191, 198). Cultural differences that were initially seen as exciting can become negative in a student's mind.

A way to understand students' ability to cope with their host environments are intensity factors described by R. Michael Paige. He says that intensity factors are "situational variables and personal attributes that can influence the psychological intensity or stress associated with intercultural experiences."

Some intensity factors include cultural differences, cultural isolation (lack of interaction with family and friends at home), lack of language skills leading to social isolation and frustration, status issues (not getting the respect they feel they should), expectations (unrealistic expectations leading to a psychological letdown), and the loss of control leading to varying levels of anxiety. Being aware of the intensity factors can help students and administrators understand challenges and how to "develop more effective coping and learning strategies" (Paige 2013).

When a student experiences feelings of anxiety and frustration, he/she is entering the culture shock or crisis phase of the W-Curve (Hamline University 2013). Culture shock can be defined as "anxiety that results from losing all familiar signs and symbols of social intercourse" (Oberg 2013). The dip down from the initial honeymoon stage may only be slight for some students, while others may experience great stress.

Despite its negative association, culture shock can have positive outcomes. When students experience culture shock, they begin to learn about themselves, their beliefs, and their values. Because of the anxiety caused by culture shock, this process is not always pleasant to witness or experience. However, culture shock is what causes students to start to question their new environment. They acknowledge differences and go through a period of introspection that can be the "catalyst for a positive personal change" (Fernández-Cruz 2013). Many factors can affect how long a student will experience culture shock, including: the student's maturity level, their motivation to study abroad, and their interest in the language and culture.

Complaints

One main result of culture shock is that students start to reject the host culture and often consider their own as superior because of a lack of understanding of mostly culturally based things. At this point, students tend to stay even closer together, and often criticize the host culture. Most complaints stem from not understanding how things work (buying things, doing paperwork, handling money, registering for classes, daily schedules, and so on). Food may cause misunderstanding between a host family and a student, such as when a student is served a very common dish and doesn't know what it is or how to eat it, often thus rejecting it.

Students seek comfort in friends and family back home and the host country may not have the bandwidth to support students' "constant electronic solace" that they seek (Johnson 2013). Many U.S. students study in large cities like London, Rome, Paris, or Madrid, but most students have "limited knowledge of cities and urban life outside of the United States" (Ritsema,

Knecht, and Kruckemeyer 2011, 87). Even gestures, body language, and personal space differences can cause confusion. When students start to pull away and complain, it's important to get them involved so they aren't avoiding contact with locals, which will only lengthen the adaptation process (University of California-Irvine 2013; Oberg 2013).

Academic performance also tends to falter when students start feeling frustrated and uncomfortable. Of course, many students don't stay in their host city all the time; traveling nearly every weekend plays a role as well. If students aren't taking academics seriously, they will not be prepared when the time comes for exams. The combination of difficulties with the language, traveling too much, and not understanding the academic system in general all contribute to poor performance abroad. Perhaps a second orientation or more constant academic support could help with these issues.

Drugs and Alcohol

Because students see their semesters abroad as a break with newfound freedoms, many experiment with drugs and alcohol more so than they would at home. This can present great problems for students, because they are in an unfamiliar environment and can't recognize social cues due to a lack of cultural understanding. Additionally, U.S. students often have less nightlife experience compared with youth their age abroad, which puts them at risk. "Students have not really spent much time in social settings in which there are people that are not in their own circle..." (Vega 2013b). Combining this information with a lack of undeveloped coping skills, students may also choose to drink because they feel uncomfortable and stressed and do not know how to ask for help. While students want to blend in and do "as they see others doing," they may not know (a) how to drink as locals do, (b) where to legally drink, (c) when people drink acceptably (timetable), and (d) in what quantities. Alcohol consumption is a huge concern as students tend to abuse it, which can affect students' well-being in many ways. As a result of student trial and error, on-site staff is accountable for resolving all substance use issues including petty theft, injuries, sexual abuse, and even death. Students need to be educated about local drinking cultures so they can make educated decisions regarding the extent to which they will participate.

Under the Drug Free Schools and Communities Act (DFSCA), as a condition of receiving federal funds, schools must "prevent the unlawful possession, use, or distribution of illicit drugs by students, faculty, and staff" (Epstein and Rhodes 1999–2000). This affects domestic and international programs, and universities need to be aware of this if they are trying to decide whether to serve alcohol at school-promoted events (Epstein and Rhodes

1999–2000). Risk factors of having intoxicated students in foreign cities, where they've drank (possibly too much) at an official university event, need to be considered. "Heightened levels of interpersonal violence, including sexual assault, is the most common unwanted occurrence linked to drinking" (Epstein and Rhodes 1999–2000). However, anything and everything including theft, personal injury from a wide variety of incidents, and students vandalizing their and other's property can occur.

The Center for Global Education hosts the online SAFETI Clearinghouse, which has an alphabetical health and safety issues index that provides useful information on a wide variety of issues affecting students abroad. SAFETI also has resources for programs to use on alcohol awareness, orientation courses, and a newsletter (The Center for Global Education 2013). The NAFSA website also has a great amount of online best practice resources for professionals, including information on such topics as diversity, orientation, health and safety issues, and measuring the impact of study abroad (NAFSA 2013). Specifically in the health and safety subsection of the NAFSA website there is a section with excellent online resources to help professionals stay informed of relevant health and safety issues, put together by the Education Abroad Knowledge Community (EA KC) Health and Safety Subcommittee.

Psychological and Emotional Support

Even if a program has great orientation sessions, academic advising services, and round-the-clock assistance, some students will need additional help. Everyone has their own level of stress tolerance, and students often experience anxiety as they assimilate to a new culture (Lucas 2009, 198). Being away from family and a regular support network, dealing with frustrations of a new culture, academic stress, and just general feelings of inadequacy related to communication can all lead students to struggle. Laurie Mazzuca refers to this adjustment and crisis phase as a "sink or swim" situation. The majority of students seek answers themselves in order to adapt, and others seek help when they feel uncomfortable. The sinking student who struggles to adapt most likely is someone who doesn't seek help because they are "afraid or embarrassed to admit they can't resolve the problem on their own" and may end up leaving early or in a mental health crisis (Mazzuca 2013).

Having a counselor available is critical because certain prior mental conditions can be exacerbated while abroad. Other new issues may arise even for students who have never presented psychological problems previously (Fernández-Cruz 2013). Some programs have an on-campus counselor, while others don't have any psychological support for students at all. Resident directors normally don't have "the training to … deal with the depth and breadth of mental health issues" (Lucas 2009, 187). One way that some programs provide this service is to pay an outside counselor so students can call someone if they need counseling services. In urban areas this support may be more accessible, but in rural areas programs need to develop a plan of action in case there is a need for psychological help.

While some students are stable and can function with counseling and medication, others have very specific treatments that need to be kept constant. "What happens in the U.S. does not stay in the U.S.: If students are dealing with a problem at home like depression, an eating disorder, or a family issue, that problem will not suddenly go away when students leave the country to study abroad" (Mazzuca 2013). Often, students who are on medication and going to counseling at home want to make a clean start, and think by going abroad and stopping their treatment they'll get it. Normally, the opposite happens, and the student breaks down.

Students are encouraged to study abroad because it can be such a positive learning experience, yet "unfortunately, study abroad is not always a good choice. It can force some students beyond what they're capable of handling. And the results can be academically and personally disastrous not only for them, but also for their families and friends" (Baile 2013). If a student like this does go abroad and loses control, they not only risk their personal safety because their condition may worsen or they may cause harm to themselves, but they may also affect the whole group with a negative attitude or dangerous behavior. Staff may devote large amounts of time solely to this student, ultimately limiting time they can spend with others.

In situations where students take medication and/or go to counseling regularly or have a physical or mental disability, it's essential for study abroad programs to be in direct contact with home universities. "Developing a relationship with the disability services office on campus is one of the best ways to collaborate on data gathering and to plan proactively for the recruitment and support of students with disabilities" (Scheib 2009, 54). Students can work with their home university counselor or disability services via Skype, FaceTime, Google Voice, and so on to ensure continued support.

University and Program Collaboration

In an Alliance to Advance Liberal Arts Colleges (AALAC) workshop at Wellesley College, participants supported "greater collaboration between [home university] faculty and study abroad administrators to facilitate a more holistic approach to foreign study" (Vega 2013a). Faculty from various colleges agreed that working more closely with staff could "not only enrich the ability to advise students more effectively, but would facilitate a greater integration of curricular content and the types of programs (and providers) of most benefit to students" (Vega 2013a). Study abroad offices might not be the best place for students to seek academic advice, and faculty may not be the best source for essential study abroad information. If faculty and staff work together, students can be better advised and prepared in all aspects of study abroad.

Additionally, it's essential for the home institution to work with the host institution. Normally, when a student has a problem, communication is often inefficient because students first contact their parents, who, being so far away with little cultural knowledge, worry. Nervous parents then get in contact with the study abroad staff, who in turn get in touch with the host institution (Johnson 2013). Often small problems could be solved quickly, but they become escalated because of the number of people involved. With time differences and the nondirect channel of communication, students don't get help in a timely manner when often the shortest path would be for them to go directly to the contact person at the host institution.

Student Adjustment

Once students start to get used to the new routine (classes, daily lifestyle, using a new language, public transportation, or commutes) they often feel quite proud of living abroad and experience a new surge of excitement. They usually say they are comfortable at this point and want to see and try new things in the host city. Returning to the W-Curve, this is the initial adjustment phase, where students regain control and normalcy and feel good about it (Hamline University 2013). "It seems to take sojourners about four to six months to overcome any mood disturbances related to their entrance into a new cultural context (psychological adaptation) and to settle down and get along with everyday matters of work, life, and social communication (socio-cultural adaptation)" (Vande Berg, Paige, and Lou 2012, 9). Some students may not get to this comfortable point before they leave, if they are only studying abroad for one semester, while others may actually reach this comfort level faster. Again, this has to do with the intensity factors and each individual student's personality.

If students do reach the upswing adjustment period, they may experience a second culture shock, the mental isolation stage, as new adjustments occur and new comparisons between home and the host culture are made. While students at this point are comfortable and understand the host culture, they also miss home and how things are done there. This feeling of being "caught between two worlds" is often experienced by students who stay longer than a semester, as they are finally able to communicate in the foreign language and can contemplate their beliefs based on what they are experiencing in the host country (Hamline University 2013). If students are studying in a country where their native language is spoken, the length and depth of the adjustment phases will vary; however, varying cultural aspects will affect how students feel, more so, perhaps, than the language itself.

Acceptance and Integration

The final phase of the W-Curve is the acceptance and integration stage, where "students accept the customs of a country as another way of living" (Oberg 2013). They settle in and can function efficiently without feeling anxiety (generally) and can understand social cues because they've adapted their way of thinking (Oberg 2013). This is also referred to as the bicultural phase where someone's home culture becomes foreign and a person's "foreignness" is lessened (Oberg 2013; University of California-Irvine 2013). This is a phase that only long-term students and expats may eventually reach. Study abroad professionals should be aware of what a student may be experiencing emotionally to best help them while they are abroad.

Besides the good times that students have traveling and meeting new people, students return to their home universities feeling proud to have become more independent. Their self-confidence increases because they've had to learn to do things on their own (and often in a foreign language). Communication skills improve because they've worked on a new language and most likely have come to understand nonverbal skills, such as interpreting body language and gestures (Brewer 2011). And, by learning about a new culture, they've most likely reflected on their own beliefs and some shifts in personal values may have occurred.

Ultimately, learning about one's self is a lifelong journey, but self-awareness and introspection can be triggered by living in another culture. "In our pluralistic world, students now need to develop a global perspective while in college. They need to think and act in terms of living in a world in which they meet, work, and live with others with very different cultural backgrounds, habits, perspectives, customs, religious beliefs, and aspirations" (Braskamp, Braskamp, and Merrill 2009, 101). With workplaces and the world becoming flat, people are even more interconnected (Friedman 2005). And by understanding themselves and others better, students initiate the process of becoming global citizens, even if they don't leave their home country again after their time abroad.

References

Baile, Elizabeth. 2013. Personal communication with the author (e-mail), July 10, 2013.

Braskamp, Larry A., David C. Braskamp, and Kelly C. Merrill. 2009. "Assessing Progress in Global Learning and Development of Students with Education Abroad." *Frontiers: The Interdisciplinary Journal of Study Abroad* 18: 101–118. http://www.frontiersjournal.com/documents/FrontiersXVIII-Fall09BRaskampBRaskampMerrill.pdf.

Brewer, Elizabeth. 2011. "Study Abroad and the City: Bringing the Lessons Home." *Frontiers: The Interdisciplinary Journal of Study Abroad* 20 (Spring): 195–213. http://www.frontiersjournal.com/documents/Brewer-FrontiersXX-2011.pdf.

Casado, Margarita. 2013. Conversation with the author, July 10, 2013.

The Center for Global Education. 2013. SAFETI Clearinghouse Project Accessed July 18. http://globaled.us/safeti/safeti_index.asp.

Chaney, Phyllis. 2013. Personal communication with the author (e-mail), July 23, 2013.

Epstein, Joel C., and Gary Rhodes. 2000. "A Discussion About Alcohol and Student Exchange." *SAFETI Online Newsletter* 1, 2 (Spring/Summer). http://globaled.us/safeti/v1n22000ed_alcohol_and_student_exchange.asp.

Fernández-Cruz, Eduardo. 2013. Conversation with the author, July 9, 2013.

Forum on Education Abroad. 2013. "Standards of Good Practice." Accessed August 5. http://www.forumea.org/standards-index.cfm.

Friedman, Thomas L. 2005. *The World is Flat: A Brief History of the Twenty-First Century.* New York, N.Y.: Farrar, Straus and Giroux.

Gullahorn, Jeanne F., and John T. Gullahorn. 1963. "An Extension of the U-Curve Hypothesis." *Journal of Social Issues* 19:33–47.

Hamline University. 2013. "The W-Curve and the First Year of College." Accessed August 6. http://www.universityparent.com/2009/09/01/making-the-transition-to-college-the-w-curve.

Harris, Elizabeth. 2013. Personal communication with the author (e-mail), July 11, 2013.

Hoppes, Allen. 2013. Personal communication with the author (e-mail), July 11, 2013.

Institute of International Education. 2012. *Open Doors 2012.* New York, N.Y.: Institute of International Education. http://www.iie.org/Research-and-Publications/Open-Doors/Data.

Johnson, Christopher. 2013. Personal communication with the author (e-mail), July 15, 2013.

Kehl, Kevin, and Jason Morris. 2007–2008. "Differences in Global-Mindedness between Short-Term and Semester-Long Study Abroad Participants at Selected Private Universities." *Frontiers: The Interdisciplinary Journal of Study Abroad* 15 (Fall/Winter): 67–79. http://www.frontiersjournal.com/documents/KehlMorrisFRONTIERSJOURNALXVWinter2007-08.pdf.

Kruse, Julia and Cate Brubaker. 2007. "Successful Study Abroad : Tips for Student Preparation, Immersion, and Postprocessing." *Die Unterrichtspraxis/Teaching of German* 40, 2 (Fall): 147–152. http://www.jstor.org/stable/20479956.

Larson, Paul. 2013. Conversation with the author, July 8, 2013.

Leggett, Karen. 2007. "Active Engagement." *International Educator* 16, 3, (May/June):30–37.

Lucas, Jim, Paige Sindt and Austin Melcher. 2013. "Student Learning & Development." Accessed October 22. http://www.president.msu.edu/documents/Student_Develolpment_Estry.pdf.

Lucas, John. 2009. "Over-stressed, Overwhelmed, and Over Here: Resident Directors and the Challenges of Student Mental Health Abroad." *Frontiers: The Interdisciplinary Journal of Study Abroad* 18 (Fall): 187–215. http://www.frontiersjournal.com/documents/FrontiersXVIII-Fall09-JLucas.pdf.

Martínez, Alicia. 2013. Personal communication with the author (e-mail), July 11, 2013.

Mazzuca, Laurie. 2013. Personal communication with the author (e-mail), September 2, 2013.

NAFSA. 2013. "Best Practices." Accessed August 7. http://www.nafsa.org/Find_Resources/Supporting_Study_Abroad/.

Oberg, Kalervo. 2013. "Culture Shock & the Problem of Adjustment to New Cultural Environments." Consortium for International Education & Multicultural Studies. Accessed August 9. http://www.worldwide.edu/travel_planner/culture_shock.html

Ogden, Anthony. 2007–2008. "The View from the Veranda: Understanding Today's Colonial Student." *Frontiers: The Interdisciplinary Journal of Study Abroad* 15 (Fall/Winter): 35–55.

Paige, R. Michael. 2013. "Theory Reflections: Intensity Factors in Intercultural Experiences." Accessed August 15. http://www.nafsa.org/_/file/_/theory_connections_intensity.pdf.

Pennsylvania State University-Altoona. 2013. "The Gullahorn 'W-Curve' Transition Model." Accessed August 9. http://www.altoona.psu.edu/fts/docs/WCurve.pdf.

Ritsema, Mieka, Barbara Knecht and Kenneth Kruckemeyer. 2011. "Learning to Unlearn: Transformative Education in the City." *Frontiers: The Interdisciplinary Journal of Study Abroad* 20 (Spring): 87–102. http://www.frontiersjournal.com/documents/Ritsema-Knecht-KruckemeyerFrontiersXX-2011.pdf.

Rubin, Kyna. 2009. "Overseas Internships Jumpstart Careers." *International Educator* 18, 3 (May/June):58–70.

Sanford, Nevin. 1967. *Where Colleges Fail: A Study of the Student as a Person.* San Francisco, Calif.: Jossey-Bass.

Scheib, Michele. 2009. "Tracking Students With Disabilities Who Study Abroad." *International Educator* 18, 2, (March/April): 52–55.

University of California-Irvine. 2013."Culture Shock." Accessed August 9. http://www.cie.uci.edu/prepare/shock.shtml.

Unite for Sight. 2013. "Module 2: Overview of Cultural Adjustment and Culture Shock." Accessed August 9. http://www.uniteforsight.org/cultural-competency/module2.

University of York. 2013. "Adjusting to University Life." Accessed October 23. https://www.york.ac.uk/students/support/health/problems/adjusting/.

Vande Berg, Michael, R. Michael Paige, Kris Hemming Lou, eds. 2012. *Student Learning Abroad: What Our Students Are Learning. What They're Not, and What We Can Do About It.* Sterling, Virginia: Stylus Publishing.

Vega, Carlos. 2013a. "Bringing Study Abroad Home: Integrating the Experience Abroad with the Liberal Arts Campus." Paper presented at the Alliance to Advance Liberal Arts Colleges Workshop, Wellesley, Mass.: March 1–2.

Vega, Carlos. 2013b. Personal communication with the author (e-mail), July 10, 2013.

fghanistan • Albania • Algeria • Andorra • Angola • Antigua and Barbuda • Argentina • Armenia • Aruba •
ustralia • Austria • Azerbaijan • Bahamas, The • Bahrain • Bangladesh • Barbados • Belarus • Belgium •
elize • Benin • Bhutan • Bolivia • Bosnia and Herzegovina • Botswana • Brazil • Brunei • Bulgaria • Burkina
aso • Burma • Burundi • Cambodia • Cameroon • Canada • Cape Verde • Central African Republic • Chad •

PART V
MANAGING AN EDUCATION ABROAD OFFICE

Kiribati • Korea, North • Korea, South • Kosovo • Kuwait • Kyrgyzstan • Laos • Latvia • Lebanon • Lesotho •
Liberia • Libya • Liechtenstein • Lithuania • Luxembourg • Macau • Macedonia • Madagascar • Malawi •
Malaysia • Maldives • Mali • Malta • Marshall Islands • Mauritania • Mauritius • Mexico • Micronesia • Moldova
• Monaco • Mongolia • Montenegro • Morocco • Mozambique • Namibia • Nauru • Nepal • Netherlands •
Netherlands Antilles • New Zealand • Nicaragua • Niger • Nigeria • Norway • Oman • Pakistan •
Palau • Palestinian Territories • Panama • Papua New Guinea • Paraguay • Peru • Philippines • Poland •
Portugal • Qatar • Romania • Russia • Rwanda • Saint Kitts and Nevis • Saint Lucia • Saint Vincent and the
Grenadines • Samoa • San Marino • Sao Tome and Principe • Saudi Arabia • Senegal • Serbia • Seychelles •
Sierra Leone • Singapore • Sint Maarten • Slovakia • Slovenia • Solomon Islands • Somalia • South Africa •
South Korea • South Sudan • Spain • Sri Lanka • Sudan • Suriname • Swaziland • Sweden • Switzerland • Syria
• Taiwan • Tajikistan • Tanzania • Thailand • Timor-Leste • Togo • Tonga • Trinidad and Tobago • Tunisia •
Turkey • Turkmenistan • Tuvalu • Uganda • Ukraine • United Arab Emirates • United Kingdom • Uruguay •
Uzbekistan • Vanuatu • Venezuela • Vietnam • Yemen • Zambia • Zimbabwe • Afghanistan • Albania • Algeria

CHAPTER 18

PORTFOLIO MANAGEMENT

by Catherine S. Meschievitz

Office Mission, Vision, and Goals

Any new director of a university study abroad office (SAO) has several resources to use as guides to help establish office mission, vision, and goals. The job description issued for recruitment purposes ideally outlines the core duties the director will be expected to perform and also describes the functions of the office. Most existing offices will have a standard description and statement about the office's work. However, not all offices will have a vision statement or a clear link between an office mission, vision, and goals.[1]

Any existing mission, vision, and/or statement of goals should be studied to see if they are appropriate and up-to-date. This may include what expectations have been placed on the table for exploration, and what changes have been suggested. If there is no clear direction or a vacuum of ideas, the new director needs to talk to various constituency groups across the institution (e.g., faculty, fellow directors of key offices, and the direct reporting office supervisor) in order to establish the mission, vision, and goals that can be can embraced going forward. Finding faculty is key, since they can describe their working ties to the study abroad office, and their impressions of what has been done and what could be done. It is equally important to get advice from peers and colleagues in other SAOs, who can fill in details and offer impressions, office history, and ideas.

The new SAO director also needs to gain a clear understanding of the overall institutional priorities of the university or college. Does its institutional mission and vision contain a clear statement of the value of international education, study abroad, or international university partnerships? Many schools have made international activities a primary feature for their educational undertaking. In such a fortunate situation, the SAO must describe and align its ongoing activities to take maximum advantage of

---

[1] There are different models to choose for establishing an office mission and vision, outlining goals, and/or creating objectives that will the advance the SAO on its mission. No single system is mandatory, but to be most effective it is best to adopt the nomenclature and style commonly used at the institution for campus planning and assessment. It is advisable to meet as early as you can with the director of the university's assessment and institutional effectiveness team, as they typically drive the assessment process and data systems.

being part of the campus plan.[2] If the campus plan does not have a clearly stated priority for international education or study abroad, the SAO director can identify other aspects of the campus plan to link to and support. For example, study abroad can enhance undergraduate education (e.g., through honors work, innovative course development, experiential learning, new majors, and internships), support student retention efforts, graduate a talented workforce for development, build student résumés for their career search, and foster global citizenship and multicultural understanding. Shaping descriptions of study abroad programs and faculty engagement in them as part of a larger university effort will build long-term support for study abroad and the SAO among faculty and campus leaders.

The SAO in Institutional Context

The SAO director must understand the organizational structure and ascertain the SAO's visibility within the institution. To whom does the SAO director report? Most study abroad offices are located in academic affairs, and report directly or indirectly to the provost or chief academic officer. What is the hierarchical power ladder, and how are decisions on programs and finances made that affect the SAO? If the SAO director is the official or de facto senior international officer (SIO), what other individuals in the academic structure nonetheless need to review plans for new programs, exchanges, policies, and procedures? The latter picture of required or advisable consultation, and then required decisionmaking, will show the path to other offices necessary for smooth SAO operations. Equally important is the subtle (and at times not so subtle) notion of institutional culture and study abroad. What is the traditional role of the faculty and deans of the academic schools or colleges? What bureaucratic channels and norms exist that must be mastered? Are there old histories or sensitivities to watch out for? Again, advice from long-standing faculty advocates of study abroad to gain insight into these issues can be quite useful.

A helpful tool for institutional culture is the creation of a faculty advisory council for the SAO. If there is no faculty council, the SAO director should consider creating one to act as an advisory group for the SAO. Faculty are a valuable asset to any SAO, as faculty drive most programming and are key to student recruitment for overseas programs.[3] Such a council can signal the

---

[2]Most campus strategic plans determine the allocation of scarce university resources, so being part of the plan (or being perceived to advance an aspect of the plan) can assist the SAO in requests for more staff and budget allocations. See the ACE Internationalization Toolkit samples of university mission statements and strategic plans at http://www.acenet.edu/news-room/Pages/Internationalization-Toolkit.aspx.

[3]Catherine S. Meschievitz, "Meeting the Global Imperative: International Education at Florida Atlantic University," (unpublished essay available from author, February 2011), 4, 7–8.

importance placed on faculty engagement in a shared governance institution, be an important tool in building an international education community across the university, and act as a communication channel for the SAO and the colleges. Councils also advise on policy issues that arise common to all study abroad programs, such as minimum GPA requirements or faculty reimbursement levels. Lastly, a faculty committee can help build consensus for new initiatives and activities to be advanced.[4] Knowing the proper process to get approval to constitute such a council will also help answer the questions above on hierarchy and decisionmaking.[5]

Selecting Overseas Programs

The basic "portfolio" issue facing the SAO is selecting the overseas programs that students will be allowed to go on. To answer this question, the SAO director must ask for advice and input from a widening campus constituency (i.e., the SAO staff, faculty, other university staff) about such issues as (a) what programs students have gone on in the recent past, and which of those are the most successful, (b) how willing faculty are to develop and lead short-term programs, (c) if the school supports reciprocal student exchange traffic and all that entails, (d) whether academic departments are able and willing to approve credit for work done abroad, and lastly (e) what financial needs students face in going abroad.

Most institutions offer a combination of faculty-led, short-term programs, reciprocal student exchanges, and provider programs. The SAO director needs to review what programs are done well, determine what "problem programs" should be eliminated, and identify new programs to be started or added. It is also vital to examine the types of provider programs used. Few schools have the capacity to create all "homegrown" programs, so some use of provider options is common. It may make sense for the SAO to join a consortium of schools offering cooperative programs. Cooperation from (a)

---

[4] The faculty advisory council at the author's current institution has a faculty member for each of the nine academic colleges, appointed by the dean. The SAO director chairs this group. The faculty member serves for two years and can be reappointed. The council meets 2-3 times a semester to discuss current issues and advise on arising policy issues. The group was first constituted with the consent and approval of the provost and the dean's council. In fall 2012 we added new permanent members to represent admissions, the international student and scholar services office, graduate college, and division of research. The expanded council was a logical group to serve as a task force in AY 2012–2013 to create a report for the provost on top needs in international education at our university. See "Top International Education Needs at Florida Atlantic University—A Report of the International Education Task Force," an unpublished report available at http://fau.edu/goabroad/pdf/International%20Education%20Task%20Force%20Report%20June%202013.pdf

[5] A campuswide council differs from faculty committees or advisory groups formed to support specific programs. Large campuses may have multiple programs serving a single language, e.g., Italian or Spanish, and see the need to create a committee of faculty to advise and build academic support and student interest for these specific programs.

university departments for credit approvals, (b) the registrar for transfer credit recognition, and (c) financial aid for access to appropriate aid packages are all needed to allow other types of shared programs the chance to be used successfully at the home institution.

Most SAOs have a small core of short-term, faculty-led programs that run every summer and during breaks. Large schools with a long history of study abroad may have more programs and even semester-long faculty-led programs; in other cases, programs may be very college-specific. It is advisable to support annual programs that feature known, reliable content, since repeated annual programs build student recognition and interest and make it easier for students to plan an abroad experience during their student career.

Adding new faculty-led programs each year is also important, as it takes advantage of expanding faculty interests and new faculty hires. New programs can attract new pools of interested students. Tactics for identifying potential faculty leaders include offering periodic informational sessions prior to the deadline for program proposals, and targeted e-mails to specific faculty or chairs of departments. Current program leaders can also encourage their peers to create a new program.[6]

Most institutions offer reciprocal student exchange programs since they can be very cost effective for the students. Maintaining popular and successful exchanges and adding new exchange options over time is a time-consuming process, but it can add a vital element to an institution's portfolio. Adding new exchange partners will engage the SAO director's time and energy, as it requires the assistance of faculty and deans. In determining the ideal or preferred balance of programs in the school's portfolio, the capacities of the SAO staff should be factored in as well as the size of the student body.

There may be a need to balance the more labor-intensive faculty-led programs and reciprocal student exchanges with student access to academically approved provider programs. Outsourcing logistical support and planning to reputable travel agencies or custom program providers can help with some faculty-led programs, and can offer great pricing, too. But do not overlook mandatory university guidelines for vendors and service providers, since they often need to be realigned to meet the needs of overseas vendors and service situations. The more flexible a university purchasing and financial services office can become, the easier time the SAO will have to locate and utilize vendors and service providers abroad.

---

[6]Be sensitive to the fact that some colleges and departments may discourage nontenured faculty from engaging in study abroad activities, as that participation may be seen as a hindrance in their quest for tenure.

Office Systems for Superior Service

Clear Job Assignments

The SAO director must outline clear job assignments and responsibilities to each staff member, including the SAO director position. Linked to job clarity will be a system for office management, staff meetings, and annual performance review. The actual division of labor between available staff (i.e., who does what) is less important than the clarity of the scheme—each staff member needs to understand their responsibilities, their job expectations, and the relationship of what they do in association with other staff.

Most SAO directors are tasked with specific areas of responsibility in addition to overall direction, goal setting, and office representation. Much will depend on the size of the institution and job expectations. As an example, for a modest-sized office, the director might take the lead for university partnership and exchange formation, meeting with faculty to help design short-term programs, federal fellowship advising, visitors, and special projects. At larger institutions, some of these tasks would be delegated to staff, but it is always the case that the SAO director will be the lead contact to faculty as well as the upper-level administration of the institution. The SAO director will also be called upon to enforce requests for assistance from units across the university, when other SAO staff are not getting the responses (or a response) needed to answer posed questions.

Advisers are the frontline for student services and program management. Effective advising is critical as it can help students better integrate study abroad into their degree program.[7] Advising assignments can be by region (e.g., someone does all of Europe, someone else does Asia), by program type (e.g., all exchanges, or all providers) or by college (e.g., someone does business programs and another does arts and letters). There is no single "correct" system, since many different arrangements can work. Whatever the system adopted, three rules of thumb should be followed: (1) assign programs to match staff skills and backgrounds to meet advising needs, (2) make sure there is an even distribution of the heavy advising programs and the less heavy advising programs, and (3) annually review the assignments to make sure recent growth of new options has not accidentally increased someone's load disproportionately. It is also a good idea to consider switching programs among staff every 2–3 years; cross-training allows staff to build new skills, meet new faculty with whom to work, and creates some backup capacity if staff are out sick. It can also provide staff relief if a particular faculty member or college is more challenging to work with.

---

[7] Forum on Education Abroad, *Standards of Good Practice for Education Abroad*, 4th Edition (Carlisle, Pa.: Forum on Education Abroad, 2011) 29–29.

Large institutions may have strong college-based study abroad programs and their own advising staff. The SAO should clarify what advising will be done in the college and what will be done by the SAO staff. In addition, other core activities best done by the central SAO should also be clarified with large colleges employing their own study abroad staff.

Other common office tasks that need to be assigned include:

EMPLOYEE	JOB FUNCTIONS
Office Manager Administrative Assistant	Financial, payroll, event assistance, meeting set up, file management
Student Workers Graduate Students	Reception, general welcome advising, data entry, outreach across campus

The larger the operation, the larger the staff, and therefore the more detailed subdivision of labor. Lastly, the SAO director needs to set a preferred schedule for staff meetings (how often) and establish the staff evaluation processes for performance throughout the year and at the end of every 12-month period.

Faculty Guidelines for Overseas Programs

Guidelines for faculty and departments on how to create a faculty-led program need to be announced at the time the SAO issues a call for new program proposals. The campus approval processes will dictate when to set a deadline for receipt of new program proposals. Part of the guidelines should explain the approval process and what the SAO will do to assist in recruitment, program registration, financial arrangements, and predeparture orientations for faculty and students. It is advised to place the guidelines on the SAO website for easy access and reference.

Program Enrollment

Students going abroad, whether on faculty-led programs, exchanges, or through providers, need to apply to the SAO, and therefore the SAO needs to create a system that manages enrollment, receipt of applications, and any fees they need to pay, and records student assent to the rules and policies of the program.[8] The SAO student application packet is probably the single most important document you have to create. The study abroad application can

---

[8]Institutions have different practices toward students who enroll at an overseas institution directly and then bring back their credits as transfer credits through the registrar office. The SAO needs to clarify procedures for such cases with the registrar and when they will be considered a study abroad student for the home institution. This status is often critical for financial aid purposes.

collect a wealth of data on the student that the SAO needs, and it can be used to inform the student of obligations, mandatory features such as application and program fees, health insurance, refund policies, and even student behavior codes. Most study abroad offices also add the standard student waiver and release of liability language. Institutional legal counsel should review the application for these aspects regularly. Online application systems are more common and can be very useful, but the content of the forms still need to be checked by university legal counsel.

Marketing

Marketing and outreach to the campus to recruit students for abroad programs need to be planned each year. Program information can be shared through program flyers or brochures that can be on the website and available at the SAO. Create an attractive reception area where program information can be placed. General answers to the most common questions from students can be tasked to the student workers at the front, and SAO advisers can establish a pattern to handle more in-depth questions on a walk-in basis and by setting up appointments for specific students. It can also be helpful to create an inquiry form process to answer predictable questions and channel students to focus their attentions. The inquiry forms can be fulfilled by the student workers and sample program materials delivered to students, who then study the program options and make an appointment to see an adviser to go over their interests in more detail.

Publicity about the array of program options can be shared with students through targeted classroom visits, regular weekly or daily information tables in key student traffic areas across campus, information sessions led by the faculty program leader, and regular study abroad fairs. Faculty program leaders and advocates who take part in these outreach activities can be very influential in building student interest.

Since most students have ready and even 24/7 access to smart phones, tablets, and laptop computers, it is essential to have a social media strategy and a plan to actively manage them on a regular basis. Websites are the most basic, and can be robust sites for full information on all the SAO does. Some schools have website protocols that must be followed, but within these frameworks the SAO can create easily accessed contact information, e-mails, phone numbers, and logical menu picks. An SAO Facebook page is also increasingly popular; however, both a website and a Facebook page are only good if maintained regularly. Other social media and technology tools to explore include Skype, video conferencing to reach faculty and groups at other physical campus locations, GotoMeeting for webinars, Twitter, Doodle for setting up meetings, and the use of videos and blogs. SAO staff capacity to learn these skills and maintain them in a proactive way is key, as are good relations to the university technology team.

Other marketing strategies include an annual study abroad photo contest, study abroad fairs, and student/faculty activities during International Education Week (IEW).

Scholarships

Most SAOs have some study abroad scholarship funding to assist students in going abroad. SAOs also have to handle federal fellowship programs such as the Gilman and Boren programs and the U.S. Student Fulbright program. Clear processes to apply for the various funds must be distributed and available on the SAO website. It is advised that no SAO staff be on the evaluation and review committees of the applications for an award, so there can be no claims of partiality on the part of the SAO staff.

Predeparture Orientations and Safety

As students prepare to go abroad, the SAO must create a multitiered system of preparations for their time abroad. At least one predeparture orientation led by the SAO staff is mandatory, as it is for the faculty member if the program is faculty-led. Students going on an exchange or provider program also need a predeparture orientation that goes over general guidelines for travel abroad. At the overseas school site, the exchange partner or provider program will offer a program-specific orientation upon their arrival abroad.

Complementing the orientation will be a general student study abroad manual for those going abroad. The manual should contain a thorough review of all the aspects of studying abroad, tips for their safety and study success, and a review of the guidelines they have agreed to adhere to while abroad. Some schools have students sign a form acknowledging they have received and read the manual. Having that form in SAO files can help later if there are discipline or academic disputes arising from the program with a particular student. The SAO should create a counterpart exchange student manual for incoming students attending your school, describing the experience they will have, tips on how to succeed in their studies and cultural immersion in the United States, and the rules governing their academic studies. Both manuals need to be available online to the staff and updated annually.

The SAO director and staff also need to establish and update regularly the safety and security processes that faculty and students will need to follow while abroad. Study abroad offices need to choose an emergency health insurance policy for students and establish the protocols for when (if at all) the requirement can be waived.[9] Faculty-led programs should prepare an emergency and safety plan in advance, noting the access while abroad at their site for hospitals, police, and U.S. consulates. The safety plan should also instruct students where to go in case of an emergency, so participants can plan to assemble at the predetermined gathering place in case they get split up. Faculty should also collect the cell phone numbers of all students, if using them abroad, and make sure students know faculty cell phone number(s) while abroad. The safety plan should be reviewed at the predeparture orientation and available to students during the trip. Faculty should follow SAO instructions on how and when to report incidents that happen abroad and be familiar on the insurance provided and how to access health services while overseas.[10]

Record Keeping

The well-run SAO needs an infrastructure to create, maintain, and store the paper and electronic records of the office. Much of the processes noted above have forms to be completed with signatures acknowledging receipt of information and agreement to follow policies, procedures, and to pay the fees required for their program. Sensitive personal information must be stored in secure locations and redundant systems used to record payments received (including what was paid when, by whom, and who received it on behalf of the SAO). Most schools have some or all elements of the application process stored in electronic fashion (such as a secure shared drive for the SAO), but it is advisable to consult with the campus financial management offices and the university's Office of Inspector General for guidance on what the SAO needs to keep in hard copy format and for how long. SAO staff are also advised to keep good notes of any in-person conversations or phone conversations with students or parents, in case of any discrepancies or differences of opinions on application or payment status down the road. Contracts with outside vendors for faculty-led programs should follow standard university vendor processes, cleared by appropriate campus legal review, and stored with the program administrative materials for that year.

There is a natural timetable for most SAO activities that will be revealed once you have gone through a typical 12-month period. The SAO should

---

[9]Many schools allow their own institutional health insurance requirement to be waived if the student is going on an approved external program that includes an equivalent insurance coverage. A clear policy in these situations needs to be articulated. For more information on insurance, see chapter 11.

[10]It is advisable to create an incident report form that faculty can complete at the time of a major incident, such as medical emergency, robbery, assault, or student behavior problem. Such reports should to be completed in the first 24-48 hours while the incident and information is fresh. The incident report form can then be used if there is any need for student affairs follow up or health care referrals. How to complete an incident report can be part of the faculty member predeparture orientation led by the SAO staff.

anticipate the periods in which students will be applying to go abroad, when they depart, and when exchange students first come to campus. The SAO will have ready for recruitment purposes the programs and their information and pricing and payment plans, and a process to receive applications and take in payments. Program cycles for summer, semester, and annual departures can help set deadlines for marketing efforts, student enrollment, bill payments, and predeparture orientations throughout the year. These will be linked closely to the university academic calendar. During the year staff can plan to review application materials, and all forms and policies to be ready for the new round of programs. To avoid endless updating of program materials—unless there is a particular error that needs to be corrected—most schools will find it best to have forms for students ready in the fall of each school year (as students come back to campus and contemplate a time abroad in the future) and forms for the faculty ready in the spring of each year at the time the SAO calls for short-term programs proposals.

Once a study abroad office has established a good working routine for the annual academic cycle, and key processes for tasks linking other campus entities (e.g., financial affairs, registrar, housing) have been confirmed, a study abroad office operations manual should be compiled. The manual needs to be succinct but thorough, and show screen images and samples of completed forms that are needed. The manual serves as an ongoing resource for all staff, and a training tool for new staff. The manual should be kept in a common location in hard copy format, and on an easily accessed common electronic file storage drive or cloud. Each year the calendar also needs to show a date (usually in the summer when things are slower) to check to see if the manual needs to be updated.

A final annual written document that needs to be prepared is the SAO annual report. In most cases, the SAO annual report will be done over the summer by the SAO director to record the tasks and activities of the previous academic year. The annual report records annual growth in student and program numbers, builds a constituency across the institution, acknowledges the help received from faculty, staff, and deans, and is a repository of what the SAO has done in case of a review or a call for information to be included in a campus report or speech. The SAO needs to send the annual report to a wide range of university officials and faculty as well as external supporters, donors, and friends of the office (i.e., the international education community) and place it in a visible location on your SAO web page.

Fostering Innovation: Taking on Special Projects

Study abroad offices need to be alert for opportunities to make the study abroad experience more visible and more mainstream across the institution. Program directors and advisers should watch for opportunities to engage with other university offices on projects that will, immediately or over time, garner more attention and buy-in for study abroad activities. For example, in recent years many institutions have launched large, campuswide efforts to enhance undergraduate education. These are often provost or chancellor/president-level initiatives, and study abroad offices have benefited from partnering with faculty and units in grant competitions to build new models of programing abroad. In other situations, SAOs have taken steps to be part of the institution's reaccrediting process and create an area of academic priority to invest campus resources. Special projects on a smaller scale can be powerful as well—the study abroad office at Florida Atlantic University has had success joining the campus career and civic engagement offices to host student information sessions on experiential learning.

As helpful as it can be to broaden awareness for study abroad via special projects, one does have to be cautious and not deviate too far from the stated office mission and goals. As a case in point, my own office has had to turn down occasional college requests to organize and pay for travel and hosting of college visiting scholars and faculty, citing lack of staff and budget capacity. We are not a travel agency, and have limited hospitality funding. In other instances, we were willing to join early efforts to create formal international student recruitment activities. While abroad on a typical university partnership visit, we also attended several international student recruitment fairs on a trial basis and covered the costs associated with them. More recently, however, we have indicated other offices more clearly suited for this (at our school this is admissions and enrollment management), that must take the lead on overseas recruitment projects in regard to both the staff time and out-of-pocket costs for travel and fair fees. We still attend occasional meetings to share ideas and be supportive.

Final Remarks on Benchmarking for Excellence

Good university managers understand the value and practice of peer benchmarking. No one knows everything there is to know about study abroad, international education, higher education, or general management. A SAO director must feel comfortable asking for advice and gather data and information on what others do, as an aid to shaping policy and practice choices. The savvy SAO director will reach out to nearby peers, and moreover target those institutions excelling in study abroad and international education to learn as much as possible about what they are doing that makes them so successful. Fortunately, most people enjoy being asked for their advice and solutions, and don't mind sharing information with their peers.

Formal benchmarking typically involves phone calls, travel to the benchmark school by a team of SAO staff and faculty, and/or a consultancy by appropriate staff of the benchmark school. Formal benchmarking costs money. If the SAO budget does not allow for the more elaborate versions, one can still garner valuable advice from peers by attending professional conferences and networking at them during down periods or conducting informal consulting through informal e-mail surveys. To simplify the process, craft any survey questions as succinctly as possible, and make it easy to reply by return e-mail or SurveyMonkey. It is also best to limit the number of surveys sent around to a few per year, since even the most generous colleagues will tire from endless survey requests. As a courtesy, whenever possible, summarize the responses received and send them out to participating colleagues at some point, so all can benefit from the survey results.

Additional Resources

American Council on Education Campus Internationalization Toolkit
http://www.acenet.edu/news-room/Pages/Internationalization-Toolkit.aspx
Website with useful models of templates, concept papers, and policies and procedures, including administrative structure, faculty policies and procedures, student mobility and collaboration and partnerships.

Forum on Education Abroad Toolkit
This is a series of volumes to guide study abroad offices. They include Code of Ethics for Education Abroad (2011), *Standards of Good Practice for Short-Term Education Abroad Programs* (2009), *Standards of Good Practice for Education Abroad* (4th Edition 2011), *Education Abroad Glossary* (2011) and *A Guide to Outcomes Assessment in Education Abroad*, edited by Mell Bolen (2007).

Florida Atlantic University Report
International Education Task Force. 2013. Top International Education Needs at Florida Atlantic University. Unpublished report from Florida Atlantic University. Available at http://fau.edu/goabroad/pdf/International%20 Education%20Task%20Force%20Report%20June%202013.pdf.

References

NAFSA. 2011. *Internationalizing the Campus 2011: Profiles of Success at Colleges and Universities.* Washington, D.C.: NAFSA: Association of International Educators.

American Council on Education. 2012. *Mapping Internationalization on U.S. Campuses: 2012 Edition.* Washington, D.C.: American Council on Education.

Burnett, Sally-Ann. 2010. "Universities' Responses to Globalisation: The Influence of Organisational Culture." In *Journal of Studies in International Education* 14, 2: 117–142.

Mehaffy, George L. 2012. "Challenge and Change." *EDUCAUSE Review* 47, 5.

Meschievitz, Catherine S. 2011. "Meeting the Global Imperative: International Education at Florida Atlantic University." Unpublished essay available from author.

Mestenhauser, Josef. 2011. *Reflections on the Past, Present, and Future of Internationalizing Higher Education: Discovering Opportunities to Meet the Challenges.* Minneapolis, Minn.: University of Minnesota.

Spencer, Sarah E. and Kathy Tuma, eds. 2002. *The Guide to Successful Short-Term Programs Abroad.* Washington, D.C.: NAFSA: Association of International Educators.

Trubek, David M. 2001. "The Future of International Studies." In *Changing Perspectives on International Education.* Edited by Patrick O'Meara, Howard Mehlinger and Roxana Ma Newman. Bloomington, Ind.: Indiana University Press: 298–319.

CHAPTER 19

HUMAN RESOURCES IN EDUCATION ABROAD

By Steven Duke

Among the numerous challenges education abroad professionals face is the need to manage their human resources. Many education abroad professionals feel stretched to do all of things that seem vital to their office's core missions: advising and preparing students, coordinating strong and effective education abroad programs, and ensuring the health, safety, and well-being of students. Many also feel a strong need to increase participation in study abroad, advocate for internationalization on campus, integrate study abroad into the curriculum, and promote a global mindset among students. These tasks and goals can feel daunting, particularly amid concerns about a weak economy, rapidly rising tuition, and other financial pressures. For these reasons, it is important that educational abroad directors and professional staff work together to achieve their objectives.

Office Staff and Assignments/Responsibilities

When thinking about human resources, it helps to start with the office staff. Each institution is unique, so it is no surprise that the number of education abroad staff in an office is shaped largely by the past. Some institutions have had an education abroad office for several decades, and a large, well-organized staff has developed over time. Education abroad offices at other institutions may have been established more recently; colleagues at some work in a "one-person office." The size of institutions also varies, so it is logical that a large "flagship" public university might have multiple study abroad offices across a large campus, while other institutions, both public and private, have only one office, with just 2-4 staff members.

In addition, the titles used in education abroad offices vary widely. Although there has been discussion within the field for several years regarding standardizing titles, it is still common for numerous titles to be used very differently across multiple institutions. Someone with a title of "education abroad adviser" at one institution could easily have the title of "associate director" in another institution. The Forum on Education Abroad's "Pathways to the Profession Survey 2008" found 146 different titles among 309 individuals who participated in the survey (n.d., 9).

Regardless of the number of staff in the education abroad officer's office or the titles they currently have, it is useful to think broadly and creatively about the current roles of staff, as well as the strengths and weaknesses of those individuals. Developing a clear set of written responsibilities as well as expectations for how individuals with different roles will work together can be key to leveraging the talents and previous work and academic experiences of office staff. Common responsibilities include:

- Advising students about program options
- Processing student applications, whether in paper or online
- Preparing students to study abroad, including predeparture orientations
- Assisting students in selecting courses and housing
- Enrolling students into courses or coordinating this process with a registrar's office
- Developing marketing materials
- Holding events such as education abroad fairs, cooking classes, intercultural learning sessions, reentry workshops or conferences, etc.
- Maintaining accurate data regarding students and student participation in programs, typically using a database (see chapter 20)
- Working with a parent office and other offices regarding core functions such as the office budget (see chapter 21), travel procedures, building maintenance, etc.
- Conducting site visits and program reviews, and establishing protocols for assessments of student learning and program management (see chapter 24)
- Working with existing programs regarding budgets, program fees, academic and admissions policies, student support services, visas, etc.
- Working with faculty committees to establish policies, review proposals for new programs, review student applications, and manage partnerships
- Working with faculty and staff committees to identify student learning outcomes and to conduct assessments of student learning abroad
- Developing new programs or establishing new student exchange relationships, and managing a portfolio of programs (see chapter 18)
- Working with overseas staff or partner organizations regarding budgets, program fees, student support services, student visas, enrollment processes, academic policies, internships, building maintenance, student housing and homestays, etc.
- Reviewing and approving transfer credit (if not done in a registrar's office)
- Working with academic departments and/or dean's offices regarding transfer of academic credit, financial aid and scholarships, probation, misconduct, etc.
- Developing protocols for health, safety, security, and crisis management

- Responding to emergencies abroad
- Coordinating a peer adviser program
- Working with a human resources office regarding compensation and benefits, job descriptions, employment status and titles, salary increases, handling complaints, etc.
- Holding events to recognize faculty champions and program directors

With such a long list of responsibilities, it is no wonder that many education abroad professionals feel stretched thin. It is easy to get pulled largely toward student advising and events, with less time to stand back and look at the "big picture" of how the office functions internally, its role within the institution, and how office staff and other stakeholders want the office to grow or change. However, with time, patience, and a long-term approach to the challenges as well as opportunities within your institution, you and your colleagues can make a difference in the lives of students, and in the functioning of the institution.

Staffing Models

Regardless of the size of your office, it is common for individual staff members to be assigned unique roles where they can specialize in a given area, in addition to roles shared jointly by several individuals (such as advising). In some offices, education abroad advisers are assigned advising duties based on world region, so they can advise all students going to a particular country or area. In other cases, assignments are made by program type, so some staff work with semester programs while others work with summer or faculty-led programs, or with student exchanges. It is also common for individuals to become the "point person" for certain tasks, such as scholarships, coordinating student peer advisers, liaising with other offices on campus, coordinating education abroad fairs and other events, working with marketing and publicity, and so on.

Deciding which staff should have which assignments and then communicating the logic and process by which assignments are made is key. Office directors generally solicit the input of office staff before assignments are made in order to obtain insights regarding the background, interests, and current workload of staff. In some cases, advisers compete to work with a popular program or country, or to avoid less-popular programs or locations. Effective office directors ensure that assignments are communicated clearly and concerns are resolved throughout the year and throughout application cycles and fiscal years.

When new staff is hired, it is a good time to review the programs for which everyone advises and other general responsibilities. Duties can be shifted, when appropriate, to capitalize on the individual skills, knowledge, and experience of the new staff member. The Center for International Programs Abroad at Emory University has found that these occasional shifts of responsibilities can also serve as good opportunities for cross-training, and can also serve to motivate staff to learn something new and different.[1]

In cases where an office has several staff, it can be tricky to balance the workload and assignments of office staff. The reason is that workloads can vary depending on the time of year and amount of effort required to handle core functions, such as submitting applications to a partner organization, processing student visas, leading predeparture orientation sessions, conducting overseas visits or program reviews, or coordinating events or other tasks. In some cases it may be appropriate to make assignments based on the number of students who participate in a portfolio of programs so that all advisers have a roughly equal number of advisees.

In other cases the number of advisees is not a good metric for workload, so one adviser may work with more students than another adviser. Several teams of education abroad professionals, working with the Forum on Education Abroad, have conducted national surveys and analyses of workload issues in education abroad. These surveys, "State of the Field," "Forum Pathways," and "Program Management," can be found on the Forum's website (www.forumea.org) or by contacting Forum staff. In addition, various Forum committees and working groups also collect data regarding workloads and staffing in the field.[2]

Several models exist for student advising and program management. One common model is for professional advisers to handle all aspects of certain programs, meaning that they advise all students applying to those programs as well as process applications, work on course selection and enrollment procedures, do marketing/publicity, and coordinate with overseas staff. A contrasting model is to separate the advising process from program management, so that one adviser meets with students while other staff coordinate enrollment, student visas, program handbooks, and so on. The University of Wisconsin-Madison's International Academic Programs office, one of several offices that serve study abroad at a large university, has created "triangle teams" involving three individuals: a study abroad adviser who advises students and coordinates orientations, an enrollment specialist who processes applications and course equivalencies, and a financial specialist who handles finances. These teams work well because responsibilities are divided and staff

---

[1] Personal communication between the author and Kristi Hubbard (director, Center for International Programs Abroad, Emory University), November 5, 2013.

[2] The data collection section on the Forum on Education Abroad's website, http://www.forumea.org, includes survey results for the "State of the Field," "Institutional and Program Resources," and other topics.

can assist one another with a set of programs they know well.[3] Some institutions, as well as provider organizations, assign certain staff to recruit outside students through campus visits, study abroad fairs, and other methods of outreach. Each of these approaches has strengths and weaknesses in terms of staff assignments and balancing workloads within an office.

Variations also exist regarding program management, depending on how and when programs were first created and the involvement of upper administration and faculty. One common model is for all programs to be managed directly from an education abroad office. In this case, overseas staff officially report to the office director or an assistant/associate director, who is also responsible for negotiating contracts, dealing with program budgets and enrollment costs, dealing with fluctuations in currency, and arranging student housing, among many other tasks. In contrast is another common model in which home-campus faculty members serve as directors of individual programs. In this case, the faculty director supervises overseas staff, oversees program budgets, and arranges student housing, while education abroad staff work with students and on-campus activities.

The consortium-program model is a variation of the direct-management model. In this model, a group of institutions forms a consortium, generally with a formal agreement that describes how the consortium will function, including the process for new members to join or existing members to leave the group. One institution serves as the lead institution, with other institutions contributing students, input, and advice. In one version of the consortium-program model, each member institution must supply a faculty member to serve as on-site director on a rotating basis. The lead institution then provides oversight of the program, and members of the institution meet regularly to discuss the program, course selection, budgets, staffing, and other relevant matters.

Of course, other program models also exist. Student exchange programs require different levels of interaction, both with the partner organizations as well as with inbound and outbound students and international student support staff. Maintaining relationships with direct-enrollment programs, in which outbound students enroll directly at a foreign institution, and partner organizations or "third-party providers" may require the involvement of multiple individuals in an education abroad office.

Regardless of the number and type of education abroad programs your institution operates or offers to students, it is important to identify high-priority tasks that always need to be done, as well as less-critical tasks that

---

[3]Personal communication between the author and Julie Lindsey (associate director, International Academic Programs, University of Wisconsin-Madison), January 7, 2014.

should be attended to as time permits. Then create a list of assignments for which staff will do which tasks, or a timeline for when those tasks need to be completed each semester or year.

Professional Development: Internal, External, and Cross-Training

In addition to creating a clear list of tasks and responsibilities for staff, it is also important to develop plans for their professional development. Professional development opportunities can be lumped into three main groupings: internal, external, and cross-training.

"Internal" professional development refers to opportunities for continuing development that are available inside the institution. Many colleges and universities host a range of different programs and learning activities that are open to staff. For example, many institutions offer functional training on databases, website design, and software packages such as Microsoft Office. These short courses may be free or relatively low in cost. In addition, institutions often offer other professional development opportunities focused on topics such as leadership, delegating, budgeting, theories and approaches to student affairs, communication skills, project management, leadership, and more. Taking advantage of these local learning opportunities can help staff develop new skills and insights that will assist them in doing their work and helping them develop professionally, often at little or no cost to the office. Emory University has found that team-building exercises facilitated by their own human resources staff can be very helpful in cultivating a positive group dynamic. Where possible, it is appropriate for staff to attend such trainings during their regular work day and as part of their job responsibilities.

Numerous external professional development opportunities are also available outside of your institution. Professional conferences are important for professional development because they enable staff to learn best practices, develop core competencies, and build networks of contacts who are leaders in certain areas or who deal with similar challenges.

Conferences are also a great place where your staff can share lessons learned or programs developed for your students and gain valuable experience in making professional presentations. Many professional conferences, including NAFSA's annual and regional conferences, now offer preconference workshops and short courses on a wide range of topics, from introductions to the education abroad field to topics such as financial aid, best practices in assessment, working with students from diverse backgrounds, current trends in marketing and social media, and others.[4] In addition, the Forum

---

[4] The NAFSA website, **www.nafsa.org**, includes numerous resources about best practices, training opportunities, conferences, publications, professional networks, and more.

on Education Abroad is now organizing one-day workshops on individual standards, plus one-day Standards of Good Practice Institutes on different topics. Program provider conferences are also expanding beyond narrow conversations about their own programs to full-fledged professional conferences with a wide variety of topics. There can be interesting and relevant sessions at professional conferences in related fields such as student affairs, financial aid, registrars, and so on. Many offices find it best to send some staff to certain conferences or workshops while others stay in the office to handle routine and emergency issues that may arise, and then rotate attendance at other conferences.

In addition to attending professional conferences and workshops, visiting programs and sites abroad is also essential to the work of education abroad professionals. Education abroad advisers and directors need to know as much as possible about the programs they manage and advise for, and visiting programs is invaluable in their advising and program management responsibilities. On-site visits also serve to strengthen relationships with institutional partners and on-site staff. Even if staff can only participate in one international site visit per year, it is important not only to allocate the money for such trips, but also the time needed to make them effective.

Site visits should be carefully planned and purposeful, allowing education abroad directors and staff to meet on-site staff or partners, attend classes (when authorized), visit housing or homestay options, and meet with students. Most on-site visits run 10-12 hours per day and are demanding physically, intellectually, and linguistically. Where possible, education abroad professionals should try to travel to the site the same way students are expected to travel. For example, taking the train or bus from the airport (where doing so is safe) allows a director or adviser to anticipate common challenges students might experience, so they can adjust the advising process accordingly. Taking public transportation or walking between housing and academic buildings (again, where doing so is safe) will help you better understand the challenges your students will face in each location. It goes without saying that those participating in site visits should also evaluate health, safety, and security practices and protocols, and recommend improvements when needed.

The third type of professional development relates to cross-training staff. It is great when roles and responsibilities are clear and when staff members have the skills and experience to perform their individual tasks effectively. But what happens when a key staff member is out due to illness, family concerns, travel, or vacation? It is important to have other staff learn enough about the tasks done by others so that the entire office does not fall apart when key staff members are away. Important functions to consider for cross-training include front office reception/intake, processing and filing paperwork, financial aid documentation, database updates, conducting pre-departure orientations, and managing student health crises or emergencies abroad. Documenting the steps for each task and role can be useful not only when cross-training others, but also in making improvements in day-to-day work. You don't need a full-scale adviser's manual in order to document these functions and cross-train staff.

Education abroad professionals are deeply committed to their work and the needs of students. Taking the time to develop plans for their professional development will improve the quality and depth of their work with students and programs, and will also increase their global awareness.

Hiring New Employees

As you work on the professional development of your staff, address the advising and personal needs of students, and strengthen programs, you may have the opportunity to hire a new team member. Hiring new education abroad professionals or support staff can be an exciting process. New staff often brings new energy and ideas to an office. New employees tend to be enthusiastic about getting to know their institution, learning about programs, trying new and creative methods to reach more students, and investigating new ways to do their work. When open positions are advertised through SECUSS-L, NAFSA, the Forum on Education Abroad, or other electronic platforms, it is not uncommon to receive hundreds of applications from interested candidates.

When a position becomes open, either through the retirement or departure of an existing employee or through the opportunity to create a new position, there are a number of steps that should be followed. The following is a list of common steps. Check with the human resources office at your institution to learn how the hiring process unfolds where you work.

- Develop a position description: this should contain core details of the position, as well as the skills, experience and education that are required.
- Identify a salary range for the position, including the maximum and minimum salaries that can be offered. This may require comparison of similar positions at your institution, including in other offices or departments. Be prepared to answer questions about salary ranges from potential applicants.
- Identify the source or sources of funding for the position and obtain written approval to access those funds; find out if the funding is available immediately or not until a future date.

- Develop a timeline for the hiring process, beginning with a target date for announcing the position opening; include several weeks for reviewing applications and interviewing; and allow several weeks or even months for the person who is offered the position to move to your location or to leave an existing position.
- Speak with your human resources office to confirm your institution's policies regarding affirmative action and equal opportunity in the hiring process, so you will know what steps are required, what types of questions are permissible in the interview process,[5] and what reports or updates you are expected to provide throughout the process.
- Confirm whether your institution uses an online application system for candidates to apply for the position, whether you can accept applications submitted via e-mail or "hard copy," and what type of system should be used for tracking candidates, reviewing cover letters and résumés, and informing human resources about the status of each candidate at different stages of the review and interview processes.

Once you have completed these steps, you are ready to begin advertising the open position. To cast a wide net, consider posting notices for the position on the SECUSS-L e-mail listserv, as well as on websites of NAFSA, the Forum on Education Abroad, and other professional organizations. Circulate the position notice among education abroad professionals who may know of eligible candidates or among schools that offer master's degrees in international education. Ensure the deadline for applicants is prominent in all publicity. If you wish to accept applications submitted after the closing date, it is important to include words such as "the review of applications will continue until the position is filled."

After the closing date has passed, it is time to review applications. This can be a daunting task, especially if hundreds of applications were submitted. Many institutions use search committees to spread out the time-consuming work of reviewing cover letters and résumés. Human resources staff could also review applications, assuming that you have given them a good list of items to screen for, such as educational background, previous work experience, languages spoken, time spent abroad, and so on. Consider having other office staff help in reviewing applications, or include one or more trusted faculty or staff from other offices to assist. Be careful to follow institutional and affirmative action/equal opportunity policies. One strategy for reviewing applications is to create a rating system with three to five categories, such as

---

[5]The website of the Society for Human Resource Management, http://www.shrm.org, includes information about sample interview questions and other resources.

highly qualified, unqualified, or moderately qualified. Another strategy is to create a grid or chart to track required skills or experience, plus other desirable experience or traits.

The interview process may vary, depending on the number and quality of candidates and your timeline. It is common to conduct phone interviews with 5–10 candidates, and then to select 2–4 candidates for on-campus interviews. Phone interviews typically last 15–30 minutes and cover additional details of the position and office and an ideal timeline for the hiring process. For entry-level positions, it may be appropriate to discuss potential salary ranges. Keep your hiring manager informed as candidates are removed from consideration. Confirm whether someone in human resources will notify those individuals no longer under consideration.

On-campus or in-office interviews are your best opportunity to learn more about the finalists and explore their skills, experience, and background in detail. Communicate clearly with all candidates regarding potential interview dates, travel and logistics, what time the interviews will start and end, and how and when they will be reimbursed for any travel costs incurred. Finalists will appreciate you sending them more details about your office and institution, such as data reports, program review reports, descriptions of how the office interacts with faculty and faculty committees, and key projects the new employee will undertake. Give all finalists a timeline for when they will hear from you, and stick to that timeline, even if you can only tell them a decision is still pending.

Extending a job offer can be an enjoyable process, depending on how closely the salary fits with the candidate's expectations, as well as variables such as relocation expenses, official start date, office space, and so on. Before extending a formal job offer, be sure to double-check with your human resources office concerning benefits and hiring procedures. Confirm that the funding and necessary approvals have been obtained. It is common for the person extending the job offer to do so verbally first, followed by a written letter that includes details about salary and benefits as well as details about the formal hiring practices, such as a background check. Your institutional policy or process governs how and when an offer is extended.

Throughout the hiring process, be positive with candidates and existing staff. The application and interview processes can be exhausting and nerve-racking, so take time to thank and recognize those individuals who pitched in to help with the process or who took on extra work while a new team member was hired. Hopefully, everyone concerned will be pleased when the hiring process is completed and your new employee comes on board.

New Employee Orientations

Naturally, the hiring manager will want to pay careful attention to helping new staff get "up to speed" quickly after being hired. According to Tyson (2006, 183), a high percentage of new employees leave an organization within a few years of joining it. Education abroad directors can help new employees to overcome the natural stresses of starting a new job by carefully planning their introduction to your organization and helping them integrate into the office staff and office procedures. Continue to work with your human resources office for "onboarding" procedures. Best practices for bringing new employees into an existing office include the following:

- Introduce new staff to all employees in the education abroad unit and its parent office, typically on the person's first day of work.
- Allow time for the new person to complete federal tax forms, human resources forms, and benefit applications, some of which must be done on the first day or two of employment.
- Prepare a detailed, multiweek plan for new staff to meet with staff inside and outside the education abroad office to discuss detailed aspects of their roles and responsibilities.
- Review procedures for advising, academic requirements, procedures for working with the office of the dean of students, and other on-campus procedures.
- Review protocols for health, safety, security, and well-being of students abroad.
- Discuss how programs are managed at your institution.
- Review the programs that are usually available to your students in detail, including application deadlines and procedures, how and when acceptance decisions are made and by whom, and how acceptance or rejection is communicated to students.
- Meet staff in offices that interact with the education abroad office, such as student financial aid, bursar or student financial services, registrar, housing and residence life, etc.
- Meet faculty or staff in key academic departments or academic deans' offices.

It is important to realize that new staff need to experience one or two full cycles of programs, often lasting a full year or longer, to truly understand how all the pieces fit together. There will likely be aspects of recruitment and advertising that will work better the second or third time around, simply because advising and program management are iterative processes, in which a person's work improves over time across a natural learning curve. For this reason, consider scheduling time to revisit key issues and processes at later points, such as three or six months after a new employee is hired, to discuss what has been accomplished, to plan additional training activities, and to learn how the new employee is feeling about his or her work. This is a good time to identify and address any concerns that have arisen. It is not necessary to wait until an official performance review to discuss concerns or to consider whether the new-employee training was adequate for the tasks and responsibilities given.

Staff-Peer Mentor Program

It seems nearly universal in our field that there is always more work than there is time. Many institutions have developed peer mentoring programs to take advantage of the time, energy, enthusiasm, and creativity of students who have returned from abroad. Several varieties of such programs exist. In one variation, a peer mentor program is intended for the professional development of the peers, who may spend just one or two hours per week developing events, meeting with interested students, or assisting with predeparture orientations. In this case, peer mentors might not be paid for their time or efforts, but receive professional development opportunities that engage them with education abroad programs. In another variation, peer mentors are hired for ten or fifteen hours per week and play a much greater role in speaking with students, helping with marketing and recruiting, and planning events.

When considering whether to create or change a peer mentor (sometimes called peer adviser) program, it is important to consider the staff time that is needed to train and coordinate the work of peer mentors. Student peer mentors become an extension of your office and may be viewed as official representatives, whether or not they are paid for their time. For this reason, it is essential to provide initial training for them, as well as ongoing monitoring and professional development, albeit on a smaller scale than for full-time employees. For example, an initial training session might last three hours, rather than three weeks. Another best practice is to meet regularly with peer mentors, such as every two or three weeks, to coordinate efforts and events, provide feedback as a group, and to discuss their insights and concerns. Assigning one experienced staff member to coordinate student peer mentors is essential to the success of this type of program.

Interns and Research Assistants

Hiring an intern or research assistant is another way to extend the scope and the reach of your office without hiring a full-time employee. At institutions that have graduate programs, there may be opportunities to hire a graduate student to work in your office. In some cases, graduate programs are able to cover a portion of the cost of hiring a graduate research assistant. In other cases, you may need to provide the full compensation, which might include tuition support as well as salary and benefits. Research assistants can provide invaluable help with such items as data reporting and analysis, processing applications, and helping with events, in addition to doing research for curriculum integration efforts or other projects.

Hiring an intern for a short period offers another opportunity to expand your reach. Interns could be one of your own students after graduation, or could be graduate students in one of the many master's degree programs that focus on international education, higher education leadership, or intercultural communication. Many students in those degree programs are required to complete a practicum or internship. Interns are generally paid for their work, but the overall cost of hiring a short-term intern might be lower than bringing on a full-time employee.

Front Office Operations vs. One-on-One Student Meetings

One area of critical importance to the work and flow of an education abroad office is the front office or reception area. Students, faculty, parents, and other visitors who come to your office should be welcomed in a professional and supportive manner. Some students may be apprehensive on their first visit and may have many questions about the process. Many of those questions might seem silly or off-base to someone who has traveled widely. It is essential that whoever works in your reception area be able to handle a wide range of questions and issues with diplomacy and tact.

Although the office may have one full-time staff member who is assigned to greeting visitors and setting appointments, it is important that multiple staff be cross-trained in the essential parts of these various processes. As noted above, members of your team may be out for illness, vacation, personal time, or family commitments, so it is important that others who work in the reception area are prepared to handle the types of questions and issues that may arise. This includes the possibility that students or faculty abroad might call your main office number in an emergency, so the person answering phone calls needs to know what types of information should be obtained from callers.

In many education abroad offices, students will want to meet one-on-one with an adviser or the office director. One common practice is to ask students to fill out an advising sheet, which the person advising the student can use to write notes on and document what advice was given or questions were raised. This document can then be used again at future meetings, both to track each student's progress toward studying abroad and to identify potential issues of concern. Advising sheets plus other documentation should be filed in such a way that they can be retrieved and consulted as necessary. Each institution has a "records retention" policy that governs where such records should be housed, how long such records must be maintained, and when they should be destroyed. There may be exceptions given for exceptional circumstances.

Managing Staff and Dealing with Concerns

Education abroad offices are not immune to the complications that can come from stress, including finding a positive work-life balance and the strain that comes from differences of opinion regarding student advising, program management, working with students and faculty, and more. Education abroad directors face challenges of identifying problems and then addressing them, often amid the stresses of institutional policies and tight finances. The University of California–Berkeley has published a resource on its website called *Guide to Managing Human Resources.*[6] It includes useful information on recruiting, managing staff, interaction in the workplace, managing conflict, wellness, and employee relations. Moreover, your own human resources office can assist with additional resources for addressing in-office stresses and inter-personal challenges.

Managing Space

One of the other key issues that affect every office is where offices are located, how much space is available for staff, and how that space is managed. It seems nearly universal that education abroad offices need more or better space. In some cases, the space that once was adequate when an office had just a few staff becomes inadequate when additional staff are hired. In other cases, the education abroad office is located on the edge of campus or in a hard-to-find building, far away from student "foot traffic." Occasionally, staff members share cubicles or desks, making it hard to have private conversations with students.

Education abroad directors should do their best to use and manage the space that is available to the office. Because each institution is different, what works at one college may not work at another. Advocating for additional space or a different location can feel like an uphill battle, because space is generally limited at most colleges and universities. Networking with key faculty and administrators can often be helpful. For example, working with

---

[6]See http://hrweb.berkeley.edu/guides/managing-hr.

campus facilities to make sure signs around campus direct visitors to the study abroad office and making sure that campus maps include the location of the office is a good form of networking and outreach. In addition, it is helpful to know the staff who clean and care for your building and those who supervise the campus physical facilities when addressing any core concerns that may arise from the space.

Regardless of where your office is located, keep in mind the many valuable reasons why students should go abroad, and how they and the institution might benefit from their international experience.

References

The Forum on Education Abroad. 2012. The Forum on Education Abroad State of the Field Survey 2011. Carlisle, Pa.: The Forum on Education Abroad. http://forumea.org/documents/ForumEA-StateofFieldSurvey-2012.pdf.

The Forum on Education Abroad. N.d. *The Forum Pathways to the Profession Survey 2008: Report and Results*. Carlisle, Pa.: The Forum on Education Abroad. http://forumea.org/documents/ForumEAReportPathways2008.pdf.

Tyson, Shaun. 2006. *Essentials of Human Resource Management, Fifth Edition*. Oxford, UK: Butterworth-Heinemann.

University of California–Berkeley. N.d. *Guide to Managing Human Resources*. Berkeley, Calif.: University of California. http://hrweb.berkeley.edu/guides/managing-hr.

CHAPTER 20

EFFECTIVE UTILIZATION OF INSTITUTIONAL DATA FOR STRATEGIC EDUCATION ABROAD PLANNING AND CAMPUS ADVOCACY

By Anthony C. Ogden

In an era of increasing standardization and accountability, it is strategically important that education abroad professionals be able to produce data that reinforce the importance of education abroad programming and demonstrate how international education can enhance and extend institutional missions, values, and priorities. This chapter provides a basic overview of the importance of accurately gathering and effectively utilizing institutional and external data for long-term strategic planning and campus-based advocacy. In particular, the chapter presents a series of emerging questions or key challenges frequently posed to education abroad professionals. It summarizes the commonly used datasets available at most colleges and universities, which can be accessed or reframed to address these questions and thus further bolster the role of education abroad in the curriculum. Common pitfalls and related methodological considerations are explained, and suggestions are offered for effectively partnering with strategic offices or units to compile, analyze, and use essential information.

Purposes for Data Collection

In recent decades, education abroad programming has moved from the margins toward the center of the undergraduate curriculum. Once the purview of a small number of academic departments, education abroad today is acknowledged and integrated into curricula across most disciplines (Braskamp 2008; Streitwieser, Le, and Rust 2012). The popularity of education abroad programming has been driven largely by the ubiquitous rhetoric around globalization, which poses major pressures and competing challenges for those who facilitate education abroad. In addition to fighting the long-held perception of education abroad as a mere touristic enterprise, and keeping the profit motive and exploitative commercialization at bay (Ogden, Streitwieser, and Crawford 2013), education abroad professionals must also ensure quality over quantity in spite of pressures to "get the numbers up" from senior administration. To name just a few of the many challenges, professionals must produce rigorous evidence-based assessment and research that justifies the expense and effort, compile sophisticated enrollment reports with multiyear projections, and produce detailed strategic plans based on metrics and baseline data. Common among these many challenges is the need for reliable data that are accessible, easily transferable, and—as is often needed—persuasive and predictive.

In daily practice, education abroad practitioners most often rely on existing national and institutional datasets when called upon for such information. The most common requests generally fall within five broad categories, as follows:

- **Advocacy.** Providing data for effective campus-level advocacy is often an essential function of most education abroad offices. Campus-level advocacy initiatives include, for example, leveraging data on underrepresented students to advocate for new institutional funding, providing major-specific enrollment information to advance curricular integration efforts, or positioning noncredit-bearing travel enrollment data to advocate for a blanket travel medical insurance requirement.

- **Benchmarking.** Comparing one's processes and performance metrics with peer institutions is common practice in U.S. higher education and certainly, education abroad professionals must similarly benchmark within the profession and know how to leverage benchmarking data to advance initiatives on one's home campus.

- **Strategic Planning.** Every three to five years, most institutions regroup to establish a new strategic plan, alongside which each college and/or department must develop unit-specific strategies supported by methodologies and measures of assessment. Education abroad offices that are poised to provide colleges/departments with enrollment data may be more successful with integrating education abroad programming within the measurable goals of units throughout the institution.

- **Outcomes Measures.** As institutions have begun to direct more attention to documenting practices that effectively maximize student success, increasing attention has turned to understanding what students learn through international education programming (Bolen 2007; Ogden and Brennan 2013). No longer is it simply enough to claim in this environment that education abroad is a "good thing" for students without offering specific evidence to support such assertions. Like others in higher education, education abroad professionals must also demonstrate the value of their efforts with valid and reliable outcomes data.

- **Grant Proposal Writing.** Whether it is to identify sources of potential funding, to provide faculty members with needed data, or to partner with another unit in writing a grant proposal, education abroad offices are increasingly invited into grant proposal processes, or initiating grant proposals themselves. Usually only basic enrollment trend data are needed, but there are times when a grant proposal calls for more persuasive and complex data that are not readily accessible, such as understanding the interplay between socioeconomic status and the likelihood of participating in an education abroad program.

While education abroad practitioners are expected to be engaged in this complex panoply of issues and related demands for data, even the most well-intentioned professional faces challenges, both in data collection and in consuming data for practical application. For many, the day-to-day demands of an education abroad office can overshadow the task of collecting, analyzing, and utilizing data, which can be viewed more as an optional task than as an integral function of a high-performing office. Moreover, some education abroad directors may be of a generation for which rigorous assessment and data collection methodologies were not part of their training or paradigm, and as a result, they may have a limited knowledge of how to collect data, or may not see the potential in leveraging data to bolster the position of education abroad programming (Ogden, Streitwieser, and Crawford 2013). Even though outcomes assessment research has grown increasingly sophisticated and useful, it can still be quite difficult to extrapolate practical applications from much of the literature.

It is similarly important to note that even the most actively engaged education abroad professionals face real obstacles with data collection. For example, progress can be hindered by the lack of direct access to datasets and raw data without incurring significant expense or undergoing time-consuming training. Similarly, accessing reliable data is dependent on the extent to which the data have actually been collected and organized into databases and related information management systems. Unless data are coded and correctly entered into an institution's student information system (for example, Banner, SAP, PeopleSoft), the ability to extract reliable information is limited. If there is no code or tracking mechanism for education abroad participation, for instance, then to calculate comparative graduation rates of those who studied abroad versus those who didn't will be difficult, if not impossible.

Data Utilization

Data collection is not new to U.S. higher education, and certainly education abroad professionals have a long history of collecting and sharing institutional data. Since 1949, the Institute for International Education (IIE) has conducted its annual statistical survey of the international students in the United States, now commonly known as *Open Doors*. Information on undergraduates studying overseas on U.S.-sponsored education abroad programs however was not systematically represented prior to the mid-1980s. As such, available data on how many students participated in education abroad and where they chose to study contained numerous gaps and inaccuracies. Until 1978–79, IIE gathered and published data collected only from foreign institutions, not from U.S. institutions as is done today. When IIE began collecting statistics directly from U.S. institutions, it did so only for academic-year programs, thus omitting summer study, and often, overseas direct enrollment as well. In the early 1980s, IIE developed a new reporting mechanism, surveying U.S. colleges and universities on the number of students who earned credit toward their home-campus academic degrees. However, consistent and reliable *Open Doors* reports with more extensive and detailed information on education abroad programming did not begin until 1994–95 (Ogden, Soneson, and Weting 2010).

While the annual *Open Doors* report has become arguably the most widely known and reliable dataset on U.S. education abroad enrollment, the report collects only basic enrollment data; it provides little to no interpretation of the data beyond enrollment trends and student demographics, nor does it position the data within the broader U.S. higher education landscape. Fortunately, the data collected by IIE over the years have become more sophisticated, and now the *Open Doors* report provides summary data on leading destinations, institution type, duration, fields of study, and basic information on the student profile, including academic level, gender, and race and ethnicity. It was not until 1993 that IIE began to collect data on race and ethnicity, and that data confirmed that there existed very little racial and ethnic diversity among students studying abroad. As IIE does not yet collect national-level data on other populations that have long been considered underrepresented, institutions must do so internally, and then reflect on the data relative to the broader student population. Among these populations are students from lower socioeconomic backgrounds, first-generation college students, transfer students, nontraditional students, and so on. LGBTQ students have often been considered underrepresented students, and yet very few institutions collect this information.

Education abroad offices are generally involved in numerous other forms of data collection beyond enrollment reporting. For example, education abroad offices that oversee student scholarships must often report on the utilization of funds, which is useful for both auditing purposes and for providing information to strategic campus partners. Offices that are actively engaged in promotion and outreach activities are best served when they collect data over time on factors such as attendance at education abroad promotional events, utilization of student advising spaces, or recurring topics discussed with student peer advisers. These data are best managed in a database that can be used to (a) track students in the recruitment and advising process; (b) do direct outreach to particular demographic groups; and (c) project staffing needs throughout the academic year.

Education abroad offices must also continually scan institutional enrollment patterns and related information that may potentially influence education abroad enrollment behaviors. For example, if a larger percentage of students are coming to the institution with significant prematriculation international experience, ongoing orientation programs must be adjusted to accommodate that more sophisticated student population. As institutions compete for and enroll greater proportions of high-achieving students, the education abroad portfolio may need to be further enhanced with research abroad programming, honors programming, and related features. If the institution enrolls more traditionally underrepresented students, then additional scholarships, advising structures, or curricular innovations may need to be leveraged to effectively appeal to these students (Salisbury, Paulsen, and Pascarella 2011). With a sophisticated understanding of the institution and its enrollment trends, the education abroad office can be better positioned to respond to changing student demographics and curricular demands.

Due to the need to understand what motivates students and engages faculty, education abroad offices have long conducted program evaluations. Whether such evaluations are quantitative or qualitative, it is essential that education abroad professionals engage students and faculty as part of an ongoing mission to continually assess and improve programming and services. For example, the education abroad office can regularly evaluate students at all phases of the education abroad process, namely at predeparture, while abroad, and upon reentry. Evaluations should seek to generate information that is timely to each phase and is as informative for the student's self-reflection process as it is for providing feedback to the education abroad office. The evaluations can be conducted using multiple formats, including electronic surveys, open-ended narratives, or focus group interviews. Similarly, seeking feedback from faculty members is instrumental, especially if the data are analyzed across a number of years to show change in faculty responsiveness or engagement with education abroad programming.

Education abroad offices must also partner with other stakeholders who rely on careful record keeping and reporting. With the release of the 2012 handbook on reporting campus crime, for example, the application of the Jeanne Clery Disclosure of Campus Security Policy and Campus Crime Statistics Act to education abroad programming has changed. While primarily once a domestically focused law, its inclusion of noncampus property abroad now requires education abroad offices to partner with campus security personnel to collect and report crime-related data via the institution's annual security report. Others organizations are similarly turning to education abroad offices with requests for such data. For example, the Forum on Education Abroad requests that its members submit brief synopses of student incidents abroad to its Critical Incident Database (CID). With this information, Forum member institutions can observe trend data, whether targeted to a particular location or in terms of the type of incidents that occur.

Whether reporting for *Open Doors,* for external constituencies, or for internal campus advocacy purposes, education abroad professionals are expected to be actively engaged in collecting, analyzing, reporting and utilizing data to understand and advance education abroad programming.

Key Questions and Potential Approaches[1]

At the 2013 Forum on Education Abroad annual conference, a well-attended session was offered on effectively utilizing data for strategic education abroad planning and campus advocacy (Ogden, Sideli, and Wiseman 2013). At the outset of the session, those in attendance were asked to share their more common requests for education abroad related data. An overwhelming 82 percent reported being asked for enrollment figures, of which most were requests for numbers or percentages of students studying abroad. Nearly a third of those requests were specifically for destination information, enrollment by major, class standing, demographic data, or program type (e.g., internship, exchange, etc.). In addition to enrollment data, attendees reported being asked for retention and persistence data (e.g., time to graduation, graduation rates), outcomes data (e.g., learning outcomes, job placement rates), and campus internationalization data (e.g., campus climate, credit transfer rates). Other requests included alumni tracking, faculty and staff mobility rates, and budgetary projection data. In the ensuing discussion, attendees identified other more complex issues, including requests from senior administration wanting to know the extent to which students are taking courses abroad in their major disciplines, the efficacy of campuswide efforts with curriculum integration, and differential outcomes by program type(e.g., internships vs. service-learning,).

To be sure, education abroad professionals share similar challenges with respect to effectively collecting and utilizing data for strategic planning and

---

[1]The data utilized in this chapter to illustrate approaches to these key questions are fictional and used only for explanatory purposes.

advocacy. Of the many key issues discussed at the aforementioned conference and even more broadly throughout the professional community, this section addresses seven of these key questions. With each question, considerations are discussed, and when appropriate, an approach to data collection or a particular dataset will be presented.

Who Are Our Underrepresented Populations and How Do We Foster Greater Inclusion?

Based on *Open Doors* data, the typical education abroad student profile can be inferred to be white, female, without any disability, majoring in the humanities, social sciences, or business, and studying in Europe on a program of less than eight weeks (IIE 2012). This student profile is perhaps most helpful when comparing education abroad enrollments to other national trends in higher education. For example, despite the fact that there has been significant growth in the participation rates of racial and ethnic minority students in U.S. higher education since the civil rights movement and the passage of the Higher Education Act of 1965, participation rates of these students in education abroad programming remain substantially disproportionate (NCES n.d.). However, this student profile is not consistent across individual institutions, and thus without a clear understanding of one's own enrollment populations, it is difficult to determine who is underrepresented in order to develop appropriate strategies to foster greater inclusion.

Table 1 provides a sample illustration of a fictional institution's education abroad enrollment in relation to the overall enrollment of the specific population within the broader institutional environment. In this example, African American students represent 6.6 percent of the total education abroad enrollment, which is quite comparable to the enrollment of African American students at the institution. In this sample, then, African American students are not underrepresented, and compared to the *Open Doors* 2011 report, this institution's efforts to foster greater inclusion seems to be working. It is obviously important to track this data annually to ensure sustainability as well as to investigate potential factors that may be skewing the data (e.g., one large program targeting a specific population). Table 2 points to categorical data not collected by IIE, namely first-generation status, class standing, honors enrollment, and transfer status. At this same institution, the data suggest that its most high-achieving students are disproportionately overrepresented and more work must be done to enroll first-generation students and transfer students.

TABLE 1. Underrepresentation, by Race/Ethnicity

Race/Ethnicity	% of 2010-11 Education Abroad Enrollment	% of 2010-11 Campus Enrollment	National Average (IIE, 2011)
African American	6.6%	6.5%	4.7%
Asian American/ Pacific Islander	3.6%	2.7%	7.9%
Caucasian/White Non-Hispanic	80.5%	79%	78.7%
Hispanic American	2.2%	1.8%	6.4%
Multiracial	0.9%	0.6%	1.9%
Native Amer./ Alaskan Native	0.2%	0.2%	0.5%
Prefer Not to Answer/Other	5.9%	4.2%	n/a
Nonresident Alien	n/a	5.0%	n/a
Other	0.2%	n/a	n/a

Note: Fictional data are used for explanatory purposes.

TABLE 2. Underrepresentation, by Gender, First-Generation Status, Class Standing, Honors, and Transfer Status

Profile Category	% of 2010-11 Education Abroad Enrollment	% of 2010-2011 Campus Enrollment	National Average (IIE, 2011)
Male	35.6%	50.8%	36.5%
Female	64.4%	49.2%	63.5%
First Generation	9.3%	23.2%	n/a
Not First Generation	47.3%	76.8%	n/a
Unreported	43.4%	0%	n/a
Undergraduate	92.0%	71.7%	n/a
Graduate	8.0%	28.3%	n/a
Honors	14.6%	4.0%	n/a
Not Honors	85.4%	96.0%	n/a
Transfer	11.3%	20.9%	n/a
Not Transfer	88.7%	79.1%	n/a

Note: Fictional data are used for explanatory purposes.

In sum, it is important that education abroad professionals not only understand national enrollment trends, but also understand enrollment trends within their own education abroad enrollment, relative to the campus population. Failure to understand who is underrepresented within one's own programming, and a failure to strategize accordingly, can potentially lead to missed opportunities for particular populations to realize the benefits of education abroad.

What Are the College/Department-Specific Priorities for Education Abroad and What Information Is Needed?

In relation to working effectively with faculty, perhaps the "platinum rule" should apply, which would state, "Do unto the faculty as they themselves would have done unto them" (Bennett 1998). In other words, rather than continually entreating the faculty to support education abroad programming, offices that position themselves in service to the faculty, and who fit with the language and culture of that faculty, may be better received. That is, education abroad offices need to understand the international education priorities of each college or department and work in support of realizing those goals and objectives. In addition to providing resources and assistance as requested, education abroad offices need to provide direction and good counsel on integrating education abroad programming within the measurable goals of each academic unit. Toward this aim, college or department-specific education abroad enrollment data must be readily available and easily understood.

Most often, colleges or departments request only general enrollment information, such as total enrollment growth over time, proportion of graduating class that earned credit abroad, or enrollment data by particular majors (see Table 3). While providing comparative data across units throughout the institution may be helpful with gauging internal momentum (and promoting a degree of internal competition), most academic units respond more readily to comparative data across comparable colleges or departments. For example, the nursing faculty may be more responsive to data from nursing programs at peer institutions or benchmarks, coupled with analyses or observations from the education abroad office.

TABLE 3. College-Level Enrollment, by Year, Total EA Enrollment, and College Proportion

College	2010-11 Enrol.	2011-12 Enrol.	% of Total EA Enrol.	2012 Grad. Rate
College of Liberal Arts	224	250	28.3%	15.6%
College of Business	96	116	13.1%	12.2%
College of Agriculture	66	93	10.5%	8.6%
College of Engineering	39	81	9.2%	6.7%
College of Communications	45	76	8.6%	13.4%
College of Education	25	53	6.0%	3.0%

Note:: Fictional data are used for explanatory purposes.

In order to provide data on demand, it is increasingly common for education abroad offices to produce a comprehensive annual enrollment report that is disseminated throughout the institution. More recently, online dashboards are being created to allow end users to generate custom reports on education abroad enrollment trends, including college or departmental-level reports by major, demographics, destinations, and more. These interactive dashboards potentially allow academic units to monitor their own exchange balances, faculty-directed program enrollments, and enrollment trends over time by major, destination, program type, and so on.

Is Our Education Abroad Portfolio Responsive to Our Institutional Demographic?

It is essential that education abroad offices analyze enrollment patterns to ensure that the program portfolio is responsive to the demographic of the student body and to the institution's broader enrollment trends. In other words, a diverse portfolio of offerings can boost diverse student participation and strengthen institutional efforts toward internationalizing the curriculum (Ogden 2010). But first, an office must be able to access and utilize the types of data that can guide the development of this range of offerings. Tables 4, 5, and 6 present different ways to assess portfolio responsiveness by program duration, experience type, and destination.

Table 4 presents a simple enrollment analysis of student demographic by program duration, and the data suggest that duration does in fact appeal differently to particular student populations. For example, first-generation and nontraditional students are disproportionately drawn to course-embedded programs. Summer and embedded programs appear to be the most feasible way for undergraduates to study abroad. The dataset also demonstrates that particular fields of study are disproportionately represented in embedded programs, such as agriculture, engineering, and physical sciences, all of which are known for regimented curricular requirements that make it difficult to study abroad.

TABLE 4. Student Demographic by Program Duration, in Percentages

	Semester	**Summer**	**Embedded**	**AY**
Race/Ethnicity: White	44.0%	22.8%	32.0%	1.2%
Race/Ethnicity: Minority	38.8%	21.8%	37.4%	2.0%
Male	39.5%	20.6%	38.4%	1.5%
First Generation	33.4%	20.8%	44.3%	1.5%
Nontraditional	5.4%	10.1%	84.2%	0.3%
Freshmen & Sophomores	4.6%	24.2%	70.4%	0.8%
Science & Engineering	28.7%	17.1%	52.2%	2.0%

Note:: Fictional data are used for explanatory purposes.

Increasingly, the term "education abroad" is preferable to "study abroad," which is viewed as one category among other program experience types, such as research abroad, intern abroad, teach abroad, and international service learning. Table 5 provides a snapshot of how particular populations may respond differently to program experience types. Although study abroad is the most popular experience type across all demographics in this sample, this data suggest no particular trends favoring a particular enrollment type by race/ethnicity.

TABLE 5. Student Demographic by Program Experience Type, in Raw Numbers

Race/Ethnicity	Study Abroad	Research Abroad	Intern Abroad	Teach Abroad	Service Abroad
African American	41	2	2	0	3
Asian American/ Pacific Islander	14	0	1	0	0
Caucasian/White Non-Hispanic	632	28	39	8	22
Hispanic American	17	2	0	0	1
Multiracial	24	0	2	0	1
Native Amer./ Alaskan Native	2	0	0	0	0
Prefer Not to Answer/Other	77	5	4	3	8

Note: Fictional data are used for explanatory purposes.

Although female students have long dominated education abroad enrollments, it may be useful to understand how male and female students respond differently to an institution's education abroad program portfolio. In Table 6, male students enroll in programs in Asia at almost twice the rate of female students. If this enrollment pattern is consistent over time, it may be useful to investigate the factors behind this trend to determine what is driving male enrollment numbers up or female enrollment numbers down.

Does Education Abroad Impact Persistence/Retention? How So?

As institutions direct more attention to documenting practices that maximize student success, education abroad professionals are increasingly being asked to demonstrate the extent to which education abroad programming impacts retention and persistence to graduation. Not surprisingly, many institutions are producing data such as that reflected in Table 7, which shows 4-, 5-, and 6-year graduation rates of those who studied abroad versus those that did not (Rhodes, Ogden, and Berquist 2013). At first glance, the data in this sample suggest that those who study abroad are more likely to graduate within four years, but this does not necessarily mean that studying abroad increases the probability of graduating. Such tables are potentially problematic.

TABLE 6. Student Gender by Destination of Study

Region/Gender	2012-2013 EA Enrollment	Percentage of Enrollment by Gender
Africa		
Male	9	3.0%
Female	37	6.3%
Asia		
Male	48	15.8%
Female	49	8.4%
Europe		
Male	179	59.1%
Female	346	59.2%
Latin America		
Male	55	18.2%
Female	121	20.7%
Middle East		
Male	2	0.7%
Female	2	0.3%
North America		
Male	4	1.3%
Female	6	1.0%
Multiple Regions		
Male	0	0.0%
Female	8	1.4%
Oceania		
Male	6	2.0%
Female	15	2.6%

Note: Fictional data are used for explanatory purposes.

TABLE 7. Graduation Rates, by Education Abroad Participation

Cohort		First Fall Enrollment (N)	4 Year Degree Completion %	5 Year Degree Completion %	6 Year Degree Completion %
2000	No	2913	29.4	52.1	57.9
	Yes	58	48.3	82.8	89.7
	All	2971	29.8	52.7	58.6
2001	No	3067	30.0	52.8	60.3
	Yes	62	46.8	75.8	82.3
	All	3129	30.4	53.3	60.7
2002	No	3574	27.5	49.8	56.0
	Yes	130	47.7	77.7	86.2
	All	3704	28.2	50.8	57.0
2003	No	3513	30.8	52.7	57.0
	Yes	170	45.9	82.9	90.6
	All	3683	31.5	54.1	58.6
2004	No	3712	30.8	50.6	55.0
	Yes	223	59.6	91.5	95.5
	All	3935	32.4	52.9	57.3
2005	No	3493	31.5	51.1	55.5
	Yes	331	57.7	88.2	93.4
	All	3824	33.8	54.3	58.8
2006	No	3774	28.0	48.6	
	Yes	344	57.0	85.8	
	All	4118	30.4	51.7	
2007	No	3474	29.9		
	Yes	361	64.0		
	All	3835	33.1		

Note: Fictional data are used for explanatory purposes.

Such comparisons between the graduation rates for students who studied abroad and those who did not may not be entirely proper because studying abroad and retention are confounded. In other words, the number of students who study abroad in their freshman year is typically very small. Thus, for a student to be assigned to a "study abroad group" he or she usually has to be retained at least for the second year, which in and of itself increases the probability of graduating. To control for this, it is important to look at those who were retained for the second year and for those who were retained for the third year. It is also important to control for other characteristics that may affect graduation rates and the number of years to graduation. For example, first year GPA, residency status, gender, and race are generally known to affect graduation rates and time to graduation. Table 8 presents inferential data of when such factors are controlled. While the mean graduation rate for those who studied abroad is lower, when adjusting for gender, residency, race, and first year GPA, the differences are negligible and not significant. A positive inference from this data sample could be that studying abroad does not, on average, increase time to graduation.

TABLE 8. Graduation Rates, by Education Abroad Participation (Adjusted)

Year Graduated	Study Abroad Participants		All Other Students		Mean Difference	Adjusted Mean Difference	T-test for comparing adjusted means	P-value
	N	Mean	N	Mean				
2011-2012	365	4.59	2155	4.92	-0.33	-0.06	-0.85	0.3967
2010-2011	356	4.49	2130	4.90	-0.41	-0.14	-2.35	0.0190
2009-2010	315	4.53	2039	4.78	-0.25	0.02	0.41	0.6804
2008-2009	281	4.50	2150	4.81	-0.30	-0.02	-0.26	0.7916
2007-2008	210	4.55	2230	4.77	-0.21	-0.03	-0.46	0.6443
All years	1527	4.53	10704	4.83	-0.30	-0.04	1.55	0.1213

Note: Fictional data are used for explanatory purposes.

Other approaches are being utilized to address this question, such as minimizing self-selection bias as a threat to reliability by investigating behaviors of those who applied but did not eventually study abroad (Barclay Hamir 2011). A systemwide analysis in Georgia found that African Americans who participate in education abroad are 13 percent more likely to graduate from college in four years and have a higher GPA than their peers (Sutton and Rubin 2004). Although researchers are continuing to employ new methodologies, causal data that confirm the extent to which education abroad leads to higher persistence and graduate rates is still inconclusive. For now, higher education administrators often point to Kuh's (2008) theoretical model on student success or Tinto's longstanding model of student retention (1975).

What Role Does Education Abroad Have in Student Recruitment and Admissions?

It has become rather commonplace for institutions to highlight education abroad in recruitment materials and outreach initiatives to prospective students. Because a large proportion of incoming freshmen indicate that they have plans to study abroad (NSSE n.d.), it has become increasingly important for institutions to showcase education abroad programming to prospective students. Coupled with the potential of enrolling high-achieving students by strategically leveraging education abroad, data now suggest that students who opt to study abroad are more active and engaged. Such students are more likely to successfully persist to graduation.

The National Survey of Student Engagement (NSSE) collects information at four-year colleges and universities about student participation in programs and activities that institutions provide for their learning and personal development. NSSE provides participating institutions with data on how undergraduates spend their time and what they gain from attending college. Table 9 presents a sample of weighted means of 2007, 2009, and 2012 incoming freshman students, which suggests that the incoming students in this sample are expecting to be more academically and socially engaged. The data also suggest that those students who plan to study abroad are even more academically and socially engaged than those not yet decided or not planning to study abroad. For example, in the area of "Active and Collaborative Learning," students who plan to study abroad indicate that they are asking more questions in class, working with classmates outside class, and tutoring other students. In the area of "Enriching Educational Experiences," these same students claim to have serious conversations with students of different beliefs, race, or ethnicity, and spend more time in cocurricular activities, community service, and volunteering. Significance testing (utilizing z-test values due to sample sizes) indicates that these two groups are indeed significantly different across each NSSE category, at either the 0.05 or 0.01 level. Strategic use of such data can influence the type of advocacy in which education abroad professionals engage, whether with the faculty, administration, or students. Table 10 offers a comparison of senior students who've studied abroad with those who did not. Here again, those who did study abroad remained academically and socially engaged students and the differences are significant across all category levels, at (p < .05) or greater.

TABLE 9. NSSE 2007, 2009, And 2012 Freshman Participants, Weighted Means of NSSE Benchmark Scores by Study Abroad Plans

Freshmen		Number	Aca-demic Chal-lenge	Active and Collab-orative Learning	Student Faculty Interac-tion	Enriching Educational Experi-ences	Sup-portive Campus Environ.
2007	Not decided or do not plan to study abroad	416	51.68	34.46	28.78	23.08	56.13
	Plan to or studied abroad	376	52.11	39.43	32.52	28.60	55.40
2009	Not decided or do not plan to study abroad	525	52.51	38.27	31.87	24.46	58.72
	Plan to or studied abroad	461	55.66	44.07	36.87	31.41	61.05
2012	Not decided or do not plan to study abroad	314	54.37	44.07	33.04	25.65	62.20
	Plan to or studied abroad	364	56.75	48.64	37.61	31.79	64.08
All yrs.	Not decided or do not plan to study abroad	1255	52.70	38.47	31.14	24.30	58.74
	Plan to or studied abroad	1201	54.88	44.00	35.74	30.65	60.20

Note: Fictional data are used for explanatory purposes.

TABLE 10. NSSE 2007, 2009, And 2012 Senior Participants, Weighted Means of NSSE Benchmark Scores by Study Abroad Plans

Freshmen		Number	Aca-demic Chal-lenge	Active and Collab-orative Learning	Student Faculty Interac-tion	Enriching Educational Experi-ences	Sup-portive Campus Environ.
2007	Not decided or do not plan to study abroad	609	53.89	46.67	39.66	37.74	52.71
	Plan to or studied abroad	82	53.09	51.22	44.23	55.97	52.52
2009	Not decided or do not plan to study abroad	978	54.91	47.94	40.92	38.33	53.57
	Plan to or studied abroad	173	56.72	50.24	45.75	57.38	57.88
2012	Not decided or do not plan to study abroad	722	55.36	48.50	40.30	37.98	56.01
	Plan to or studied abroad	186	57.26	51.40	46.38	55.13	57.67
All yrs.	Not decided or do not plan to study abroad	2309	54.78	47.78	40.40	38.06	54.10
	Plan to or studied abroad	441	56.24	50.91	45.72	56.18	56.76

Note: Fictional data are used for explanatory purposes.

Further analyses of individual NSSE items for senior students in this particular sample data suggest that those who participated in an education abroad experience are not only more academically and socially engaged overall, but are more interested in foreign language coursework. These students report significantly more involvement with faculty members on activities other than coursework, particularly with research projects outside of program requirements. Those who studied abroad are also significantly more likely to have been involved in enriching activities such as service learning, volunteer work, and internships, as well as clinical assignments. These students are significantly more engaged in independent research and work that culminates in a senior capstone experience. Perhaps an ideal talking point for admissions and recruitment officers, these students also report that their home institution is providing them with the support they need to thrive socially and succeed academically.

How Do We Monitor Noncredit-Bearing International Travel? Why Should We?

Due to increasing concerns on managing institutional risk management, many education abroad offices are being asked, at the very least, to track noncredit-bearing, international group travel. Senior administrators are emphasizing the need to account for all students who travel abroad under the auspices of the institution, whether on credit-bearing or noncredit-bearing programming. Consequently, education abroad offices are increasingly being asked to provide risk management and student services to choir members traveling abroad for performances in much the same way as the office is asked to provide services to credit-bearing, education abroad participants. In the event of an emergency, the education abroad office must account for all students abroad and have communication protocols and insurance and evacuation coverage in place.

As education abroad professionals, risk management officers, and other campus stakeholders maneuver to implement protocols to ensure that noncredit-bearing travel is monitored, at least three major concerns have arisen. First, when there are institutional policies in place that govern education abroad programming, these policies seldom include noncredit-bearing international travel. Institutions that have not traditionally required noncredit-bearing programming to be vetted and monitored have had to develop new systems and communicate protocols across the institution.

Second, the systems required to monitor noncredit-bearing international travel must be developed in order to conduct a uniform query of students abroad in the event of an emergency. Newer enrollment management systems, such as Terra Dotta's TDS for Study Abroad software, allow for an easy locator search for all students who are in a particular country or region on a given date. In the event of a real emergency, any locator search of this nature should not require compiling information from various data sources or engaging multiple personnel; a centralized and accessible data system is essential.

Finally, the administrative resources required to provide support services to noncredit-bearing international travel often go unreported and become unfunded mandates. The use of persuasive data can help education abroad offices advocate for the resources needed to provide these services. The sample data in Figure 1 demonstrate that noncredit-bearing international travel enrollment accounts for a growing proportion of student involvement. In this particular sample, noncredit-bearing travel has moved from 18.8 percent of the population in 2011–12 to 29.8 percent in 2012–13. Such growth may have significant staffing and resourcing implications that need to be communicated to senior administration.

FIGURE 1. Enrollment by Credit-Bearing and Noncredit-Bearing Participation

	For Credit	Not For Credit
2010-11	637	182
2011-12	884	205
2012-13	887	377

Note: Fictional data are used for explanatory purposes.

How Does Financial Need Impact Education Abroad Enrollment Trends?

All too often, education abroad professionals are reminded that studying abroad is expensive and that students cannot afford it. Although we frequently counter with information on scholarship opportunities or emphasize that not all programs are expensive, most education abroad offices simply don't know much about the actual socioeconomic status of their students. Similarly, IIE does not collect information on financial need or socioeconomic status, and yet the general understanding is that the typical education abroad student is of middle to upper-middle socioeconomic class. In fact, there is very little generalizable data which show the degree to which financial need actually impacts participation.

In 2010, an institution-specific analysis of financial need was conducted with a sample size of 8,415 students at a large east coast public institution (see Table 11) (Ogden 2010). Data were gathered primarily through the institution's student information system and/or exported from individual education abroad program applications. Nearly half of these students (48.3 percent) had no demonstrated financial need or no FAFSA on record at the time of studying abroad. Based on this finding, it is possible to conclude that financial need may not actually deter studying abroad to the extent expected at this particular institution. However, this data only accounts for those students that did in fact successfully study abroad and were thus represented in the sample. It does not account for students that opted out of studying abroad due to financial need or related reasons. Because such datasets only include information on actual education abroad participants, Salisbury et al. (2009) chose to instead look at the likelihood of studying abroad. They concluded that lower income students (i.e., students from families eligible for federal financial aid) are less likely to plan to study abroad than higher income students, and those students who receive federal financial aid are 11 percent less likely to intend to study abroad than are those not receiving federal aid. By examining likelihood ratios, these authors were able to conclude that insufficient financial capital does significantly inhibit the likelihood of participation, even in the earliest stages when the beginnings of predisposition, plans, or intentions to study abroad are being formed.

TABLE 11. Financial Need and Education Abroad Participation

Need Index (n=8,415)	Frequency	Percentage
No FAFSA	2,351	27.9%
0	1,714	20.4%
1-49	1,508	17.9%
50-99	2,238	26.6%
100	604	7.2%

Note: The data are fictional and used only for explanatory purposes.

Another way of understanding the extent to which financial need impacts education abroad participation has been to investigate the behaviors of Pell-eligible students or Pell recipients. For example, Table 12 documents the percentages of those students who received a Pell Grant in academic years 2010–11 and 2011–12 with those who had earned credit abroad with the total population. Whereas roughly 24 percent of total student body received a Pell

Grant at this institution, only 17–18 percent of students who studied abroad were receiving a Pell Grant. As such, this sample data suggest that financial need does impact participation.

Generating such data can be useful for determining underrepresented populations, but the data must be understood in context of other strategies being used to foster inclusion of those with financial need. For example, this same analysis as reflected in Table 12 found a statistically significant difference between the six-year graduation rates of Pell Grant recipients who studied abroad compared to Pell Grant recipients who did not study abroad, even after adjusting for the first fall GPA (p-value < 0.001). Based on this sample, it could be argued that strategically investing in Pell Grant recipients by financially supporting their education abroad can positively impact student graduation rates. As suggested earlier, engaging students in high-impact experiences such as studying abroad benefits students and improves their retention and graduation rates (Kuh 2008).

TABLE 12. Pell Recipients and Education Abroad

Bachelor's Degree Students: Academic Years 2010–2011 and 2011–2012				
	2010–11		**2011–12**	
	Number	**% with Pell Grants**	**Number**	**% with Pell Grants**
Education Abroad	567	17.11%	690	17.97%
All Students	20,613	24.42%	20,894	24.61%

Note: Fictional data are used for explanatory purposes.

Datasets and Effective Partnerships

As education abroad offices rally to gather and effectively utilize data for long-term strategic planning and campus-based advocacy, it is critically important to have access to reliable datasets as well as strategic partners that can assist with data generation and analysis. While most offices regularly consult institutional datasets and *Open Doors* with some degree of regularity, it is essential to be knowledgeable of other datasets that might be generated by the education abroad office, the institution, or national or international research. In addition to the datasets already mentioned, consider the following datasets and their potential use:

- **Cooperative Institutional Research Program** conducts the well-known Freshman Survey and follow up assessments such as the Your First College Year (YFCY) and the College Senior Survey. The Freshman Survey provides useful data on education abroad participation by institution type.

- **Project Atlas** provides a global picture of international student mobility for major sending and host countries. Project Atlas also features country-level data as well as analysis of global trends.
- **National Center for Education Statistics** is the primary federal entity for collecting and analyzing data related to education in the United States and other nations. The U.S. Department of Education's College Affordability and Transparency Center[2] is generated via NCES data.

Education abroad offices must establish strategic partnerships with units within the institution that have the ability to both code and query education abroad data. Many of these units can assist with data generation and analyses. Consider the following strategic units:

- **Institutional Research.** Most institutions have a unit that is responsible for preparing and analyzing data for official reports to the institution, state, federal, and other external agencies. These units provide useful data on institutional enrollment trends and are usually willing to generate customized reports and analyses upon request.
- **Bursar and Student Accounts.** The institution's bursar or student accounts office can also be an ally in generating financially oriented data. Whether it is determining student financial need indices or related billing information, these offices can usually generate helpful information on the student profile.
- **Admissions and Registrar.** With recent significant advances in the automation and tracking of admissions and registration, these offices are often able to generate student information that can be useful in understanding the student profile and in recruitment and outreach initiatives.

Conclusion

This chapter has provided a basic overview of the importance of accurately gathering and effectively utilizing institutional and external data for long-term strategic planning and campus-based advocacy. In an era of increasing standardization and accountability, it is strategically important that education abroad professionals produce and disseminate data that reinforce the impact and importance of education abroad programming.

---

[2]For more information, see http://collegecost.ed.gov/catc/.

References

Barclay Hamir, Heather. "Go Abroad and Graduate On-Time: Study Abroad Participation, Degree Completion, and Time-to-Degree." Unpublished PhD dissertation, University of Nebraska, 2011. http://digitalcommons.unl.edu/cgi/viewcontent.cgi?article = 1065&context = cehsedaddiss.

Bennett, Milton. 1998. "Overcoming the Golden Rule: Sympathy and Empathy." In *Basic Concepts of Intercultural Communication,* ed. Milton Bennett, 191–214. Yarmouth, Maine: Intercultural Press.

Bolen, Mell, ed. 2007. *A Guide to Outcomes Assessment in Education Abroad.* Carlisle, PA: The Forum on Education Abroad.

Braskamp, Larry. 2008. "Developing Global Citizens." In *Journal of College and Character* 10, 1.

Institute of International Education (IIE). 2012. *Open Doors Report on International Educational Exchange.* Retrieved from http://opendoors.iienetwork.org.

Kuh, George. 2008. "High-Impact Educational Practices: What they Are, Who Has Access to Them, and Why They Matter." Washington D.C.: AAC&U. http://www.aacu.org/leap/hips.

National Center for Education Statistics. *Fast Facts.* U.S. Department of Education Institute of Education Sciences. Retrieved March 30, 2013, from http://nces.ed.gov/fastfacts/display.asp?id = 98.

Ogden, Anthony. 2010. *Education Abroad and the Making of Global Citizens: Assessing Learning Outcomes of Course-Embedded, Faculty-Led International Programming.* Saarbruecken, Germany: VDM Publishing.

Ogden, Anthony and Sharon Brennan. 2014. "International Outreach Education." In *Education in North America,* eds. D.E. Mulcahy, D.G. Mulcahy, and Roger Saul. New York: Bloomsbury Academic. http://www.bloomsbury.com/us/education-in-north-america-9781472510709/.

Ogden, Anthony, Kathleen Sideli, and Ana Marie Wiseman. 2013. "Effective Utilization of Institutional Data for Strategic Education Abroad Planning & Campus Advocacy." Presentation at the Forum on Education Abroad Annual Conference, Chicago, Ill. http://www.forumea.org/documents/EffectiveUtilizationofInstitData.pdf.

Ogden, Anthony, Heidi Soneson, and Paige Weting. 2010. "The Diversification of Geographic Locations." In *A History of U.S. Study Abroad: 1965 to the Present,* eds. William Hoffa and Stephen DePaul. Carlisle: PA: The Forum on Education Abroad.

Ogden, Anthony, Bernhard Streitwieser, and Emily Crawford. (Forthcoming). "Empty Meeting Grounds: Situating Intercultural Learning in U.S. Education Abroad." In *Internationalization of Higher Education and Global Mobility*, ed. Bernhard Streitwieser. Oxford Studies in Comparative Education. Symposium Book Series.

Rhodes, Gary, Anthony Ogden, and Brett Berquist. 2013. "Making Education Abroad a Campus Priority: Measuring and Enhancing the Impact of Education Abroad on Student Success." Presentation at the AIEA Annual Conference, New Orleans, La.

Salisbury, Mark, Paul Umbach, Michael Paulsen, and Ernest Pascarella. 2009. "Going Global: Understanding the Choice Process of the Intent to Study Abroad." In *Research in Higher Education* 50, 2:119–143.

Salisbury, Mark, Michael Paulsen, and Ernest Pascarella. 2011. "Why Do All the Study Abroad Students Look Alike? Applying an Integrated Student Choice Model to Explore Differences in the Factors that Influence White and Minority Students' Intent to Study Abroad." *Research in Higher Education* 52, 2:123–150.

Streitwieser, Bernhard, Emily Le and Val Rust. 2012. "Research on Study Abroad, Mobility, and Student Exchange in Comparative Education Scholarship." In *Research in Comparative and International Education* 7, 1:1–4.

Sutton, Richard and Donald Rubin. 2004. "The GLOSSARI Project: Initial Findings from a System-Wide Research Initiative on Study Abroad Learning Outcomes." In *Frontiers: The Interdisciplinary Journal of Study Abroad* 10, 65–82.

Tinto, Vincent. 1975. "Dropout from Higher Education: A Theoretical Synthesis of Recent Research." *Review of Educational Research* 45, 1:89–125.

United States Department of Education. 2011. *The Clery Act*. Higher Education Center. Retrieved from http://www2.ed.gov/admins/lead/safety/handbook.pdf.

CHAPTER 21

MANAGING AN EDUCATION ABROAD BUDGET

By Corrine Henke

Managing the budget and cash flow of an education abroad office is critical to a program's growth and expansion. However, many international educators are never formally trained in the budget and financial management process. This chapter emphasizes the concepts of planning, patience, and creativity. Planning is critical to the budget process, but plans must be nimble to react to changes, and to manage the unexpected. Patience is essential; it can take years for some projects to be successful or to be approved by upper administration. Having a creative or entrepreneurial spirit is a unique concept. While higher education institutions are different and some cannot be entrepreneurial, creativity is a benefit to all, and offices need new ideas to move their mission forward.

Creating an Operational Budget

Operating budgets are carefully created budgets that focus on managing current expenses. An operating budget ensures there are funds to maintain the continued operation of an office, and that funds are distributed in a cost-efficient manner.

Those working with budgets need to ask themselves the following questions:

- What is the framework in which budget decisions are made?
- Who is responsible for planning and preparing the budget?
- How can changes in budget be programmed and targeted?
- What activities will be needed complete the work?
- What resources will be needed to conduct these activities? Include travel, supplies, consultants, postage, telephone, and so on.
- Which staff will work on the program and for what percentage of their time? Include salaries and benefits.

Once the budget is created, management should identify sources of revenue to meet the budgetary needs. It is also critical to understand the framework regulating budgets. It is essential to find out the following:

- How does the budget process work at the institution?
- When are budgets established? Annually? Every two years? Which funds are encumbered? Salaries, travel, etc.?

Understanding encumbrances is important at many institutions. Encumbrance is the name given to funds that have been reserved for a specific purpose. The purpose and main benefit of encumbrance accounting is to avoid budget overspending (University of California-Riverside 2013).

Operational Expenses

Common expense categories are salaries, benefits, operating expenses, and travel.

Here is a sample budget from University A.

TABLE 1. Sample Budget A

EXPENSES	
Salary & Benefits	
Salaries	$80,000
Benefits	$22,400
Subtotal	**$102,400**
OPERATING EXPENSES	
Equipment rental	$100
Insurance	$500
Meals and refreshments	$1,300
Office supplies	$2,200
Other expenses	$500
Postage/mail services	$750
Printing	$1,500
Professional development	$1,200
Room rentals	$600
Student employees	$12,000
Travel	$5,000
Web Services	$500
Subtotal	**$26,150**
Total Expenses	**$128,550**

Note: Fictional data are used for explanatory purposes.

Revenue

Revenue can be derived from a number of sources. Some sources of revenue are institutional support, application fees, user fees, tuition capture, or other activities.

Institutional Support

In the perfect scenario, all the funding for salary, travel, and operating expenses are funded by the institution. Institutional support allows for consistency, stability, and the need for additional revenue decreases.

As an example, College B has 100 percent institutional support for the expenses of the education abroad office.

TABLE 2. Sample Budget B

College B Education Abroad Office	
REVENUE	
Institutional support	$293,000
Subtotal Revenue	**$293,000**
EXPENSES	
Staff Salaries	$200,000
Benefits	$60,000
Student Help	$5,000
Operating Expenses	$20,000
Travel	$8,000
Subtotal Expenses	**$293,000**
Revenue minus Expenses	**$0**

Note: Fictional data are used for explanatory purposes.

However, funding to institutions of higher education is changing rapidly and a variety of budget models are possible. These models will be discussed in a later section.

Application Fees

One method of revenue generation is application fees. Amounts vary by institution. At Boise State University, a fee of $100 is charged for each direct exchange application. Across the United States, application fees for education abroad applications range from no fee to $300. For example, the University of

Nevada-Las Vegas education abroad office does not charge students an application fee, as the office is funded 100 percent by institutional support.[1]

It is critical to involve the institution's budget and finance office in the review process of application fees, including the refund policy, to ensure that it is clear to students as well as in compliance with institutional regulations. Most application fees are nonrefundable unless the student is not accepted to a program. For administrative purposes, making the application fee nonrefundable in all circumstances is the simplest and most efficient policy. This limits the burden on clerical staff to issue refunds.

User or Administrative Fees
Another form of revenue is the "user fee" or "administrative fee" for education abroad. Students are charged a set amount (typically per term) for studying abroad. These funds are utilized to fund positions, travel, and operating expenses. Again, being clear with students about why the fee is charged and whether it is refundable is important. The timing of the fee can be critical. If the office provides a large amount of student support prior to departure and the student cancels before the fee is charged, there may not be enough funding to cover expenses.

Tuition Capture
Another source of revenue is tuition capture. At institutions that offer exchange programs, the education abroad office receives the tuition for outbound exchange students. The office uses these funds to support staff and operating expenses. The benefit of this model is that it provides an incentive to send students on direct exchange, and as enrollments increase, the office has more funding to use for operations and staffing. While it may be difficult to negotiate, this model could generate significant revenue when compared to application fees or user fees.

Other Revenue Sources
In recent years, some education abroad offices have become U.S. passport acceptance facilities (PAF). A PAF is authorized by the U.S. State Department to accept passport applications. Passport acceptance facilities ensure proper completion of passport applications and forms, accept and process payments for passport fees, and must be open to the public. Many also provide photograph services. Passport acceptance facilities charge a fee of $25 for each application processed. The fee cannot be changed or modified in any way.

---

[1] Ryan Larsen (assistant director of education abroad, University of Nevada-Las Vegas), in discussion with the author, September 20, 2013. Las Vegas, Nev.

However, the PAF can charge for photos or other services (e.g., making photocopies) (Rausch 2012).

Becoming a PAF has a number of possible benefits, such as convenience for students and faculty members preparing for study abroad, and increased local community awareness of the education abroad office. Additionally, application fees provide a source of revenue. Many offices use the funds for education abroad scholarships, but the funds can also be used for operating expenses or salaries. Boise State University has awarded $20,000 in scholarship funding from passport acceptance fees since August 2011 (Henke 2013, 2).

Self-Supporting or Hybrid Office and Program Models

Education abroad offices have a variety of budget models. Two of the more common ones are the self-supporting and the hybrid model. In the self-supporting office model, the office supports itself completely from revenue it generates. In most cases, revenue comes from user fees, application fees, or other revenue sources.

The education abroad office at University C is self-supporting from application fees and administrative fees. This university sends 300 students abroad per year and charges a $125 application fee, generating $37,500 per year. They charge a $300 per student, per term administrative fee for education abroad. Since the fee is charged per student, the amount of revenue generated from the administrative fee is $90,000 (or $300 times 300 students). Because the fee is charged per term, the annual revenue is higher. By term, the institution has 100 students abroad in the fall, 250 in the spring, and 50 in the summer. The 100 fall students are year-long students, and are charged the education abroad administrative fee in both the fall and the spring. Therefore, the 400 students cited in the graph actually refer to the number of terms being charged, not the actual number of students. This is an important distinction to make for *Open Doors* reporting; students cannot be counted twice (IIE 2013).

TABLE 3. Sample Revenue Generated from Administrative Fees

University C Participation Numbers		
Education Abroad Participation	**Number of Students**	**Revenue Generated (From administrative fees)**
Fall enrollment	100	$30,000
Spring enrollment	250	$75,000
Summer enrollment	50	$15,000
Total	**400**	**$120,000**

Note: Fictional data are used for explanatory purposes.

TABLE 4. Self-Supporting Model Sample Budget

University C (Self-Supporting Model)	
REVENUE	
Institutional support	$0
Application fees	$37,500
Administrative fees	$120,000
Subtotal Revenue	$157,500
EXPENSES	
Staff salaries (director, adviser, administrative assistant)	$100,000
Benefits	$30,000
Student help	$4,000
Operating expenses	$15,000
Travel & staff development	$5,000
Subtotal Expenses	**$154,000**
Revenue Minus Expenses (reserve for next year)	**$3,500**

Note: Fictional data are used for explanatory purposes.

While it is possible to support an office completely on application and administrative fees, it can be a stressful situation to manage. It is difficult to move forward with innovative ideas if staff members are under pressure to keep enrollments high to fund their positions. If the institution cannot fund of all the office's expenses, it is wise to use the hybrid model with a mix of institutional funding and funds generated from other sources. In a hybrid budget model, the office receives some funding from the institution and other expenses are covered by revenue sources.

On page 363 is State College D, which is a hybrid model. The institution has one director, two advisers, an administrative assistant, and two peer advisers. It sends 500 students abroad per year.

TABLE 5. Hybrid Model Sample Budget

State College D Education Abroad Office (Hybrid model)	
REVENUE	
Institutional support	$ 75,000
Application fees	$ 50,000
Administrative fees	$ 150,000
Subtotal Revenue	$ 275,000
EXPENSES	
Staff Salaries (director, advisers, administrative assistant)	$ 170,000
Benefits	$ 51,000
Student help	$ 8,000
Operating expenses	$ 30,000
Travel and staff development	$ 10,000
Subtotal Expenses	**$ 259,000**
Revenue Minus Expenses (reserve for next year)	**$ 6,000**

Note: Fictional data are used for explanatory purposes.

Self-Supporting Program Model

In addition to the self-supporting office model, individual education abroad programs can be self-supporting; this is particularly true with faculty-led programs. Faculty-led education abroad programs are growing in popularity and prevalence. Some institutions are unable to cover faculty expenses or salaries to administer faculty-led programs; as a result, the program becomes self-supporting and runs without support from the institution. In a self-supporting program model, the students bear the costs of the program.

In the model on page 364, State University E uses a self-supporting program model for its faculty-led program to Rome. All of the program costs, including faculty salary, are covered by student participants. The disadvantage of this model is that the costs can become quite high, and it is critical to set a minimum number of participants for the program to run. Ten students is the most common breakeven number for many such programs.

TABLE 6. Self-Supporting Faculty-Led Program

Rome Through the Ages Professor Jones July 4–July 18 (two weeks) Based on 10 participants One credit		
Program Expenses	**Cost per unit**	**Total cost**
Tuition	$726/credit	$7,260
Education abroad administrative fee	$100/student	$1,000
Faculty Expenses		
Faculty salary & benefits	$3,500	$3,500
Faculty travel costs (airfare and accommodations)	$2,046	$2,046
Faculty meals or per diem	$500	$500
Cell phone	$172	$172
Faculty entrance fees	$75	$75
Student Program Expenses		
Insurance	$9/week	$180
Accommodations	$215/person	$2,150
Ground transportation	$240	$2,400
Airfare (round trip)	$1,800	$18,000
Guest speakers/tour guides	$400 (flat)	$400
Entrance fees	$75	$750
TOTAL		**$38,083**
Indirect fund (to cover currency fluctuations) 5%		**$1,904**
Cost per student (total cost divided by number of participants)		**$3,999**

Note: Fictional data are used for explanatory purposes.

For additional resources, NAFSA offers an e-learning course on faculty-led programs, providing participants hands-on training with various budget models.

Budget Cuts and Funding Strategies

To understand funding strategies, we will study the budgets of an imaginary institution. University X is a small university with an enrollment of 7,000 students. University X has a study abroad director, an administrative assistant, and two peer adviser positions. Education abroad participation at University X is approximately 70 students per year, but participation is growing.

In the budget example below, institutional support has not increased since fiscal year 2012. Therefore, in fiscal year 2013, the education abroad office instituted an application fee of $100 for its 70 study abroad students, resulting in $7,000 in new revenue.

For fiscal year 2013, institutional support did not increase. Therefore, in fiscal year 2014, the office will charge a $200 per student administrative fee to cover expenses. Office X is collecting more in revenue and building a small reserve fund (revenue minus expenses). The reserve fund will prove critical, because it is likely that institutional support may never increase again. The office will need a reserve fund to cover expenses or to weather budget cuts. The office projects a modest increase in student applications, from 72 students, to 75 students, to 80 students in fiscal year 2014.

TABLE 7. Sample Education Abroad Office Operating Budget

University X Education Abroad Operating Budget				
REVENUE	**FY 2012**	**FY 2013**	**FY 2014**	**FY 2015**
Institutional support	$128,550	$128,550	$128,550	$128,550
Application fees	0	$7,000	$7,500	$8,000
User/administrative fees	0	0	$14,000	$16,000
TOTAL REVENUE	**$128,550**	**$135,550**	**$150,050**	**$152,550**

TABLE 7. Sample Education Abroad Office Operating Budget (Continued)

EXPENSES	FY 2012	FY 2013	FY 2014	FY 2015
SALARY & BENEFITS				
Salaries	$80,000	$84,000	$88,200	$92,610
Benefits	$22,400	$23,520	$24,696	$25,931
Subtotal	**$102,400**	**$107,520**	**$112,896**	**$118,541**
OPERATING EXPENSES				
Equipment rental	$100	$125	$200	$210
Insurance	$500	$1,200	$1,260	$1,323
Meals and refreshments	$1,300	$1,300	$1,300	$1,300
Office supplies	$2,200	$2,310	$2,426	$2,547
Other expenses	$500	$525	$551	$579
Postage/mail services	$750	$788	$827	$868
Printing	$1,500	$1,575	$1,654	$1,736
Professional development	$1,200	$1,260	$1,323	$1,389
Room rentals	$600	$630	$662	$695
Student employees	$12,000	$12,600	$13,230	$13,892
Travel	$5,000	$5,050	$5,513	$5,788
Web Services	$500	$525	$551	$579
Subtotal	**$26,150**	**$28,088**	**$29,492**	**$30,966**
TOTAL EXPENSES	**$128,550**	**$135,608**	**$142,388**	**$149,507**
REVENUE-EXPENSES (Reserve fund)	**$ -**	**$143**	**$7,662**	**$3,043**

Note: Budget example adapted from NAFSA (2013b, 36).

Encumbrances can be important during budget cuts because they can be done strategically. For example, if budget cuts are in the foreseeable future, it may make sense to hire a new position as soon as possible to encumber the funds for the next fiscal year. This approach can provide staffing and give administrators a year or two to establish new revenue sources.

Professional Development Opportunities

Professional development opportunities are critical to all employees. International educators may feel isolated on their campus if "no one understands" their work, or if the campus is small with few international education staff. Conferences, workshops, and other opportunities allow for revitalization, new skills development, and critical job information.

These opportunities should be built into the operating budget and planned like other expenses. In large offices, opportunities may need to be shared among multiple staff members. Managers and supervisors should have employee development plans for all staff members, which mesh with the opportunities and funding availability. When a new staff member is hired, their attendance at conferences may be the highest priority.

There are a number of ways to reduce the costs of conference attendance. Volunteers are sought for the NAFSA annual conference, and this can reduce the registration price to the conference attendee. Volunteering at the conference allows education abroad staff to meet NAFSA staff/leaders, or colleagues at other institutions. At some institutions, it may be expected that employees present posters or lead sessions in order to attend conferences. Encourage staff to submit proposals to conferences, and also encourage new staff to seek out opportunities to gain new skills or meet with international partners.

Many NAFSA regions offer travel grants to new members, and regional conferences tend to be closer for staff travel, and less expensive. A few of the regions, for example NAFSA Region 1, include some meals in the conference fee to minimize additional out-of-pocket expenses for conference participants. As of August 1, 2013, their fall 2013 conference included a plenary luncheon, an opening reception, and a gala auction, which included food. The Forum on Education Abroad also holds a popular conference. The Forum offers travel grants which can offset the cost of travel for newcomers or those presenting at the Forum annual conference (Forum 2013).

Aware that budgets may not allow for conference attendance, NAFSA now offers a number of e-learning courses. These are relatively low-cost and designed as a quick start plan for new employees or individuals without formal EA training (NAFSA 2013a). E-learning courses are offered on a variety of topics, such as faculty-led program development and education abroad advising. The courses are self-paced, which allows the learner to gain the information in a reasonable timeframe based on their goals and time constraints.

Webinars are another affordable option, offering timely information on a variety of topics. Webinars allow larger numbers of participants. Typically, one registration will cover as many individuals as can fit in a room (NAFSA 2013d).

Professional development should be seen as critical and essential part of the education abroad operating budget. There are creative ways to reduce costs and allow staff professional development to do their jobs well and successfully. Staff can volunteer at conferences to reduce registration fees. Webinars and e-learning courses are affordable ways to encourage professional development when budgets do not allow for conference attendance. Professional development should be seen as an investment in staff and budgeted as an operating expense.

Promotional and Marketing Materials

At most institutions, marketing and promotion are still critical to promote education abroad to students. There are a variety of low-cost options that every office can utilize.

Social media is an affordable and effective way to promote education abroad. Pinterest, Facebook, and Twitter are all being used by institutions.

Websites remain an important form of information and marketing for education abroad programs. In addition, there are also databases that serve as websites, application clearinghouses, and enrollment management systems. Some of the more popular education abroad databases are AbroadOffice, Horizons, and StudioAbroad. The fees for set up, maintenance and add-ons vary by program. Currently, AbroadOffice is free to all users.

E-newsletters are another way to reach students, faculty, or staff. These newsletters are offered by a number of providers, who generally charge a fee. It will depend on the budget and campus dynamics if an e-newsletter makes sense.

Additionally, older methods of communication may prove effective. Fliers are a traditional method. Program details and photos are described on a piece of paper and distributed across campus. Fliers can be expensive, however, and the cost should be compared to the amount of student interest generated. Mailing letters to students about education abroad programs can also be expensive, but may be more effective, since very few students still receive "snail mail." Promotion and marketing efforts should be assessed as part of annual plan and report of the education abroad office.

Education abroad fairs are one way to market programs and to engage the campus population in education abroad. It is important to assess whether a fair makes sense on campus. If the campus does not allow students to utilize outside program providers, having a fair may not make sense. It might be better to organize a smaller event to promote the institution's programs instead. If the office is understaffed, it may be too difficult to organize a fair. However, tasking an intern or energetic student employee with the event may make it possible.

Education Abroad Fairs

Education abroad fairs should break even financially or be a minimal investment. Typical costs include event marketing, parking for program representatives, meals and/or coffee, and room or equipment rentals. The fair registration cost should be based on average of all costs divided by number of participants.

TABLE 8. Sample Education Abroad Fair Budget

Sample Education Abroad Fair Budget		
	Costs	**TOTAL**
Parking	$50 (flat rate)	$50
Boxed lunch and morning coffee	$15/person	$150 (based on 10 meals)
Fliers and other marketing	$500	$500
Rentals (easels and display boards)	$4/table	$40
Supplies (chalk, name tags, photocopies)	$50	$50
TOTAL FAIR COSTS		**$790**
Average cost		**$79/registrant based on 10 registrations**

Note: Fictional data are used for explanatory purposes.

Seeking Out Grant Opportunities

Finding grant funding can be a long and difficult process. Some questions to ask when seeking funding or reviewing grant opportunities.

- What problem am I trying to solve?
- What am I trying to achieve?
- What am I trying to develop and to grow?

- When reviewing a grant possibility, ask these questions:
- Is the institution eligible?
- Is the grant aligned with the mission and goals of the office?
- What are your chances?
- Is it worth the time and effort?
- What is the plan to sustain the project when the funding ends? Donors prefer projects that will continue in the future.

To find funding there are a number of options. Most institutions have a grant or research office, which may provide search engines on their website. In addition, there are ways to receive automatic e-mails about funding options based on keywords.

It is critical to work closely with the campus institutional research office to ensure there is no conflict with others on campus who may be seeking funding from the same entity. Some grants only allow one application per institution, and failure to communicate a plan to apply for funding could ruin a larger research agenda. It is possible that the education abroad staff may be discouraged from applying or asked to apply in a different year; this is part of process of applying for grants.

Networking
Networking is a key aspect of grant funding. Talk to colleagues who have received grants, particularly those in international education. Attending conferences and visiting the exhibit hall may yield grant opportunities in the future or stimulate ideas for funding. Participating in funding panels gives detailed insight into the grant funding process, and some grants may encourage applicants to visit their administrative offices to learn more about the grant and increase the chance of success. For more information on managing and applying for grants, watch for trainings sponsored by the campus institutional research office.

Managing Grants
There are three main aspects of grant management: financial, reporting, and compliance.
- **Financial.** Managing the funds.
- **Reporting.** Reporting outcomes to the donor.
- **Compliance.** Complying with rules and regulations of the grant.

Tracking grant funding is a critical component of grant management. Many institutions have grants managers who assist with managing the funds. If there is no such person, there may be a budget manager in the same reporting line that may be able to track the funds. If there is no such person, it might be necessary to have the education abroad administrative staff track the budget.

Communication with donors is critical. Some important questions to keep in mind throughout the grants management process include:

- What flexibility is there to move funds around?
- Is permission needed from the donor to make changes in the plan?

The largest warning to those applying for grant funding, is to only apply for funding that will advance the goals and mission of the education abroad office. There are funding opportunities that may arise that do not exactly fit with the office's mission and goals. However, the funding may be substantial, and it may seem a grant is an excellent opportunity even if its purpose is not in line with the scope of the education abroad office. It is recommended that you do not apply for this type of funding. Grants are a great deal of work and effort, and if a grant does not meet real goals of the education abroad office, it will pull staff away from mission critical functions. Save energy and time for grants that are most in line with the future goals and mission of the education office.

Building Rationale for Increasing Resources

Nearly all education abroad offices are not as well funded as desired. It is necessary to advocate for additional resources.

Data Collection

Data collection is one of the most critical ways to demonstrate what the office does and the success of outcomes. Send data to deans, provosts, and vice presidents on an annual basis. The data can focus on how the college is doing with education abroad participation. Showing success over time and how successes align with the university's mission and goals is an important way of demonstrating how education abroad activities have merit. It is also important to have a formal communication plan in place regarding data. The campus should be regularly informed what the education abroad office does. Please review chapter 20 for an in-depth discussion of data collection.

Mission Critical Initiatives

Universities and colleges are complicated entities and it can be challenging to remain focused. On an annual basis, the education abroad office should summarize the goals achieved during the academic year and the goals for the upcoming year. Summer is an easier time to do strategic planning because there are fewer faculty members and students needing assistance from the education abroad office. It is an old saying, but a true one, that education abroad leaders need to "have a plan, and work the plan." The plan should be revisited regularly to ensure the office is on track with its goals.

As new leaders enter positions or institutions, it is essential to focus on what will work and what is needed at the current institution. It may not be the same as other institutions. The institution may be less or more developed internationally, and what worked at one place, may not work at another. It is essential to understand the campus climate, culture, and political landscape.

The state of current political climate should be taken into account when advocating for additional funds. Is the time right to ask for funds? If the institution is focused on a particular issue, or there are concerns about budget cuts or funding shortfalls, it may not be wise to ask for funding at the present time. Along with politics comes timing. Is the timing right to ask for new funding? Is there new upper administration that may want to take education abroad to a new level? Does the campus need what the office offers at this particular time?

Site Visits and Program Development

Site visits and program development are essential components of due diligence and should not be seen as "optional." From an outside view, or a perspective outside of international education, site visits are seen as "exotic" and "fun." The reality is that site visits are an incredible amount of work. Institutions need to be able to verify the information provided to students about safety, academic facilities, housing, and transportation. Visiting program sites can invigorate and inform student advising, increase faculty engagement, and strengthen campus awareness of program offerings. However, site visits should have a clear rationale and be part of the overall strategic plan for the education abroad office. Funding for site visits should be included in the operational budget. Sandi Smith of Global Learning Semesters offered her perspective on site visits.

> *As part of your due diligence, you should be sending people to visit sites and assessing them. Institutions should have articulated reasons for the site visit, a set of guiding questions to assess the site, and a list of desired outcomes upon return to campus. From a provider perspective, it's important to get people to our sites so advisers and faculty understand the quality of the programs and the environment in which students will engage. Providers understand that participants are comparing sites, but having carefully articulated goals and outcomes will allow them to assess all sites in a similar manner.*[2]

---

[2]Sandi Smith (director of institutional relations, Global Learning Semesters), in conversation with the author, August 26, 2013. Reston, Va.

Most program providers offer site visits annually or biannually to their institutional affiliates to allow advisers and administrators to assess their program sites. Cost sharing is typical. The provider may cover in-country transportation, meals, and accommodations, and require the participants to pay for the airfare or some other expenses. It may be possible to add on additional time to visit other partner sites. The provider may need to approve a visit to another site before or after the site visit if they are arranging or purchasing flights. The provider has specific goals for the site assessment visit and it is essential to remain focused on the program being assessed.

If budgets are extremely tight, managers or staff may wish to add on professional time to a personal vacation abroad. The office could reimburse staff for per diem, meals, hotels, and ground transportation to the sites. The office may choose not to reimburse for the international flight because the primary goal of the trip was personal. Administrators and staff will need to establish an agreement fair to both parties. This tactic allows staff to remain engaged in their field and provides an affordable option to the office.

Summary and Additional Resources

Managing and developing the education abroad budget is a critical skill. There are a number of resources available through NAFSA and other professional organizations to enhance budget skills. Revenue can be increased through a variety of methods and leaders should consider creative or new ideas to bring in revenue. It is important to plan carefully and demonstrate patience with the budget process to have a successful office. Professional development of staff is critical to the success of an office and should be budgeted like all other expenses. Managers and staff should learn as much as possible about budgets, revenue, and take advantage of opportunities to enhance their skills.

Online Resources

NAFSA

NAFSA offers a wealth of information on its website, including recorded or captured "collegial conversations," which include topics on funding for education. View the conversations at http://www.nafsa.org/Connect_and_Network/Join_a_Conversation/.

The One Person Office (OPO) Member Interest Group (MIG) at NAFSA has resources for funding education abroad, creating faculty-led program budgets, and low-cost marketing options useful to offices of all sizes. The Member Interest Group can be subscribed to at http://www.nafsa.org/groups/home. aspx?groupid = 30.

Faculty-Led Budget Creation

NAFSA's One Person Office budget creation information: http://www.nafsa.org/Resource_Library_Assets/Migs/OPO_SIG/How_to_Create_a_Budget_for_a_Faculty_Led_Program/.

Mississippi State University's faculty information for creation of faculty-led programs: http://studyabroad.msstate.edu/faculty/budget.html.

Grants

The National Education Association (NEA) has good information for grant writers at http://www.neafoundation.org/pages/resources-writing-tutorial.

Boise State University is one of many universities that offers information for grant writers: http://research.boisestate.edu/osp/grant-management/.

Acknowledgments

The author would like to acknowledge and thank the contributions and guidance provided by the following field experts: Ryan Larsen, assistant director for education abroad at the University of Nevada-Las Vegas, Sandi Smith, director of institutional relations at Global Learning Semesters, and Julie Van-Vechten-Smith, western regional director at Academic Programs International.

References

Forum on Education Abroad. "Forum Annual Conference Travel Grant." Retrieved August 2013 from http://www.forumea.org/TravelGrantSD14.cfm.

Go Abroad. *Education Abroad Fair Calendar.* Retrieved on August 20, 2013 from http://fairs.goabroad.com/.

Rausch, Kyle. 2012. "Setting up a Passport Facility on Campus." In Melibee Global. Retrieved February 18, 2014 from http://www.melibeeglobal.com/2012/06/setting-up-a-passport-acceptance-facility-on-campus/.

Henke, Corrine. "International Learning Opportunities Annual Report 2012-2013." Unpublished annual report, Boise State University, 2013.

Institute of International Education. *Open Doors Survey Forms.* Retrieved September 1, 2013 from http://www.iie.org/Research-and-Publications/Open-Doors/Survey-Forms.

NAFSA. 2010. *Maximizing Funding for Education Abroad.* Washington, D.C.: NAFSA: Association of International Educators.

NAFSA. 2013a. "NAFSA e-Learning." Retrieved August 14, 2013 from http://www.nafsa.org/Attend_Events/Online/E_Learning/NAFSA_e-Learning/.

NAFSA. 2013b. "Financial Management." In *Managing the Education Abroad Office* participant workbook. Washington, D.C.: NAFSA: Association of International Educators.

NAFSA. 2013c. "Region I." Retrieved August 1, 2013 from http://www.nafsa.org/Connect_and_Network/Engage_with_a_Community/NAFSA_Regions/Region_I/.

NAFSA. 2013d. "Online Professional Learning & Training." Retrieved August 1, 2013 from http://www.nafsa.org/Attend_Events/Online/Online_Professional_Learning___Training/.

University of California-Riverside. "What is an Encumbrance?" Retrieved August 20, 2013 from http://cnc.ucr.edu/encumbrances/info.html.

CHAPTER 22

PARTNERSHIPS AND ADVOCACY

By Emily Gorlewski

Introduction

Partnerships and advocacy are essential at all levels of education abroad administration and advising. No one person or one office can accomplish all of the tasks expected of an office of education abroad in any given day. Leveraging the skills of one's campus community and maintaining relationships with partners all over the world are two skills necessary for success as an education abroad administrator or adviser. Using these skills to advocate for students, programs, the education abroad office, and for the internationalization of higher education in the United States and in the world is a central responsibility in these positions.

In this chapter, we will explore the goals of partnerships and advocacy. We will use the goals as a framework to talk about partnerships and advocacy on the home campus, working with partners, and different levels of advocacy. When goals and objectives are clear and made explicit, interactions with these various partners and stakeholders become more focused and fruitful.

Goals of Partnerships and Advocacy

An education abroad office may have many different goals for partnerships and advocacy. Staff members may wish to advance internationalization at their own institution or in U.S. higher education in general; they may wish to advance their own careers through networking and professional development, or cultivate an education abroad opportunity for one particular student who has come to them for help. Ultimately, though, the overarching goals for the partnerships and advocacy practiced in the office every day should align with the mission and vision of the institution itself (Barnes 2011). If one's own goals and initiatives conflict with those of the college or university, it is time to reevaluate and decide whether to take steps to change the institution, change one's own goals, or move on to an institution that is a better fit ideologically.

Institutional Mission and Vision

What value does an institution place on international education? Often, an indication can be found in the mission statement of the college or university.

Many institutions include some global dimension in their mission and vision statements, and incorporate internationalization in the institutional strategic plan. While infusion throughout the institution of international initiatives is the ideal under the philosophy of comprehensive internationalization (Hudzik 2011), not all institutions have embraced this philosophy. If a given institution does not include global or international elements in its mission statement, vision statement, or strategic plan, it does not necessarily mean international education is not valued; conversely, if these elements are included, sometimes international education professionals view this as largely symbolic, without any real support behind the inclusion.

Office Mission and Vision

After determining how the mission, vision, and strategic plan of the institution provide for international initiatives such as education abroad, the education abroad office must shape its own mission and vision aligned with institutional plans. The alignment of the missions and visions of the unit and of the institution is vital, though not all education abroad offices emphasize this in their plans. The education abroad office can create and foster partnerships within and outside of the university based on this alignment. For example, if the institutional strategic plan includes internationalization of the curriculum as a goal, the education abroad office can help a department to integrate study abroad programs into its curriculum, thus working toward a goal of the strategic plan while forming a partnership that increases education abroad participation (assuming this is a goal of the education abroad office; it is not always the case). Indeed, at some institutions, allocation of resources is directly tied to whether any given initiative furthers the goals and objectives of the strategic plan.

Though the alignment discussed above between the institutional and education abroad office's strategic plans is paramount, there are goals the study abroad office may have that are outside what the institution has explicitly laid out in terms of international programs. These may include such efforts as ensuring student health and safety abroad, increasing participation in education abroad, increasing internship opportunities, diversifying the education abroad portfolio, and advocating for education abroad and the internationalization of higher education at the individual, departmental, institutional, state, regional, and national levels. In order to meet all of the institutional and office goals, partnerships must be developed and maintained. This is true for any type of institution of higher education; no education abroad professional works in a vacuum.

On-Campus Partnerships

"It takes a campus to run a study abroad program," (White 2002, 51). On-campus partnerships help an education abroad office fulfill its many functions and implement its plans. Some of these partnerships are more obvious than others, but no area of campus should be overlooked when seeking out potential partners. Often, a seemingly unlikely partner can provide something that benefits the office in unexpected ways. For example, an office of education abroad might not always see a university writing center, staffed by graduate students of English, as a potential partner. However, if said office does not have a staff member dedicated to helping students apply for study abroad scholarships, the writing center staff can be a great asset in showing students how to craft their application essays to showcase their qualifications. Partners can be found in upper administration, academic affairs, student affairs, and administrative services offices on college and university campuses (White 2002). The staffing structure for these personnel may be different at different institutions, but the main partnership activities and partners will be similar.

Upper Administration and Governing Bodies

Regardless of the reporting line at the institution—whether the education abroad office is under academic affairs, student affairs, or a separate international division with its own associate provost or other executive-level administrator—upper administration and governing bodies must be partners in order for the office to meet its goals. Frontline education abroad advisers may not always interact directly with boards, presidents, provosts, vice presidents, deans, college senates, and other top-level institutional officials and bodies, but they are partners nonetheless. These individuals and groups set policy and procedure for the institution and create the missions, visions, and strategic plans that guide the institution forward.

Depending on the culture and structure of the institution, there are various ways in which the education abroad office can collaborate with upper administration and governing bodies. These also may vary depending on the level at which the education abroad adviser or administrator is employed at the institution. For example, at some institutions, education abroad advisers are at the level of other academic professionals and can sit on committees and participate in governance, but at some institutions this kind of work is reserved for administrators and faculty. Some institutions have high-power distance cultures, and one must be careful to observe strict protocols and reporting lines when communicating with officials or governing bodies. At other institutions, any level of employee can approach the president at any time with an idea.

At most institutions, education abroad advisers and administrators are able to work with upper administration and governing bodies in various capacities, and may have more opportunity than they think they do to influence institutional plans, policies, and procedures. Maneuvering through the culture and structure of the institution in order to do this can be tricky, but can result in desired changes, increased funding, and any number of other benefits. In general, persistence, diplomacy, and a willingness to take on additional work are traits that are helpful in working with these partners. If an education abroad administrator serves on a university committee, for example, and does good work in this capacity, he or she shows their commitment to the institution and may gain time with upper administration and faculty to discuss the goals of the education abroad office.

Academic Partnerships Within the Institution

Upper administration plays a role in advancing the goals of the education abroad office, but the members of the academic staff of the institution are also extremely important partners. Though education abroad encompasses many different facets of higher education, it is a fundamentally academic pursuit. Without the support and partnership of deans, department chairs, academic program directors, and individual professors, lecturers, instructors, and academic advisers, education abroad is destined to remain at the fringes of the institution, at best an external addition to a student's educational program.

Academic staff at different levels help to integrate education abroad into the curriculum, generate education abroad programming, and disseminate academic information about education abroad to students. Those with leadership roles in departments, colleges, and other academic units work with international education professionals to ensure that study abroad programs are academically rigorous. They also provide many of the leaders (faculty members) for academic programs abroad, and generate interest among students toward education abroad. Faculty members and departments are also the drivers behind successful, strategic university partnerships, which help not only with study abroad and exchanges, but also in internationalizing the institution at different levels (Sutton and Obst 2011).

At the college level, partners may include deans or directors. These administrators can be the catalysts for internationalizing their colleges and the departments within them. Depending on the degree to which international programs are centralized or decentralized at any given institution, colleges may hold their own exchange and partnership agreements, run their own study abroad or international internship programs, and even staff their own education abroad offices. If there is only one central education abroad office, then the colleges and their administrators must be allies in advancing the education abroad office's goals, whether these goals are to increase participation, improve student intercultural learning, or others. Colleges can help with many initiatives, from coordinating efforts to recruit more faculty leaders for study abroad programs, to providing financial resources for scholarships or other support for education abroad.

Department chairs can serve some of the same functions as the leaders of colleges in partnering with education abroad, but they may be more involved in the day-to-day operations. Department chairs may approve faculty-led study abroad program proposals and course equivalencies or transfer credit for exchange or provider programs, or they may work with the leaders of their colleges in order to do this. Department chairs can be the guardians of academic rigor in education abroad: by approving a course or faculty-led program, a department chair is certifying that the content and level are appropriate and at least equivalent to what the student would encounter on campus. There is a delicate balance here in terms of partnering with education abroad. In order to increase participation, many education abroad staff wish department chairs would approve more courses so that they fit in with students' degree programs. However, education abroad advisers and the department chairs themselves must recognize the importance of academic rigor and the department chairs' role in maintaining it.

Personnel in different academic areas, such as service learning, student teaching, and internship coordinators, as well as others, may serve some of the same functions as department chairs. While these professionals may not actually approve courses or programs, they may assist with the development of international opportunities for students. They may administer, or help to administer, programs. Regardless of the autonomy of these programs, education abroad professionals should collaborate with these personnel to the extent that it is possible. This collaboration may yield a streamlining of administrative functions, for example reducing duplication of efforts in risk management, or new knowledge of best practices in marketing or student services.

Faculty members are such important partners to education abroad advisers and administrators that one of their main education abroad functions, leading faculty-directed education abroad programs, is discussed extensively elsewhere in this guide (see chapter 14). Faculty can also be collaborators in serving on advisory councils for education abroad programming, mentoring future faculty leaders, and advocating for internationalizing curriculums in their departments. Having a strong ally in a faculty member opens many doors for education abroad advisers and administrators who may lack the academic credentials and experience to be regarded as colleagues by professors, department chairs, and other academic staff.

Finally, among academic personnel, academic advisers can be the strongest allies or the worst enemies of education abroad. Academic advisers can promote education abroad better than anyone else on campus by letting their students know it is an option, and showing them how to fit it into their academic plans. If academic advisers are knowledgeable about study abroad programs, courses, and financing, they can serve as additional study abroad personnel on campus. If they do not have this knowledge, or if they do not see the importance of education abroad, they may not mention it to their students, or worse: they may tell their students, "You're a ____ major; you can't study abroad."

Cultivating relationships with academic advisers is the responsibility of the education abroad office. Communication is very important in these relationships. Holding meetings with individual academic advisers, developing advising materials such as worksheets for each major, collaborating with them on curriculum integration or course articulation, and checking in with them on individual students or programs are all ways to help them become more familiar with education abroad offerings and understand how their students can participate. In order for academic advisers to understand the importance of education abroad, administrators should consider sending them on site visits, familiarization trips, or faculty seminars, whether these are offered by program providers or planned by the education abroad office. An academic adviser may not have traveled for educational purposes before, so letting them have the experience for themselves may be the most effective way to show them how transformative it can be.

Student Services Partnerships on Campus

Colleagues in student services are just as important as academic colleagues in performing the functions of an education abroad office. Generally speaking, these professionals help with a number of goals, including risk management and crisis response, promotion and marketing of education abroad programs, predeparture and reentry programming, and financing education abroad opportunities. Because each of these goals is discussed in greater detail elsewhere in this guide, the following are brief descriptions of partnering with student services personnel and offices on these goals. For further details, please consult the relevant chapters. In these relationships, it is worth remembering that these student services partnerships should not exist only to serve the education abroad office. If there is something an education abroad adviser can do to reciprocate help given by a student services professional, this can keep relations friendly and collegial.

Risk management and crisis response cannot be handled in the vacuum of the education abroad office, even if that office is fortunate enough to have a professional on staff who is dedicated to health and safety of students abroad. Continuous collaboration and support are necessary from the units that are responsible for such functions on campus. These may include public safety or campus police, a risk management officer, the student health insurance officer, legal counsel, the office responsible for responding to sexual harassment and assault complaints, student development, the counseling and student medical centers, and any other staff or office that handles emergencies or risk mitigation. The most important aspect of these partnerships is constant communication; that is, one must not wait until a crisis is in progress to reach out to these personnel. Meeting a few times a year to debrief emergency situations and develop plans is essential to being able to respond to time-sensitive crises when they happen.

In keeping with emergency preparedness, many of these same partners can help with predeparture programming. They can review what the education abroad office has put together for accuracy and add their own advice, or they can come to predeparture meetings and present on various topics. Balancing these presentations with the required cultural orientation can be tricky, though; the campus police should not take up an hour of a half-day predeparture orientation. For reentry programming, different partners may come on board. A career center, for example, can be a valuable resource for reentry programming, showing students how to translate their education abroad experiences into marketable skills to list on their résumés or showcase in interviews, and helping students find career opportunities abroad. Again, finding ways to help the career center, possibly with other programming, would be beneficial in maintaining the relationship and ensuring that these professionals are available to help with reentry.

For the promotion of education abroad programs and recruitment of students, there are other student services offices that can help, if one cultivates and maintains partnerships with them. Multicultural or diversity centers on campus might be of help in getting information out to populations that are underrepresented in education abroad at the institution. Recognizing that these offices' goals and priorities are not exactly the same as those of the education abroad office and agreeing to help their staff to work toward their goals as well as one's own will be effective here as well. Student activities offices can be helpful in connecting the education abroad office to student organizations, which may be happy to have education abroad staff come and present in their meetings but have not known they were available. Honors programs, which may serve academic as well as student services functions, are another potential partner for promoting education abroad, as are nontraditional student programs, LGBTQ centers, and disability services offices.

Financing study abroad, for many students, is not possible without scholarships or financial aid. The offices in charge of these must be allies in order for the education abroad office to advocate for its students. They can help identify sources of aid the education abroad office might not be aware of, as well as help education abroad staff and their students understand the regulations for federal student aid and existing scholarships. Veterans and student athletes may have other offices on campus helping them with special funding they receive, so working with them may be necessary from time to time. Again, it is better to have this contact in place before there is a student in need. Scholarship or fellowship offices may also be instrumental in helping students applying for nationally competitive study abroad scholarships such as Fulbright, Boren, and Gilman scholarships. Foundation, alumni, and development offices can be great partners for financing as well; their fundraising campaigns can generate donations for study abroad scholarships, and they can help education abroad offices stay in touch with their alumni for other purposes as well.

Administrative Services

Administrative services personnel, such as billing and receivables, the bursar, purchasing, travel offices, legal counsel, and others, are instrumental in running education abroad programming. The degree to which each of these offices is involved varies from institution to institution, and is discussed in other areas of the guide. They help with logistics, purchasing, and compliance with national and international regulations as well as university policies and procedures.

Centralized and Decentralized Models of Education Abroad Administration

Education abroad in U.S. higher education is administered in a number of different ways. Some models are centralized, meaning that there is one education abroad office in charge of all activity undertaken for academic credit in other countries, and some are decentralized, meaning that there is more than one unit responsible for these functions. There are advantages and disadvantages to models at each end of the continuum, and no one model is right for every institution. The administration of education abroad should most likely, in the end, mirror that of the institution itself, and be aligned with its mission and goals.

If there is more than one unit on campus administering education abroad programming, then there are many different forms the administration can take. There may be a central education abroad office, and then several smaller education abroad offices across campus, in different colleges, for example. Or, in addition to the central education abroad office's programs, departments may run their own faculty-led programs, provider programs, or exchange partnerships.

Centralized Models

The centralized model of education abroad administration offers many advantages. In this model, any decision made in policies and procedures can be very quickly applied to all programs, thus reducing confusion about, for example, a GPA requirement to study abroad. Risk management can be easier; if there is a natural disaster in a certain country, it is relatively easy to ascertain how many students of the institution are in that country at the time, in order to make sure they are all safe and accounted for. Communication with off-campus partners can be less confusing as well; multiple, contradictory messages to a partner from different units within the institution are minimized.

There are disadvantages to centralized models as well. When all education abroad functions are in one office, that office can be a "silo" of outgoing international activity. This runs counter to comprehensive internationalization, in which international activities should be infused throughout the entire institution. The education abroad office in such a model can be seen as obstructionist and draconian, not allowing individual faculty members or departments to run programs the way they would like to, and policing every international initiative at the institution. This model also means a great deal of work for the education abroad office, since it is running and keeping track of all programs itself, and thus may be more suitable for small- to mid-sized institutions than for very large research universities.

Decentralized Models

Decentralized models of education abroad administration offer many advantages as well. Most importantly, having different units on campus participating in education abroad opportunities can help with comprehensive internationalization of the institution by taking these activities out of a "silo." This model can mean there are more personnel collaborating on education abroad programming, thus reducing the per capita workload which can be heavier in a more centralized office. Different units might also understand the needs and academic programs of their students better than a centralized education abroad office can, thus ensuring more targeted and appropriate programming.

The disadvantages to this model include a possible lack of communication and collaboration between the different units. This can result in poor communication with partners, inefficiencies related to the duplication of efforts, and can make risk management and crisis response more difficult. There also may not be anyone at the institution using this model who has a clear idea of the big picture of education abroad programming, so strategic planning and a vision for where international education is headed can be difficult to grasp. Large, comprehensive research universities sometimes have an administrative model that is decentralized, and this may reflect how many of the other administrative functions in such a university are handled.

Off-Campus Partnerships

In addition to the many on-campus collaborations detailed above, education abroad administrators and advisers must maintain partnerships with institutions and organizations off campus. These include foreign higher education institutions, education abroad providers (whether these are other U.S. higher education institutions, nonprofit organizations, or businesses), and vendors such as travel agents and insurance companies. There are many functions of off-campus partnerships—some related to international education and some not—that are not part of education abroad advising and administration; this chapter will focus mainly on the functions that are directly related to education abroad.

Foreign Institutions

One of the main types of entities with which education abroad personnel must maintain relationships is the overseas partner institution. There are many reasons to partner with institutions abroad, including raising the profile or reputation of the home institution, recruiting degree-seeking international students, research or grant application collaboration, and others (Sutton and Obst 2011), but in terms of education abroad, these partnerships are about student exchange agreements. Exchanges and their administration are described in the chapter on portfolio management (see chapter 18), but this chapter will describe the partnerships necessary for them to function.

Depending on the administration of international education at the institution, all agreements with foreign institutions may be handled by the education abroad administrator. Whether or not this is the case, the education abroad office must help to set the policies and procedures related to such agreements, or at least be aware of them. In a decentralized model, colleges and departments may maintain their own agreements and have their own policies related to them. In the centralized model, the education abroad administrator or other administrator in charge of the agreements must set policies for who can initiate agreements, who approves and signs them, who administers the programs created under the agreement, and who maintains the relationship.

There should also be consideration of vetting or evaluating potential partners, and a clear procedure for this should be adopted.

The agreements created under these policies and procedures vary greatly, but for education abroad purposes there are two main types. These are memoranda of understanding, or MOUs, and implementing agreements, or memoranda of agreement. Generally, an MOU is a universitywide, one- or two-page, legally nonbinding agreement, mainly describing the intent of two institutions to work together. It does not commit any money or labor on behalf of either institution, and is signed by the presidents, chancellors, rectors or equivalent officials of both institutions. The implementing agreement is the student exchange agreement, or a detailed agreement for a different type of collaboration. These agreements may be institutionwide or signed at the college or department level, and are, in contrast to the MOU, legally binding. They may still be signed by the president or equivalent, but may also be signed by a college dean or other official.

Some institutions require an MOU, but administrators at other institutions see MOUs as superficial and unnecessary, and prefer to have only agreements that lead to concrete activities. This reflects a difference in institutional goals and philosophies. The number of agreements has been seen as an indicator of internationalization, with a greater number of agreements supposedly equaling a greater degree of internationalization at an institution. However, the recent trend has been toward strategic partnerships (Sutton and Obst 2011), ones that help advance goals of teaching, research, scholarship, service, or student exchange. Institutions can complement each other in these areas. For example, a newer university in a developing country may not have a music department, but have a goal to establish one. A U.S. university can provide the expertise to help the academic personnel at this institution found a music department, which provides research and study abroad opportunities to faculty and students at the U.S. university. Collaboration of this type is becoming more and more important as reduced state funding and higher costs worldwide necessitate sharing resources and staff.

The benefits of collaboration are many, but there are also challenges, and some partnerships are not sustainable. Cultural differences are one reason for this. For example, a staff member at one university may have an open and frank negotiating style, while her counterpart at the other university has a more guarded style and finds the candor of the first staff member off-putting or rude. The first staff member may find the other university's representative sneaky and dishonest. Even international educators are susceptible to cultural misunderstandings. Another challenge is funding. The Atlantis program of the Fund for the Improvement of Postsecondary Education and the European Union was a good example of this (Obst and Kuder 2009). These transatlantic dual-degree partnerships were established with generous funding, but the funding was finite. The institutions involved had to figure out how to sustain the partnerships after the grant money was spent, which proved difficult in some cases.

For U.S. institutions wishing to begin or strengthen their international partnership strategies, the Institute of International Education (IIE), through its Center for International Partnerships in Higher Education, Global Partnerships Service, and International Academic Partnership Program, offers institutional assistance in this area. On an individual scale, the Fulbright International Education Administrators programs are a way for individual administrators to meet their counterparts in different countries and learn about the different educational systems in which they work. There are also various programs run by the governments of other countries, which provide a way for U.S. administrators to connect with administrators in those countries.

Study Abroad Providers

Study abroad providers are another type of external partner. Information about their different program models and advice for how to work with them are included elsewhere in this guide, so this chapter will include information only on how they function as partners. Study abroad providers may be other higher education institutions, based either in the United States or abroad, nonprofit organizations, or businesses. Providers can expand an education abroad office's portfolio of programs, assist with promotion and marketing of education abroad, and perform a great deal of the academic, health and safety, and logistical functions of running programs.

Depending on the institution's and the provider's policy, affiliation agreements may or may not be necessary in order for students to participate in a provider's programs. The agreement may become necessary if students need to use financial aid in order to participate (an agreement solely for financial aid is sometimes called a consortium agreement), or if the home institution needs the agreement in order to issue academic credit for a program transcripted by a provider. In cases in which an institution will only accept a transcript from another U.S. accredited higher education institution, a provider may use a school of record (SOR). The arrangements for this type of partnership are complicated; guidelines for establishing this type of arrangement have been developed by The Forum on Education Abroad and are available at the Forum's website.

Agreements with study abroad providers may be less complicated than those for reciprocal exchanges; they provide for credit approval or transfer, selection of students, payment, application deadlines, and sometimes scholarships for students from the signing university, or payment of an annual stipend to the signing university for use in education abroad marketing. Some institutions will not allow offices to take these payments for marketing, so understanding institutional policy before signing the agreement will avoid trouble later on.

Advocacy

Throughout preceding portions of this chapter, the word "advocacy" has signified interceding with upper administration, academic and student affairs partners, administrative services, and development on behalf of students, goals and objectives, or programs. This is advocacy at the institutional level, which is made possible through all of the different partnerships described. Advocacy at the institutional level is part of every study abroad adviser and administrator's position description. Advocacy at the state, national, or international public policy level may be more difficult for study abroad personnel to influence, but it is vital to the advancement of the internationalization of higher education in the United States and around the world. Every international educator is affected by public policy at these levels, and every international educator has opportunities to help influence this policy. For international educators based in the United States, membership organizations, governmental organizations, and legislators can be partners in working toward the goal of public policy that supports international higher education.

NAFSA: Association of International Educators may be the sponsor of this guide and the most visible individual membership organization working on public policy, but there are a number of other organizations that U.S. international educators should be aware of. These organizations usually provide other benefits such as professional development, conferences, networking, and resource sharing, but some have a focus on public policy. NAFSA, for example, works on advocacy for international education through its Connecting Our World social media campaigns, which send out messages for members to write to and communicate with their legislators and encourage others to do the same; Advocacy Day, in which members are organized for a trip to Washington, D.C. to meet with policymakers; and the Grassroots Leadership Program, in which member cohorts are trained to advocate for a specific issue. Advocacy issues for NAFSA have included immigration reform, the Senator Paul Simon Study Abroad Act legislation, opening up travel to Cuba, and other issues that advance education abroad, enable international students to come to the United States, and otherwise promote internationalization.

Other international education organizations doing work on public policy include The Forum on Education Abroad, the Association of International

Education Administrators (AIEA), and the Alliance for International Educational and Cultural Exchange. In addition, NAFSA member regions participate in advocacy to varying degrees, and the state organizations under these NAFSA regions do as well, again to varying degrees. There are state and regional organizations, such as the Boston Area Study Abroad Association (BASAA), the Education Abroad Professionals of Minnesota (MSAP), and the Kentucky Council on Education Abroad (KCEA), which are not affiliated with NAFSA, but may have advocacy as well as professional development missions. Higher education organizations such as the American Association of State Colleges and Universities, Association of American Colleges and Universities, and others belong to coalitions that advocate for internationalization issues.

With all of these large organizations working on advocacy and public policy, individual international educators may not realize that there are actions they as professionals and voters can take that can make a difference. Much of NAFSA's work in the area of advocacy involves mobilizing members in letter writing campaigns and other ways of communicating with the legislators who represent them as voters. These legislators pay attention to their constituents, possibly more so than to large organizations whose headquarters are not in their areas of representation.

Some other considerations for international educators who are inspired to accept the responsibility for advocacy: they should advocate for all issues involving international education, and make sure they are taking action as individuals, not as representatives of their institution. Immigration policy affects all international educators, not just those who work with international students and scholars. When visa regulations make it difficult for international students to come to the United States, other countries respond by making immigration regulations more difficult for U.S. students going abroad. And if fewer international students and scholars can come to the United States, international education as a whole is affected. Taking action as an individual and not an institutional representative means writing to the legislators who represent the area where one lives, not where one works, because these legislators want to hear from the voters in their area. An institution may not allow individual employees to advocate on its behalf, and in any case, citizens vote as individuals, so personal e-mail addresses and home computers should be used to reach out to representatives.

Summary

The complexity of education abroad administration—the many different considerations, from health and safety to academic excellence—makes it necessarily a collaborative effort. On-campus partners such as academic affairs, student affairs, and administrative services; off-campus partners such as overseas institutions and study abroad providers; and advocacy at the individual, institutional, and policy levels, all are essential in helping education abroad advisers and administrators accomplish the goals of their offices and institutions. Keeping these goals in mind while also helping partners work toward their own goals and objectives is the key to building partnerships that work. In this chapter, we have discussed the different partners with whom an education abroad office must collaborate and innovate, around the framework of its own mission.

Additional Resources

Web Resources

IIE Center for International Partnerships in Higher Education
http://www.iie.org/What-We-Do/International-Education-Services/
Center-for-International-Partnerships.

American Council on Education/CIGE Publication on Institutional Partnerships
Includes sample agreements and templates for different types of partnerships
http://www.acenet.edu/news-room/Pages/International-Partnerships-
Guidelines-Colleges-Universities.aspx.

Forum on Education Abroad Guidelines for School of Record Relationships
http://www.forumea.org/SchoolofRecord.cfm.

NAFSA and Alliance Exchange information on advocacy
http://www.connectingourworld.org.
http://www.nafsa.org/Explore_International_Education/Advocacy_and_
Public_Policy.
http://www.nafsa.org/uploadedFiles/NAFSA_Home/Resource_Library_
Assets/Public_Policy/advocacy_handbook.pdf.
http://www.alliance-exchange.org.

Other Publications

The Forum on Education Abroad. 2011. *Standards of Good Practice for Education Abroad.* 4th edition. Carlisle, Pa.: The Forum on Education Abroad. http://www.forumea.org/standards-standards.cfm.

NAFSA: Association of International Educators. 2009. "NAFSA's Statement of Ethical Principles." Washington, D.C.: NAFSA, Association of International Educators. https://www.nafsa.org/Learn_About_NAFSA/Governance_Documents/Ethics_And_Principles/Statement_Of_Ethics/NAFSA_s_Statement_of_Ethical_Principles/.

References

Barnes, Tim. 2011. "Intentionality in International Engagement: Identifying Potential Strategic International Partnerships." In *Developing Strategic International Partnerships: Models for Initiating and Sustaining Innovative Institutional Linkages.* Edited by Susan Buck Sutton and Daniel Obst, 1–6. Global Education Research Reports. New York, N.Y.: Institute of International Education and the AIFS Foundation.

Hudzik, John K. 2011. *Comprehensive Internationalization: From Concept to Action.* Washington, D.C.: NAFSA, The Association of International Educators. http://www.nafsa.org/uploadedFiles/NAFSA_Home/Resource_Library_Assets/Publications_Library/2011_Comprehen_Internationalization.pdf.

Obst, Daniel, and Matthias Kuder, eds. 2009. *Joint and Double Degree Programs: An Emerging Model for Transatlantic Exchange.* New York, N.Y. : Institute of International Education and Freie Universität Berlin.

Sutton, Susan Buck, and Daniel Obst, eds. 2011. *Developing Strategic International Partnerships: Models for Initiating and Sustaining Innovative Institutional Linkages.* Global Education Research Reports. New York, N.Y.: Institute of International Education and the AIFS Foundation.

White, Dawn. 2002. "Internal Support Systems: It Takes a Campus to Run a Study Abroad Program." In *The Guide to Successful Short-Term Programs Abroad.* Edited by Sarah E. Spencer and Kathy Tuma, 51–62. Washington, D.C.: NAFSA, Association of International Educators.

CHAPTER 23

POLICIES AND PROCEDURES

By Holly R. Carter

A spotlight has been focused recently on how institutions handle emergencies and crises, as well as how everyday decisions in the international education (IE) office could impact the outcome of a student experience or study abroad program. Study abroad professionals are familiar with small incidents that happen day-to-day in their own international education offices, but there are also larger incidents reported on the news that make headlines (Herrmann 2009). What can an office do when an incident occurs? The answer is to be prepared before something happens.

> **Best Practice:** *All study abroad offices should have a policies and procedures manual that details both the everyday running of the office and emergency procedures.*

Having policies and procedures written and clearly organized has many benefits. It has the benefit of being a roadmap for new employees; it also is extremely helpful when there is a shift in work from one employee to another. There are many other benefits, too, such as giving the university community an idea of how things in the international education office work, and what to expect when dealing with the office. It also guides the institution in times of concern or uncertainty. To be able to refer back to a written set of guidelines is valuable in making difficult decisions. Policies and procedures will also help in times of great crisis. When the worst events come to pass, one of the main questions that will be asked is whether there was a policy or procedure in place and whether it was followed. In addition to providing clarity to the international education office, employees, and to the wider community, a policy and procedure manual will also help the institution to know that it has taken appropriate action in times of concern or crisis.

What are policies and procedures? A policy is a rule that governs how something needs to be done, while a procedure is how the policy is implemented. Procedures can change over time as we obtain new technology or new staff, while policies can take a long time to change or may be resistant to change (University of California-Santa Cruz 1994). Policies and procedures give clear structure to an organization, something that every organization and office or department within that organization can benefit from, including the international education office. Policies and procedures are not something that are simply written once, put on a shelf, and checked off a list. These are documents that need to be continually reviewed, updated, and changed. The office may find that a once-a-year review will work to update some minor issues, but policies may also need to be updated after debriefing an incident or crisis. Most of the time, offices reflect on policies after finding an exception, or that one small thing that was never considered. All of these are times to reflect on the document and to remember that it is a living manual. It must change at times to be current and correct.

The most important item to note when starting to put together policies and procedures is that the international education office does not control everything. There are some decisions and some control that must come from other areas within the university. This can be a very good thing for an international education office, but it is one that must be carefully considered when starting to write the policy and procedure manual.

> **Best Practice:** *Consider where policies already exist within the institution's structure and which ones apply to the international education area. Using policies and procedures that are already in place will help guide the international education office and tie the office to the larger university context.*

There are many places on campus to consider reaching out to for existing policies and procedures. Consider the following offices or areas: student life, the dean of students, accounts payable, finance, travel, academic advising, deans or chairs of academic departments, the vice president for academic affairs or provost, student financial services, the registrar, and student housing. There may be more departments than this to reach out to, but ask these offices for direction on other offices or units to speak with. It is also important to remember that these offices and departments can be placed in many different areas depending on the structure of the institution.

At a large research institution, an international education office wanting to cover travel regulations in its manual may need to reach out to a travel office or perhaps to a member of the leadership team within its own department to get clarity on the regulations; where a small private university may not have a travel office and may simply need to reach out to finance and ask how travel is paid through e-mail or a phone conversation. At my own small private university, the budget is allocated and the IE director determines how these resources are spent, while large universities and public universities may need to follow strict regulations for travel, including many forms and preapproval processes.

An example of the latter can be found in Western Kentucky University's *Faculty-Led Study Abroad Policy Manual,* where the policy states, "After program approval, the WKU Controller's office shall establish an account for the [program leader] for use to deposit payments (revenue) and to pay expenses as listed on the budget. All WKU purchasing policies and procedures are in force with this account. [The program leader] must apply for a procurement card and attend training" (Western Kentucky University 2011).

The following are some offices to consider interviewing for potential policy issues/connections.

Financial Policies

- Travel policies
- Cash advance/ petty cash policies
- Reimbursement policies
- Policies on incidental items
- Time frames for returning of receipts
- Payment to vendors policies

Discipline Policies

- Student behavior guidelines
- Alcohol guidelines
- Academic dishonesty guidelines
- Due process procedures
- Sexual harassment policies

Academic Policies

- Contact hours for granting credit
- Teaching qualifications for subject areas
- Summer pay for teaching guidelines
- Syllabus guidelines
- Registration procedures
- Academic advising procedures

When making these appointments, it is important to remember some basic organizational issues about universities. Academic institutions are generally divided into three governing areas: Faculty, staff, and students.

The work of faculty within academic affairs is typically governed by an overarching rule of academic freedom. This simply means that the academic, who is a subject-matter expert, will determine the areas that need to be taught or addressed in a class or in a curriculum. This is often a tense meeting with the international education office, as the professor has the ability to determine the way a subject is being taught, which sometimes does not work abroad or with the resources available in an international setting (Goonen and Blechman 1999). An example of academic freedom and international education potentially being in conflict is when the professor is set on taking students to a certain location in order to achieve academic goals, but perhaps the international education office has policies against traveling to this particular country. In attempting to resolve this issue, the international education office may offer an alternative location, but the professor would be able to determine ultimately if the course would work in that area as it is a critical academic issue.

Academic affairs also has a strict hierarchy. Faculty members hold rank, which is their place on the ladder of professionals within their department. A chair is generally who a faculty member reports to, and a chair reports to a dean, and a dean to a vice president of academic affairs or provost. These reporting structures can vary from institution to institution, but most have organizational charts published on their website for staff and faculty. It is a good idea to become familiar with these hierarchies. It is most unlikely that any of these individuals will ever report directly to the international education office, however, which makes it difficult at times with assessment or working relationships.

International education policies can never dictate that someone in the academic arena reports directly to them in most cases (Schloss and Cragg 2012). If a professor from public health wishes to run a program in Africa, that professor will not become an international education employee during the duration of the international education component of the course, but will still be supervised by a chair and a dean. This can be a difficult situation if issues with a faculty member arise. Most institutions report through the chain of command, so one needs to be familiar with the hierarchy in order to reach out and get help or to work with others in their own structures. An example of this can be seen in the University of Georgia's study abroad program manual as follows: "The curriculum is appropriate and sufficiently rigorous, commensurate the department/college, including content and pedagogical method(s) appropriate with other courses in to the discipline (traditional lecture, field research, lab research, internship, service-learning, etc.), and appropriate number and types of assignments" (University of Georgia 2012).

Staff members throughout the university generally report to a director. Most directors report to vice presidents. Staff members may be helpful to the international education office in many ways, such as academic advising or careers services; however, it is important to see them as partner departments and not as a part of international education services or controlled by the international education office.

Students will have a code of conduct which should be spelled out in a student handbook. Students will be held responsible by the appropriate offices on the campus for behavior that breaks this code. The student handbook will spell out a chain of events that must happen, so students are awarded their due process. It is not for the international education office to determine punishment for students, even if a student is expelled from a program. It is rather the responsibility of the international education office to turn over the infraction to the appropriate office, most often the dean of students, and then allow the process to determine the outcome (Waryold and Lancaster 2008). The University of Central Oklahoma states this in its study abroad manual as:

> [The Office of Student Conduct] supports CGC in determining responsibility of alleged policy violations by students participating in study tours and/or study abroad programs. During predeparture orientation meetings, the Office of Student Conduct educates and reminds students of the university disciplinary policies, which remain in effect while participating in off-campus travel activities, sponsored by the university. Additionally, the Office of Student Conduct encourages students to be positive ambassadors of the University of Central Oklahoma and maintain an awareness of the potential personal, legal, and professional consequences that may ensue due to violations of university policies and/or laws. (University of Central Oklahoma 2012).

Students are also subject to academic honor codes and can be sanctioned for academic dishonesty. Students who plagiarize, cheat, or violate other academic honor codes will need to be turned over to the appropriate office on campus, generally the vice president of academic affairs office, for due process in this matter.

In all of these cases and in many more at universities, there are already rules and regulations in place. It is important to determine what policies are already in place and how the policies apply to international education. If policies need to be altered to fit into the international education arena, then conversations must be arranged. It can take some time to change policies, a process that is detailed in this chapter also. Be mindful of items such as travel, reimbursement, payment, and other financial policies when writing the manual as well. Do your best to incorporate policies that already exist into the international education manual, and determine where the areas that should apply to the international education office come into play.

Creating and Implementing Study Abroad Policies and Procedures

Creating policies is a two-step process. First, determine which policies are already set by the university and refer to them, and then take a look at what the office is already doing within the international education arena. As discussed in the previous section, there are many areas for which policy already exists and the office simply needs to use this policy.

Once all of the areas where there is existing policy to refer to have been identified, it is time to consider what policies and procedures are needed for international education. These are typically two types of items:

- Procedures for the work that the office needs to accomplish; and
- Policies for those who interact with the office.

Collecting information and visiting the offices where policy will be drawn from is a great first start. The next step is to identify the procedures within the international education office. One of the best ways to do this is to brainstorm a list of everything that must be accomplished within the office. Once that list has been brainstormed, the next step is to look at the process a student follows to get there. Map this on a flowchart or in bullet points or numbered steps. These steps are the makings of the procedures. Remember to do this for every goal that the office must accomplish.

The second item needed are the policies that must be followed by those who interact with the office. These can easily be broken down by constituency—faculty, staff, and students. Starting with students, reflect on this question: what are the rules that apply to students? Consider the rules that can be referred to (such as academic dishonesty) and then consider the rules that come from the international education office. Is there a minimum GPA requirement to participate in programs? Is there a deadline for program applications? Brainstorm a list of all of the rules for each category.

Remember to start working from where the office currently is, not trying to imagine an ideal state. Think of the rules that anyone who comes into contact with the international education office must follow, and these will inspire the link to policies. Once these have been identified, it would be a good exercise to consider why these are the rules that exist. Are they university rules that cannot be changed, or are they rules that have always existed, and thus one must consider if they are still useful? Often offices create rules because of one circumstance, or even one student. Is this how the rules came about, or were they inherited? Many international education offices were created after international programs had been running for years. There may be programs that predate the international education office, and have systems that were in place before the office existed, too. For example, my international education office inherited a course approval form that a faculty member created many years ago to ensure students registered for classes. This form was very complicated and no longer worked with the new system of academic advising that the university had created; however, the international education office continued to use the form, and had expanded its use to more programs. When we considered this form when writing our own manual, it became clear there was a much easier way to have courses approved in our online system.

The other possibility when considering rules is that more may be needed. Is it clear who can apply for a scholarship, or has that been handled on a one-off basis, where an adviser who likes a student can decide? All of these should be carefully considered when looking at the rules of the office. Once these are identified, start to match them to the procedures areas. Matching policies and procedures will be quite clear in some cases and complex in others. For example, if the institution has a registration process, then the international education office can work within that process to register students who will be studying abroad. It can be more complex when the policies and procedures are not clearly linked. For example: Are the university alcohol policies still enforced while abroad, or should there be an on-campus policy and a study abroad policy? Many countries allow students to consume alcohol legally under the age of 21, and the university policy may explicitly state that any student under age 21 caught with alcohol will be sanctioned. Matching the policies and procedures, and facing these tough issues and questions, will get the manual off to a good start.

After collecting the policies and procedures through these brainstorming exercises and also through research and conversation on campus, it is time formalize the writing of the manual. The first question is: can all issues be addressed in one manual, or if it is preferable to have one for faculty and staff—addressing those who work for the university and organization—and one for students?

Best Practice: *It is advisable to have information for faculty/staff and information for students in separate places, as the audience is vastly different.*

Once a decision is made regarding how many manuals are needed and the information necessary to include in each, it would be a good time to think about governance. When one writes a manual that focuses on financial issues in international education, it is important to have financial services review it. When writing a manual that is for faculty, see if the governing faculty council will review it or have a conversation about it before it is finished. Letting the appropriate people or committees and councils know what the international education office is doing and why may save a lot of time, conversation, and pain in the long run.

The next step is writing the manual. Most technical writing is straightforward and to the point. It must be clear and concise, but easy for the reader to follow (Weiss 2005). Make sure to include a table of contents, and to organize the materials logically in chapters. Start at the beginning. If it is a student manual, what does the student need to know first? Perhaps the types of issues handled in the international education office are a good place to start before discussing the application procedure. Make sure that the manual makes logical sense and flows with the materials as they are needed. Create subheadings and sections to make matters more clear.

Best Practice: *Policies should be spread throughout the procedures. It isn't very friendly to tell a student how to apply and then to list all of the rules that make them ineligible for programs, so make sure to embed the policies so that they make sense. Some policies take more explanation; for example, if some programs take a higher GPA to be eligible to apply, then the office might want to explain why.*

Remember to direct the reader to the full policies that are referred to. When writing in the faculty manual that university rules that govern travel apply to international education programs, make sure to either include a complete listing of the travel rules or provide a link to the travel rules. Never assume that others know the rules, where to find them, or what they say. Placing them within the document and citing them will be a big help.

Once finished with the initial draft of the document, get feedback on it. Ask other departments to read it and see where they are referenced. Make sure to have accurately portrayed their policies and procedures. Have a colleague proof the document and give feedback. Some of the most difficult things to write are the things that you know well, so a second set of eyes will be invaluable. Ask strategic players within the university to read the manual. Perhaps a student government leader may like to look at the student manual, as well as students who have used the office's services successfully or those who may have had issues. By asking these opinions, one will be able to see if what the manual meant to communicate has been communicated effectively. Taking these extra steps requires time and collaboration. It may take several tries to get different offices or departments to approve the manual, but this will allow the manual to be more accepted and easier to implement.

Best Practice: *All study abroad manuals should have a section addressing emergency policies and procedures.*

One of the most important reasons to have a policy and procedures manual is that it guides the institution in times of crisis. During a crisis that involves a program or a participant, it is often difficult to remember all of the steps involved in making the right decisions and keeping the correct information. Having the procedures in front of the crisis team and in written form will help everyone involved; it also may be the best protection an institution can have when things don't go as planned. Remember that in writing policies and procedures for emergencies abroad there are several things that the institution cannot control. The institution cannot control the laws of the countries where the accident or emergency happens. The institution cannot control some circumstances, such as natural disasters or terrorism. The institution can control the response of the university being in line with the written policies and procedures.

Every manual should have a section on emergencies abroad, even if the university has never experienced one. There may be a considerable amount of work already done through risk management, legal counsel, faculty leadership, or insurance on this issue, and these are the first offices or colleagues to ask. Many policies and procedures may be written on what to do if there is an incident on campus or within the United States, so it may mean referring to some of these policies or working with the appropriate offices to expand them to an international setting. After looking at the already existing policies and determining what could work and what needs to be added, write this chapter in the manual.

Areas to consider for this chapter include:

- What is considered an emergency by the university
  - One may want a sliding scale, from small things such as a student being injured, to larger incidents, such as earthquakes or other natural disasters.
- How insurance coverage while abroad is determined
  - Every student who is abroad needs to be covered by insurance. The international education office may purchase this for participants or may require them to purchase it and show proof of purchase.
- What information is given to students before they commit to a program and before they travel abroad
  - Typical information is provided from the U.S. Department of State (http://travel.state.gov/travel/tips/emergencies/emergencies_1212.html) (http://studentsabroad.state.gov/emergencies.php); Centers for Disease Control and Prevention (http://wwwnc.cdc.gov/travel) ; and the World Health Organization (http://www.who.int/ith/en/).
- The point of contact for a student in crisis
  - This is typically the professor with the group or provider of the program.
  - Ensure that the student has these phone numbers, as well as a 24-hour phone number for the university
- The point of contact for a professor in crisis
  - There needs to be a point person reachable at all times to those abroad.
- Who will need to be notified once the university contact person has been notified
  - Many universities develop a response team for emergencies and crises.

- A reporting format or report form to keep good notes of the situation
- What funds are available for action to be taken if necessary
- The point of contact for the media
- Who will contact family members or emergency contacts if necessary
- Who will contact embassies or other government officials if necessary

Once all of these issues are identified and put down in writing, there are still two very important steps: Communicate the policies and procedures and train those who need to know them for when there is an emergency. Communication is vital. If faculty members are traveling with students, make sure that professor has a copy of the emergency procedures, which should be available to them at all times. It may be a printed copy in case the electronic copy is not available. They must have access to emergency phone numbers at all times as well; it is advisable for them to program it into their phones before leaving the United States. When an emergency happens, there can be little time to think. Those involved with the response also need to have the procedures and polices close at hand at all times. Consider putting it on the international education website and providing everyone involved a copy of the document, perhaps laminated or on colored paper.

Policies and Procedures Training

The next exercise is training. All members going out into the field need to be trained every year on the policies and procedures (Fischer 2010). This means an annual meeting of those who will be abroad with students. Also consider including the international education staff in these meetings, as many crises will touch their students or areas of advising. Have the staff meet with the faculty leaders or in a separate meeting, but remember to include them in annual trainings. In these meetings, review the policies and procedures and provide case studies. Having the policies and procedures written is only half the battle; it is using them correctly in times of crisis that will save the day. Practice makes perfect. It shows commitment to the teams abroad to do so, and offers them a chance to get to know those who they would be working with in an emergency. This is truly an advantage when a crisis or emergency happens unexpectedly abroad. Those in the field and those coordinating the response at the university will be ready and trained and can ensure that all policies and procedures are followed, which in some circumstances can mean the difference between life and death.

Once the manual is finished the final step is to make it public and to implement it. This can actually be the trickiest step. There is a possibility that international education on the campus has never had a comprehensive policy and procedures manual, which may mean that some individuals were able to do things that will not be in line with the new policies. This can be controversial. There are several things that can be done to make this smoother, although it may always be a battle to convert to a new manual.

- Understand that there are politics involved with everything. There will be politics involved with the new manual as well. Ensure that everyone up the chain of command has read and supports the manual.
- Consider where to place the manual. It needs to be readily accessible to all of those who need it.
- Publicize the fact that the new manual is available. Perhaps a newsletter or e-mail to all affected. If the university has a daily communication about happenings on campus, consider placing a notice here. Contact key players directly and let them know it has been posted.
- Be open to hearing concerns about a new way of doing things, or simply having a written way of doing things. Having the manual is the right thing to do, but those who still like to operate with a handshake will be skeptical.
- Be prepared to discuss the manual and the process of writing it with those who are concerned. This may take time and meetings, but it will be worth it in the end.
- Have an update schedule and keep the manual up-to-date. People will not take the manual seriously if it is out-of-date.
- Remember that change is always a challenge and it will be a challenge of implementing a new manual. Be patient, everyone will come to terms with the new system and abiding by it, but it may be rocky at first.
- Use allies on campus. Remember the committees and individuals who reviewed the manual and provided input and feedback. Perhaps an international education committee, made up of other bodies on campus, can be helpful in the transition.

Once the policies and procedures are set, there will be time to determine if they are effective and working. One of the ways to do this is by determining if the office is reaching its goals and outcomes. For example, policies should allow for students to apply for programs in a smooth manner; one should periodically ask the students and advisers if this is the outcome. If one finds that the policies that are set in the office are too complex, too difficult, or too restrictive, they may need to be changed. If the international education office determines that other policies outside of the international education office are the policies that are not working, it will take more time and effort to get those changed—if it is possible to change them at all.

Many policies that are set by a state or other government entity may not be able to be changed. For example, if the state sets policies on how monies can be spent, and it is contrary to what a study abroad program needs to spend money on, it would be almost impossible to change this policy. Likewise, some institutional policies can take many councils or committees to vote before passing something on to a larger vote. For example, if the course withdrawal policy needs to be more flexible in study abroad because semesters have different start dates around the world, this may be a policy that has to go through many committees and structures to be changed.

Whether it is the international education office's rules or others, it is vital to always evaluate policies and determine if the office is making progress forward. If so, take the time to consider if there are still improvements that can be made. If not, then consider how the policies and procedures can be changed to help make the progress that is wanted and needed. No manual will ever be perfect, especially not the first time. It will always be a work-in-progress.

Having a policies and procedures manual that clearly articulates the work of the international education office and the steps that are needed to accomplish this work and the greater goals of the office is imperative. Working without these policies and procedures gives a sense of uncertainty to those who work within international education at the institution as well as in the greater international education community. It will strengthen the international education office and the institution as a whole. Such policies and procedures will be there in time of crisis and emergencies, and will provide guidance for all when needed.

References

Centers for Disease Control and Prevention. N.d. *Traveler's Health*. Atlanta, Ga.: Centers for Disease Control and Prevention. http://wwwnc.cdc.gov/travel.

Fischer, Karen. 2010. "Study-Abroad Missteps Remind Colleges of Need to Train Trip Leaders." *The Chronicle of Higher Education*. http://chronicle.com/article/Study-Abroad-Missteps-Remind/65690/.

Goonen, Norma and Rachel Blechman. 1999. *Higher Education Administration: A Guide to Legal, Ethical, and Practical Issues*. Westport, Conn.: Greenwood Press.

Schloss, Patrick and Kristina Cragg. 2012. *Organization and Administration in Higher Education*. Hoboken: Taylor and Francis.

Spencer, Sarah and Kathy Tuma. 2007. *The Guide to Successful Short-Term Programs Abroad.* Washington, D.C.: NAFSA: Association of International Educators.

Herrmann, Michele. 2009. "UW Strengthens Study Abroad Policy." *University Business.* Professional Media Group.

University of California-Santa Cruz. 1994. *Guide to Writing Policy and Procedure Documents.* Policies and Procedures Team. Santa Cruz, Calif.: University of California. http://policy.ucsc.edu/resources/index.html.

University of Central Oklahoma. 2012. *Study Abroad Policy Manual.* Edmond, Okla.: University of Central Oklahoma.

University of Georgia. 2012. *Study Abroad Program Manual.* Athens, Ga.: University of Georgia.

U.S. Department of State. "What the Department of State Can and Can't Do in a Crisis." Washington, D.C.: Bureau of Consular Affairs. http://travel.state.gov/content/passports/english/emergencies/crisis-support.html.

U.S. Department of State. N.d. "Students Abroad." Washington, D.C.: Bureau of Consular Affairs. http://studentsabroad.state.gov/emergencies.php.

Waryold, Diane and James Lancaster., 2008. *Student Conduct Practice: The Complete Guide for Student Affairs Professionals.* Sterling, Va.: Stylus Publishing.

Weiss, Edmond. 2005. *The Elements of International English Style: A Guide to Writing Correspondence, Reports, Technical Documents, and Internet Pages for a Global Audience.* Armonk, N.Y.: M.E. Sharpe.

Western Kentucky University. 2011. *Faculty-Led Study Abroad Policy Manual.* Bowling Green, Ky.: Kentucky.

World Health Organization. "International Travel and Health." Geneva, Switzerland: World Health Organization. http://www.who.int/ith/en/.

CHAPTER 24

THE THEORY AND PRACTICE OF OUTCOMES ASSESSMENT IN EDUCATION ABROAD

By Nick Gozik

Internationalization efforts have led to an upsurge in the number of students participating in education abroad activities. Over the past two decades alone the number of U.S. students participating in study abroad has more than tripled, and continues to maintain a steady pace (IIE 2012). This trend has led many to ask what students are gaining from their experiences abroad. It is often pointed out that students are developing critical skills—including independence, intercultural competency, language proficiency, adaptability, and knowledge of other cultures and histories—which are integral to a well-rounded undergraduate experience as well as preparation for post-graduation employment and education. But how do we know what students are actually learning? Additionally, how do we know whether our administrative and programmatic infrastructures are helping to facilitate anticipated outcomes? To answer these questions, education abroad professionals have turned to assessment.

If the need for assessment has become apparent, the actual process of getting started can be overwhelming. Assessment represents an addition to all of the other duties that must get carried out to ensure students: (a) are prepared to go abroad; (b) have meaningful experiences while abroad; and (c) are integrated successfully back onto U.S. campuses. Moreover, many feel like they are not adequately qualified to assess, as they do not have the necessary training and experience. However, assessment need not be an intimidating or overly burdensome process. It requires planning and can be facilitated by leveraging expertise and resources already on hand.

In this chapter, we begin with a basic overview of assessment and the factors that motivate education abroad professionals to engage in it. We then explore how assessment can be conceptualized at different levels of education abroad work, steps for beginning the process of assessing, and resources that can assist in developing a deeper knowledge of the topic.

Assessment in U.S. Higher Education

Assessment has received great attention over the past several decades within the field of international education, with a proliferation of committees, projects, conference sessions, and publications. Many of these efforts have been guided by professional organizations such as NAFSA: Association for International Educators, the American Council on Education (ACE), the Association of International Education Administrators (AIEA), and the Forum on Education Abroad. Evidence demonstrates that the conversation on assessment is trickling down to individual institutions and education abroad offices in a very real way. ACE's 2006 report, *Mapping Internationalization on U.S. Campuses*, demonstrated that 45 percent of more than 2,000 institutions surveyed had articulated internationally oriented student learning outcomes; six years later, 55 percent—or an increase of 10 percent—of institutions had developed learning outcomes (ACE 2012, 13).

All of this activity may lead us to assume that assessment is new. In fact, as early as the 1940s, Ralph Tyler (1949) helped to pioneer an "objectives-based" approach to education in schools. Shortly after, Benjamin Bloom contributed to the development of outcomes-based curricula through his publication of *A Taxonomy of Educational Objectives* (1956). In subsequent years, scholars have added to these early models, leading to the development what is referred to as the "logic model," which includes the dimensions of inputs, activities, outputs, outcomes, and impact. This model has been used widely within private, public, and nonprofit sectors (Deardorff 2009b, 353), as it provides a useful approach for evaluating the efficacy of programs.

Today, there are many definitions of assessment, which vary based on discipline or field. A taskforce led by NAFSA's Teaching, Learning, and Scholarship Knowledge Community offers a general definition which applies to education abroad: "assessment focuses on judging the quality of what stakeholders want to learn about, using standards of excellence, criteria, and points of views of the stakeholders" (NAFSA 2010, 3). The authors explain that quality may focus on: "how and what students learn and develop as global citizens; characteristics of program, activities, and the entire institution; policy implications; and indicators of campus outreach, research initiatives, and collaboration among institutions across nations." Assessment can take place at multiple levels of an organization and factor in a variety of stakeholders, including students, faculty, administrators, government agencies, parents, alumni, and funders.

Assessment is considered by some to be a holistic and ongoing process, which is cyclical in nature, and thus essential that the "mission, goals, pedagogy/curriculum/program, and assessment methods/tools are aligned" (Deardorff 2009b, 356). Education abroad professionals may enter the process at different stages of the cycle, based on their existing assessment efforts. Many, for example, have long been collecting program evaluations and other data to serve as a starting point for a conversation around a more comprehensive assessment plan. For assessment to be effective, however, all of the components need to be linked together. This way, learning outcomes are aligned with the institutional mission and goals. Rather than having a discrete end point, assessment is a practice that needs to be continuously reviewed and revised, to guarantee that data collection and distribution are ultimately keeping up with changing organizational objectives.

Motivating Factors for Assessment

Education abroad professionals may engage in assessment for a variety of reasons, both internally and externally driven. Many begin by responding to outside requests, e.g., from an accreditor or senior-level administrator, while others seek to understand the value and effectiveness of their programs and later adjust their processes to comply with external regulations. Regardless of the initial impetus, it is essential to determine why and for whom assessment is being conducted. Noted below are a few of the reasons prompting education abroad professionals to engage in assessment.

External Factors

Accreditation

One of the primary external reasons for engaging in assessment involves complying with accreditation requirements. According to the Council for Higher Education Accreditation (CHEA), accreditation is "a review of the quality of higher education institutions and programs ... it is a major way that students, families, government officials, and the press know that an institution or program provides a quality education" (2013). Accrediting practices vary significantly from one country to another. It is common for a governmental agency such as the ministry of education to monitor and sanction institutions. The United States takes a different approach in that a nongovernmental organization, the CHEA, regulates accreditation at the postsecondary level. Reviews are carried out by regional accrediting entities, which follow standards outlined by CHEA and the U.S. Department of Education, yet are fully independent. Some regional bodies have moved more quickly to incorporate assessment into reviews, thus creating an uneven pattern of expectations across the United States.

Accreditation has required institutions to demonstrate that they have made strides in assessment, leading to the formation of campuswide assessment committees and/or offices to monitor, assist, and collect results. Those that have not been able to demonstrate effectively that they are assessing have been put on monitoring status, with a real risk of losing their accredited status. Assessment has thus become a high priority on many campuses, if not always viewed in a positive light. Some education abroad offices have not been required to comply as part of accreditation, at least in any formal sense. However, the overall creation of a "culture of assessment" on campuses, as prompted by accreditation, has led these offices to initiate their own assessment initiatives.

Additionally, other types of oversight can have a bearing on education abroad activities. This includes monitoring by national faith-related accreditors, who accredit religiously and doctrinally based institutions, and programmatic accreditors, who accredit specific programs, professions and freestanding schools, e.g., law, medicine, engineering, and health professions (Eaton 2012). The Accreditation Board for Engineering and Technology (ABET), for example, has long been requiring engineering schools to integrate assessment into their curricula, which in turn has impacted study abroad programs intended for students in this field.

Institutional Demands

Education abroad offices may also be required to assess due to institutional demands. As noted above, the institution may be responding to requirements as part of an accreditation process, though this is not always the case. Others have found that they simply want to know whether their teaching and learning are truly producing the results that are expected. This can be particularly important when resources are limited. Campus leaders are understandably averse to funding activities that are not viewed as helping students attain desired learning outcomes. Particularly in public institutions and systems, which rely on the state government for a portion of their budget, leaders have found it increasingly necessary to demonstrate success to state legislators and others with budgetary control. A downturn in the economy and reduced tax base, among other factors, make this justification all the more essential. At the same time, both public and private institutions are beholden to a variety of stakeholders, including alumni, donors, funding agencies/organizations, parents, and students, who likewise want to see progress through year-end reports and other mechanisms. For all of these reasons, institutional leaders have placed pressure on units, including education abroad offices, to assess and report on their findings.

Internal Factors

Student Learning

Among the internal factors that motivate education abroad professionals to assess, many have sought to answer the key question of whether are students are actually attaining desired learning outcomes. Through one's own time abroad and in talking with returned students, the transformational nature of an abroad experience may be palpable and unmistakable. While anecdotal evidence can help to formulate hypotheses, it does not provide a sufficient analysis that demonstrates, for example, whether all students are actually learning as a result of organized education abroad activities, the degree to which individual students may attain certain skills, and the extent to which particular programs may be enhancing students' abilities. Systematic and comprehensive analysis helps professionals to fine tune what works, as well as determine what might need to be tweaked in order to maximize students' success abroad. Results about student learning outcomes affect all other aspects of education abroad, including program development, marketing/advocacy, and advising.

Program Quality

Many have relied similarly on assessment to ensure that their programs offer both quality and value. Postprogram surveys have long been used to verify that students are content with housing, academics, facilities, activities, and the responsiveness and care of on-site staff. Health and safety, too, have been a concern, leading to reviews, for example, of students' access to health care facilities (e.g., proximity to hospitals and clinics for both physical and mental health concerns), the safety of housing and other facilities (e.g., noting if there are smoke detectors, emergency evacuation plans), and the extent to which programs are contracting with companies that are adequately insured. Increasingly, greater efforts have been made to consider the extent to which program models and activities are helping students achieve learning outcomes. Scholars and practitioners alike have applauded this latter trend, arguing that assessment instruments need to go beyond simply gauging customer satisfaction (Vande Berg et al. 2012).

Advising

Evaluations and other forms of assessment likewise have served as a source of feedback on advising and predeparture processes. During site visits, advisers can gather plenty of information from classroom observations, meetings with on-site staff, students, host families, and others, as well as tours of facilities. They can also gain an on-the-ground understanding of a program by receiving input from students. Student responses should be put into context and aggregated to offset the tendency for outliers; for example, students most likely to respond are those who feel either very positively or very negatively about a program. With this caveat noted, students are a valuable source of information about how programs function and what they learn while abroad.

Advocacy

Finally, with tightening budgets and more competition for resources (Aulenbach 2010), education abroad professionals have leveraged assessment findings for advocacy purposes. Some have found that data can help to establish credibility and demonstrate the efficacy of programs. One strategy has been to develop a fact sheet, which might include participant demographics (e.g., ethnicity/race, family income, majors/minors, and gender), composition of programs (e.g., countries where they are located, subjects taught), and showcase examples of student success (e.g., gains in language proficiency, examples of research, or other projects completed). Another approach has been to provide reports on assessment efforts for upper-level administrators, boards, and other stakeholders; these may range from a one-page executive summary to a much longer analysis, either of the results of one particular instrument or a wider array of assessment efforts. In these and other examples, data have become powerful tools in garnering resources which allow for the expansion of staff, access to better facilities, and heightened status on campus.

Levels of Assessment

While there is a lot of talk about assessment, especially around developing an "assessment plan," it is not always clear what is being assessed. An assessment plan is often used to refer to the evaluation of student learning outcomes, which is undoubtedly an integral component. However, for assessment to be effective it needs to take into account multiple levels of analysis—what might be called "units of analysis" in social science research—which may include the institution, department/office, program, and student. A multilayered approach aligns more closely with the idea of "comprehensive internationalization" (Stearns 2009, Hudzik 2011), thus ensuring that international activities are integrated throughout all areas of teaching and learning on campus. Here, a brief overview is provided for each of the levels of assessment.

FIGURE 1. Levels of Assessment

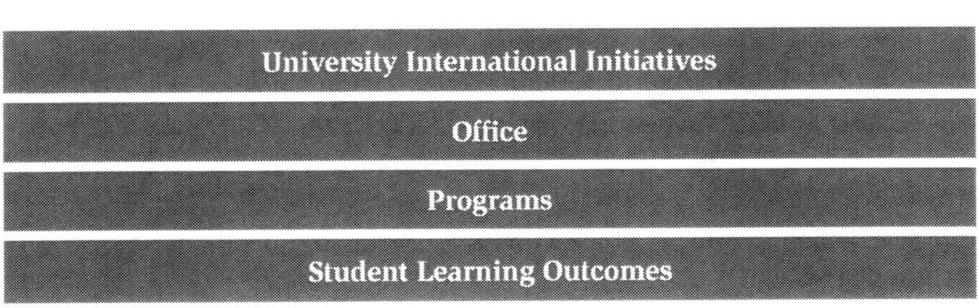

University International Initiatives

Office

Programs

Student Learning Outcomes

Source: Nick Gozik

Institution/University International Initiatives

In determining the role and impact of education abroad, it is helpful to begin by evaluating the extent to which internationalization has been incorporated into an institution's mission statement and strategic plan, as well as how institutional leaders have defined internationalization. Even if a clear definition may not be articulated—something that is more often than not the case (Altbach and Knight 2007)—an environmental scan of websites, speeches, and other documents can provide important clues to leaders' understandings of this term. It may be asked, for example, whether internationalization is considered primarily to be a checklist of study abroad, international student services, and service learning programs, or as a broader, all-encompassing plan that bridges academic and administrative spheres. For institutions with certain areas of specialization, such as a provider that offers marine biology programs or a technical college concentrating in science and engineering, it may become clear that internationalization has a very specific connotation tied to the focus of the organization.

Instruments such as the American Council of Education (ACE)'s Mapping Internationalization Assessment Tool can be helpful in evaluating internationalization and global engagement efforts. This ACE tool assesses six major categories, which cover a broad array of activities: (1) articulated institutional commitment; (2) administrative structure and staffing; (3) curriculum, cocurriculum, and learning outcomes; (4) faculty policies and practices; (5) student mobility; and (6) collaboration and partnerships. Other resources offered through NAFSA include John Hudzik's *Comprehensive Internationalization: From Concept to Action* (2011) and Madeleine Green's *Measuring and Assessing Internationalization* (2012). These works are designed to help leaders move toward a comprehensive internationalization plan and assessment strategy.

Office/Department

At the level of an individual unit such as an education abroad office, it too is necessary to consider both strategy and operations. Education abroad offices can easily become reactive rather than proactive, with an emphasis more on everyday tasks instead of on developing a longer-term plan. As with the overall institution, the first task is to determine whether a mission statement exists, and if so, whether it continues to reflect what the office has set out to accomplish. The mission of the office should fit with the overall institutional aims.

Additionally, an office-level assessment typically encompasses daily operations and the office structure, which might include a review of the organizational chart, budget, office dynamics, marketing/messaging, emergency plans, and relationship with other units on campus. The review may reveal, for example, that the office does not have the necessary technology or staffing to meet the needs of students, staff, and faculty, information that can help when advocating for additional resources. At the same time, it is useful for reviewers to take into account the history of the office, where it fits into the university structure, and its location on campus. Answers to these questions can provide a sense of why the office was originally set up and whether the mission may have changed over time. The placement of the office, both in terms of hierarchy and physical position, moreover, may indicate the office's ability to garner necessary resources, attract students, and gain credibility with academic departments and other units on campus.

Office reviews can be handled in a variety of ways, though preferably they are conducted by those outside the office, who can bring an objective perspective. On some campuses, an education abroad office may be evaluated on a regular and cyclical basis, as part of a systemic academic or administrative review process. In other cases, an office may choose to be reviewed, either by other institutional members or an external review committee. The decision to do one or the other may be based largely on resources, as an external review would include travel costs and perhaps honoraria.

Programs

Here, a program refers specifically to an education abroad enrollment option designed to result in academic credit, which is not to be confused with all of the other ways that this term is used on campuses, e.g., to refer to a degree- or certificate-granting unit on campus. Program types vary considerably and include both programs that the institution manages directly and those offered by a provider, which can be either a college or university that accepts outside students, or a separate organization, either nonprofit or for-profit. When students are going abroad through a provider, an education abroad office has less direct control and ability to assess the program. The office can rely on student evaluations and send staff to conduct site visits. If there are any shortcomings, reviewers can make suggestions to the provider, and ultimately if the provider is unwilling or unable to make changes, the office can decide to no longer send students on the program.

For programs that are run directly by the institution, an office has much greater latitude in evaluating and making changes on the program. Regardless of type, program assessments include many of the same criteria. In its Standards of Good Practice for Education Abroad, for example, the Forum on Education Abroad outlines nine categories that should be examined as part of a comprehensive program review: (1) mission; (2) student learning and development; (3) academic framework; (4) student preparation for the learning environment abroad; (5) student selection and code of conduct; (6) policies and procedures; (7) organizational and program resources; (8) health, safety, security, and risk management; and (9) ethics and integrity. Within each category, subtopics and queries guide organizations and institutions to test their programs against the standards. At first glance, this queries section may be overwhelming. It can help to address broad topics first, and then focus on individual questions.

One of the most common tools used by programs is the evaluation completed by students following an education abroad experience. These evaluations are still, primarily, "customer satisfaction" instruments, which help gauge whether students are satisfied with housing, classroom facilities, activities, on-site support, and faculty engagement. While such characteristics are important for improving students' comfort and safety, they do not necessarily speak to the quality of the academics and cultural learning. Institutions have begun to revise postprogram evaluations to add other forms of assessment, especially direct measures such as observations and tests, to help gain a greater grasp of students' gains. Some have taken to adding a question or short essay in the program application or in the predeparture stage, which can be repeated in the postprogram evaluation; by having students respond to the same question before and after their experience abroad, it is possible to assess the extent to which students have attained outcomes over time. Such questions also prompt critical reflection, thus helping students gain more from education abroad. Rubrics and/or coding can be a way to evaluate the results of such open-ended questions.

Additionally, program reviews can be used to assess a program, and may be adapted based on time and funding. Without leaving an office, an evaluator draws from existing materials such as student evaluations, reports on student courses and grades, reports from faculty and staff, the program website and brochures, and incident reports. Reviewers or a review team can prepare using the same materials above, and yet ideally have the added benefit of visiting program facilities as well as meeting with students, faculty, and staff at the program site. Recruiting reviewers from outside the organization is generally preferable in gaining objective feedback, though there may be additional costs in doing so. It is important that program reviews should be clearly defined as such, and not confused with more regular site visits. All participants at the program site should understand when a review is taking place. Additionally, a systematic approach should be taken when conducting the review, and results should be shared with key constituents.

Student Learning Outcomes

When offices develop an "assessment plan," they are often referring to a strategy for gauging student learning outcomes. These outcomes should be established and measured as part of a holistic assessment cycle, which includes a mission statement, goals, learning outcomes, methods of assessing, and the distribution of results. The assessment cycle begins with a review of the institutional and office mission statements, as well as other relevant websites and materials which articulate organizational priorities and values. This process ensures that goals and learning outcomes are aligned with, and ultimately contribute to, broader institutional aims. Once the mission(s) has been identified, assessors will develop a manageable list of goals, e.g., language learning, intercultural competence, adaptability, and knowledge of the host culture. This list is far from being a template, or comprehensive, for all institutions. For each of the goals, it is then advisable to develop a subset of learning outcomes. Unlike goals, which are broader, learning outcomes are more specific and measurable. Some prefer to merge goals and outcomes, and while this approach is not problematic, it is essential to ensure that each of the goals and/or outcomes can be measured through specific instruments.

After learning outcomes have been established, it is time to select assessment instruments, which may be homegrown or purchased from an outside vendor. Whatever the source, it is necessary to verify that the tools are aligned with the stated outcomes. Many vendors, for example, have developed tests designed to capture some element of global competence, yet each measures different characteristics and skills. Being specific about what outcomes are being measured will help in selecting the appropriate instrument. It is also recommended that research be done on the validity and reliability of tools.

Homegrown tools, or tools developed in-house, can also be effective—and sometimes more so than standardized ones in meeting an individual institution's needs—though they do need to be carefully constructed. In the case of postprogram evaluations, it is necessary to ensure they comply with best practices in survey development. Moreover, questions that do not serve a purpose can be eliminated, so as to keep the evaluation short and easy to complete.

As with other units of analysis, it is essential to share assessment results with all relevant parties, so as to close the assessment loop. In doing so, the office demonstrates that assessment is a worthwhile activity while also helping to create a "culture of assessment" on campus. Results may be shared with a variety of groups, ranging from students to parents, staff, faculty, senior-level administrators, and funding agencies. Each of these groups may want to see the results in a different type of format: a senior-level administrator may only want a one or two-page executive summary, while prospective students may want to see responses to open-ended questions, which will help them choose between programs. Data should be stripped of any identifiers, e.g., students' names, unless there is a specific purpose, and permission is given by the student.

FIGURE 2. Assessment Cycle

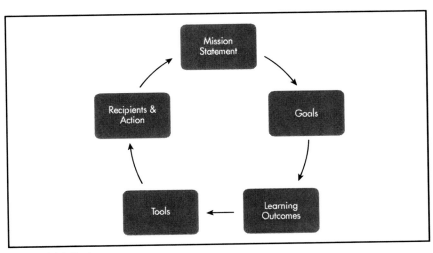

Source: Nick Gozik

Getting Started

Assessment may seem like an intimidating process, which requires a great amount of expertise and time. While assessing does require planning, it can be manageable with any level of resources by following the tips below:

- **Assessment Team:** Assessment is made easier by forming a team. Ideally the group will include members from outside the education abroad office such as a representative of the on-campus assessment office, if one exists, as well as faculty with relevant proficiency. Inviting outsiders is particularly useful for a one-person office, where the lone staff member will greatly benefit from additional support. Even in a larger office, outsiders can offer skills that complement those of the staff. Not all members may need to attend each meeting; those with particular areas of expertise may join the group at certain points within the planning process.
- **Meetings:** A newly formed assessment team will want to establish a regular schedule for meetings in order to stay on track. Even at a busy time of the year, it can help meet in order to stay motivated and focused. It is likewise useful to develop a list of short- and long-term projects and deadlines. At each meeting, team members should report

on their progress, so as to keep all accountable and help the group track progress toward long-term objectives.

- **Reasonable Expectations:** While perfection is admirable, the reality is that assessment can be a messy and uneven process. It is better to remain nimble and try different methods, realizing that it may take several attempts, for example, to find an instrument that effectively measures desired learning outcomes. Likewise, it is better to gain success with a lot of smaller tasks and projects, with an understanding that they will eventually lead to a larger goal.

- **Use Existing Data:** When developing an assessment plan, it can be easy to forget about all of the data that already exists. A lot can be accomplished in a little time by mining data that have already been collected. For example, the registrar can provide data on grades and courses taken, while the financial aid office can offer statistics on students with financial need. Findings may also be culled from large-scale surveys such as the Cooperative Institutional Research Program (CIRP) Freshman Survey and the National Survey of Student Engagement (NSSE). Moreover, it may be possible to obtain data from partner institutions, including providers and overseas exchange partners.

- **Attain Buy-In:** Lastly, one of the challenges is to attain buy-in among faculty, staff, and students. In doing so, offices have a much easier time in collecting and distributing data. Whenever possible, it is helpful to bring faculty into the process, either as part of the assessment team or in an advisory capacity. Faculty can give valuable advice, as well as become advocates on campus for the work being done. It is good to start with faculty who are already supportive of the office and can encourage their colleagues to assist with assessment. It is also necessary to report results back to key constituents, as noted above, so that it becomes clear that assessment results are being used and acted upon to make changes to programs and activities. Students are more apt to complete surveys, for instance, if they know that their responses will lead to improvements that will help future students.

Additional Resources

This chapter is designed to provide a general overview of the assessment process and strategies for conceptualizing and implementing assessment activities. Of course, this is just the beginning; many other valuable resources are available for becoming more proficient in this area. For additional resources and support networks, the following are recommended.

Print Publications

A number of books and articles on assessment in education abroad have been released over the past several years. Among these, Madeleine Green's *Measuring and Assessing Internationalization* (2012) zeroes in on institutional performance and the outcomes of student learning as two complementary frameworks for evaluating the results of internationalization. *A Guide to Outcomes Assessment in Education Abroad* (2007), edited by Mell Bolen, offers rationales for assessing education abroad, theoretical concepts, and terminology. Two other volumes that include chapters specifically on the assessment of global citizenship and intercultural competency, respectively, are *The Handbook of Practice and Research in Study Abroad: Higher Education and the Quest for Global Citizenship* (2009), edited by Ross Lewin, and *The SAGE Handbook of Intercultural Competence* (2009), edited by Darla Deardorff. Additional publications are listed within NAFSA's *Assessment and Evaluation for International Educators* (2010).

Websites

In addition to print publications, much information can be found online. For examples and tips related to education abroad specifically, readers find a host of online publications through NAFSA's website. The American Council on Education (ACE) has likewise been a forerunner in providing samples of learning outcomes and case studies through its Internationalization Toolkit. Similarly, the Forum on Education Abroad will soon be launching an Outcomes Assessment and Research Toolbox, which will allow for access to samples of instruments; examples of best practices; a glossary of assessment terminology; case studies; a bibliography of research and texts related to assessment; and a list of outside resources. The National Institute for Learning Outcomes Assessment (NILOA) provides more general resources on outcomes assessment.

Instruments

As noted in this chapter, assessment tools should be selected based on one's institutional needs, as outlined through an assessment plan. For homegrown options, it can be helpful to consult with colleagues who have created their own survey or rubric, for example, while understanding that these tools will need to be adapted. For standardized tools, the array of choices can be overwhelming. To gauge aspects of students' attitudes towards other cultures, for instance, one might select from the Intercultural Development Inventory (IDI), Global Perspectives Inventory (GPI), and Beliefs, Events, and Values Inventory (BEVI), among others. It is recommended that practitioners consult the available literature and talk to experts to determine which instrument will be most effective for the intended use.

Conferences and Other Meetings

One of the best ways to learn more, as well as to develop an assessment network, is to reach out to others in the field. This can be accomplished by attending annual conferences organized by international education professional associations such as NAFSA: Association of International Educators, the Association of International Education Administrators (AIEA), and the Forum on Education Abroad, as well as through providers like the Council on International Educational Exchange (CIEE) and Institute for the International Education of Students (IES). Outside of the United States, a growing number of associations have likewise begun to focus on assessment, including the International Education Association of Australia (IEAA), European International Education Association (EIEA), and the Canadian Bureau for International Education, among others. On a regional level, conferences organized by NAFSA and other regional associations such as the Boston Area Study Abroad Advisors Association (BASAA) can provide a less costly way to train staff, as travel and conference costs tend to be lower.

Acknowledgments

A special thanks to Steven Duke and Kelly McLaughlin for providing comments on various drafts of the chapter.

References

Bolen, Mell, ed. 2007. *A Guide to Outcomes Assessment in Education Abroad.* Carlisle, PA.: Forum on Education Abroad.

Altbach, Philip and Jane Knight. 2007. "The Internationalization of Higher Education: Motivations and Realities." *Journal of Studies in International Education* 11: 290-305.

American Council on Education. 2003. Mapping Internationalization on U.S. Campuses. Washington, D.C.: American Council on Education.

Aulenbach, Kris. 2010. *Leading Internationalization in Times of Fiscal Restraint: A Report on the NAFSA 2010 Conference Symposium on Leadership.* Washington, D.C.: NAFSA.

Bloom, Benjamin. 1956. *Taxonomy of Educational Objectives, Handbook I: The Cognitive Domain.* New York: David McKay.

Braskamp, Larry, et al. ed. 2009. *Assessment and Evaluation for International Educators.* Washington, D.C.: NAFSA.

Council for Higher Education Accreditation. 2013. "Information about Accreditation," March, 17, 2013, Accessed August 1, 2013, www.chea.org.

Deardorff, Darla, ed. 2009a. *The SAGE Handbook of Intercultural Competence*. Thousand Oaks, CA.: SAGE Publications.

Deardorff, Darla. 2009b. "Understanding the Challenges of Assessing Global Citizenship." In The *Handbook of Practice and Research in Study Abroad: Higher Education and the Quest for Global Citizenship*. Edited by Ross Lewin. New York, N.Y.: Routledge.

Eaton, Judith S. 2012. *An Overview of U.S. Accreditation*. Washington, D.C.: Council for Higher Education.

Green, Madeleine. 2012. *Measuring and Assessing Internationalization*. Washington, D.C.: NAFSA.

Hudzik, John K. 2011. *Comprehensive Internationalization from Concept to Action*. Washington, D.C.: NAFSA.

Institute for International Education, "*Open Doors* 2012: International Student Enrollment Increased by 6 Percent," November 12, 2012, accessed August 1, 2013, http://www.iie.org.

Lewin, Ross, ed. 2009. *The Handbook of Practice and Research in Study Abroad: Higher Education and the Quest for Global Citizenship*. New York, N.Y.: Routledge.

NAFSA. 2010. *Assessment and Evaluation for International Educators*. Washington, D.C. NAFSA: Association of International Educators.

Stearns, Peter N. 2008. *Educating Global Citizens in Colleges and Universities: Challenges and Opportunities*. New York, N.Y.: Routledge.

Tyler, Ralph. 1949. *Basic Principles of Curriculum and Instruction*. Chicago, IL.: University of Chicago Press.

Vande Berg, Michael, R. Michael Paige, and Kris Hemming Lou, eds. 2012. *Student Learning Abroad: What Our Students Are Learning, What They're Not, and What We Can Do About It*. Sterling, VA: Stylus.

"Information About Accreditation" Council of Higher Education Accreditation website, accessed September 8 2014, http://www.chea.org/public_info/index.asp.

INDEX

A

academic advisers
> education abroad applications, 44
> partnerships overview, 382
academic disciplines. *see also* specific areas of interest
> advising documents, 30
> strategic planning, 215–216
academic freedom considerations, policies and procedures, 395–396
academic goals. *see* institutional goals; student goals and expectations
academic honor code for students, policies and procedures, 397
academic outcomes. *see* learning outcomes
academic partnerships within institution, 380–382. *see also* partnerships
academic planning and preparation. *see* student and family preparation
> and orientation
academic policies and procedures, 395. *see also* policies and procedures
acceptance and integration stage, 295. *see also* experience of students on site
acceptance notifications, 273
accessibility considerations, comprehensive internationalization and, 118,
> 122–123. *see also* underrepresented student groups
accommodations (for disabilities), 155, 293
accommodations (housing). *see* housing
accreditation as factor, 239, 409–410
Accreditation Board for Engineering and Technology, role of, 410
address data element, 50
adjustment stage, 294–295. *see also* experience of students on site
administration of programs. *see* program administration
administrative assistant, job functions, 306
administrative entities, strategic planning role, 218–219. *see also specific concerns
> and entities*
administrative fees, 360–365. *see also* fees
administrative services, partnerships with, 384. *see also* partnerships;
> *specific aspects*
admissions office
> data collection and use, 353
> student and family preparation and orientation, 68
admissions, student
> data collection and use, 345–349
> student and family preparation and orientation, 68

advising sheets, 327–328

advocacy. *see also specific aspects*

 conclusion, 391

 data collection and use, 331–353

 goals, 372

 individual initiative, 106–107

 introduction, 372, 377–378

 levels of, 389

 making a difference, 390

 marketing overview, 8–9, 16

 motivating factors for assessment, 412

 organizations working on, 389–390

 use of term, 389

affiliation agreements, partnerships overview, 388–389

affirmative action in hiring, 323

Africa. *see also specific countries*

 program destination data, 216

 strategic planning, 221

African American students data examples, 337, 338, 345

airport security information, 202–203

alcohol and drug use

 experience of students on site, 291–292

 insurance coverage and exclusions, 185

 policies and procedures, 399

alert systems, 194

Alliance to Advance Liberal Arts Colleges workshop, 293–294

alumni lists, 102

alumni phase. *see* post-study abroad phase

American Red Cross library, 196

Americans with Disabilities Act regulations, 154–155

AMIDEAST, Egypt program, 85

anchored instruction model, 53, 55

annual reports, 310, 340

anorexia nervosa, 152

anxiety disorders, 152, 155. *see also* stress

application fees, 48, 359–365. *see also* fees

applications for education abroad. *see* education abroad applications

apps, web. *see* web apps

arrests, questions for responding to emergencies, 209

arts students

 education abroad applications, 48

 student and family preparation and orientation, 71

Asia. *see also specific countries*
    program destination data, 216
    strategic planning, 216, 221
    teaching abroad, 256–257
assessment of outcomes. *see* outcomes assessment
assumption of risk documents, 151
attention deficit hyperactivity disorder, 152
audience for book, xiv–xv
Austin College, reentry program, 99
Australia, insurance coverage and visas, 178
automatic teller machines, 85
automobile accident case study examples, 164

B

background considerations. *see specific areas of interest, e.g.,* post-study abroad
        phase
background of book, xiii, 75, 125
bank accounts, crisis management, 194
Barcott, Rye, 286
Bellarmine University, intervention model, 78
benchmarking. *see also* quality considerations
    data collection and use, 332
    portfolio management, 311–312
bicultural stage, 295
bipolar disorder, 151
blanket trip policies, 183
blogs and vlogs, post-study abroad phase, 99, 108–109. *see also* technology and
        social media
Boise State University, fees, 359, 361
branch and/or satellite campuses. *see* overseas branch and/or satellite campuses
budget management. *see also* financial planning; *specific aspects*
    benchmarking for excellence, 312
    conclusion, 373
    education abroad fairs, 369
    exchange program model, 233
    faculty-led program model, 229–230
    funding strategies and budget cuts, 365–367
    funds access for emergencies, 194
    grant opportunities, 369–371
    hiring process, 322
    hybrid program model, 238
    introduction, 357
    island program model, 235
    marketing, 15, 368–369

operational budget, 357–358, 365–367
operational expense categories, 358
outcomes assessment, 410
professional development opportunities, 367–368
rationale for increasing resources, 371–373
revenue sources, 357, 359–361
self-supporting or hybrid models, 361–365
while abroad phase, 85
work, internship, and volunteering abroad programs, 248
bulimia nervosa, 152
bursar, data collection and use, 353
Bush, George W., 130

C

campus committees, strategic planning role, 218. *see also specific concerns*
campus emergency response. *see* crisis management
campus leadership, strategic planning role, 218–219. *see also specific concerns and roles*
campus life office, student and family preparation and orientation, 69
campus programs as partners, 80. *see also* partnerships; *specific program areas*
career considerations for students. *see* professional considerations for students; work, internship, and volunteering abroad programs
career counseling field, marketing tools, 5
career services office
    education abroad applications, 44
    post-study abroad phase, 96
CASVE Cycle, marketing for advisers, 5–7
cell phones. *see* telephones
Center for Global Education
    education abroad research overview, 127
    risk management planning, 170
centralization, program administration, 266–267, 384–385
chat software, 81. *see also* technology and social media
Cities in the 21st Century Program, 289
citizenship data element, 50
Clarion University, program administration, 267
classroom presentations, marketing, 10
class standing data example, 337, 338
Clery Act, 168, 276–277, 335–336
clinician verification forms, 153
cognitive structural theory overview, 23
collaborations. *see* partnerships
college of education, student and family preparation and orientation, 62
Colorado State University, Peer Advisor Program, 93

commodification of higher education, 117–118

communication considerations. *see also* technology and social media; *specific aspects and concerns*

    CASVE Cycle, 6–7

    crisis management, 196, 197–200, 349–350

    experience of students on site, 294, 295

    health and safety considerations, 153, 156

    job interviews, 324

    outcomes assessment, 416–417

    partnerships overview, 385

    policies and procedures, 402–403

    post-study abroad phase, 101–107

    program administration, 267, 272–273, 277–278

community engagement and integration

    experience of students on site, 288–289, 295

    post-study abroad phase, 96, 107

    while abroad phase, 76, 81

comprehensive internationalization

    critiques, 119

    data collection and use, 121–122

    definitions, 54, 115–116

    education abroad goals and, 120–122

    education abroad research overview, 130–131

    equity considerations, 118, 122–123

    history of higher education, 116–117

    introduction, 115

    motivations and rationales, 117–118

    outcomes assessment, 412–413

    outside of United States, 119

computer technology. *see* technology and social media

conduct code for students, policies and procedures, 396–397

conferences

    assessment networks, 420

    benchmarking for excellence, 312

    budget management, 367–368

    professional development, 320–321

    reentry conferences, 94, 98

confidentiality considerations

    health information, 153, 156

    portfolio management, 309

consortium agreement, use of term, 388

consortium-program model, 319

consular information sheets, 201–202

contacts, emergency. *see* emergency contacts

content considerations. *see specific areas of interest, e.g.,* post-study abroad phase
contract record keeping, 309
contract signing, 48
Cooperative Institutional Research Program, 352–353
co-op model, 260
Costa Rica case study example, 164
Council for Higher Education Accreditation, role of, 409
Council for the Advancement of Standards in Higher Education, risk management planning, 168–169
Council on Standards for International Educational Travel, insurance guidance, 175
course approval form example, 398
credit cards
    crisis management, 194
    medical services, 178
criminal history, on education abroad applications, 48
crisis management. *see also* risk management planning
    communication response planning, 197–200
    conclusion, 204
    considerations, 191–195
    crisis response teams, 192, 195
    introduction, 191
    monitoring conditions abroad, 193, 200–204
    noncredit-bearing travel, 349–350
    overview of book, xv
    partnerships overview, 382–383
    plan and protocol development, 191–192, 195–197
    policies and procedures, 393–394, 400–402
    portfolio management, 308–309
    program administration, 272, 273
    questions for responding to emergencies, 207–210
    risk/crisis management team composition, 162–163
    training, 192–193, 196–197
Critical Incident Database, 336
cross-campus considerations for program administration, 271
crowdsourcing, marketing for advisers, 15
cultural adjustment curve. *see* W-Curve
cultural considerations for agreements, 387
Cultural Experiences Abroad, live chats, 81
culture of education abroad, creating, 8
culture shock
    experience of students on site, 289–290
    health and safety considerations, 153, 155
    student and family preparation and orientation, 53

culture shock or crisis stage, 290
currency exchange rates, 85
current issues, study abroad correlation with, 106
curriculum integration, education abroad research overview, 135
curriculum internationalization as goal, 120. *see also* comprehensive
    internationalization
customized program type, 32
Czech Republic, student and family preparation and orientation, 79

D

data collection and use. *see also* research on education abroad; *specific aspects*
    budget management, 361, 371
    college/department-specific priorities, 339–340
    comprehensive internationalization, 121–122
    conclusion, 353
    education abroad applications overview, 41–52
    financial need and enrollment, 350–352
    introduction, 331
    key questions and potential approaches, 336–352
    marketing overview, 15–16
    noncredit-bearing travel, 349–350
    outcomes assessment, 332, 371, 418
    partnerships and datasets, 352–353
    portfolio and demographics, 340–342, 343
    purposes, 331–333
    quality considerations, 126–127, 333
    raw data and research portals, 126–127
    student persistence and retention, 342, 344–345
    student recruitment and admissions, 345–349
    underrepresented student groups, 334, 337–339
    utilization overview, 333–336
    while abroad phase, 87–88
date of birth data element, 50
deadlines
    education abroad applications, 47
    portfolio management, 310
deans
    partnerships overview, 380–381
    policies and procedures, 396
    portfolio management, 302
    strategic planning, 218
deaths
    case study examples, 164
    questions for responding to emergencies, 209

repatriation of remains coverage, 172, 177
suicide prevention, 155
debriefing
crisis management, 197
policies and procedures, 394
program administration, 278
decentralization, program administration, 266–267, 384–386
degree programs, twinning agreements, 120–121
degree requirements, education abroad advising overview, 30
demographics, student. *see* student demographics
department chairs
partnerships overview, 381
policies and procedures, 396
strategic planning, 218
departments, organizational. *see* organizational departments;
specific departments
deposits, education abroad applications, 48
depression, 151, 289
developmental theory overview, 22–25
developmental vs. prescriptive advising, 25
development of programs. *see* program development and management
digital media. *see* technology and social media
direct enrollment programs. *see also specific aspects and concerns*
education abroad advising overview, 32
education abroad models, 230
human resources, 319
portfolio management, 306
program administration, 268, 275
directories and databases, marketing for advisers, 11
directors' liability insurance, 185–186, 187
disabilities, students with. *see* students with disabilities
discipline policies and procedures, 395–397. *see also* policies and procedures
distance/online vs. in-person learning, 77
diversity considerations. *see also* underrepresented student groups;
specific groups
different advising for different groups, 26–28
education abroad research overview, 139–140
post-study abroad phase, 108–109
while abroad phase, 86
drowning case study example, 164
drug and alcohol use. *see also* medications
experience of students on site, 291–292
insurance coverage and exclusions, 185
policies and procedures, 399

Drug Free Schools and Communities Act, 291–292
duration of programs. *see* program duration
dysthymia, 151

E

earthquake case study example, 163
eating disorders, 152, 155
education abroad advising. *see also specific aspects*
    applications overview, 41–52
    checking in with students, 82
    conclusion, 38
    content, 28–35
    different advising for different groups, 26–28
    evaluating efficacy, 37
    introduction, 21
    marketing overview, 3–17
    models and adviser role, 25–26
    motivating factors for assessment, 411
    overview of advising, 21–38
    overview of book, xiv
    portfolio management, 305–306
    post-study abroad overview, 91–109
    preparation and orientation overview, 53–72
    principles and goals, 21–22
    programming and techniques, 36–37
    student development theory, 22–25
    while abroad overview, 75–89
education abroad applications
    conclusion, 51–52
    content of applications, 43, 45–49
    data collection, 49–51
    format of applications, 45–46
    goals and objectives, 41–43
    introduction, 41
    portfolio management, 306–307, 309–310
    program administration, 270
    stakeholders, 43–45
education abroad as term, 341
education abroad case study development, 163–165
education abroad fairs
    budget management, 369
    marketing overview, 10
Education Abroad Glossary, definitions, 57–58
Education Abroad Knowledge Community, 169

education abroad models. *see also specific aspects and models*
  advising overview, 31–33
  budget models, 361–365
  comprehensive internationalization, 121
  conclusion, 240
  data collection and use, 342
  exchange programs model, 230–233
  faculty-led programs model, 227–230
  human resources, 319
  hybrid programs model, 236–238
  introduction, 226
  island programs model, 233–236
  junior year abroad model, 127–128
  office/department assessment level, 414–415
  overview of book, xv
  program administration, 267–268, 279–280
  reentry models, 93–94
  research overview, 131–132
  strategic planning, 221–223
  study abroad organizations, 238–240
  while abroad phase, 77
education abroad office management. *see also specific aspects*
  budget management overview, 357–373
  data collection and use overview, 331–353
  human resources overview, 315–329
  office mission, vision, and goals, 301–302, 371, 378
  outcomes assessment overview, 407–420
  overview of book, xv
  partnerships and advocacy overview, 377–391
  policies and procedures overview, 393–404
  portfolio management overview, 301–312
education abroad research. *see* research on education abroad
education abroad value, research overview, 133–140. *see also*
        outcomes assessment
educational context, research overview, 130–131
education department, student and family preparation and orientation, 62
efficacy, evaluation of. *see* outcomes assessment
Egypt program example, 85
e-learning courses, for budget management, 367–368
e-mails. *see also* technology and social media
  crisis management, 194, 198, 200
  education abroad applications, 49
  program administration, 272
  SECUSS-L listserv, 322–323

survey return, 312

while abroad phase, 80

embassies and consulates, crisis management, 201–202

emergency assistance coverage, 171–173

emergency contacts

crisis management, 192–194, 196, 198, 200

education abroad applications, 47

health and safety considerations, 156

policies and procedures, 401–402

portfolio management, 309

program administration, 272

emergency response. *see* crisis management

emerging adulthood, use of term, 24

Emerson, Ralph Waldo, 106

emotional and psychological support, 292–293. *see also* health and safety
        considerations

employee considerations. *see* human resources

employment considerations for students. *see* professional considerations for
        students; work, internship, and volunteering abroad programs

e-newsletters, 368

English as a foreign language, teaching, 256–257

entertainment, campus, 10–11

equal opportunity in hiring, 323

equity considerations, comprehensive internationalization and, 118, 122–123. *see
        also* underrepresented student groups

essays, education abroad applications, 42, 47

essential learning outcomes, 55–57. *see also* learning outcomes

ethical guidelines

marketing overview, 11, 14

program administration, 269–270, 280

risk management planning, 167

ethnic groups. *see also* underrepresented student groups

data collection and use, 337, 338, 341–342

ethnicity data element, 50

Europe. *see also specific countries*

experience of students on site, 285

history of higher education, 116

program destination data, xiii, 216

strategic planning, 216, 221–222

work, internship, and volunteering abroad programs, 246

European Association for International Education, 246

evacuation insurance

crisis management, 193

for individuals, 179–180

order of priority, 187
for programs and institutions, 185
risk management planning, 172
evacuation providers, 185, 193
evaluation of efficacy. *see* outcomes assessment
events and programming. *see* programming and events
exchange programs. *see also specific aspects and concerns*
comprehensive internationalization, 121
education abroad advising overview, 32
human resources, 319
models overview, 230–233
partnerships overview, 386–388
portfolio management, 303–304
program administration, 268
strategic planning, 222–223
teaching abroad opportunities, 257
expense and budget considerations. *see* budget management
experience of students on site. *see also specific aspects and concerns*
academic program, 287–288
acceptance and integration, 295
adjustment, 294–295
community engagement, 288–289
complaints, 290–291
culture shock and stress, 289–290
drugs and alcohol, 291–292
host staff interaction with students, 286–287
housing, 285–286
introduction, 283–284
orientation, 284–285
overview of book, xv
psychological and emotional support, 292–293
university and program collaboration, 293–294
experiential/constructivist narrative, 139
experiential learning/volunteer office, post-study abroad phase, 95
experiential programs. *see* work, internship, and volunteering abroad programs

F

Facebook. *see also* technology and social media
education abroad advising overview, 37
portfolio management, 307
post-study abroad phase, 100
while abroad phase, 87
faculty. *see also* human resources; *specific concerns*
academic partnerships within institution, 380–382

crisis management, 192
data collection and use, 339–340
education abroad applications, 44
education abroad models, 229, 234
experience of students on site, 293–294
overseas engagement and, 121–122
policies and procedures, 395–396, 399–400, 402
portfolio management, 302–304, 306
post-study abroad phase, 97
program administration, 274–275
program guidelines, 306
risk/crisis management team composition, 162–163
strategic planning, 215–216
teaching abroad program type, 256–257
while abroad phase, 80
faculty advisory council, creation and role, 302–303, 381, 399
faculty-led programs. *see also* short-term programs; *specific aspects and concerns*
budget management, 363–365
crisis management, 192
education abroad advising overview, 33
experience of students on site, 283
models overview, 227–230
portfolio management, 303–304, 309
program administration, 268
strategic planning, 221–223
faith-based organizations
outcomes assessment, 410
work, internship, and volunteering abroad programs, 246, 254
families. *see* parents and families
Federal Aviation Administration, crisis management, 202
Federal Emergency Management Agency, crisis management, 196–97
Federal Trade Commission, risk management planning, 167
fees
budget management, 359–365
comprehensive internationalization, 118
education abroad advising overview, 35
education abroad applications, 48
education abroad models, 239–240
marketing overview, 15
work, internship, and volunteering abroad programs, 259–260
field study/field based program type, 33
finance/business administrative office
budget management, 360
education abroad models, 232, 235

policies and procedures, 395
strategic planning role, 218
financial aid. *see also* scholarships
    comprehensive internationalization, 122–123
    data collection and use, 350–352
    disclosure requirements, 168
    education abroad advising overview, 34–35
    education abroad applications, 44
    partnerships overview, 384
    portfolio management, 304, 308
    work, internship, and volunteering abroad programs, 258–260
financial planning. *see also* budget management; *specific aspects*
    crisis management, 194
    education abroad advising overview, 34–35
    marketing overview, 14–15
    policies and procedures, 395
    risk management and, 171
    strategic planning overview, 218, 220–221, 224
financial worksheets, education abroad applications, 48
fire case study example, 164
first-generation college students
    data collection and use, 337, 338, 341
    different advising for different groups, 28
    first generation in college data element, 50
    post-study abroad phase, 108
    student and family preparation and orientation, 71
first generation to study abroad data element, 50
fliers, use of, 368
Florida Atlantic University, special projects, 311
foreign governments. *see also specific countries*
    comprehensive internationalization, 119
    crisis management, 203
    partnership assistance, 388
    work, internship, and volunteering abroad programs, 255–256
foreign institutions as partners, 386–388. *see also* partnerships; *specific aspects*
foreign language learning. *see* language learning considerations
foreign liability insurance, 183
Forum on Education Abroad
    budget management, 367
    data collection and use, 336
    education abroad research overview, 126
    insurance guidance, 176
    job listings, 322–323
    outcomes assessment, 414–415

professional development, 320–321

risk management planning, 167

work, internship, and volunteering abroad programs, 246–247

foundations, marketing for advisers, 11

4Ps of marketing, 8, 14–15

France

case study example, 163

insurance coverage and visas, 178

Frontiers: The Interdisciplinary Journal of Study Abroad, research overview, 126

Fulbright International Education Administrators programs, 388

Fulbright Program history and scope, 117

full range advising model, 25

funding and budget considerations. *see* budget management

fundraising, marketing for advisers, 11, 15

G

gender as factor

data collection and use, 338, 341–343

gender data element, 50

women in study abroad, research overview, 129–131, 138

women's moral development theory overview, 23

generalized anxiety disorder, 152

Georgetown Consortium Project, 102

Global Internship Conference, 247

globalization vs. internationalization, 115–117. *see also* comprehensive internationalization

Global Leadership Program, 58

Global Scholar website, 78

global university rankings, comprehensive internationalization and, 118

goals of book, xiv–xv

good practices, use of term, 166–167

Goucher College, program administration, 280

governing bodies, partnerships with, 379–380. *see also* partnerships; *specific entities*

grade point average data element, 50

graduate students

interns and research assistants, 326–327

job functions, 306

student and family preparation and orientation, 71–72

graduation rates, data collection and use, 342, 344–345

grants. *see also* financial aid

budget management, 367, 369–371

data collection and use, 332–333

partnerships overview, 387–388

Guatemala case study example, 164
guided reflection
    while abroad phase, 82, 84–85
    work, internship, and volunteering abroad programs, 245, 257
guidelines, use of term, 166

H

hard waiver policy, 184. *see also* waivers
hashtags, 100. *see also* technology and social media
health agencies, crisis management, 203–204. *see also specific entities*
health and medical insurance. *see also* evacuation insurance; insurance
    claims payment, 178, 184
    crisis management overview, 193
    for individuals, 177–179
    order of priority, 187
    portfolio management, 308–309
    for programs and institutions, 184
    reasons for requiring, 177
    risk management planning, 171–173
    travel assistance, 181
    U.S. plan considerations, 177–178, 184
health and safety considerations. *see also specific aspects*
    accommodations and support, 155
    crisis management overview, 191–204, 207–210
    culture shock as factor, 153
    education abroad applications, 47
    experience of students on site, 289–293
    health care case study example, 164
    insurance overview, 175–188
    introduction, 151
    medical information forms as tool, 153, 154, 156
    medications, 152–154, 156, 293
    mental health issues, 151–152, 164, 292–293
    monitoring conditions abroad, 200–204
    on-campus and community assessments, 155
    on-campus network development, 154
    outcomes assessment, 411
    overview of book, xv
    partner establishment, 155–156
    portfolio management, 308–309
    potential issues abroad, 160
    predeparture orientation, 153–154
    questions for responding to emergencies, 207
    risk management planning overview, 159–174

standards and good practices documents, 165–171
student and family preparation and orientation, 68
student consultations, 154–155, 173
volunteering in medical settings, 253–254
while abroad phase, 85–87
work, internship, and volunteering abroad programs, 253–254, 258
health and safety officer, role of, 194
hiring considerations. *see* human resources
A History of U.S. Study Abroad: 1965--Present, research overview, 129
A History of U.S. Study Abroad: Beginnings to 1965, research overview, 129
home fees, 35. *see also* fees
home institution infrastructure considerations, 270–271
homestays, 272, 285–286. *see also* housing
honeymoon stage, 280. *see also* experience of students on site
honor code for students, policies and procedures, 397
honors student data example, 337, 338
horizontal roots, 107
hospitalization, insurance coverage. *see* health and medical insurance
hostage incidents, questions for responding to emergencies, 209
host institution emergency contacts. *see* emergency contacts
host institution infrastructure considerations, 271–272
housing
    experience of students on site, 285–286
    outcomes assessment, 411
    program administration, 272, 273, 276–277
    property insurance, 182–183
    work, internship, and volunteering abroad programs, 259
human resources. *see also specific aspects and roles*
    application review process, 323–324
    cross-training, 321–322
    employee orientations, 325–326
    exchange program staffing, 232
    faculty-led program staffing, 229
    front office operations, 327
    hiring process, 322–324, 326–327
    host staff interactions with students, 286–287
    hybrid program staffing, 237–238
    interns and research assistants, 326–327
    interview process, 324
    introduction, 315
    island program staffing, 235
    job assignments and responsibilities, 305–306, 315–317, 322
    job offers, 324
    job titles, 315

managing office space, 328–329

managing of staff, 328

one-to-one student meetings, 327–328

peer mentoring, 326

policies and procedures, 396, 399–400

professional development, 320–322, 326, 327, 367–368

program administration, 271, 274–275, 277–278

risk/crisis management team composition, 162–163

staffing models, 317–320

student and family preparation and orientation, 79–80

work, internship, and volunteering abroad programs, 258–260

workload issues, 318–319

hybrid budget model, 361–363

hybrid programs. *see also specific aspects and concerns*

education abroad advising overview, 33

models overview, 236–238

program administration, 268

I

identity theory overview, 23–24

immigration policy advocacy, 390. *see also* passports and visas

implementing agreement, use of, 387

incident reports, 309, 336

in-country contact information, crisis management, 193, 194. *see also* emergency contacts

in-country element of crisis response team, 195

Indiana University, education abroad history, 127

information technology department, education abroad applications, 44

infrastructure considerations. *see specific areas of interest, e.g.,* post-study abroad phase

in-person vs. distance/online learning, 77

inquiry form process, 307

Instagram ideas, 100. *see also* technology and social media

Institute for International Education

data collection background, 333–334

partnership assistance, 388

institutional academic purpose, strategic planning, 214–215

institutional culture, strategic planning, 217–219

institutional data, collection and use of. *see* data collection and use

institutional demands, as motivating factor for assessment, 410

institutional goals

budget management, 371–372

education abroad applications, 42

education abroad models, 226

partnerships and advocacy, 377
program administration, 266, 270
strategic planning, 215–219, 220, 222–223
institutional mission
budget management, 371–372
education abroad advising overview, 28
outcomes assessment, 416–417
partnerships and advocacy, 377–378
program administration, 266
strategic planning, 213–214, 222–223
institutional partners. *see* partnerships
institutional policies and procedures. *see* policies and procedures
institutional research. *see* research
institutional research office, student and family preparation and orientation,
68–69
institutional support, as revenue source, 359
institutional vision
partnerships and advocacy, 377–378
program administration, 266
institution/university international initiatives level, 412, 413
institution, use of term, 265
insurance
conclusion, 188
coverage and exclusions, 178–179, 183–186
coverage types, 172
crisis management, 193, 196
for individuals, 171–173, 176–183
introduction, 175–176
medication laws, 156
order of priority, 187
outcomes assessment, 411
overview of book, xv
policies and procedures, 401
portfolio management, 308–309
for programs and institutions, 171, 183–187
request for proposals, 186–187
risk management planning, 169, 171–173
work, internship, and volunteering abroad programs, 258
intake forms, tips for, 29
integrated university study program type, 32
integration and acceptance stage, 295. *see also* experience of students on site
intellectual and ethical development theory overview, 23
Interassociational Advisory Committee on Safety and Responsibility in
Study Abroad

insurance guidance, 175–176

risk management planning, 166–167

intercultural competence, education abroad research overview, 137–140

intercultural learning, program interventions, 77–79

international currency, 85

international health agencies, crisis management, 203–204. *see also specific entities*

international industry, study abroad connections with, 106

internationalization, definitions, 54, 115–116, 413. *see also* comprehensive internationalization; *specific aspects*

international research office, grants and, 370

international students. *see also specific concerns*

comprehensive internationalization, 116–120

different advising for different groups, 27

education abroad models, 231, 239

student and family preparation and orientation, 72

international student services, post-study abroad phase, 95, 101

International Studies Abroad services, 79

International Volunteer Programs Association, 246

Internet. *see* technology and social media

internship organizations, 251, 252

internships abroad program type, 250–252. *see also* work, internship, and volunteering abroad programs

interns, hiring, 326–327

island programs. *see also specific aspects and concerns*

education abroad advising overview, 33

models overview, 233–236

program administration, 268

Italy, case study example, 164

J

Japan case study examples, 163

Jeanne Clery Disclosure of Campus Security Policy and Campus Crime Statistics Act. *see* Clery Act

judicial affairs, education abroad applications, 44

Juniata College, institutional mission, 214

junior year abroad model, 127–128

K

kidnappings, questions for responding to emergencies, 209

L

language learning considerations

education abroad advising overview, 30

education abroad applications, 47
education abroad research overview, 127–128, 138
experience of students on site, 283–284, 287–288, 295
language institute program type, 33
marketing overview, 12, 14
language teaching opportunities, 256–257
Latin America. *see also specific countries*
program destination data, xiii, 216
strategic planning, 216, 221
law students, student and family preparation and orientation, 71
leader for a day program, 79
learning outcomes. *see also* outcomes assessment; outcomes research;
specific aspects
education abroad research overview, 133–134
motivating factors for assessment, 410–411
post-study abroad phase, 75–76, 92–93
student and family preparation and orientation, 55–57, 59–60
student learning outcomes assessment level, 412, 416–417
work, internship, and volunteering abroad programs, 244–245
learning theory overview, 24
legal considerations. *see also specific areas of concern*
background of book, xiii
education abroad applications, 44, 48
education abroad models, 232, 235
experience of students on site, 291–292
health and safety issues, 152, 154–156
hiring process, 323
policies and procedures, 400–401, 404
portfolio management, 307, 309
program administration, 275–277
risk management planning, 161–162, 165–170
strategic planning, 219
legal department, education abroad applications, 48
Lessons From Abroad returnee conference, 94, 98
letters of recommendation, education abroad applications, 47
LGBTQ students
data collection and use, 334
different advising for different groups, 27
student and family preparation and orientation, 70
liability insurance. *see also* insurance
for individuals, 182–183
order of priority, 187
for programs and institutions, 183, 185–186
risk management planning, 169, 172

Liberal Education and America's Promise (LEAP) campaign, 55–56

Lincoln Commission, formation of, 130

LinkedIn ideas, 100. *see also* technology and social media

local governments and policy changes, 404

location choice, data analysis, 51. *see also* program destination

logic model, development of, 408

logistics
    evacuation providers, 185, 193
    exchange program model, 233
    faculty-led program model, 230
    hybrid program model, 238
    island program model, 236
    program administration, 270–271, 273–274

M

major depression, 151

major medical coverage, 172. *see also* health and medical insurance

major/minor data element, 50, 51

Mapping Internationalization Assessment tool, 413

maps, marketing and, 8

marketing
    background and infrastructure, 3–4
    budget management, 368–369
    conclusion, 17
    introduction, 3
    marketing funnel, 69
    outreach content, 12–15
    partnerships, 8–9, 383
    portfolio management, 307–308
    post-study abroad phase, 108–109
    principles, 4–7
    programming and events, 9–11
    strategies, 7–8
    student groups, 15–17
    technology and social media, 11–12

Massachusetts Institute of Technology, institutional mission, 213–214

media relations, crisis management, 199, 200

medical considerations. *see* health and medical insurance; health and safety considerations

medical information forms, 153, 154, 156

medications, health and safety considerations, 152–154, 156, 293

memoranda of agreement, use of, 387

memoranda of understanding, use of, 387

mental health considerations. *see* health and safety considerations mental isolation stage, 294–295

Middle East. *see also specific countries*

 case study example, 163

 program destination data, 216

 program example, 85

Minnesota study abroad returnee conference, 94, 98

minority students. *see also* underrepresented student groups

 different advising for different groups, 27

 education abroad research overview, 139–140

 student and family preparation and orientation, 70

missing students, questions for responding to emergencies, 208

models for education abroad programs. *see* education abroad models

moral development theory overview, 23

Morocco Exchange program, 288–289

multicultural affairs office, post-study abroad phase, 95

murder case study example, 164

music students

 education abroad applications, 48

 student and family preparation and orientation, 71

N

NAFSA

 advocacy work, 389–390

 education abroad research overview, 127

 health and safety considerations, 169, 292

 job listings, 322–323

 professional development offerings, 320, 367–368

 work, internship, and volunteering abroad programs, 246

National Association of Colleges and Employers, 247

National Center for Education Statistics, 353

National Society for Experiential Educators, 246–247

National Survey of Student Engagement data analysis, 346–349

natural disasters. *see also* crisis management

 case study example, 163

 evacuation insurance, 180

 questions for responding to emergencies, 210

networking. *see also* technology and social media; *specific aspects*

 benchmarking for excellence, 312

 grants, 370

 human resources, 328–329

 outcomes assessment, 420

New England study abroad returnee conference, 94, 98

news media, crisis management, 199, 200

New Zealand case study example, 164

noncredit-bearing travel, monitoring, 349–350
Northern Virginia Community College, institutional mission, 214

O

Obama, Barack, 105
objectives-based approach, development of, 408
obsessive-compulsive disorder, 152
off-campus partnerships. *see* partnerships
office/department assessment level, 412, 413–414
office management. *see* education abroad office management
office manager, job functions, 306
officers' liability insurance, 185–186, 187
offices, organizational. *see* organizational offices; *specific offices*
office space considerations, 328–329
office staff considerations. *see* human resources
Oklahoma State University, reentry program, 93
on-campus and community psychological assessments, health and safety
        considerations, 155
on-campus element of crisis response team, 195
on-campus network development, health and safety considerations, 154
on-campus partnerships. *see* partnerships
online technology. *see* technology and social media
on-site element of crisis response team, 195
on-site staff as partners, 80. *see also* human resources; partnerships
on-site student experience. *see* experience of students on site
Open Doors report
    contributing to, 51
    data collection and use, 333–334, 361
    education abroad research overview, 125
operational budget and expenses. *see* budget management
organizational departments. *see also* partnerships; *specific departments*
    academic partnerships within institution, 380–382
    advising documents, 30
    college/department-specific priorities, 339–340
    data collection and use, 339–340
    office/department assessment level, 412, 413–414
    policies and procedures, 394, 396
    portfolio management, 304, 306
    program administration, 268
    as siloed, 120
    strategic planning, 218
organizational hierarchy
    human resources, 319
    office/department assessment level, 414

policies and procedures, 396
portfolio management, 302
organizational offices. *see also* partnerships; *specific offices*
    comprehensive internationalization, 121
    office/department assessment level, 412, 413–414
    program administration, 268
    risk/crisis management team composition, 162–163
    as siloed, 385
    special projects, 311
orientation of students and families. *see* student and family preparation and
    orientation
outcomes assessment
    assessment cycle, 416–417
    assessment plans, 412, 416
    assessment team formation and role, 417–419
    buy-in, 418
    comprehensive internationalization, 119
    data collection and use, 332, 371, 418
    debriefing vs. assessment, 278
    definitions, 408
    education abroad advising overview, 37
    education abroad research overview, 133–140
    instrument selection, 416, 419–420
    introduction, 407
    levels of, 412–417
    motivating factors, 409–412
    networking and, 420
    program reviews as tool, 415
    site visits and, 280–281
    student and family preparation and orientation, 55
    student evaluations as tool, 415
    in U.S. higher education, 407–409
    work, internship, and volunteering abroad programs, 258–259
outcomes-based curricula, development of, 408
outcomes, learning. *see* learning outcomes
outcomes research. *see also specific aspects*
    academic outcomes overview, 134–136
    professional/career outcomes overview, 136–137
    universal outcomes overview, 137–140
outreach. *see* marketing
outside groups, marketing and, 11
overseas branch and/or satellite campuses. *see also* island programs
    as comprehensive internationalization goal, 120
    education abroad advising overview, 32

models overview, 233
Overseas Security Advisory Council
    crisis management, 202
    risk management planning, 168
overview of book, xiv–xv

P

panic disorder, 152
parents and families. *see also* student and family preparation and orientation
    crisis management, 200
    education abroad advising overview, 34–35
    education abroad applications, 45
    experience of students on site, 294
    health consultations, 155
    insurance coverage for students, 177
    learner characteristics, 59–60
    post-study abroad phase, 96, 107
partnerships
    academic partnerships within institution, 380–382
    administrative services, 384
    centralized and decentralized models of administration, 384–386
    conclusion, 391
    contract record keeping, 309
    data collection and use, 335–336, 352–353
    foreign institutions, 386–388
    goals, 372
    health and safety considerations, 155–156
    institutional mission and vision, 377–378
    introduction, 372
    marketing overview, 8–9
    off-campus partnerships overview, 386–389
    office mission and vision, 378
    on-campus partnerships overview, 379–386
    post-study abroad phase, 95–97
    program administration, 268–269
    special projects, 311
    strategic planning, 219–221
    student and family preparation and orientation, 54–55, 60–61, 68–69
    student service partnerships on campus, 382–384
    study abroad providers, 388–389
    university and program collaboration, 293–294
    upper administration and governing bodies, 379–380
    while abroad phase, 79–80
    work, internship, and volunteering abroad programs, 260

passports and visas
    education abroad applications, 48, 50
    immigration policy advocacy, 390
    insurance coverage and visas, 178
    passport acceptance facilities, 360–361
    student and family preparation and orientation, 68
    while abroad phase, 86–87
    work, internship, and volunteering abroad programs, 248
pastoral element of programs, education abroad models, 228, 231
pay-for-service crisis management, 204
peace through educational exchange doctrine, 117
peers, student
    marketing overview, 16
    peer advisers, 36
    post-study abroad phase, 93
    staff-peer mentoring, 326
    while abroad phase, 80, 82
peer-to-peer program model, 93
Pell Grant data element, 50
Pell Grant data example, 351–352
performance recordings, education abroad applications, 48
personal community, building, 105–107. see also specific elements
personal considerations for students. see also student goals and expectations;
        specific areas of concern
    marketing overview, 14
    post-study abroad phase, 105
    student and family preparation and orientation, 67
    while abroad phase, 84–85
personal liability and property insurance
    for individuals, 182–183
    order of priority, 187
    for programs and institutions, 186
    risk management planning, 172
personal travel services, 182
Peru case study example, 164
phobias, 152
phones. see telephones
photos
    education abroad applications, 48
    post-study abroad phase, 100
physical health considerations. see health and safety considerations
place, in 4P's, 8
policies and procedures. see also specific issues and policy areas
    academic freedom considerations, 395–396

brainstorming, 398–399

conclusion, 404

creating and implementing, 397–402

definitions, 393

education abroad advising overview, 28

evaluating, 403–404

existing policies and procedures, 394–395, 397

introduction, 393–394

organizational hierarchy and, 396

student academic honor codes, 397

student code of conduct, 396–397

study abroad manuals, 307, 310

training and implementation, 402–403

updates and changes, 403–404

writing guidelines, 399–400

policy advocacy. *see* advocacy

political turmoil evacuation insurance, 180

political unrest

case study example, 163

questions for responding to emergencies, 210

portfolio management

benchmarking for excellence, 311–312

conclusion, 311–312

data collection and use, 340–342, 343

faculty guidelines for programs, 306

institutional context, 302–303

job assignments, 305–306

marketing and, 307–308

office mission, vision, and goals, 301–302, 311

orientations and safety, 308–309

program enrollment, 306–307

program selection, 303–304

record keeping, 309–310

scholarships, 308

special projects, 311

strategic planning, 219–221

positivist narrative, 139

post-study abroad phase

background and infrastructure, 91–93

conclusion, 109

content delivery modes, 101

continued international engagement, 108

desired outcomes, 92

focus on, 75

importance to student learning, 91

introduction, 91

investing in learning outcomes, 92–93

marketing, 13, 108–109

partnerships and programming, 383

program administration, 273

programming and events, 97–98

programming models, 93–94

stakeholders and collaboration, 95–97

student groups, 108–109

technology and communities, 101–107

technology and programming, 99–100

posttraumatic stress disorder, 152

preexisting conditions, exclusion of, 177–179. *see also* health and safety considerations

preparation of students and families. *see* student and family preparation and orientation

prescriptive vs. developmental advising, 25

price, in 4P's, 8, 14–15

Privacy Act, 202

privacy considerations for health information, 153, 156

procedures and policies. *see* policies and procedures

product, in 4P's, 8

professional community, building, 102–104. *see also specific elements*

professional conferences. *see* conferences

professional considerations for students. *see also* student goals and expectations; work, internship, and volunteering abroad programs

academic credit and professional development, 247

education abroad research overview, 136–137

marketing overview, 13

student and family preparation and orientation, 66

while abroad phase, 83–84

professional development for employees. *see also specific areas of interest*

budget management, 367–368

human resources overview, 320–322, 326, 327

professional organizations. *see also specific organizations and concerns*

budget management, 367–368

comprehensive internationalization, 122

outcomes assessment, 408, 420

partnerships overview, 389–390

work, internship, and volunteering abroad programs, 246–247

program accreditation organizations, 410

program administration. *see also specific aspects*

balance considerations, 272

centralization and decentralization, 266–267, 384–385

conclusion, 281

debriefing and assessment, 278

definitions, 265–266

expectations and communication, 272–273

faculty and staff preparation, 274–275

feedback, value of, 278

home institution infrastructure considerations, 270–271

host institution infrastructure considerations, 271–272

housing, 272, 273, 276–277

implementation and on-site administration, 267–278

introduction, 265

lessons learned, 278–281

logistics, 270–271, 273–274

models for programs, 267–268, 279–280

partnerships overview, 384–386

planning for programs, 270–276

plan tracking, 275–276

relationship management, 268–269

site visits, 280–281

staff support and communication, 277–278

strategic planning, 265–270

student orientations, 271, 275, 276

updates to resources, 279

work, internship, and volunteering abroad programs, 257–260

program assessment level, 412, 414–415

program choices, education abroad applications, 47

program destination as factor. *see also specific destinations*

data analysis, 51

data collection and use, 342–343

strategic planning, 216, 221–223

work, internship, and volunteering abroad programs, 248

program development and management. *see also* specific aspects

budget considerations, 372–373

education abroad models overview, 227–240

human resources, 318–319

overview of book, xv

program administration overview, 265–281

strategic planning overview, 213–225

student experiences on site overview, 283–295

work, internship, and volunteering abroad programs overview, 243–260

program duration

data analysis, 51

data collection and use, 341

education abroad advising overview, 33–34

program administration, 279–280

strategic planning, 221–222

work, internship, and volunteering abroad programs, 251, 254–256

program in progress, tracking plans, 275–276

program interventions

education abroad research overview, 139

while abroad phase, 77–78

program management and development. *see* program development and
management

program marketing. *see* marketing

programming and events. *see also specific aspects and types*

marketing overview, 9–11

post-study abroad phase, 97–98

student and family preparation and orientation, 61–62

while abroad phase, 81–82

program models/types for education abroad. *see* education abroad models

program provider organization model. *see* study abroad organization program
model

program quality considerations. *see* quality considerations

program selection

education abroad advising overview, 30–31

education abroad applications, 42

portfolio management, 303–304

program structures. *see* education abroad models

program success, determining, 223–225. *see also* outcomes assessment

Project Atlas, 353

promotion and marketing. *see* marketing

promotion, in 4P's, 8

property insurance

for individuals, 182–183

order of priority, 187

for programs and institutions, 186

psychological and emotional support, 154, 292–293. *see also* health and safety
considerations

psychological assessments, 155

psychosocial development theories, 22–23

Public Announcements (U.S. government), 201

public policy advocacy. *see* advocacy

Q

quality considerations. *see also* outcomes assessment

data collection and use, 332, 333

motivating factors for assessment, 411

portfolio management, 311–312
research on education abroad, 125–126
risk management planning, 167

R

racial groups. *see also* underrepresented student groups
 data collection and use, 337, 338, 341–342, 345
 research on, 140
rape and sexual assault
 case study examples, 164
 questions for responding to emergencies, 208
reception area
 front office operations, 327
 marketing, 307
record keeping
 data collection and use, 335–336
 human resources, 328
 portfolio management, 309–310
reentry conference model, 94, 98
reentry course model, 94
reentry phase. *see* post-study abroad phase
registrar
 data collection and use, 353
 education abroad applications, 44
 education abroad models, 232, 234, 237, 239
 portfolio management, 304, 306
relationship management, in program administration, 268–269. *see also*
  partnerships
relativist narrative, 139
repatriation of remains coverage, 172, 177
request for proposals, insurance and, 186–187
research assistants, hiring, 326–327
research on education abroad. *see also specific areas of interest*
 academic outcomes, 134–136
 complications, 133
 comprehensive internationalization, 115–123
 conclusion, 140
 critiques, 131–133
 current research overview, 128–140
 data collection and use, 353
 educational context, 130–131
 educational value and student learning, 133–140
 historiography of literature, 128–130
 history of education abroad, 127–128

introduction, 125–126
overview of book, xiv
overview of research, 125–140
professional/career outcomes, 136–137
quality considerations, 125–126
raw data and research portals, 126–127
student and family preparation and orientation, 68–69
universal outcomes, 137–140
résumés, education abroad applications, 48
return phase. *see* post-study abroad phase
revenue and budget considerations. *see* budget management
"Review of Global Studies Literature," research overview, 127
review sites, marketing for advisers, 12
risk management office
partnerships overview, 382–383
strategic planning role, 218, 219
risk management planning. *see also* crisis management; health and safety
considerations
case study development, 163–165
conclusion, 173–174
evaluation of risks, 161–162
exchange program model, 233
faculty-led program model, 230
hybrid program model, 238
identification of risks, 159–161
insurance and emergency assistance coverage, 171–173
insurance as risk management, 175
introduction, 159
island program model, 235
noncredit-bearing travel, 349–350
overview of book, xv
partnerships overview, 382–383, 385
program administration, 274–275
reduction of risk, 173
risk/crisis management team composition, 162–163
standards and good practices documents, 165–171
strategic planning overview, 218–219
risk matrix, 161
robbery case study example, 164
roots, horizontal and vertical, 107

S

SAFETI Clearinghouse, 170, 292
safety considerations. *see* health and safety considerations

satellite and/or branch campuses. *see* overseas branch and/or satellite campuses

scholarships. *see also* financial aid

    education abroad advising overview, 35

    marketing overview, 11, 15

    partnerships overview, 384

    portfolio management, 308

    strategic planning, 217

    student and family preparation and orientation, 67

Science, Technology, Engineering, and Mathematics students. *see* STEM students

security travel assistance, 181

SECUSS-L listserv, 322–323

self-supporting budget model, 361–365

semester and year-long programs. *see also specific aspects, concerns, and types*

    education abroad advising overview, 34

    experience of students on site, 283

    portfolio management, 304

    program administration, 268

    research on education abroad, 127

    strategic planning, 221–222

    work, internship, and volunteering abroad programs, 251, 254, 256

service-learning and volunteering abroad program type, 253–254. *see also* work, internship, and volunteering abroad programs

sexual assault and rape

    case study examples, 164

    questions for responding to emergencies, 208

shoebox metaphor, 91

short-term programs. *see also* faculty-led programs; specific aspects, concerns, and types

    education abroad advising overview, 33–34

    education abroad applications, 51

    education abroad models, 234

    experience of students on site, 283

    insurance overview, 183, 186

    portfolio management, 303–304

    program administration, 268, 279–280

    research on education abroad, 127

    risk management planning, 169

    strategic planning, 217, 221–222

    use of term, 34

    work, internship, and volunteering abroad programs, 251, 254–256

should, use of term, 166–167

signature documents, 170

silo effect, 120, 385

single reentry session model, 93

sink or swim situations, 292
site visits
    budget management, 372–373
    human resources, 321
    program administration, 280–281
Smart Traveler Enrollment Program, crisis management, 202
Smith College, education abroad history, 127–128, 130
social media. *see* technology and social media
social unrest case study example, 163
software. *see* technology and social media
Spain case study example, 164
special projects, taking on, 311
staff considerations. *see* human resources
stakeholders. *see also specific concerns and types*
    education abroad applications, 43–45
    outcomes assessment, 410
    post-study abroad phase, 95–97
state governments
    outcomes assessment, 410
    policies and procedures, 404
State University of New York
    institutional mission, 214
STEM students
    data collection and use, 341
    different advising for different groups, 27
    engineering school assessments, 410
    marketing overview, 16–17
    strategic planning, 215–216
    student and family preparation and orientation, 70
Stetson University, Global Leadership Program, 58
strategic planning. *see also specific aspects*
    academic disciplines and faculty, 215–216
    academic purpose, 214–215
    budget management, 371–372
    checklist, 269–270
    conclusion, 224–225
    culture, 217–219
    data collection and use, 331–353
    goals, 215–219, 220
    introduction, 213
    mission, 213–214
    partners and portfolio management, 219–221
    partnerships and advocacy, 378
    portfolio management, 302

program administration, 265–270

program location, design, and structure, 221–223

program success, 223–225

stress

    experience of students on site, 289–292

    health and safety considerations, 152, 153, 155

    human resources, 328

student academic honor code, policies and procedures, 397

student accounts office, data collection and use, 353

student admissions. *see also* admissions office

    data collection and use, 345–349

    student and family preparation and orientation, 68

student and family preparation and orientation. *see also specific aspects and concerns*

    background and infrastructure, 57–66

    conclusion, 72

    content examples, 66–67

    crisis management, 194

    definitions, 57–58

    education abroad advising overview, 29–30

    education abroad applications overview, 41–52

    essential learning outcomes, 55–57

    experience of students on site, 284–285

    financial planning, 67

    focus on, 75

    goals, 72

    health and safety considerations, 68, 153–154

    institutional partners, 68–69

    introduction, 53–57

    learner characteristics, 59–60

    marketing overview, 12–13

    partnerships and programming, 54–55, 383

    passports and visas, 68

    policies and procedures, 401

    portfolio management, 308–309

    post-study abroad phase, 93

    program administration, 271, 275, 276

    technology and social media, 62–66

    underrepresented student groups, 69–72

    while abroad phase, 83

    work, internship, and volunteering abroad programs, 258

student complaints, experience of students on site, 290–291

student conduct code, policies and procedures, 396–397

student demographics. *see also* data collection and use; student groups;

underrepresented student groups
    data collection and use, 340–342, 343
    strategic planning, 220
    student and family preparation and orientation, 59–60
student development theory overview, 22–25
student enrollment. *see also* data collection and use; student participation
    portfolio management, 306–307
    trends, 350–352
student entertainment, marketing overview, 10–11
student enthusiasm, capitalizing on, 106–107
student essays, education abroad applications, 42, 47
student exchange programs. *see* exchange programs
student experience on site. *see* experience of students on site
student goals and expectations
    education abroad advising overview, 28–29
    education abroad applications, 45
    experience of students on site, 285
    marketing overview, 14
    strategic planning, 220
    student and family preparation and orientation, 66
    while abroad phase, 83–84
student groups. *see also* underrepresented student groups; *specific groups*
    data collection and use, 340–342, 343
    different advising for different groups, 26–28
    education abroad research overview, 139–140
    marketing overview, 15–17
    post-study abroad phase, 108–109
    student and family preparation and orientation, 69–72
    while abroad phase, 87–89
student health considerations. *see* health and safety considerations
student honor code, policies and procedures, 397
student identification, data collection and use, 16
student ID number data element, 50
student judicial affairs, education abroad applications, 44
student leadership
    post-study abroad phase, 97
    while abroad phase, 79
student learning outcomes. *see* learning outcomes
student-led programming model, 94
student mobility, as internationalization goal, 120, 121
student organizations, marketing and, 10
student orientation. *see* student and family preparation and orientation
student outcomes. *see* learning outcomes
student participation. *see also specific aspects*

different advising for different groups, 26–28
strategic planning, 216–217, 224
work, internship, and volunteering abroad programs, 245–246
student peers. *see* peers, student
student persistence and retention, data collection and use, 342, 344–345
student preparation. *see* student and family preparation and orientation
student profiles, post-study abroad phase, 99
student recruitment, data collection and use, 345–349. *see also* marketing
student services, partnerships with, 95, 382–384. *see also specific aspects*
students of color. *see also* underrepresented student groups
 data collection and use, 337, 338
 different advising for different groups, 27
students with disabilities
 accommodations and support, 155
 different advising for different groups, 27
 experience of students on site, 293
 student and family preparation and orientation, 71
study abroad applications. *see* education abroad applications
study abroad center programs. *see also* island programs
 education abroad advising overview, 33
 models overview, 233
 strategic planning, 222–223
study abroad director, portfolio management and. *see* portfolio management
study abroad office management. *see* education abroad office management
study abroad organization program model. *see also* partnerships; *specific aspects*
 comprehensive internationalization, 121
 education abroad applications, 45
 models overview, 238–240
 partnerships overview, 388–389
study abroad providers, partnerships overview, 388–389
study tour program type, 33
suicide
 case study example, 164
 psychological assessments, 155
surveys, conducting. *see also* data collection and use
 benchmarking for excellence, 312
 data collection and use, 333–334
 marketing overview, 15–16
 outcomes assessment, 411
 while abroad phase, 87

T

teaching abroad program type, 256–257. *see also* work, internship, and
 volunteering abroad programs

technology and social media. *see also* data collection and use; *specific aspects*
    budget management, 367–368
    crisis management, 194, 200, 349–350
    education abroad advising overview, 36–37
    education abroad applications, 46–49, 307
    hiring process, 323
    in-person vs. distance/online learning, 77
    marketing overview, 11–12, 15
    online dashboards, 340
    portfolio management, 307–308
    post-study abroad phase, 99–109
    program administration, 272–273
    risk management planning, 170–171, 173
    social media integration theory model, 64
    social media landscape, 65
    student and family preparation and orientation, 62–66
    while abroad phase, 80–81, 85, 86, 88–89
telephones. *see also* emergency contacts
    crisis management, 192, 196, 198
    front office operations, 327
    health and safety considerations, 155
    hiring process, 324
    phone number data element, 50
    portfolio management, 309
    program administration, 272
    risk management planning, 172, 173
    while abroad phase, 80
term selection, data analysis, 51. *see also* program duration
Terra Dotta software, 170–171, 349–350
terrorist acts, questions for responding to emergencies, 210
Texas Christian University, program administration, 266
text messages. *see also* technology and social media
    education abroad applications, 49
    text alert systems, 194
third-party organization program model. *see* study abroad organization program
    model
throwback Thursday trend, 100
time abroad phase. *see* while abroad phase
training for employees. *see* professional development for employees; *specific*
    areas of interest
transcripts
    education abroad applications, 47
    education abroad models, 232, 237, 239
    partnerships overview, 388

transfer status data example, 337, 338
transportation arrangements as factor, 273, 321
transportation case study examples, 164
Transportation Security Administration, crisis management, 203
Travel Alerts, 161
travel assistance
    for individuals, 176–177, 180–182
    order of priority, 182
travel insurance
    for individuals, 176–177, 180–182
    order of priority, 187
    for programs and institutions, 183
travel, noncredit-bearing, 349–350
travel policies and procedures, 394–395. *see also* policies and procedures;
        specific aspects
Travel Warnings
    crisis management, 201–202
    insurance overview, 180, 183
    risk management planning, 161, 168
    strategic planning, 219
triangle teams, 318–319
tribe, building of, 9
trip cancellation/interruption insurance
    for individuals, 176–177
    order of priority, 187
    for programs and institutions, 183
tsunami case study example, 163
tuition. *see also* financial aid; financial planning
    comprehensive internationalization, 118
    education abroad advising overview, 34–35
    refund insurance, 183
    tuition capture, 360
twinning agreements, as comprehensive internationalization goal, 120–121

U

underrepresented student groups. *see also* student groups; *specific groups*
    comprehensive internationalization, 119, 122–123
    data analysis, 51
    data collection and use, 334, 337–339
    different advising for different groups, 26–28
    education abroad research overview, 139–140
    marketing overview, 16–17
    post-study abroad phase, 108–109
    strategic planning, 217

student and family preparation and orientation, 69–72
    while abroad phase, 88–89
United Educators, risk management planning, 169
United Kingdom, accommodations offices, 155
universal element of crisis response team, 195
universal outcomes research overview, 137–140
University of California
    institutional mission, 213
    reentry conference, 98
    risk management planning, 170
University of Central Oklahoma, policies and procedures, 397
University of Cincinnati, reentry night, 93
University of Delaware, education abroad history, 127–128, 130
University of Georgia, policies and procedures, 396
University of Kentucky
    leader for a day program, 79
    live chats, 81
University of Michigan, work, internship, and volunteering abroad programs,
    245–246
University of Minnesota, education abroad research overview, 135
University of Nebraska, reentry program, 94
University of Nevada, fees, 359–360
University of Texas, education abroad research overview, 135–136
University of Wisconsin, triangle teams, 318–319
university rankings, comprehensive internationalization and, 118
updates to resources, 279
upper administration, partnerships with, 379–380. see also partnerships
U.S. Centers for Disease Control and Prevention, risk management planning, 168
U.S. Congress, education abroad research overview, 130
U.S. Education Department
    data collection and use, 353
    outcomes assessment, 409
U.S. embassies and consulates, crisis management, 201–202
user fees, 360, 365. see also fees
U.S. government. see also specific entities
    crisis management, 201–203
    risk management planning, 161–162, 168
    work, internship, and volunteering abroad programs, 252, 256
U.S. Justice Department, risk management planning, 167
U.S. Peace Corps, risk management planning, 170
U.S. State Department
    crisis management, 201–202
    insurance overview, 180, 183
    passport acceptance facilities, 360

risk management planning, 161, 168

strategic planning, 219

V

vacations, adding professional time to, 373

vaccinations, 154

Valid Assessment of Learning in Undergraduate Education (VALUE) initiative, 55–56

value of education abroad, research overview, 133–140. *see also* outcomes assessment

vertical roots, 107

veterans, student and family preparation and orientation, 72

video conferencing. *see also* technology and social media

    health and safety considerations, 155

    while abroad phase, 80

virtual advising, 37. *see also* technology and social media

virtual fairs, marketing for advisers, 12

visas. *see* passports and visas

vlogs and blogs, post-study abroad phase, 99, 108–109. *see also* technology and social media

volunteering abroad and service-learning program type, 253–254. *see also* work, internship, and volunteering abroad programs

W

waivers

    education abroad applications, 48

    health and safety considerations, 151

    insurance overview, 184

    portfolio management, 307

    risk management planning, 171

Wake Forest University, reentry course, 94

W-Curve, 284, 290, 294–295

web apps. *see also* technology and social media

    risk management planning, 173

    while abroad phase, 81, 89

webinars. *see also* technology and social media

    budget management, 368

    post-study abroad phase, 99

Western Europe. *see* Europe

Western Kentucky University, policies and procedures, 394–395

while abroad phase

    background and infrastructure, 75–77

    content delivery examples, 78–80

    content needs, 82–87

in-person vs. distance/online learning, 77
interventions, 77–78
programming and events, 81–82
program type, 77
student groups, 87–89
technology and social media, 80–81
Willamette University, intervention model, 78
women in study abroad, research overview, 129–131, 138
women's moral development theory overview, 23
workers' compensation insurance, 185–186, 187
work, internship, and volunteering abroad programs
    administrative commitment, 257–260
    advising considerations, 249–250, 257–260
    community engagement, 288
    conclusion, 260
    definitions, 243–244
    external resources, 260
    as high impact, 245
    institutional commitment of resources, 248–249, 257–260
    institutional context, 257–260
    introduction, 243
    learning outcomes research, 244–245
    marketing overview, 14
    participation data, 245–246
    post-study abroad phase, 96
    professional associations and, 246–247
    program administration, 268
    program referrals, 258–259
    program types, 250–257
    student worker job functions, 306
    while abroad phase, 82, 83–84
    work abroad vs. study abroad, 247–249
work permit and placement program type, 254–256. *see also* work, internship, and volunteering abroad programs
world wide travel assistance, 180–181
writing of policies and procedures, guidelines for, 399–400. *see also* policies and procedures

Y

year-long and semester programs. *see* semester and year-long programs